SCIENCE AND CIVILIZATION IN ISLAM

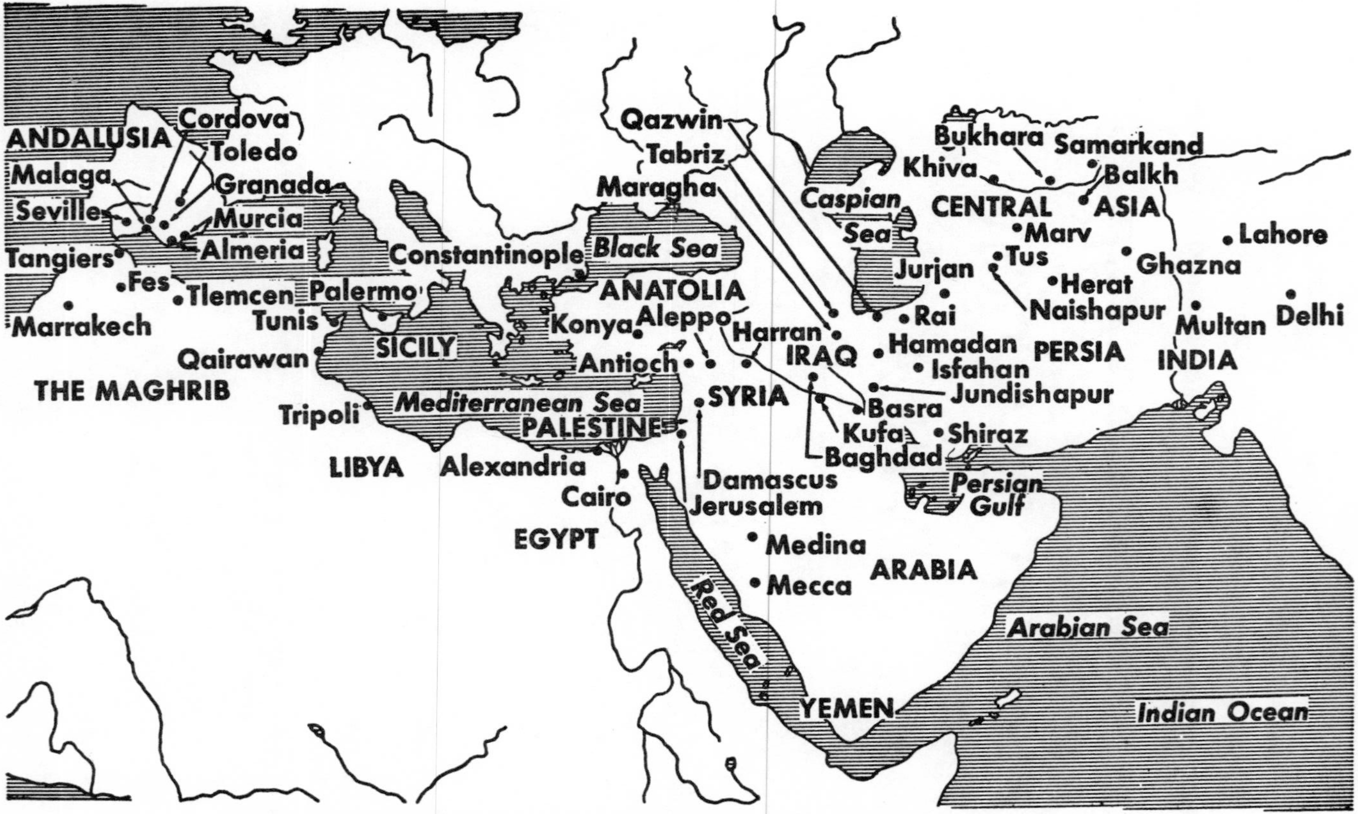

Some of the Important Centers of Islamic Science and Culture.

SCIENCE AND CIVILIZATION IN ISLAM

by
Seyyed Hossein Nasr

With a Preface by
GIORGIO DE SANTILLANA

BARNES & NOBLE
BOOKS
NEW YORK

To S. Maryam (Sussan)

This edition published by Barnes & Noble Inc.
by arrangement with Seyyed Hossein Nasr

1992 Barnes & Noble Books

ISBN 0-88029-878-2

Printed and bound in the United States of America

M 9 8 7 6 5 4 3 2

PREFACE

I

The portrayal of Islamic science which follows may surprise some readers both West and East, if for very different reasons. There can be no question as to the author's qualifications or his familiarity with our Western point of view. Seyyed Hossein Nasr, an Iranian by birth, breeding, and early education, also studied in Europe and graduated in physics from the Massachusetts Institute of Technology, where he developed in his undergraduate years a strong interest in the history of scientific thought as I was teaching it. He went on then to Harvard for graduate studies in geology and geophysics, but soon decided to make history of science a career, and obtained a Ph.D. in the subject in 1958. He has been teaching it ever since at the University of Tehran. His Western background makes it all the more significant that we should find here the passionate, direct, and uncompromising statement of a modern Muslim, who deeply believes in the coming rebirth of his own civilization.

His text is a new departure in many ways. Islamic culture is too often presented as the indispensable link between Antiquity and our Middle Ages, but the achievement of its historic mission is implied when it has handed on the texts and techniques of the Greeks. This is a way of turning a great civilization into a service department of Western history. It is the merit of Dr. Nasr to have shown convincingly that the mind and culture of Islam embrace a far wider arc, and that the cultivation of the Greek heritage is only a phase in the development of an essentially independent thought.

What is central in other histories becomes here incidental. The figure of Aristotle is commonly accepted as the great shaping influence of Islamic thought. He was for the Muslims "the Philosopher" par excellence, his systems and logical distinctions harmonizing so well with their taste for encyclopedism and grammatical sharpness. Yet for the author, "philosophy" in that sense remains a foreign body, and Aristotle is shipped back unceremoniously to the West where he belongs, together with Averroes, his greatest disciple.

The fact is that for Dr. Nasr Islamic thinking is still profoundly alive, and Aristotle only a monument of the past. No Neo-Thomist nostalgias here. If there is something enduring, an immortal spirit in Muslim thought, it is, in the mind of Dr. Nasr, to be found in its retreat from the rationalizing and secular attitude of Hellenistic tradition—in its retreat even from the trials and tumult of history—to become more fully conscious of its own vocation as a Near Eastern religious community. If Greek thought had fueled the phase of splendor and expansion, there is a further phase which to the outside (critical) historian may look like stagnation and squalid decay, but seen from the inside may reveal itself as a maturing of consciousness, the moment of spiritual insight and timeless *ḥikmah* (wisdom) to replace time-bound discursive philosophy. And indeed in Islam we see, from the time when it recedes from the forestage of history, the growth of an imposing new metaphysics which took the name of Sufism, in which the Greek Neoplatonic element inspires the unitary vision of Justice, Harmony, and controlled Order extending to the whole cosmos and reflecting back on man's life.

From the earliest beginnings of Near Eastern thought, the cosmos is regarded as a unified entity which embraces the whole of being; so that human societies have to reflect the divine rulership. This is what endures. Islamic philosophy makes its way through Greek science, through the emanations and intelligences of Plotinus, to concentrate upon the one divine principle from whom all being is derived, in whose overwhelming Presence all reality is dissolved into the "world of similitude," all conscious existence becomes a Surrender—*islām*. Directly from that Presence issues the Prophet, the "Cosmic Man," and what he institutes is as complete and immovable as the Cubic Stone of the Kaaba.

This is the vision, and it implies a complete order and hierarchy in the Universe, from the ninth heaven to the rock buried deep in the earth, and that order is reflected in the law and the order of society. As temporal justice and tangible society decay beyond repair, the mind of the sage retreats into the invisible order entrusted to God's chosen ones, the unknown Saints in their hierarchy, ever headed by the mystical Pole, the *Quṭb*, who still protect the Community of the Faithful. Thus the four-square integrity of the whole remains invariant, but with the passing of time a growing part of it is removed from the visible to the suprasensible realm. Dr. Nasr has shown that the withdrawal begins, not with the fracturing of the political body of Islam, but before it, in the midst of the golden age of success, before the ascendancy of the metaphysical doctrines of Sufism. The change belongs thus to the intrinsic nature of the Community, and a unitary evolution is seen over the whole arc of time to the present. Something very similar occurred in the Christian West, if we are to believe so Roman Catholic a writer as François Mauriac, who wrote that Christendom had been changing from a visible cathedral into a stellar system.

This line of evolution is conceived as beginning very early in the life of the new faith, and continued right into our own times. It is the story of a thought which goes on forever inside an orthodoxy, and never breaks out sharply into secularism as has happened with us. This is also, we should add, what allows the religious ideas of other Eastern cultures to converge into it through the centuries. The transition from the time-bound into the timeless, from reason to the suprarational, does not take place at one point either, nor does it coincide simply with political decay, as appears too often in the clichés about history. It did not in the Near East any more than it did in Antiquity. In showing the early thickening web of suprarational elements in ʿUmar Khayyām and Avicenna, Dr. Nasr has proved his thesis.

One wishes only at times that he had not drawn so tight the web of orthodox piety as to leave in an uncomfortable and slightly alien position, along the course of time, men who stand out more clearly as representing the scientific temper. These men do not belong to the phase of withdrawal, but to the phase of world leadership; they are good Muslims and true, and a glory of their civilization. Therefore, since this is a history centered on science, I feel they should have been presented in bolder relief. In al-Bīrūnī, the greatest scientist of Islam, we meet a mind in no wise different from the Western lay scientific mind at its best. His religious faith is secure but carried lightly, without protestations. It does not impede his freedom of judgment, his love of fact, his free-wheeling curiosity, his easy sarcasm, his strict and watchful cult of intellectual integrity. We recognize soon, in al-Bīrūnī, the Scientist without qualifications as we mean him, as he has been understood again and again, and the same may be said of the other great men of his ilk—observers, experimenters, analysts, such men as Rhazes, Alhazen, al-Battānī, Averroes. This is what the Islamic intellect was able to bring forth during the golden age, as well as later, and they surely need no apologies for their perhaps-a-shade-too-secular attitude, nor deserve the hint that they were out of step with their own culture.

In any case, they would have been equally out of step with the culture of our own Middle Ages. Let us then simply conclude—and the author, who entertains such warm brotherly feelings for that culture, would certainly agree—that Islam has throughout retained medieval characteristics. It has in fact reinforced them in the passing of time, returning to a science of the soul which almost blots out the science of nature. This will tell us why the pious clause, the unremitting reverence, the *sensus eminentior,* take a place in these texts which might seem excessive to the modern Western eye. The conciliation of many shades of thought, of many voices, in an intellectual harmony and a kind of inbred concordance was of the very nature of Islamic wisdom. But as in law, so in philosophy, it did not prevent organic differences from taking shape. The clauses of style of a civilization deeply imbued with orthodoxy and pious wisdom cannot but sound foreign and sometimes wearisome to us. On the other hand, of the intellectual elements, very few will escape recognition to the Western mind, since they can, most of them, be traced back to the great Alexandrian melting pot. The conceptual elements of Islamic mysticism itself are to be found already in Neoplatonic literature. The author sometimes seems to forget it. But it is his merit to have made us feel that they live a new and charmed life in the delicate fervor of Islamic piety.

II

Fervor cannot go without partisanship, and Dr. Nasr refers more than once with a touch of scorn to the "unilateral" quantitative character of modern science. Of that unilateral aspect we are only too sadly aware, but the way to overcome it has been more often discoursed upon than clearly marked. We hope that Dr. Nasr's treatment may do something toward dispelling the clouds. We all are ready to wish that someone could reveal to us how the merely quantitative element beclouds the "true relations"—qualitative, intuitive—which seem to shine forth in the activity of *natura naturans;* but it remains a wish. Beyond this wish there are staggering philosophical hurdles to be overcome. Science has forever been going the other way. Johann Kepler himself, a witness whom Dr. Nasr can hardly refuse, wrote: "As the eye for colors, as the ear for sounds, so the mind is made for grasping quantitative relations." He deeply believed in the virtues of Pythagorean magnitudes, but he had come to the conclusion that the "Light of nature" only shines intelligibly on the strict mathematical plane. He would have answered Jābir the alchemist with his numerology as ironically as he answered Robert Fludd, the master of Hermetic theosophy, who also claimed a hidden science of numbers and impulses issuing from nature herself.

All in all, in passionately defending the essential wholeness and integrity of his culture down to modern times, Dr. Nasr is willing to lay himself open to doubt, but the issues he raises in our minds are so rewarding as to force our gratitude even when we disagree totally.

Thus, the silence of later Muslim astronomy with respect to the Copernican system is in his mind the result of a considered choice, and a choice dictated by wisdom. "As long as the hierarchy of knowledge remained preserved and intact in Islam, and *scientia* continued to be cultivated in the bosom of *sapientia,* a certain limitation" of the physical domain was accepted in order to preserve the freedom of expansion and realization in the spiritual domain. "The wall of the cosmos was preserved. It was as if the old scientists and scholars foresaw that the breaking of those walls would also destroy the symbolic content of the cosmos . . . and so, despite all the technical possibility, the step toward breaking the traditional world view was not taken."

One might wonder whether the author is not making a virtue of necessity. He does not raise the question whether the condition and prestige of Muslim astronomers from A.D. 1650 on, four centuries after al-Ghazzālī had "saved orthodoxy by depressing science," would have allowed them to propose such a bold innovation without being lynched as Suhrawardī was. The simple fact is that they stayed put, and the author does not gloss over the consequences: that up to our days, the traditional curriculum of Muslim universities has gone on teaching Ptolemaic astronomy, embedded in a frame of geocentric cosmology and philosophy, with a "modern" system available as an option but presented as "hypothesis." This last is an ancient term, which means simply that it is separated from all its implications. Can "one modern system" be taught without the whole framework of modern science? Or does the student use its elementary schemes as *quodlibeta* to play with as against the theory of the equant? In what way does he preserve his intellectual integrity?

These are questions the author leaves unanswered, but he allows them to stand out starkly in our mind. At least he stands up for his past and does not throw it into the ashcan, as so many of his contemporaries do. Nor does he shun the confrontation with the West, as Muslims are often apt to do. With true brotherly feeling, as I said, he insists on the parallelism between the Muslim and the Christian Middle Ages, which seem to him to have expressed a common truth. But once the common frame has been set up, comparisons force themselves upon us. Copernicus and Kepler believed in cosmic vision and wholeness as much as any Muslim ever did, but when they had to face the "moment of truth" they chose a road which apparently was not that of *sapientia:* they felt they had to state what appeared to be the case, and that on the whole it would be more respectful of divine wisdom to act thus. In so doing, they did more than save science: they saved the intellectual integrity of generations to come, and with it our own civilization. The split between *sapientia* and integrity is one of the most disturbing issues of the book. But that intellectual integrity should be claimed by no one as a privilege. Does Dr. Nasr think that al-Bīrūnī would have behaved any differently from Copernicus and Kepler, had he lived in their time? All that we know of that sage tells us that he would not. The ideal of knowledge of the great Islamic astronomer was as exacting as theirs. But, even as happened in Greece, there came a time in Islam when science thought it could not take chances, that it had to yield to the "higher reasons" of philosophy. Here as there, it meant that irreparable change had set in; in both cases, historians have been largely right in speaking of decadence and stagnation and squalor. In both cases, however, something was being born. In the West, it was that utterly new and startling thing, Christianity, brought in from the Near East. In Islam, it came from its own Eastern roots, closer to it than science had ever been: it was Sufism. As Christian Europe, already a thousand years old, opened itself to new secular adventures, Islam was closing in on its origins.

The decline of science inside a great culture is in itself a fascinating study and a terrible object lesson. We can find here the key, in the documents that allow us to judge for ourselves, of the showdown between Averroes and al-Ghazzālī. Averroes speaks with the clarity and passionate honesty that we would expect of him, for here was the great Greek tradition at bay, whereas al-Ghazzālī's famous eloquence, undistinguished intellectually as it is, and to us ethically uninspiring, went to building up the whirlwind of intolerance and blind fanaticism which tore down not only science, but the very School system and the glorious *ijtihād,* the Interpretation of the Quran. For giving us those documents straight, the author has earned our gratitude, for he well knows that we are bound to read them our own way. As we have said, his comments are as significant as the texts themselves, since they show us the difference between two worlds. On one point only we would take exception: his likening of al-Ghazzālī to Aquinas. The two personalities are not commensurable. If anything, al-Ghazzālī's chief argument that physical causes are not true causes, but only "occasions" for God's direct intervention, shows him to be, paradoxically enough, the counterpart of men like Malebranche in our world. But the great and candid mind of Malebranche knew how to turn "occasionalism" to a far different purpose: it provided, in fact, the starting-point for Leibniz's profound scientific innovation. Such are the strange ways of History. Yet certain constants remain universal. We can admire the insight of Alhazen, for all that he was a "mere" scientist: "Those who would destroy science are really undermining religion." It was curtains not only for science in Islam, but for *sapientia* as well, insofar as the term refers at all to this world. We shall notice that Avicenna himself was eventually branded with heresy. Only pure contemplative gnostic "illumination" remained intact.

There is no doubt for us that after the age of the Almohades the creative vigor of Islam wanes in speculative thought as well as in poetry, and the Islamic way of life becomes a tenacious survival of something which had once been great, whole, and new. But it should be considered that while by that time the legal and theological structure of both the Sunni and the Shiite wings of that culture had been concluded and consolidated, the political issues were being deadened by the expanding hegemony of the Turks. The crumbling secular system could no longer hold men in line for great collective enterprises, but in lieu of it came the invisible, subtle, overall presence of the personal mystical experience.

In fact, let me quote on the present thesis an appraisal by Sir Hamilton Gibb, than whom there is no one more qualified to speak on Islamic thought:

> Whence the mystical cosmology came and how it entered Sufi thought has been set out for the first time by Seyyed Hossein Nasr in full and scholarly detail. It is almost a startling revelation that its foundations were laid by the philosophical schools of the "Golden Age," and that no other than Avicenna himself, the "second master" of Aristotelian philosophy, furnished it with its cosmological symbolism. That it was the heirs of Hellenistic culture who generated the final flowering of Illuminationist Sufism seems the greatest paradox of all.

This paradox, Sir Hamilton agrees, can only be explained by the working of an inner reason which worked toward a final elaboration of the central theme.

GIORGIO DE SANTILLANA

FOREWORD

When *Science and Civilization* was published originally in 1968 by the Harvard University Press, it was the first work in the English language to deal with the whole of Islamic science. Based on a century of scholarship by Western historians of science and Islamicists as well as the scholarship of Muslim scholars, the work sought to present Islamic science not as a chapter in the history of Western science, but as an integral aspect of Islamic civilization and the Islamic intellectual tradition. Since the book departed from the Western norm of studying the history of science, it faced criticism not only from many Western scholars imbued with the positivistic philosophy which has dominated the history of science in the West since Ernst Mach, but also from Westernized Muslim scholars, not to speak of the so-called fundamentalist Muslims who, while rejecting verbally Western thought, often accept scientism without the least resistance or critical examination. Nevertheless, the work has continued to be read extensively in both the Islamic world and the West.

Since its first printing, *Science and Civilization in Islam* has appeared not only in paperback in America but also in local editions in Pakistan and Malaysia. It has been translated into Italian and French and also Urdu and Persian, and it has incited a great deal of debate among Muslim thinkers concerned with the nature of Islamic science, how it should be studied and the relation between Islam and science in general.

During the twenty years since its publication, a great deal of research has been carried out in certain fields of Islamic science. Later astronomy of the School of Maraghah is now much better known than when we wrote this work. Mamluk astronomy and astronomical activity in Yemen have become new fields of research. A number of important studies in early Islamic mathematics have added much to our knowledge of this central branch of Islamic science. Many new discoveries have been made in Islamic medicine and pharmacology especially of later centuries. A number of significant works have appeared in certain types of cosmology such as that of the early Ismā'īlīs and also later philosophical and mystical writers, while the whole relation between

Islamic science, philosophy and Sufism has received extensive attention by scholars especially those in the Islamic world.

To write a new book on Islamic science would require integrating all such studies into a comprehensive work which we hope will be written one day. Likewise, the present book would need certain revisions in the sections dealing with the history of each discipline if it were to be re-written, but the general contour of the historical accounts remains valid. As for the conceptual framework and the ideas presented in this work concerning the meaning of Islamic science, methods to study it, the relation of Islamic science to other branches of Islamic thought, the place of science in Islamic education, the figure of the teacher, and the ultimate goal of knowledge, they have not changed for us as a result of the scholarship of the past two decades. On the contrary, our own research and what we have learned from the works of other scholars confirms even more firmly than before the perspective presented here and formulated when this book was first conceived some thirty years ago. We continue to stand by not only the translations and the choice of citations from various Muslim scientists and thinkers presented here, but also the conception of Islamic science, its meaning and how it should be studied from within the Islamic perspective as developed in this book.

During the past two decades, gradually a number of Muslim scholars and scientists have come to realize the gravity of the situation created by the blind emulation of Western science and technology, and many have awakened from the slumber of an earlier Muslim generation which did not perceive the dangers confronting the Islamic world and which continued to extol its own civilization solely on the basis of the fact that it had created a science which had in turn contributed to Western science. Today many realize that Islamic science is not Islamic simply because it was cultivated by Muslims but because it is related to the principles of Islam. This group has become to an ever greater degree aware of the fact that Islamic science, although of great influence upon Western science, is another type of science of the natural domain than what today in the West is called science in an "absolute" sense. Such thinkers have begun to speak of the Islamization of knowledge and the creation of an Islamically oriented educational system within which science could be taught.

The present book has played and continues to play a humble role in this historic debate. It continues to be taught and studied in many universities in both the Islamic world and the West. We are therefore pleased that it is being reprinted. May the new edition help those who are concerned with the question of Islamic science in its relation to Islamic civilization as well as the relation between Islam and science today to benefit from those wise Muslim scientists, savants and *ḥakīms* whose thoughts and words are translated and studied in this book. Their thoughts and words are precious because they transmit to us a science which is always rooted in God while studying His creation; a science which reflects systematic knowledge of nature without ever forgetting the Author of Nature Who has inscribed His Wisdom upon every leaf and stone and who has created the world of nature in such a way that every phenomenon is a sign (*āyah*) singing in silent music the glory of His Oneness.

SEYYED HOSSEIN NASR

Washington, D.C.
12 Dhu'l-Qa'dah 1407 (A.H.)
July 9, 1987

TRANSLITERATION

Arabic Letters

symbol	transliteration
ء	'
ب	b
ت	t
ث	th
ج	j
ح	ḥ
خ	kh
د	d
ذ	dh
ر	r
ز	z
س	s
ش	sh
ص	ṣ
ض	ḍ
ط	ṭ
ظ	ẓ
ع	ʿ
غ	gh
ف	f
ق	q
ك	k
ل	l
م	m
ن	n
ه	h
و	w
ي	y
ة	ah; at (*construct state*)
ال	(*article*) al- *and* 'l (*even before the antepalatals*)

Long Vowels

اى	ā
و	ū
ي	ī

Short Vowels

َ	a
ُ	u
ِ	i

Diphthongs

ـَو	au
ـَي	ai
ـِيّ	iy (Final Form ī)
ـُوّ	uww (Final Form ū)

Persian Letters

پ	p
چ	ch
ژ	zh
گ	g

CONTENTS

In the Name of God Most Merciful and Compassionate

INTRODUCTION

A. The Principles of Islam

THE HISTORY OF SCIENCE is often regarded today as the progressive accumulation of techniques and the refinement of quantitative methods in the study of Nature. Such a point of view considers the present conception of science to be the only valid one; it therefore judges the sciences of other civilizations in the light of modern science and evaluates them primarily with respect to their "development" with the passage of time. Our aim in this work, however, is not to examine the Islamic sciences from the point of view of modern science and of this "evolutionistic" conception of history; it is, on the contrary, to present certain aspects of the Islamic sciences as seen from the Islamic point of view.

To the Muslim, history is a series of accidents that in no way affect the nontemporal principles of Islam. He is more interested in knowing and "realizing" these principles than in cultivating originality and change as intrinsic virtues. The symbol of Islamic civilization is not a flowing river, but the cube of the Kaaba, the stability of which symbolizes the permanent and immutable character of Islam.

Once the spirit of the Islamic revelation had brought into being, out of the heritage of previous civilizations and through its own genius, the civilization whose manifestations may be called distinctly Islamic, the main interest turned away from change and "adaptation." The arts and sciences came to possess instead a stability and a "crystallization" based on the immutability of the principles from which they had issued forth; it is this stability that is too often mistaken in the West today for stagnation and sterility.

The arts and sciences in Islam are based on the idea of

unity, which is the heart of the Muslim revelation. Just as all genuine Islamic art, whether it be the Alhambra or the Paris Mosque, provides the plastic forms through which one can contemplate the Divine Unity manifesting itself in multiplicity, so do all the sciences that can properly be called Islamic reveal the unity of Nature. One might say that the aim of all the Islamic sciences—and, more generally speaking, of all the medieval and ancient cosmological sciences—is to show the unity and interrelatedness of all that exists, so that, in contemplating the unity of the cosmos, man may be led to the unity of the Divine Principle, of which the unity of Nature is the image.

To understand the Islamic sciences in their essence, therefore, requires an understanding of some of the principles of Islam itself, even though these ideas may be difficult to express in modern terms and strange to readers accustomed to another way of thinking. Yet a statement of these principles is necessary here, insofar as they form the matrix within which the Islamic sciences have meaning, and outside of which any study of them would remain superficial and incomplete.

Islamic civilization as a whole is, like other traditional civilizations, based upon a point of view: the revelation brought by the Prophet Muḥammad is the "pure" and simple religion of Adam and Abraham, the restoration of a primordial and fundamental unity. The very word *islām* means both "submission" and "peace"—or "being at one with the Divine Will."

The creed of Islam—"there is no divinity other than God and Muḥammad is his prophet"—summarizes in its simplicity the basic attitude and spirit of Islam. To grasp the essence of Islam, it is enough to recognize that God is one, and that the Prophet, who is the vehicle of revelation and the symbol of all creation, was sent by him. This simplicity of the Islamic revelation further implies a type of religious structure different in many ways from that of Christianity. There is no priesthood as such in Islam. Each Muslim—being a "priest"—is himself capable of fulfilling all the religious functions of his family and, if necessary, of his community; and the role of the imam, as understood in either Sunni or Shia Islam, does not in any way diminish the sacerdotal function of each believer. The orthodoxy based on this creed is intangible, and therefore not so closely bound to specific formulations of dogmatic theology as in Christianity. There have been, to be sure, sectional fanaticism and even persecution, carried on either by rulers or by exoteric theologians, against such figures as al-Ḥallāj and Suhrawardī. Yet the larger orthodoxy, based on the essential doctrine of unity, has always prevailed and has been able to absorb within the structure of Islam all that is not contradictory to the Muslim creed.

In its universal sense, Islam may be said to have three levels of meaning. All beings in the universe, to begin with, are Muslim, *i.e.*, "surrendered to the Divine Will." (A flower cannot help being a flower; a diamond cannot do other than sparkle. God has made them so; it is theirs to obey.) Secondly, all men who accept with their will the sacred law of the revelation are Muslim in that they surrender their *will* to that law. When ʿUqbah, the Muslim conqueror of North Africa, took leave of his family and mounted his horse for the great adventure which was to lead him through two thousand miles of conquest to the Moroccan shores of the Atlantic, he cried out: "And now, God, take my soul." We can hardly imagine Alexander the Great having such thoughts as he set out eastward to Persia. Yet, as conquerors, the two men were to achieve comparable feats; the "passivity" of ʿUqbah with respect to the Divine Will was to be transmuted into irresistible action in this world.

Finally, we have the level of pure knowledge and understanding. It is that of the contemplative, the gnostic (*ʿārif*), the level that has been recognized throughout Islamic history as the highest and most comprehensive. The gnostic is Muslim in that his *whole being* is surrendered to God; he has no separate individual existence of his own. He is like the birds and the flowers in his yielding to the Creator; like them, like all the other elements of the cosmos, he reflects the Divine Intellect to his own degree. He reflects it *actively*, however, they passively; his participation is a *conscious* one. Thus "knowledge" and "science" are defined as basically different from mere curiosity and even from analytical speculation. The gnostic is from this point of view "one with Nature"; he understands it "from the inside," he has become in fact the channel of grace for the universe. His *islām* and the *islām* of Nature are now counterparts.

The intellective function, so defined, may be difficult for Westerners to grasp. Were it not for the fact that most of the great scientists and mathematicians of Islam operated within this matrix, it might seem so far removed as to be irrelevant to this study. Yet, it is closer in fact to the Western tradition than most modern readers are likely to realize. It is certainly very close to the contemplative strain of the Christian Middle

Ages—a strain once more evoked in part, during the modern era, by the German school of *Naturphilosophie* and by the Romantics, who strove for "communion" with Nature. Let us not be misled by words, however. The opening of the Romantic's soul to Nature—even Keats's "negative capability" of receiving its imprint—is far more a matter of sentiment (or, as they loved to call it then, "sensibility") than of true contemplation, for the truly contemplative attitude is based on "intellection."

We should be mindful here of the changing usage of words. "Intellect" and "intellectual" are so closely identified today with the analytical functions of the mind that they hardly bear any longer any relation to the contemplative. The attitude these words imply toward Nature is the one that Goethe was to deplore as late as the early nineteenth century—that attitude that resolves, conquers, and dominates by force of concepts. It is, in short, essentially abstract, while contemplative knowledge is at bottom concrete. We shall thus have to say, by way of reestablishing the old distinction, that the gnostic's relation to Nature is "intellective," which is neither abstract, nor analytical, nor merely sentimental.

Viewed as a text, Nature is a fabric of symbols, which must be read according to their meaning. The Quran is the counterpart of that text in human words; its verses are called *āyāt* ("signs"), just as are the phenomena of Nature. Both Nature and the Quran speak forth the presence and the worship of God: *We shall show them Our portents on the horizon and within themselves until it will be manifest unto them that it is the Truth* (41:53).[1]

To the doctors of the Law, this text is merely prescriptive, Nature being present in their minds only as the necessary setting for men's actions. To the gnostic or Sufi, on the other hand, the Quranic text is also symbolic, just as all of Nature is symbolic. If the tradition of the symbolic interpretation of the text of the Sacred Book were to disappear, and the text thereby reduced to its literal meaning, man might still know his duty, but the "cosmic text" would become unintelligible. The phenomena of Nature would lose any connection with the higher orders of reality, as well as among themselves; they would become mere "facts." This is precisely what the intellective capacity and, indeed, Islamic culture as a whole

[1] *The Meaning of the Glorious Koran, an explanatory translation* by Mohammad Marmaduke Pickthall (London: George Allen & Unwin Ltd.; New York: New American Library, 1953), 2:255; 24:35. All subsequent references to the Quran are to the latter edition.

will not accept. The spirit of Islam emphasizes, by contrast, the unity of Nature, that unity that is the aim of the cosmological sciences, and that is adumbrated and prefigured in the continuous interlacing of arabesques uniting the profusion of plant life with the geometric crystals of the verses of the Quran.

Thus we see that the idea of unity is not only the basic presupposition of the Islamic arts and sciences: it dominates their expression as well. The portrayal of any individual object would become a "graven image," a dangerous idol of the mind; the very canon of art in Islam is abstraction. Unity itself is alone deserving of representation; since it is not to be represented directly, however, it can only be *symbolized*—and at that, only by hints. There is no concrete symbol to stand for unity, however; its true expression is negation—not this, not that. Hence, it remains abstract from the point of view of man, who lives in multiplicity.

Thus we come to the central issue. Can our minds grasp the individual object as it stands by itself? or can we do so only by understanding the individual object within the context of the universe? In other words, from the cosmological point of view, is the universe the unity, and the individual event or object a sign ("phenomenon," "appearance") of ambiguous and uncertain import? Or is it the other way around? Of these alternatives, which go back to the time of Plato, the Muslim is bound to accept the first—he gives priority to the universe as the one concrete reality, which symbolizes on the cosmic level the Divine Principle itself, although that cannot truly be envisaged in terms of anything else. This is, to be sure, an ancient choice, but Islam does inherit many of its theories from preexisting traditions, the truths of which it seeks to affirm rather than to deny. What it brings to them, as we have already said, is that strong unitary point of view that, along with a passionate dedication to the Divine Will, enabled Islam to rekindle the flame of science that had been extinguished at Athens and in Alexandria.

We have seen that the sacred art of Islam is an abstract art, combining flexibility of line with emphasis on the archetype, and on the use of regular geometrical figures interlaced with one another. Herein one can already see why mathematics was to make such a strong appeal to the Muslim: its abstract nature furnished the bridge that Muslims were seeking between multiplicity and unity. It provided a fitting texture of symbols for the universe—symbols that were like keys to open the cosmic text.

We should distinguish at once between the two types of mathematics practiced by Muslims: one was the science of algebra, which was always related to geometry and trigonometry; the other was the science of numbers, as understood in the Pythagorean sense. The Pythagorean number has a symbolic as well as a quantitative aspect; it is a projection of Unity, which, however, never leaves its source. Each number has an inherent power of analysis, arising out of its quantitative nature; it has also the power of synthesis because of the inner bond that connects all other numbers to the unit. The Pythagorean number thus has a "personality": it is like a Jacob's ladder, connecting the quantitative with the qualitative domain by virtue of its own inner polarization. To study numbers thus means to contemplate them as symbols and to be led thereby to the intelligible world. So also with the other branches of mathematics. Even where the symbolic aspect is not explicitly stated, the connection with geometric forms has the effect upon the mind of freeing it from dependence upon mere physical appearance, and in that way preparing it for its journey into the intelligible world and, ultimately, to Unity.

Gnosis in the Alexandrian world had used, as the vehicle for the expression of its doctrines, a bewildering maze of mythology. In Islam, the intellective symbolism often becomes mathematical, while the direct experience of the mystic is expressed in such powerful poetry as that of Jalāl al-Dīn Rūmī. The instrument of gnosis is always, however, the intellect; reason is its passive aspect and its reflection in the human domain. The link between intellect and reason is never broken, except in the individual ventures of a handful of thinkers, among whom there are few that could properly be called scientists. The intellect remains the principle of reason; and the exercise of reason, if it is healthy and normal, should naturally lead to the intellect. That is why Muslim metaphysicians say that rational knowledge leads naturally to the affirmation of the Divine Unity. Although the spiritual realities are not merely rational, neither are they irrational. Reason, considered in its ultimate rather than its immediate aspect, can bring man to the gateway of the intelligible world; rational knowledge can in the same fashion be integrated into gnosis, even though it is discursive and partial while gnosis is total and intuitive. It is because of this essential relationship of subordination and hierarchy between reason and intellect, rational knowledge and gnosis, that the quest for causal explanation in Islam only rarely sought to, and never actually managed to, satisfy itself *outside the faith,* as was to happen in Christianity at the end of the Middle Ages.

This hierarchy is also based on the belief that *scientia*—human knowledge—is to be regarded as legitimate and noble only so long as it is subordinated to *sapientia*—Divine wisdom. Muslim sages would agree with Saint Bonaventure's "Believe, in order to understand." Like him, they insist that *scientia* can truly exist only in conjunction with *sapientia,* and that reason is a noble faculty only insofar as it leads to intellection, rather than when it seeks to establish its independence of its own principle, or tries to encompass the Infinite within some finite system. There are in Islamic history one or two instances when rationalist groups did attempt to establish their independence of and opposition to the gnostics, and also to set themselves against other orthodox interpreters of the Islamic revelation. The spiritual forces of Islam were always strong enough, however, to preserve the hierarchy between intellect and reason, and thus to prevent the establishment of a rationalism independent of the revelation. The famous treatises of al-Ghazzālī, in the fifth/eleventh century, against the rationalistic philosophers of his time mark the final triumph of intellection over independent ratiocination—a triumph that did not utterly destroy rationalistic philosophy, but did make it subordinate to gnosis. As a result of this defeat by al-Ghazzālī and similar figures of the syllogistic and systematic Aristotelian philosophy in the fifth/eleventh century, the Islamic gnostic tradition has been able to survive and to remain vital down to the present day, instead of being stifled, as elsewhere, in an overly rationalistic atmosphere.

The reaction against the rationalists, of which the writings of al-Ghazzālī mark the high point, coincides roughly in time with the spread of Aristotelianism in the West, which led ultimately to a series of actions and reactions—the Renaissance, the Reformation, and the Counter-Reformation—such as never occurred in the Islamic world. In the West, these movements led to new types of philosophy and science such as characterize the Western world today, that are as profoundly different from their medieval antecedents as is the mental and spiritual horizon of modern man from that of traditional man. Europe in that period began to develop a science of Nature that concerns itself only with the quantitative and material aspects of things; meanwhile, the tide of Islamic thought was flowing back, as before, into its traditional bed, to that conceptual coherence that comprises the mathematical sciences.

Today, as in the past, the traditional Muslim looks upon all of science as "sacred," and studies this sacred science in a well-established threefold articulation. First, within the reach of all, is the Law, contained in essence in the Quran, elucidated by tradition and jurisprudence, and taught by the doctors; it covers every aspect of the social and religious life of the believer. Beyond that lies the Path dealing with the inner aspect of things, which governs the spiritual life of those who have been "elected" to follow it. This has given rise to the various Sufi brotherhoods, since it is actually a way of life, built upon communication at a personal, nonsystematic level. Finally, there is the ineffable Truth itself, which lies at the heart of both these approaches.

According to a still-current simile, the Law is as the circumference of a circle, of which the Path is the radius, and the Truth the center. The Path and the Truth together form the esoteric aspect of Islam, to which Sufism is dedicated. At its core lies a metaphysical intuition, knowledge such as comes only to the right "mode in the knower." From this spring a science of the universe, a science of the soul, and the science of mathematics, each of them in essence a different metaphorical setting for that one science that the mind strives after, each of them a part of that gnosis that comprehends all things.

This may help explain why the mathematician, who was something of a displaced person in the West right up to the late Middle Ages, plays a central role in Islam from the very start. Two centuries after the establishment in the Near East of Christianity (in A.D. 313), the Christian-dominated West was still sunk deep in barbarism. Yet two centuries after Muḥammad, the Islamic world under the Caliph Hārūn al-Rashīd was already far more active culturally than the contemporaneous world of Charlemagne—even with the latter's earlier start. What reached the West from Islam at that time was little more than dark tales of incredible wealth and wondrous magic. In Islam itself, however, the mathematician's craft, having "found its home," was already able to satisfy the civilized man's desire for logical subtlety and for intellectual games, while philosophy itself reached out into the mysteries beyond reason.

This early stabilization of the theoretical outlook of Islam extended also to the type of man who embodied it. Whereas the role of intellectual leadership in the West devolved upon several different figures in turn—the Benedictine monk, the scholastic doctor, the lay scientist—the central figure in Islam has remained almost unchanging. He is the *ḥakīm,* who encompasses within himself some or all of the several aspects of the sage; scholar, medical healer, spiritual guide. If he happens to be a wise merchant too, that also falls into the picture, for he is traditionally an itinerant person. If his achievements in mathematics are extraordinary, he may become a figure like ʿUmar Khayyām. It is clear, moreover, that such a man—be his name even Avicenna!—will never be able to develop each of his several attainments in the same fashion as the single-faceted specialist may. Such specialists do exist in Islam, but they remain mostly secondary figures. The sage does not let himself be drawn into the specialist's single-level "mode of knowing," for then he would forfeit the higher knowledge. Intellectual achievement is thus, in a sense, always patterned upon the model of the unattainable complete, that "total thing" that is not found in the Greek tradition. Ptolemy's *Syntaxis* becomes in the Muslim world the *Almagest* or *Opus Maximum*—even as Aristotle is purely and simply *al-failasūf* (the philosopher).

The title of Avicenna's great treatise, *Kitāb al-Shifāʾ*, which rivals in scope the Aristotelian corpus, means *The Book of Healing.* As the title implies the work contains the knowledge needed to cure the soul of the disease of ignorance. It is all that is needed for man to understand; it is also *as much as* any man need know. Newton's work *Principia* has an obviously far different ring: it means a foundation—essentially, a "beginning"—rather than a knowledge that is complete and sufficient for man's intellectual needs as the titles of so many medieval Islamic texts imply.

B. *The Perspectives within Islamic Civilization*

Islam came into the world at the beginning of the seventh century A.D., its initial date (the journey of the Prophet from Mecca to Medina) being 622 A.D.; it had spread over all of the Middle East, North Africa, and Spain, by the end of that same century. Just as the Islamic religion is one of the "middle way," so too did its territory come to occupy—in fact, it still occupies—the "middle belt" of the globe, from the Atlantic to the Pacific. In this region, the home of many earlier civilizations, Islam came into contact with a number of sciences which it absorbed, to the extent that these sciences were compatible with its own spirit and were able to provide nourishment for its own characteristic cultural life.

The primordial character of its revelation, and its confidence that it was expressing the Truth at the heart of all revelations, permitted Islam to absorb ideas from many sources, historically alien yet inwardly related to it. This was especially true in regard to the sciences of Nature, because most of the ancient cosmological sciences—Greek, as well as Chaldean, Persian, Indian, and Chinese—had sought to express the unity of Nature and were therefore in conformity with the spirit of Islam. Coming into contact with them, the Muslims adopted some elements from each—most extensively, perhaps, from the Greeks, but also from the Chaldeans, Indians, Persians, and perhaps, in the case of alchemy, even from the Chinese. They united these sciences into a new corpus, which was to grow over the centuries and become part of the Islamic civilization, integrated into the basic structure derived from the Revelation itself.

The lands destined to become parts of the medieval Islamic world—from Transoxiana to Andalusia—were consolidated into a new spiritual universe within a single century after the death of the Prophet. The revelation contained in the Quran, and expressed in the sacred language (Arabic), provided the unifying pattern into which many foreign elements became integrated and absorbed, in accordance with the universal spirit of Islam. In the sciences, especially those dealing with Nature, the most important source was the heritage of Greek civilization.

Alexandria, by the first century B.C., had become the center of Greek science and philosophy, as well as the meeting place of Hellenism with Oriental and ancient Egyptian influences, out of which came Hermeticism and Neoplatonism. The Greek heritage—itself to a great extent an assemblage of ancient Mediterranean views, systematized and put into dialectical form by the peculiar discursive power of the Greeks—passed from Alexandria to Antioch, and from there to Nisibis and Edessa, by way of the Christian Monophysites and Nestorians. The latter were particularly instrumental in the spreading of Greek learning, chiefly in Syriac translation, to lands as far east as Persia.

In the third century A.D., Shāpūr I founded Jundishapur at the site of an ancient city near the present Persian city of Ahwaz, as a prisoner-of-war camp, for soldiers captured in the war with Valerian. This camp gradually grew into a metropolis, which became a center of ancient sciences, studied in Greek and Sanskrit and later in Syriac. A school was set up, on the model of those at Alexandria and Antioch, in which medicine, mathematics, astronomy, and logic were taught, mostly from Greek texts translated into Syriac, but also elements of the Indian and Persian sciences were included. This school, which lasted long after the establishment of the Abbasid caliphate, became an important source of ancient learning in the Islamic world.

Aside from those more obvious avenues, there were also lines of communication with more esoteric aspects of the Greek sciences, particularly the Pythagorean school, through the community of Sabaeans of Harran. This religious community traced its origin to the Prophet Idrīs (the Enoch of the Old Testament), who is also regarded in the Islamic world as the founder of the sciences of the heavens and of philosophy, and who is identified by some with Hermes Trismegistus. The Sabaeans possessed a remarkable knowledge of astronomy, astrology, and mathematics; their doctrines were in many respects similar to those of the Pythagoreans. It was probably they who provided the link between the Hermetic Tradition and certain aspects of the Islamic esoteric doctrines, into which some elements of Hermeticism were integrated.

On the Oriental side the Indian and, to a lesser degree, the Persian sciences came to have an important bearing upon the growth of the sciences in Islam, a bearing far greater than is usually recognized. In zoology, anthropology, and certain aspects of alchemy, as well as, of course, in mathematics and astronomy, the tradition of Indian and Persian sciences was dominant, as can be seen in the *Epistles (Rasāʾil)* of the Brethren of Purity (*Ikhwān al-Ṣafāʾ*) and the translations of Ibn Muqaffaʿ. It must be remembered that the words "magic" and Magi are related, and that, according to the legend, the Jews learned alchemy and the science of numbers from the Magi, while in captivity in Babylon.

There are most likely elements of Chinese science in Islam, especially in alchemy, pointing to some early contact between the Muslims and Chinese science. Some have even gone so far as to claim—without much proof, to be sure—

that the word *al-kīmiyā'* from which "alchemy" is derived, is itself an arabization of the classical Chinese word *Chin-I,* which in some dialects is *Kim-Ia* and means "the gold-making juice." The most important influence from China, however, was to come in later centuries, particularly after the Mongol invasion, and then primarily in the arts and technology.

The totality of the arts and sciences in Islam thus consisted of a synthesis of the ancient sciences of the Mediterranean people, as incorporated and developed by the Greeks, along with certain Oriental elements. The dominant part of this heritage was definitely Graeco-Hellenistic, in translations either from Syriac or from the Greek itself, by such masters of translation as Ḥunain ibn Isḥāq, and Thābit ibn Qurrah. There were numerous translations of Greek authors into Arabic in nearly every domain of knowledge. The ideas and points of views contained in these translations formed a large part of the nutriment which Islam sampled and then assimilated according to its own inner constitution, and the foundation given to it by the Quranic revelation. In this way there developed, in conjunction with the three basic "dimensions" of the Law, the Path, and the Truth, Islamic schools which were to become an accepted part of Islamic civilization.

With respect to Greek learning itself, Muslims came to distinguish between two different schools, each possessing a distinct type of science: one, the Hermetic-Pythagorean school, was metaphysical in its approach, its sciences of Nature depending upon the symbolic interpretation of phenomena and of mathematics; in the other, the syllogistic-rationalistic school of the followers of Aristotle, the point of view was philosophical rather than metaphysical, and its sciences were therefore aimed at finding the place of things in a rational system, rather than at seeing, through their appearances, their heavenly essences. The first school was regarded as the continuation, in Greek civilization, of the wisdom of the ancient prophets, especially Solomon and Idrīs; it was therefore considered to be based on divine rather than human knowledge. The second school was looked upon, for the most part, as reflecting the best effort the human mind could make to arrive at the truth, an effort of necessity limited by the finite nature of human reason. The first school was to become an integral part of Islam, certain of its cosmological sciences being integrated into some of the branches of Sufism. The second school did have many disciples in the earlier centuries and thus left an influence upon the language of Muslim theology; after the seventh/thirteenth century, it lost ground, however, and, despite its continuation up to the present day, it has remained a secondary aspect of Islamic intellectual life.

The various levels of reference existing hierarchically within the structure of Islam are presented concisely by a sage who lived in the fifth/eleventh century, and who is probably the one Oriental figure most familiar to the modern Western public: ʿUmar Khayyām, mathematician and poet extraordinary. That he should be regarded in the Western world, on the strength of his famous quatrains, as a skeptical hedonist is itself a sign of the profound lack of understanding between the two worlds; for he was in reality a sage and a gnostic of high standing. What appears to be lack of concern or agnosticism in his poetry is merely an accepted form of expression, within which he incorporated both the drastic remedy that the gnostic applies to religious hypocrisy, and also the reestablishment of contact with reality. (Late Greeks, such as Aenesidemus, had had recourse to the same skeptical device, and with similar intentions.) In the following passage from a metaphysical treatise, Khayyām divides the seekers after knowledge into four categories:

(1) The theologians, who become content with disputation and "satisfying" proofs, and consider this much knowledge of the Creator (excellent is His Name) as sufficient.
(2) The philosophers and learned men [of Greek inspiration] who use rational arguments and seek to know the laws of logic, and are never content merely with "satisfying" arguments. But they too cannot remain faithful to the conditions of logic, and become helpless with it.
(3) The Ismailis [a branch of Shia Islam] and others who say that the way of knowledge is none other than receiving information from a learned and credible informant; for, in reasoning about the knowledge of the Creator, His Essence and Attributes, there is much difficulty; the reasoning power of the opponents and the intelligent [of those who struggle against the final authority of the revelation, and of those who fully accept it] is stupefied and helpless before it. Therefore, they say, it is better to seek knowledge from the words of a sincere person.
(4) The Sufis, who do not seek knowledge by meditation or discursive thinking, but by purgation of their inner being and the purifying of their dispositions. They cleanse the rational soul of the impurities of nature and bodily form, until it becomes pure substance. It then comes face to face with the spiritual world, so that the forms of that world become truly reflected in it, without doubt or ambiguity.

> This is the best of all ways, because none of the perfections of God are kept away from it, and there are no obstacles or veils put before it. Therefore, whatever [ignorance] comes to man is due to the impurity of his nature; if the veil be lifted and the screen and obstacle removed, the truth of things as they are will become manifest. And the Master [the Prophet Muḥammad]—upon whom be peace—indicated this when he said: "Truly, during the days of your existence, inspirations come from God. Do you not want to follow them?"
> Tell unto reasoners that, for the lovers of God [gnostics], intuition is guide, not discursive thought.[2]

Here we have, stated authoritatively, the central perspective of Islamic thought, in which the component parts fall naturally into place. Each one is a different mode of knowing. It is puzzling at first sight to find nowhere in it the mathematicians, of whom Khayyām himself was such an eminent example. Notice, however, that the Ismailis correspond quite closely with what in the early Pythagorean school had been the *Akusmatikoi*, "those who go by what is told them." It should be noticed, also, that the Pythagorean *Mathematikoi*, the "expounders of the doctrine," will be found both among the philosophers and again among the Sufis, since systematic theory remains helpless without spiritual achievement, which is precisely what mathematics is intended to lead to, by contrast with syllogistic hair-splitting. This is clearly revealed in later sections of the same work in which Khayyām describes himself as both an orthodox Pythagorean and a Sufi.

Here, too, we see the significant contrast with the Greek world. For the Pythagorean doctrines alluded to had become practically extinct there by the time of Aristotle, and were to be taken up again, and at that only after a fashion, in the Hellenistic revival; in Islam, we see them stabilized and restored almost according to their original pattern through the unitary religious idea. Islam was thus able to hand on to the West, to the extent that the latter accepted the Pythagorean tradition, something more coherent, as well as technically more advanced, than the West's own immediate heritage from antiquity.

There are other lines to be found in Khayyām's spectrum.

2 ʿUmar Khayyām. *Risālah-i wujūd* (Bayāḍī MS. in the Tehran National Library). Translated by S. H. Nasr.

The "atomistic" school of thought which flourished in Islam after the fourth/tenth century, and which in the Western perspective might be supposed to be scientific, he regards as not belonging to science at all, but to theology, for the Ashʿarites who represented this school were exactly the sort of "theologians" he described. In the writings of the followers of this school—especially al-Bāqillānī, who may be considered their outstanding "philosopher of Nature"—the continuity of external forms is broken by an "atomistic" doctrine of time and space, and by the denial of the Aristotelian notion of causality. For the Ashʿarites (as also for the Sufis), the world is annihilated and recreated at every moment; the cause of all events is the Creator and not a finite, created agent. A stone falls because God makes it fall, not because of the nature of the stone or because it is impelled by an external force. What appears as "Laws of Nature," i.e., the uniformity of sequence of cause and effect, is only a matter of habit, determined by the will of God and given the status of "law" by Him. Miracles, which seem to break the apparent uniformity of natural phenomena, are simply going against the "habit" of Nature; the Arabic word for a supernatural event means literally that which results from "rupture of habit." We are facing here a strict "consequentiality," which has its parallel in Western thought of the seventeenth century. From Descartes to the Occasionalists, the development presents curious similarities.

In the second grouping on Khayyām's list, the "philosophers and learned men," we would find assembled all the famous names of Islamic science. There is a sharp distinction, however, between two schools of "philosophical" thought, both of which profess to be disciples of the Greeks. The first is the Peripatetic school, whose doctrines are a combination of the ideas of Aristotle and of some Neoplatonists. The representative of this school who was closest to Aristotle was Averroes who, paradoxically, had less effect upon the Islamic than upon the Christian world, and should be studied more as a great member of the tradition of Western philosophy than as an integral part of Islamic intellectual life.

The science of Nature cultivated by the Peripatetic school is primarily syllogistic: it seeks to determine the place of each being, in a vast system based upon the philosophy of Aristotle. The best expression of the doctrines of this school appears in Avicenna's early writings. *The Book of Healing* is the most comprehensive encyclopedia of knowledge ever written by one person, and undoubtedly the most influential Peripatetic work in Islam.

The other Islamic school professing to follow the Greeks was much more sympathetic to the Pythagorean-Platonic than to the Aristotelian tradition. This school, which in later centuries came to be called the Illuminatist (*ishrāqī*) school, asserts that it derives its doctrines not only from the Pythagoreans and their followers, but from the ancient Prophets, the Hermetic Tradition, and even from the ancient Zoroastrian sages. The symbolic works of Avicenna, such as *Living Son of the Awake* (*Ḥayy ibn Yaqẓān*) are early expressions of the writings of this school. The greatest Illuminatist philosopher, however, is Suhrawardī, who drew his symbolism from all the many sources mentioned above.

The sciences of Nature, as well as the mathematics cultivated by certain adherents of this school, are primarily symbolic, and resemble to a great extent the writings of some Neoplatonists. Nature becomes for the writers of this school a cosmic crypt from whose confines they must seek to escape; and on their journey through it, they see in its phenomena "signs," which guide them on the road toward final "illumination." Many Illuminatists, particularly those of later centuries, have also been Sufis, who have made use of the eminently initiatic language of the Illuminatist philosophers to describe the journey of the Sufi toward gnosis. Many members of this school, and in general the learned men whom Khayyām mentions, have also been among the group that have cultivated mathematics, astronomy, and medicine; for these learned men took an interest in all the arts and sciences, and helped to keep alive the traditions of learning in those fields, as an integral part of their studies in philosophy.

The Peripatetics were very strong during the fourth/tenth and fifth/eleventh centuries, but their influence weakened during the succeeding period. The Illuminatists, on the other hand, became strong after the sixth/twelfth century and al-Ghazzālī's triumph. They have had a continuous tradition down to the present day, chiefly because of the metaphysical (as against rationalistic) emphasis in their doctrines, and also because of the use of their language by certain Sufi masters. One of the greatest exponents of Illuminatist doctrines, as interpreted and modified by the Safavid sage Mullā Ṣadrā, was Ḥājjī Mullā Hādī Sabziwārī who died in Persia less than a century ago.

The Ismailis, to whom Khayyām next refers, are a branch of Shia Islam, which was very powerful in his time, and also played a considerable role in the cultivation of the arts and sciences. Ismaili doctrines are fundamentally esoteric, being based on numerical symbolism and the symbolic interpretation of the "cosmic text." The symbolic interpretation of the Quran, which is basic in Shia Islam as well as in Sufism, was made the basis for the symbolic study of Nature. Moreover, such sciences as alchemy and astrology became integrated into their doctrines, and such texts as the *Epistles* of the Brethren of Purity, and the numerous writings of Jābir ibn Ḥayyān, the alchemist, were to have their greatest influence upon this group. The development of what has been called "Oriental neo-Pythagoreanism" is found most clearly in the treatises of the Ismailis. They were very much interested in the sciences of Nature; in integrating the rhythms and cycles of Nature with the cycles of history and with the manifestations of various prophets and imams, their works rank among the most important Islamic writings on Nature.

Khayyām mentions, finally, the Sufis or gnostics, the group to which he himself belonged. It may seem surprising that a man so well versed in the arts and sciences of his day should consider the "way of purification" of the Sufis as the best way of acquiring knowledge. His language in this regard, however, is not merely theoretical, it is almost operational: one cleanses and focuses the instrument of perception, i.e., the soul, so that it may see the realities of the spiritual world. Aristotle himself, the great rationalist, had once said that "knowledge is according to the mode of the knower." The gnostic, in employing the "right" mode of knowledge ensures that Intellection takes place in him immediately and intuitively. In this regard, Khayyām's statement becomes clearer when seen in the light of a doctrine that we shall discuss later: the doctrine of the universal man, who is not only the final goal of the spiritual life, but also the archetype of the universe.

To the extent that the gnostic is able to purify himself of his individualistic and particular nature, and thus to identify himself with the universal man within him, to that same extent does he also gain knowledge of the principles of the cosmos, as well as of the Divine realities. For the gnostic, knowledge of Nature is secondary to knowledge of the Divine Principle; yet, because of the rapport between the gnostic and the universe, Nature does play a positive role in guiding him to his ultimate goal. The phenomena of Nature become "transparent" for the gnostic, so that in each event he "sees" the archetype. The symbols of substances—geometric forms and numerical quantities, colors, and directions—these and many other such symbols are aspects of the being of things. They increase in their reality—a reality independent of personal taste or of the individual—to the extent that the gnostic divorces himself from his individual perspective and limited existence, and identifies himself with Being. For the gnostic, the knowledge of anything in the universe means ultimately knowledge of the relationship between the essence of that particular being and the Divine Intellect, and the knowledge of the ontological relationship between that being and Being itself.

Khayyām's classification did not take into consideration certain writers of great importance, who did not follow any particular school. There are also many Islamic writers, hakims, including Khayyām himself, who possessed a knowledge of several disciplines, and in whom two or more levels of his hierarchy of knowledge may be found. Some of the most outstanding of these men will be discussed in the next chapter.

Inasmuch as the hierarchy of knowledge in Islam, as it has existed historically, has been united by a metaphysical bond—much as a vertical axis unites horizontal planes of reference—the integration of these diverse views "from above" has been possible. Historically, of course, there have been many conflicts, sometimes disputes leading to violence and occasionally to the death of a writer. Such conflicts are not, however, as elsewhere, between incompatible orthodoxies. They are regarded by most Islamic commentators as due to the lack of a more universal point of view on the part of those who have only embraced a less universal one. Only the gnostic, who sees all things "as they really are," is able to integrate all these views into their principial unity.

Regarded from their own point of view, each of these schools may be said to possess a certain "philosophy of Nature," and, in conformity with it, to cultivate the sciences dealing with the universe. Some of their writings, primarily those of the Peripatetics, were to be translated into Latin to help form that Western scholasticism which was later to give way to seventeenth-century "natural philosophy." Other writings, such as those of the alchemists, were to flourish in the Western world for several centuries, only to wither away in its atmosphere of rationalistic philosophy. There were still other works, especially those of the Sufis and Illuminatists, which were to have an influence on certain Western circles such as that of Dante, and yet for the most part to remain almost unknown in the Western world, down to comparatively recent times.

In this brief introduction, it has been necessary to cover much ground that is unfamiliar and often quite difficult for a Western reader to grasp. But we felt that we had to dispel the common conception of the Muslims as merely Puritan warriors and merchants, whose strange bent for the "subtleties" of algebra and logic somehow also enabled them to become the transmitters of Greek learning to the West. As against that all too current notion, we have tried to present a brief picture of a culture whose spiritual values are inextricably tied up with mathematics and with metaphysics of a high order, and which once again fused the constituent elements of Greek science into a powerful unitary conception, which had an essential influence on the Western world up to the time of the Renaissance.

Strangely enough, it is this latter conception, half unknown at best, and then quickly forgotten in the West, which has remained, up to the present Western impact upon the Islamic world, the *major* factor in the Islamic perspective determining its attitude toward Nature and the meaning it gives to the sciences of Nature; conversely, it is those very elements of the Islamic sciences, most responsible for providing the tools with which the West began the study of the already secularized Nature of the seventeenth century, that became *secondary* in the Islamic world itself and had already ceased to occupy the main intellectual efforts of that civilization by the ninth/fifteenth century.

The Western world has since concentrated its intellectual energies upon the study of the quantitative aspects of things, thus developing a science of Nature, whose all too obvious fruits in the physical domain have won for it the greatest esteem among people everywhere, for most of whom "science" is identified with technology and its applications. Islamic science, by contrast, seeks ultimately to attain such knowledge as will contribute toward the spiritual perfection and deliverance of anyone capable of studying it; thus its fruits are inward and hidden, its values more difficult to discern. To understand it requires placing oneself within its perspective, and accepting as legitimate a science of Nature which has a different end, and uses different means, from those of modern science. If it is unjust to identify Western science solely with its material results, it is even more unjust to judge medieval science by its outward "usefulness" alone. However important its uses may have been in calendarial work, in irrigation, in architecture, its ultimate aim has always been to relate the corporeal world to its basic spiritual principle, through the knowledge of those symbols which unite the various orders of reality. It can only be understood, and should only be judged, in terms of its own aims and its own perspectives.

CHAPTER ONE

THE UNIVERSAL FIGURES OF ISLAMIC SCIENCE

THROUGHOUT ISLAMIC HISTORY, the central figure in the transmission of the sciences has been the wise man, or *ḥakīm.* He has usually been a physician, a writer and poet, an astronomer and mathematician, and, above all, a sage. In this figure of the *ḥakīm,* one can see the unity of the sciences as so many branches of a tree whose trunk is the wisdom embodied in the sage. The *ḥakīm* has always established the unity of the sciences in the minds of students, by the very fact of his teaching all of the sciences as so many different applications of the same fundamental principles. The Islamic teaching system as a whole and the classification of the sciences, which forms its matrix, are themselves dependent upon this figure of the *ḥakīm,* or sage.

Of course, not all of those who have made notable contributions to Islamic science have been masters of every field of knowledge. Some have been predominantly mathematicians, or physicians, or natural historians. With such figures we shall deal in the appropriate chapters pertaining to each subject matter. But there are a number of outstanding figures whose scope was universal, and they played an important role in several of the sciences. Today knowledge has become so compartmentalized as to make the conception of such figures very difficult for modern man. Furthermore, in dividing the Islamic sciences into subjects that conform more or less to the present-day division of knowledge, it becomes difficult to determine where to place such figures. We have therefore decided to describe briefly some of the outstanding universal figures of Islamic science in this chapter, leaving others whose contribution, no matter how important, belongs to a particular domain to be treated along with the subject matter in question. These universal figures are by no means the only ones to have made noteworthy achievements, especially in mathematics, but they are the hakims whose names appear in nearly every field of Islamic science and who have left an indelible mark upon the intellectual life of Islam.

Jābir ibn Ḥayyān (c.103/721–c.200/815)

Little is known of the life of Jābir ibn Hayyān al-Azdī al-Tūsī al-Sūfī, the founder of Islamic alchemy. It can be asserted with some certainty that his family came from the Azd tribe of Southern Arabia that had settled during the rise of Islam in Kufa. His father, a Shiite, had plotted against the Omayyads in Khurasan where Jābir was born, probably in Tus. He spent his early years there and then was sent to Arabia. Later he came to Kufa where he spent much of his life and, finally, to Baghdad where he first became known as an alchemist at the court of Hārūn al-Rashīd and was especially associated with the viziers of the Abbasids, the powerful Barmakids. He was a Sufi and a Shiite, closely connected with the circle of the sixth Imam, Jaʿfar al-Ṣādiq. With the disgrace of the Barmakids at court, Jābir also fell out of favor but is said to have survived into the reign of al-Maʾmūn, although the date of his death is by no means certain.

The number of writings that bear Jābir's name, about three thousand, most of which are short treatises, have made many doubt their authenticity and some have even questioned the historical existence of Jābir. But as E. Holmyard, a leading historian of Islamic alchemy, has clearly shown there is no doubt about the existence of such a person. The Shiite historical sources are too consistent about Jābir to enable one to deny that such a figure existed. Yet, there is no doubt that many works in the Jābirian corpus are later Ismaili accretions and in fact Jābir became, more than an historical figure, an intellectual type in whose name many later works were written. There is little reason to doubt, however, that much of the corpus does belong to Jābir and the rest to the school connected with his name.

The question of Jābir is further complicated by the fact that under his Latin name, Geber, there appeared a series of works in Latin for which there is no Arabic original while other works by "Geber" are really Latin versions of treatises belonging to the Jābirian corpus. There is, therefore, a distinction to be made between the Latin Geber and Jābir although until all of the Jābirian corpus, most of which remains unedited, is studied there is no means of determining how much of the Latin Geber belongs to a Western, most likely a Spanish, alchemist writing under the name of the outstanding master of the art of alchemy.

The important works of Jābir include *The Hundred and Twelve Books,* some of which are dedicated to the Barmakids; *The Seventy Books,* a good portion of which was translated into Latin, and *The Books of the Balance,* which outline the famous theory of the balance underlying the whole of Jābirian alchemy. Jābir did not only write on alchemy, of which he was the greatest medieval authority, but also on logic, philosophy, medicine, the occult sciences, physics, mechanics and nearly every other domain of knowledge. He expounded a particular "philosophy of nature" and a method for the study of different sciences that influenced all later alchemical and Hermetic authors as well as the Ismailis and certain schools of Imāmī, or "Twelver," Shiism and Sufism.

Abū Yūsuf Ya'qūb ibn Isḥāq al-Kindī (c. 185/801–c.260/873)

Al-Kindī, the Latin Alkindus, who is entitled the "Philosopher of the Arabs," came from the Arab tribe of Kindah. His ancestors had settled in Kufa where his father was governor. Al-Kindī spent his early life in Kufa, which had become a center of the sciences. He studied the religious sciences as well as philosophy and mathematics, and became especially interested in the philosophical sciences after going to Baghdad. At this time the major movement of translation into Arabic had already begun. He knew Syriac and perhaps some Greek and was well acquainted with Graeco-Hellenistic scientific and philosophical works. For some time he was held in high esteem in court but spent the last part of his life in obscurity.

Al-Kindī was the first of the Muslim philosopher-scientists.

His interest was encyclopedic. He wrote about two hundred seventy treatises, most of which are now lost, in logic, philosophy, physics, all branches of mathematics as well as music, medicine and natural history. He was the founder of the Islamic Peripatetic school of philosophy and was highly respected in the medieval and Renaissance West to the extent that he was considered as one of the judices of astrology and Cardano called him one of the twelve great intellectual figures of humanity. His immediate students were well-known geographers and mathematicians, while his philosophic influence is to be seen directly in the writings of al-Fārābī and later Muslim Peripatetics.

Ḥunain ibn Isḥāq (194/810–263/877)

Ḥunain, the Latin Joannitius, was one of the Christian scholars who made an important contribution to the rise of Islamic sciences as translators and transmitters of the Greek sciences. He was born in Hira, his father having been an apothecary. He studied in Jundishapur and Baghdad under the well-known physician Ibn Māsawaih (Mesue Senior), and journeyed to Anatolia to complete his knowledge of Greek. He and his immediate students, including his son and nephew, made the most exact and correct translations of Greek and Syriac texts into Arabic and played a major role in the sudden rise of interest by Muslims in the Graeco-Hellenistic sciences. Ḥunain himself was an outstanding physician whose works were cited as authority by later Muslim authors. He also wrote on astronomy, meteorolgy and especially philosophy. His *Aphorism of Philosophers* was well known in the West in its Hebrew version and he is especially noted for his study and translation of the philosophy of Galen.

Thābit ibn Qurrah (211/826 or 221/836–288/901)

Thābit hailed from the community of Sabaens in Harran, where there was a religious cult centered around the symbolism of the planets. This cult, much interested in the Pythagorean mathematical and mystical tradition, survived well into the Islamic period. Like many members of this community Thābit was well versed in mathematics and astronomy. Due to religious differences with his community he set out for Baghdad and was fortunate in meeting on the way the influential mathematician, Muḥammad ibn Mūsā ibn Shākir, who, recognizing his ability, took him under his patronage. Thābit soon gained fame in Baghdad and became the court astronomer.

Thābit was a major translator, almost as important as Ḥunain, and, like him, he wrote lasting works in medicine and philosophy. In addition he wrote many treatises on astronomy, number theory, physics and other branches of mathematics that exercised an immense influence on Muslim scientists. The echo of his scientific views, especially regarding the theory of "trepidation," was heard throughout the Middle Ages in the West.

Muhammad ibn Mūsā al-Khwārazmī (d. c.249/863)

Al-Khwārazmī, the first outstanding Muslim mathematician with whom the history of this subject among Muslims properly begins, was born in Khwarazm (usually written as Khwarizm in most European sources), the modern Khiva. Little is known of his life except that he spent some time in Baghdad and it is said by some later historians that he journeyed to India to master the Indian sciences. He became a well-known scientist at the court of al-Maʾmūn and participated in measuring the degree of arc in the company of astronomers commissioned by al-Maʾmūn for this task.

The writings of al-Khwārazmī, which represent his own works as well as the synthesis of the mathematical works of the generation before him, had an immense influence, more than that of any other single mathematician. His *Algebra* (*al-Jabr waʾl-muqābalah*), the first Muslim work on Algebra, gave its name to this science in both East and West. He introduced the Indian numerals into the Muslim world and through his work on arithmetic, the West came to know of the numerals which it calls "Arabic." He wrote the first extensive Muslim work on geography revising much of Ptolemy and drawing new geographical and celestial maps. His astronomical tables are among the best in Islamic astronomy. His influence is attested to by the fact that Algorism, the latinization of his name, al-Khwārazmī, for a long time meant arithmetic in most European languages and is used today for any recurring method of calculation which has become an established rule. It has even entered into the technical vocabulary of modern computation techniques.

Muḥammad ibn Zakarīyā al-Rāzī (c.251/865–313/925)

Al-Rāzī, the Latin Rhazes, sometimes called "the Arabic Galen," is the greatest clinical physician of Islam, well known in both the West and the East. His authority in medicine has been second only to that of Avicenna whom he excelled in his observational powers. Rhazes, as his name bears out, was born in Rai where he spent the first part of his life. He is said to have been a lute player who, at the age of thirty, turned from music to alchemy. Then, as a result of the weakening of his eyesight, relatively late in life, he devoted his whole attention to medicine in which he seems to have been interested even in his earlier years. He studied medicine and perhaps philosophy with ʿAlī ibn Rabban al-Ṭabarī. Soon he became the director of the hospital at Rai and later functioned in the same capacity in Baghdad. Students flocked to him from near and far, and he was respected both for his knowledge and kindness toward students and patients. He wrote and studied continuously until he went blind whereupon he returned to Rai to pass the rest of his days.

Al-Bīrūnī, who made a special study of the writings of Rhazes, mentions one hundred eighty-four works. Most of these are lost, especially the philosophical ones of which only a few survive. Of the medical works the most important one is *Continens* (*al-Ḥāwī*) so well known in the Latin Occident. It is the longest single Islamic work on medicine and contains many of Rhazes' own observations. His masterpiece *The Treatise on Smallpox and Measles* (known in Latin as *De Pestilentia* or *De Peste*) was read in medical circles in the West until the modern period. His alchemical works, especially the *Secret of Secrets,* have been also well known. His philosophical and ethical works, however, were never known to the West and in the East met with severe criticism from both the theologians and Peripatetic philosophers because of their "anti-prophetic" sentiment. His influence in the Islamic world as well as in the West has been primarily in the fields of medicine and alchemy. In both of these fields he was recognized as one of the indubitable masters.

Abū Naṣr al-Fārābī (c.258/870–339/950)

Al-Fārābī, the Latin Alpharabius, the second outstanding Peripatetic philosopher after al-Kindī, was born in Farab in Transoxiana where he spent the first half of his life. His father was a general and afforded him the opportunity to study with the best teachers. His early training was in religious sciences and languages in which he was very proficient. Later historians record his having known nearly every language. This means that most likely he knew many; certainly Arabic, Persian and Turkish, and probably some of the Central Asiatic dialects and local languages. Later in life he became interested in philosophy and the sciences but, unlike many similar figures in Islamic history, not in medicine. He set out for Baghdad, then the center of learning, where he studied logic with the Christian Abū Bishr Matta ibn Yūnus, the undisputed master in the field. Later he became himself the greatest authority in logic and trained such famous logicians and philosophers as the Christian philosopher Yaḥyā ibn ʿAdī. After twenty years in Baghdad, al-Fārābī set out for the court of Saif al-Daulah in Aleppo where he spent the rest of his days and where he died much respected and honored.

Al-Fārābī was the first person in Islam to classify completely the sciences, to delineate the limit of each, and to establish firmly the foundation of each branch of learning. He was for this reason called the "Second Teacher," the first having been Aristotle who accomplished this same task in ancient times and set the precedent for the Muslim philosophers. Al-Fārābī is also the first great Muslim commentator on Aristotle. Of the seventy works of al-Fārābī cited, half are devoted to logic, of which he was the real founder in Islam, including the commentary or paraphrasing of the whole of the *Organon* of Aristotle. His commentary on the *Metaphysics* helped Avicenna understand that work. He wrote independent works on physics, mathematics, ethics and political philosophy of which he was again the founder in Islam. He was a practicing Sufi and the spirit of Sufism runs throughout his works. He was also one of the foremost medieval theoreticians of music and some of his musical works have survived in the rites of Sufi brotherhoods, especially those in Anatolia, until modern times.

Abuʾl-Ḥasan al-Masʿūdī (d. 345/956)

One of the outstanding historians and scientists of Islam, al-Masʿūdī was born near Baghdad. He was a world traveler, having journeyed through Persia, Central Asia, India, and the Near East and, according to traditional accounts, having sailed through the China Sea and to Madagascar. The last ten years of his life were spent first in Syria and then in Egypt where he died.

Al-Masʿūdī belongs to the tradition of universal historians like al-Ṭabarī and al-Yaʿqūbī. His *Meadows of Gold and Mines of Precious Stones* is a notable work of its kind. It shows al-Masʿūdī as historian, geographer, geologist, and natural historian. Its pages contain many valuable scientific observations. Late in life al-Masʿūdī composed his *Book of Indication and Revision* which summarizes his philosophy of Nature and is the synthesis of his observations on Nature and history. Al-Masʿūdī also wrote works on philosophical and theological questions but it is upon the two major surviving works on history and natural history that his reputation as a scholar and scientist depend. These are sufficient to make him one of the encyclopedic figures in Islamic science, one whose innate thirst for knowledge led him to the examination of nearly every form of science and the observation of many pertinent aspects of both human and natural history.

Abū ʿAlī al-Ḥusain ibn Sīnā (370/980–428/1037)

Ibn Sīnā, the Latin Avicenna, whose compatriots have given him the honorific title *Shaikh al-raʾīs,* "Leader among Wise Men," is the greatest philosopher-scientist of Islam and its most influential figure in the general domain of the arts and sciences. Born near Bukhara in a family devoted to learning he received an excellent education, especially after the family moved to the city of Bukhara itself. His father acquired the best teachers in every domain for his remarkably precocious son who at the age of ten had already mastered grammar, literature and even some theology and knew the Quran by heart. At the age of eighteen he had mastered all the sciences of his day. At the end of his life he wrote that he knew then only what he had learned in his youth.

Because of changing political conditions in Central Asia and the death of his father, Avicenna left his birthplace and set out for the different cities of Persia beginning a life of wandering which continued to his last days. Already well known as a physician whose services were sought by all, he found willing patrons everywhere. He stayed in Rai, then for some time in Hamadan where he even became vizier and encountered political difficulties, and Isfahan where he had a relatively long period of peace. In all these cities he acted as physician to the Buwayhid princes who then ruled Persia. Finally anticipating his own death he returned to Hamadan where he died and where his mausoleum is found today.

Avicenna was a man of enormous energy. Although living in turbulent times and often occupied with state matters he wrote two hundred fifty works of different lengths, some of which were actually dictated on horseback while accompanying a ruler to some battle. His power of concentration and mental acumen have become proverbial in the East. Of his works the best known is first the *Canon of Medicine* which is the epitome of Islamic medicine, taught to this day in the Orient. It was translated into Latin and taught for centuries in Western universities, being in fact one of the most frequently printed scientific texts in the Renaissance. The second is his monumental encyclopedia, *The Book of Healing (Kitāb al-shifāʾ)*. It marks the high point of Peripatetic philosophy in Islam and also contains important chapters on logic, and mathematical and natural sciences. Sections of this work were translated into Latin in the sixth/twelfth century, first as part of the *Incunabula* and later as a separate work. Since the word *al-shifāʾ* resembles the Hebrew word *shefʿa* meaning abundance or sufficiency, and the work reached Latin through Hebrew, the title in Latin became *Sufficientia*. Moreover, only parts of the *Physics* became known as the *Sufficientia* whereas the other sections of the book gained independent titles. The section on geology and mineralogy for example became known as *De Mineralibus* and was attributed to Aristotle until modern times.

The influence of Avicenna on both East and West was immense. In the Islamic world his spirit has dominated the intellectual activity of all later periods while his philosophy and medicine have continued as a living influence to the present day. In the West he became known as the "Prince of Physicians" and dominated medical science for centuries while his scientific, philosophical and theological views left their mark upon many important figures such as Albertus Magnus, St. Thomas, Duns Scotus and Roger Bacon.

Abū ʿAlī al-Ḥasan ibn al-Haitham (c.354/965–430/1039)

Ibn al-Haitham, the greatest of Muslim physicists, known to the West as Alhazen, was born in Basra where he studied mathematics and other sciences. At that time the Fatimid dynasty of Egypt showed much interest in the sciences, and Alhazen was invited to come to Egypt to study the possibility of controlling the Nile floods. Having accepted the task, he set out for Egypt where he was received with much honor. But after failing to come up with a flood-control plan, he fell into disgrace and to protect himself from the wrath of the ruler began to feign insanity. For the rest of his life he lived quietly, often copying mathematical manuscripts to earn his living. He finally died in Cairo.

Alhazen is known to have written nearly two hundred works on mathematics, physics, astronomy and medicine, as well as on other scientific subjects. He also wrote commentaries on Aristotle and Galen. Although he made major contributions to the fields of mathematics and astronomy it is especially in the domain of physics that he made his outstanding achievements. He was an exact observer and experimenter as well as a theoretician. His major work, *Optics,* is the best medieval work of its kind, a work that influenced the optical writings of Roger Bacon, Witelo and Kepler in the West, and many later treatises by Muslim scientists. Alhazen also made significant contributions to the study of the anatomy and diseases of the eye.

Abū Raiḥān al-Bīrūnī (362/973–c.442/1051)

Some have considered al-Bīrūnī as the greatest Muslim scientist. Certainly he is among the foremost intellectual figures of Islam. Born near Khwarazm he studied mathematics with a student of the famous Abu˒l-Wafā˒ and became proficient in it. Later he journeyed extensively in the northern regions of Persia and when Maḥmūd of Ghazna conquered Central Asia, he joined the services of this powerful ruler. He even accompanied him in his conquest of India which enabled him to observe this land firsthand. After this, al-Bīrūnī returned to Ghazna where he lived the rest of his days writing and studying to the very end of his prolific life.

Every one of al-Bīrūnī's writings, of which about one hundred eighty are known, is of value since he was both a great scientist and scholar. His *India* is the best account of the Hindu religion and of the sciences and customs of India in medieval times. His *Chronology of Ancient Nations* dealing with the calendar and festivities of different nations is unique. His *Canon of al-Mas˓ūdī* dedicated to Maḥmūd of Ghazna's son, Mas˓ūd, holds the same position in Islamic astronomy as the *Canon* of Avicenna does in medicine while his *Elements of Astrology* was the standard text for the teaching of the *Quadrivium* for centuries. He also wrote outstanding works on physics, mathematical geography, mineralogy and nearly every branch of mathematics, astronomy and astrology. No one in Islam combined the qualities of an outstanding scientist with that of a meticulous scholar, compiler and historian to the same degree as al-Bīrūnī. His only misfortune as far as his later influence is concerned was that his works were never translated into Latin. In the East he has always been respected as both a scientist and scholar.

Abu'l Qāsim Maslamah al-Majrīṭī (d. c.398/1007)

Little is known of the life of this Andalusian scientist who was one of the first to introduce the study of the sciences, especially mathematics and alchemy, to the western part of the Islamic world. It is known that he was born in Madrid and later moved to Cordova where he established a school in which such figures as the historian Ibn Khaldūn and the physician al-Zahrāwī were to study later. He was also responsible for spreading the *Epistles* of the Brethren of Purity, an encyclopedia of knowledge with a Pythagorean tinge which had just become popular in the East, in Andalusia. Some attribute to him the treatise that summarizes the contents of the fifty-two *Epistles.* Although he wrote on astronomy and mathematics and in fact commented on the tables of al-Khwārazmī, his most important works are on alchemy. *The Sage's Step* and *The Aim of the Wise,* two of the best-known works in Islamic alchemy, are either by him or directly inspired by his teachings. The latter was translated into Latin as *Picatrix* and became a mainstay of alchemical literature in the West.

Abū Ḥāmid Muḥammad al-Ghazzālī (450/1058–505/1111)

Al-Ghazzālī (the Latin Algazel) was not a scientist or philosopher in the usual sense, yet he left such a profound mark upon the intellectual life of Islam that no account of the history of Islamic science can be adequate without a discussion of his role. Born in Tus, where early in life he was introduced to the teachings of Sufism, he went to Naishapur to study theology with al-Juwainī. He became so famous as a theologian and scholar of religious sciences that at a young age he was called to Baghdad to occupy a chair in the foremost university of that time, the Niẓāmīyah. But here, as a result of close study of both philosophical and scientific works, al-Ghazzālī underwent a deep spiritual crisis. He left his post and renounced his worldly position, finally finding the light of certainty in Sufism. After a period of self-discipline and ascetic practices during which he became himself an outstanding Sufi master, al-Ghazzālī returned to society. He went first to Naishapur where he taught for a while and finally retired to Tus with a few choice disciples.

His most important religious work is *The Revivification of the Religious Sciences,* which is the most outstanding Muslim work on spiritual ethics. Al-Ghazzālī also wrote on logic and philosophy. His importance in this domain, however, is not in exposition but in criticism. In *The Purposes of the Philosophers* he summarized Peripatetic philosophy so well that when this work was translated into Latin, he became known in the West as an authority on Peripatetic philosophy. *The Purposes of the Philosophers* served as the preparation for his severe criticism of the philosophers in *The Incoherence of the Philosophers* where he attacked the rationalistic tendencies inherent in Aristotelian philosophy and criticized some of the views of Avicenna and al-Fārābī. Because he was an outstanding figure personally and a forceful writer as well, he succeeded in curtailing the influence of Peripatetic philosophy in Islam, particularly in the Sunni world. At the same time he legitimized the teaching of Sufism in formal religious circles. Through these two important steps he helped more than any other single individual to bring about the intellectual transformation that took place in the Islamic world during the sixth/twelfth century. He is in every way one of the most notable religious and intellectual figures of Islam.

Abu'l-Fatḥ ʿUmar ibn Ibrāhīm al-Khayyāmī (Omar Khayyam) (b. 429/1038–440/1048, d. 517/1123–526/1132)[1]

ʿUmar Khayyām, the most famous Persian poet in the West, was also among the most notable scientists of the medieval period. Practically nothing is known of his life save that he was born near Naishapur where he spent most of his days and died in that city. His tomb is there and, to this day, is visited by people from near and far. In 467/1074–75

[1] There is so little known of the life of Khayyām that the date of both his birth and death are contested by scholars, the date of death varying by as much as twenty years.

he was already a famous mathematician and was called in by Malikshāh to reform the calendar. This calendar, known as the Jalālī calendar, is still in use in Persia and is more accurate than the Gregorian. Khayyām was highly respected by his contemporaries as a master of the sciences although he wrote little and accepted few students. In one of his treatises he calls himself a student of Avicenna, but since he lived much later this could only mean that he considered himself as belonging to the school of Avicenna and, in fact, he translated one of Avicenna's works from Arabic into Persian.

About a dozen treatises of Khayyām's on philosophy and science have survived, the most important being his *Algebra* which is the best work of its kind in medieval mathematics. He also wrote on geometry and physics as well as on metaphysical questions. His *Quatrains* translated beautifully, although somewhat freely, by Fitzgerald have made him the best known literary figure of the East in the West. But they have also depicted him as the chief propagator of the philosophy of "live, drink and be merry," whereas in reality he was a Sufi and a gnostic. He wrote his quatrains, not as a denial of the possibility of attaining certitude, but as a corrective for the kind of religious hypocrisy that mistakes relative forms for the Absolute Truth which the forms are meant to convey. Behind the apparent skepticism of Khayyām lies the absolute certainty of intellectual intuition. In the Islamic world the influence of Khayyām was foremost in the domain of mathematics and his philosophical position was judged by his metaphysical and philosophical treatises. These show him to be a true hakim as do his quatrains which contain spontaneous reflections upon different aspects of human existence and, if seen in the correct light, confirm rather than deny the gnostic background of his thought. Khayyām is perhaps the only figure in history who was both a great poet and an outstanding mathematician. Islam has produced a few other figures who have been accomplished in both domains but none with the brilliance of Khayyām.

Abu'l-Walīd Muḥammad ibn Rushd (520/1126–595/1198)

Ibn Rushd, or Averroes, the purest Aristotelian among Muslim philosophers, was born in Cordova of an illustrious family of judges and religious scholars. He studied law and medicine in Cordova and later journeyed to Marrakesh to continue his studies. He became an authority in religious law and medicine, as well as in philosophy. He was a judge in Seville and Cordova and also the personal physician of the caliph. Later in life he was attacked for his philosophical views, but was reinstated into a position of honor at court a short while before his death.

Averroes was the greatest medieval commentator on Aristotle. St. Thomas called him "the Commentator" and Dante referred to him as "he who made the grand commentary." According to H. A. Wolfson, one of the leading authorities on medieval philosophy and particularly on the commentaries of Aristotle, there are altogether thirty-eight commentaries by Averroes on different works of Aristotle in addition to short treatises devoted to particular aspects of Aristotelian philosophy. Averroes usually wrote a short, a medium-length and a long commentary on every subject he dealt with in conformity with the method of teaching in traditional schools. Upon five works of Aristotle, including the all-important *Physics* and *Metaphysics,* all three of Averroes' commentaries have survived. In addition, Averroes wrote independent works on astronomy, physics, and medicine. He sought to answer al-Ghazzālī's attack on philosophers in his *The Incoherence of the Incoherence.* However, this work did not have as much influence in the Muslim world as al-Ghazzālī's original attack. In fact as far as the world of Islam is concerned the influence of Avicenna was greater than that of Averroes.

In the West, however, Averroes must be considered as the most influential Muslim thinker. In fact, most of his works survive today in Latin and Hebrew versions rather than the original Arabic. He was translated not only in the seventh/thirteenth century into Hebrew and Latin but once again in the tenth/sixteenth century when his commentaries attracted new attention and became the subject of heated debate. Altogether, however, his image in the West as the opponent of revealed religion does not conform to his real nature and there is a difference between Averroes as a Muslim philosopher and the "Latin Averroes" seen in the West through a misunderstanding of some of his teachings.

Naṣīr al-Dīn al-Ṭūsī (597/1201–672/1274)

If we consider the whole domain of the arts and sciences and philosophy together, then no doubt after Avicenna the most dominant figure is Naṣīr al-Dīn al-Ṭūsī. Others like al-Bīrūnī displayed the same universal scientific genius but no one except Avicenna was able to leave a permanent imprint upon so many fields as Naṣīr al-Dīn. Born in Tus, Naṣīr al-Dīn studied mathematics with Kamāl al-Dīn ibn Yūnus and gained fame as an astronomer. At a time when Khurasan was being threatened by the Mongol invasion and there was much political uncertainty, Naṣīr al-Dīn began his career in the service of some of the Ismaili princes. When Hulagu conquered Persia, Naṣīr al-Dīn, knowing that there was no way of preventing massive destruction, tried to salvage all that was possible by rendering his services as an astrologer and astronomer to Hulagu. In this way he gained the Mongol ruler's confidence and saved many libraries and educational institutions. He was put in charge of religious endowments and was able to induce Hulagu to establish the Maragha observatory and scientific institution. As its director he brought mathematicians from near and far to this center and was personally responsible for the revival of the study of astronomy and mathematics in Islam. He spent most of his later years in Maragha and then at the end of his life went to Kazimain near Baghdad where he died and was buried next to the tomb of Mūsā al-Kāẓim, the seventh Shiite imam.

Naṣīr al-Dīn was a prolific writer in both Arabic and Persian. He wrote commentaries on the whole cycle of Greek mathematical texts from Euclid to Ptolemy. He also wrote independent works in both mathematics and astronomy in which he criticized Ptolemy and even proposed a new planetary model. He also participated in the compilation of the astronomical tables in Maragha named after the Ilkhānids. Naṣīr al-Dīn is the author of several definitive works on Ismaili doctrines written when he was in their hands. He revived the philosophy of Avicenna by answering the attacks made against him by theologians. He is the author of the *Nasirean Ethics,* the most widely read work of ethics in the Persian language. Being a twelver Shiite he also wrote several works on Shiite theology including the *Catharsis* (*Tajrīd*), which is the most famous work of its kind and is still studied in all Shiite religious schools. Moreover, Naṣīr al-Dīn composed an excellent treatise on Sufism and even wrote a few verses of poetry. In practically every field from theology and philosophy to mathematics and astronomy he left outstanding works. His influence in the Islamic world, particularly the eastern part of it, has been immense. In the West, however, only his astronomical and mathematical works were translated, but they became quite important and influential during the late Middle Ages and the Renaissance.

Quṭb al-Dīn al-Shīrāzī (634/1236–710/1311)

Quṭb al-Dīn, the most celebrated student of Naṣīr al-Dīn al-Ṭūsī, was born in Shiraz in a family of physicians. There he received his early education in medicine and also became a Sufi through the influence of his father. Then he set out for Maragha where he studied with Naṣīr al-Dīn who advised him to study mathematics and astronomy. He traveled throughout Persia, Syria and Asia Minor where he studied Sufism with Ṣadr al-Dīn al-Qunawī, the disciple of the famous Ibn ʿArabī, in Konya. Later he journeyed to Egypt where he stayed for some time and then returned to Persia, settling in Tabriz where he died.

Quṭb al-Dīn is one of the major commentators on Avicenna's medical works. He wrote one of the most widely read commentaries upon the *Canon*, and also composed numerous works on optics, geometry, astronomy, geography, philosophy and the religious sciences. He is the best known commentator on the Illuminatist doctrines of Suhrawardī, and was himself the author of several encyclopedic works that deal with many important physical and astronomical questions. Like most of the later figures of Islamic history, although famous in the East, he was not known in the West.

ʿAbd al-Raḥmān Abū Zaid ibn Khaldūn (732/1332–808/1406)

Ibn Khaldūn, whose significance as a "philosopher of history" and master of the science of human behaviour has been discovered only recently, belonged to a family that had come originally from the Yemen and settled in Spain. He himself was born in Tunis where he studied both the religious and philosophical sciences, being particularly interested in the teachings of Naṣīr al-Dīn al-Ṭūsī. He became a royal secretary at the court of many different princes, thus traveling throughout North Africa and Spain. Then he set out on a pilgrimage, stopping on the way in Cairo where he lectured for a while at al-Azhar. He even accompanied the Mamluk ruler of Egypt to Damascus in the campaign against Tamerlane and helped negotiate the surrender of that city. Finally he established himself in Cairo where he died.

Ibn Khaldūn, in a career which was continuously connected with positions of political power, developed into a keen observer of the political life of his times. His sense of observation and his philosophical and metaphysical training enabled him to become an outstanding student of the science of man. He wrote on mathematics, theology and metaphysics, but his outstanding work is as a historian. His *Kitāb al-ʿibar* whose full title can be translated as *Instructive Examples and Records of Origins and Events concerning the History of the Arabs, Persians, Berbers and their contemporaries who possessed Great Powers,* besides containing an excellent history of North Africa begins with the *Muqaddimah* or *Prolegomena* upon which Ibn Khaldūn's particular fame is based. In this work he analyzes the causes for the rise and downfall of civilizations and cultures and makes especially pertinent comments on Islamic civilization. Besides summarizing the sciences, he also discusses the reasons for their cultivation in particular periods and the lack of interest in them in others. This work marks Ibn Khaldūn as one of the masters of the science of man and human culture.

Bahāʾ al-Dīn al-ʿĀmilī (953/1546–1030/1621)

Even in Islamic civilization Bahāʾ al-Dīn al-ʿĀmilī is remarkable for his many-sided genius. He was born in Baalbek in present-day Lebanon into a well-known Shiite family. At the age of thirteen, his father took him to Persia which, under the Safavids, was now beginning to attract Shiite scholars from near and far. He studied in Qazwin and Khurasan and became a famous religious scholar as the *shaikh al-islām,* that is to say the chief religious authority in the country, of Isfahan, the Safavid capital. At the same time he was a fervent, practicing Sufi and he composed many Sufi works in both Persian and Arabic which are still very popular. He became one of the most famous men of the Safavid renaissance and resided in Isfahan until the end of his life when he went to Meshed where he died and lies buried today. His tomb, like that of Naṣīr al-Dīn, is visited by the pilgrims who flock regularly to the Shiite shrine cities, such as Meshed and Kazimain.

Bahāʾ al-Dīn was not only a theologian and a Sufi, but also a well-known mathematician, architect, alchemist and authority on the occult sciences. He revived the study of mathematics and wrote treatises on mathematics and astronomy to summarize the works of earlier masters. He was the last religious scholar in Islam who was also a notable mathematician. Henceforth the teaching of mathematics deteriorated in official religious schools in Persia as it had done somewhat earlier in the western lands of Islam. After Bahā᾿ al-Dīn gnostics and philosophers continued to appear, like his own student, Ṣadr al-Dīn al-Shīrāzī, who is the greatest of the later Muslim philosophers. But Bahā᾿ al-Dīn was perhaps the last of the universal figures of learning in Islam, whose genius touched every field of knowledge from gnosis and theosophy to architecture and landscape design, and who in this way personified, like his predecessors, the ideal of the unification of knowledge which Islam has always sought to propagate and realize.

CHAPTER TWO

THE BASIS OF THE TEACHING SYSTEM AND THE EDUCATIONAL INSTITUTIONS

A. The Classifications of the Sciences

THE ISLAMIC CLASSIFICATION of the sciences is based upon a hierarchy which has over the centuries formed the matrix and background of the Muslim educational system. The unity of the sciences has throughout been the first and most central intuition, in the light of which the different sciences have been studied. Starting from this unarguable intuition of the unity of various disciplines, the sciences have come to be regarded as so many branches of a single tree, which grows and sends forth leaves and fruit in conformity with the nature of the tree itself. Just as a branch of a tree does not continue to grow indefinitely, so any discipline is not to be pursued beyond a certain limit. The medieval Muslim authors regarded the pursuit of any particular branch of knowledge beyond its limits—thereby destroying the harmony and the proportion of things—as a useless, one might even say illegitimate activity, such as would be true of a branch of a tree which, by continuing to grow indefinitely, would end by destroying the harmony of the tree as a whole. The means whereby the proportion and hierarchy of the sciences were preserved was through their classification to which Muslim scholars devoted so much attention: In this manner the scope and position of each science within the total scheme of knowledge was always kept in view.

1. AL-FĀRĀBĪ AND THE CLASSIFICATION OF THE SCIENCES

Among Muslim scholars, attempts to classify the sciences began as early as the third/ninth century with al-Kindī, and multiplied thereafter. At first based on the Aristotelian division of the sciences into theoretical, practical, and productive, as described in Porphyry's *Isagoge,* these systems of classification became progressively more elaborate. Islamic disciplines were added to the ancient sciences, and religious and metaphysical knowledge in the sense of gnosis came to occupy the highest levels.

One of the earliest and most influential classifications was that of al-Fārābī, contained in his *Enumeration of the Sciences (Iḥṣāʾ al-ʿulūm)* known in the West as *De Scientiis,* from the Latin translation by Gerard of Cremona, as well as in a Hebrew translation. Although partly eclipsed by his successor Avicenna, al-Fārābī left his imprint upon most of the Muslim thinkers who followed him, as can be seen from the fact that his classification of the sciences was adopted, with only minor changes, by Avicenna, al-Ghazzālī, and Averroes.

Curiously enough, although al-Fārābī himself wrote treatises on alchemy, the interpretation of dreams, and other esoteric sciences, he did not include them in his classification. In this respect, he was followed by the more rationalistic philosophers of the later centuries.

His classification, according to the *Enumeration of the Sciences,* may be summarized as follows:

I. Science of language: syntax
grammar
pronunciation and speech
poetry

II. Logic: the division, definition and composition of simple ideas [corresponding to the content of the *Isagoge* of Porphyry, and the *Categories* and *On Interpretation* of Aristotle.] The parts of logic after the terms have been defined are five:

1. Necessary conditions for premises which would lead in a syllogism to certain knowledge [corresponding to the *Posterior Analytics* of Aristotle]
2. Definition of useful syllogisms and the means of discovering dialectical proofs [corresponding to the *Topics* of Aristotle]

3. Examination of errors in proofs, and of omissions and mistakes committed in reasoning, and the ways of escaping them [corresponding to the *On Sophistic Refutations* of Aristotle]
4. Definition of oratory: syllogisms used to bring a discussion before the public [corresponding to Aristotle's *Rhetoric*]
5. Study of poetry; how it should be adapted to each subject; its faults and imperfections [corresponding to Aristotle's *Poetics*]

III. The propaedeutic sciences:

1. Arithmetic: practical; theoretical
2. Geometry: practical; theoretical
3. Optics
4. Science of the heavens: Astrology; motions and figures of the heavenly bodies
5. Music: practical; theoretical
6. Science of weights
7. Science of tool-making (the making of simple machines and instruments for use in various arts and sciences, such as astronomy and music)

IV. Physics (sciences of nature)
Metaphysics (science concerned with the Divine and the principles of things)

Physics:

1. Knowledge of the principles which underlie natural bodies
2. Knowledge of the nature and character of the elements, and of the principle by which they combine to form bodies
3. Science of the generation and corruption of bodies
4. Science of the reactions which the elements undergo in order to form compounds
5. Science of compound bodies formed of the four elements and their properties
6. Science of minerals
7. Science of plants
8. Science of animals

Metaphysics:

1. Knowledge of the essence of beings
2. Knowledge of the principles of the particular and ob-

servational sciences (the "first philosophy" of Aristotle)
3. Knowledge of noncorporeal beings, their qualities and characteristics, leading finally to the knowledge of the Truth, that is, of God, one of whose names is the Truth

V. Science of Society:
1. Jurisprudence
2. Rhetoric[1]

2. *IBN KHALDŪN AND THE CLASSIFICATION OF THE SCIENCES*

Early attempts to classify the sciences were followed with some modification and elaboration during the next century by Avicenna in *The Book of Healing* and his *Treatise on the Classification of the Intellectual Sciences,* as well as by the Brethren of Purity in their well-known *Epistles.* Moreover, the tradition of composing works on the classification of the sciences and the description of each science gradually became further enhanced, as the various sciences became more developed. This can be seen in *The Book of Sixty Sciences* by the sixth/twelfth-century theologian, Fakhr al-Dīn al-Rāzī in which, as the name indicates, sixty sciences are mentioned and described. The most complete and detailed study of the sciences and their classification, however, appears in the writings of the authors of the eighth/fourteenth to the eleventh/seventeenth century, such as the *Happiness* of Tashkubrāzādah; the neglected Persian encyclopedia of Shams al-Dīn al-Āmulī, called *Precious Elements of the Sciences;* the *Clarification of Doubts* of Ḥājjī Khalīfah, and the well-known *Introduction to History* (Muqaddimah) of Ibn Khaldūn, which contains one of the best descriptions and classifications of the Muslim sciences.

Coming at the end of the most active period of Islamic history, Ibn Khaldūn's analysis of the sciences represents the results of the reflection upon and acute observation of, a whole epoch of history by a profound Muslim scholar and historian who, in a sense, stood outside it.

[1] See al-Fārābī, *Catálogo de las ciencias,* edición y traducción castellana por Angel Gonzales Palencia (2d ed. Madrid: Publicaciones de la Facultad de Filosofia y Letras, Universidad de Madrid, 1953), *passim.*

In his *Introduction to History*, Ibn Khaldūn also surveys the arts and sciences of the Islamic world, defining the aim and scope of each discipline. Although his *Introduction* was not itself universally read during the later periods, his classification contains in summary fashion the plan according to which the arts and sciences have, in fact, been studied in most religious Islamic schools during the past several centuries. Even if many of these schools, especially in the Sunni world, have not studied all the subjects enumerated by Ibn Khaldūn, they have usually accepted the principles of his classification, which can be considered the final version of the Islamic division of the sciences.

Ibn Khaldūn's division may be summarized as follows:

Sciences studied in the Islamic world:	philosophical and intellectual (such as can be learned by man naturally through the use of his innate reason and intelligence); transmitted (such as can be learned only by transmission, going back ultimately to the founder of the science and in the case of religious sciences to the origin of the Revelation)

Philosophical or Intellectual Sciences:

1. Logic	
2. Natural sciences or Physics:	Medicine Agriculture
3. Sciences of beings beyond Nature, or Metaphysics:	Magic and talisman; Science of the occult properties of letters of the alphabet; alchemy
4. Sciences dealing with quantity:	Geometry (plain and spherical optics); Arithmetic (property of numbers, art of calculation, algebra, commercial transactions, calculation of inheritance); Music; Astronomy (the making of astronomical tables, motion of heavenly bodies, astrology)

Transmitted sciences:

1. Quran, its interpretation and recitation
2. Ḥadīth, the sayings of the Prophets and their chain of transmission;
3. Jurisprudence, sacred law;

4. Theology;
5. Sufism *(al-taṣawwuf);*
6. Linguistic sciences, such as Grammar, Lexicography, and Literature[2]

Not all of the sciences enumerated above have always been taught in all of the institutions of learning which have constituted the most formal and official educational organizations in the Islamic world. But they have been transmitted from one generation to another through either formal instruction or private teaching, and they must therefore be regarded as a part of the intellectual life of Islam. It is, needless to say, impossible to give examples of all of these sciences in this book, even if we were to confine ourselves to those sciences which deal with the realm of Nature. We can do no more than describe briefly the institutions of learning which have been for the most part responsible for keeping alive the tradition of learning over the centuries, and to present a sample from the writings of some of the more important scientific and philosophical schools, so as to form from the bits thus assembled a mosaic which may give some indication of the rich and varied intellectual life of the Islamic world.

B. Educational Institutions

Since the teachings of Islam are essentially gnostic in nature, all forms of knowledge, even the most external, take on a sacred character, so long as they remain faithful to the principles of the revelation. It is not accidental that the first verses revealed to the Prophet Muḥammad were those of

2 Ibn Khaldūn, *The Muqaddimah: An Introduction to History,* translated from the Arabic by Franz Rosenthal (Bollingen Series XLIII. Copyright by Bollingen Foundation, New York, 1958. Distributed by Pantheon Books), *passim.* London: Routledge & Kegan Paul Ltd. Reprinted by permission.

the Chapter "The Clot," in which the primacy of knowledge is affirmed in the following words:

1. Read: In the name of thy Lord who createth,
2. Createth man from a clot.
3. Read: And thy Lord is the Most Bounteous,
4. Who teacheth by the pen,
5. Teacheth man that which he knew not.

Many of the verses of the Quran that were to follow affirmed the sacred nature of knowledge and *scientia* (*ʿilm*), one of God's names being "He who knows" (*al-ʿalīm*). The Prophet himself—although unlettered from the standpoint of human knowledge—was at the same time the channel of the revelation of the Book which is considered by all Muslims to be the *quintessential* sum of all knowledge, both human and divine. Moreover, he reaffirmed the teachings of the Quran by stressing that the acquisition of knowledge to the limits of one's abilities is incumbent upon every believer, as part of his religious duties. His sayings—such as, "Seek knowledge from the cradle to the grave," or "Seek knowledge, even in China"—were echoed through the later centuries as the most authoritative arguments for teaching and propagating knowledge (*ʿilm*), even though debates also arose as to exactly what the knowledge to which the Prophet alluded, and whose attainment he considered so essential, encompassed.

Whatever arguments arose as to the definition of that knowledge the acquisition of which was a religious duty, there is no doubt that the Quranic verses and prophetic sayings, which emphasized the importance of learning, along with the fact that the central symbol of the Islamic revelation is a book, made learning inseparable from religion. The first place in which teaching was carried on in Islam was the mosque, and ever since the very first decades of Muslim history, the institutions of learning have remained for the most part inseparable from the mosque, and have usually been supported by religious endowments.

The mosque began to serve as a school as early as the reign of the second caliph ʿUmar, who appointed "narrators," *qāṣṣ* in the singular, to the mosques of such cities as Kufa, Basra, and Damascus, for the purpose of reciting the Quran and the Ḥadīth (prophetic traditions). Gradually, instruction in Arabic grammar and literature became incorporated into this simple and rudimentary form of education, which became the nucleus of the later and more fully developed institutions of learning. Out of this early instruction in language and religion, there grew both the popular elementary school *(maktab)*, and the advanced centers of learning which were to develop into the first universities of the Middle Ages, and to serve as models for the early European universities during the eleventh and twelfth centuries.

The purpose of the *maktab*, which still survives in many parts of the Islamic world, has always been to acquaint the young with a knowledge of reading and writing and, more specifically, with the principles of religion. Both boys and girls have been given instruction, generally in a mosque, but also sometimes in private houses. The student is instructed to have reverence both for the teacher and for the subject taught; the gifted ones are recognized at this early stage and, in most cases, then encouraged to continue their studies at more advanced levels. The *maktab* has thus served both as the center for the religious and literary education of the general community and also—what is of more interest to our present study—as the preparatory stage for the advanced institutions of learning, in which the sciences have been taught and cultivated. Whether given in formal sessions held at the mosque, or through private tutoring at the houses of the wealthy, early instruction at the level of the *maktab* has shaped the basic attitude of the student toward his teachers and toward learning as such—an attitude which has usually persisted into the more advanced phases of instruction.

Most of the Islamic books on ethics, as well as those on education, have one or more chapters devoted to the ideal conditions for the upbringing and education of the young student, and to the way in which he should be prepared to undertake more advanced study.

For example, Ibn Khaldūn in his *Introduction to History*, which contains an extensive study of scientific education as well as of the sciences themselves, discusses the manner in which the student should be taught the sciences, especially the Quran, which is the first and most important subject taught to the young when they begin their formal education.

The instruction of children and the different methods employed in the Muslim cities.

It should be known that instruction of children in the Qur᾽ān is a symbol of Islam. Muslims have, and practice, such instruction in all their cities, because it imbues hearts with a firm belief (in Islam) and its articles of faith, which are (derived) from the verses of the Qur'ān and certain Prophetic traditions. The Qur'ān has become the basis of instruction, the foundation for all habits that may be acquired later on. The reason for this is that the things one is taught in one's youth take root more deeply (than anything else). They are the basis of all later (knowledge). The first impression the heart receives is, in a way, the foundation of (all scholarly) habits. The character of the foundation determines the conditions of the building. The methods of instructing children in the Qur'ān differ according to differences of opinion as to the habits that are to result from that instruction.

The Maghribī method is to restrict the education of children to instruction in the Qur'ān and to practice, during the course (of instruction), in Qur'ān orthography and its problems and the differences among Qur'ān experts on this score. The (Maghribīs) do not bring up any other subjects in their classes, such as traditions, jurisprudence, poetry, or Arabic philology, until the pupil is skilled in (the Qur'ān), or drops out before becoming skilled in it. In the latter case, it means, as a rule, that he will not learn anything. This is the method the urban population in the Maghrib and the native Berber Qur'ān teachers who follow their (urban compatriots) use in educating their children up to the age of manhood. They use it also with old people who study the Qur'ān after part of their life has passed. Consequently, (Maghribīs) know the orthography of the Qur'ān, and know it by heart, better than any other (Muslim group).

The Spanish method is instruction in reading and writing as such. That is what they pay attention to in the instruction (of children). However, since the Qur'ān is the basis and foundation of (all) that and the source of Islam and (all) the sciences, they make it the basis of instruction, but they do not restrict their instruction of children exclusively to (the Qur'ān). They also bring in (other subjects), mainly poetry and composition, and they give the children an expert knowledge of Arabic and teach them a good handwriting. They do not stress teaching of the Qur'ān more than the other subjects. In fact, they are more concerned with teaching handwriting than any other subject, until the child reaches manhood. He then has some experience and knowledge of the Arabic language and poetry. He has an excellent knowledge of handwriting, and he would have a thorough acquaintance with scholarship in general, if the tradition of scholarly instruction (still) existed in (Spain), but he does not, because the tradition no longer exists there. Thus (present-day Spanish children) obtain no further (knowledge) than what their primary instruction provides. It is enough for those whom God guides. It prepares (them for further studies), in the event that a teacher (of them) can be found.

The people of Ifrīqiyah [North Africa] combine the instruction of children in the Qur᾽ān, usually, with the teaching of traditions. They also teach basic scientific norms and certain scientific problems. However, they stress giving their children a good knowledge of the Qur᾽ān and acquainting them with its various recensions and readings more than anything else. Next they stress handwriting. In general, their method of instruction in the Qur᾽ān is closer to the Spanish method (than to Maghribī or Eastern methods), because their (educational tradition) derives from the Spanish *shaykhs* who crossed over when the Christians conquered Spain, and asked for hospitality in Tunis. From that time on, they were the teachers of (Tunisian) children.

The people of the East, as far as we know, likewise have a mixed curriculum. I do not know what (subjects) they stress (primarily). We have been told that they are concerned with teaching the Qur᾽ān and the works and basic norms of (religious) scholarship once (the children) are grown up. They do not combine (instruction in the Qur᾽ān) with instruction in handwriting. They have (special) rule(s) for teaching it, and there are special teachers for it, just like any other craft which is taught (separately) and not included in the school curriculum for children. The children's slates (on which they practice) exhibit an inferior form of handwriting. Those who want to learn a (good) handwriting may do so later (on in their lives) from professional (calligraphers), to the extent of their interest in it and desire.

The fact that the people of Ifrīqiyah and the Maghrib restrict themselves to the Qur᾽ān makes them altogether incapable of mastering the linguistic habit. For as a rule, no (scholarly) habit can originate from the (study of the) Qur᾽ān, because no human being can produce anything like it. Thus, human beings are unable to employ or imitate its ways *(uslūb)*, and they also can form no habit in any other respect. Consequently, a person who knows (the Qur᾽ān) does not acquire the habit of the Arabic language. It will be his lot to be awkward in expression and to have little fluency in speaking. This situation is not quite so pronounced among the people of Ifrīqiyah as among the Maghribīs, because, as we have stated, the former combine instruction in the Qur᾽ān with instruction in the terminology of scientific norms. Thus, they get some practice and have some examples to imitate. However, their habit in this respect does not amount to a good style (eloquence), because their knowledge mostly consists of scholarly terminology which falls short of good style, as will be mentioned in the proper section.

As for the Spaniards, their varied curriculum with its great amount of instruction in poetry, composition, and the Arabic philology gave them, from their early years on, a habit providing for a better acquaintance with the Arabic language. They were less proficient in all the other (religious) sciences, because they were little familiar with study of the Qur'ān and the traditions that are the basis and foundation of the (religious) sciences. Thus, they were people who knew how to write and who had a literary education that was either excellent or deficient, depending on the secondary education they received after their childhood education.[3]

C. Institutions of Higher Learning

As the newly formed Islamic society became more firmly established, and its energies turned from outward growth to inward development, educational institutions came into being which played a vital role in the cultivation of the arts and sciences. The first important center to be particularly concerned with philosophy and the natural and mathematical sciences was the *Bait al-ḥikmah* (House of wisdom), constructed in Baghdad by the caliph al-Ma'mūn around 200/815, to which a library and an observatory were joined. Supported by the state treasury, this famous school became the gathering place for many scientists and scholars, and particularly for competent translators, who translated almost the whole of Greek scientific and philosophical literature into Arabic, thus preparing the ground for the absorption of that literature by Islam. The amount of translation from the Greek and the

3 Ibn Khaldūn, *The Muqaddimah: An Introduction to History,* translated from the Arabic by Franz Rosenthal. (Bollingen Series XLIII. Copyright by Bollingen Foundation, New York. 1958. Distributed by Princeton University Press), vol. 3, pp. 300–303. London: Routledge & Kegan Paul Ltd. Reprinted by permission.

Syriac, and also from Pahlavi and Sanskrit, during the third/ninth and fourth/tenth centuries, by such men as Ḥunain ibn Isḥāq, Thābit ibn Qurrah and Ibn Muqaffaʿ—all of them competent scholars and scientists—was in fact so great that even today more of the writings of the Greek Aristotelians—i.e., of Aristotle and his commentators—are extant in Arabic than in any of the modern European languages. Moreover, there are many fragments of the writings of Aristotle, of the Alexandrian philosophers, the Neopythagoreans and Neoplatonists, the Hermetic corpus, and the works of such scientists as Galen, which exist today only in the Arabic translation done at al-Maʾmūn's academy or by translators who were stimulated by the activities of that institution.

The great interest in pre-Islamic or what is traditionally called *awāʾil* sciences—that is, sciences that existed "in the beginning," before the rise of Islam—became a part of the affairs of the state to an extent that cannot be explained solely by the personal interest of an individual ruler such as Hārūn al-Rashīd or al-Maʾmūn, however important such interest may have been. The real cause for this sudden interest on the part of the Islamic community at the beginning of the third/ninth century in non-Islamic sciences, especially in Greek philosophy and science, in contrast to the at best sporadic interest of the previous century, must be sought in the new challenge which Islamic society faced. This challenge came from the theologians and philosophers of the religious minorities within the Islamic world, especially the Christians and Jews. In the debates carried on in cities like Damascus and Baghdad between Christians, Jews and Muslims, the last-named group often found itself on the losing side, for they were unable to defend the principles of faith through logical arguments, as could other religious groups, nor could they appeal to logical proofs to demonstrate the truth of the tenets of Islam. The interest of the caliphate in making Greek sciences available in Arabic most likely stems from this challenge, which might very well have affected the role of religious law in Islamic society, upon which the authority of the caliphate itself was based. It was therefore for the purposes of safeguarding the interests of the Muslim community that the early Abbasid caliphs turned the attention of scholars to the study of Greek philosophy and science.

Until the fourth/tenth century, the main institution of learning, aside from the *maktab,* was the circle or "gathering" *(majlis),* which was presided over by a professor (often called shaikh, hakim or *ustādh*), and in which various sciences, both religious and philosophic, were discussed. Then, in 395/1005, the Fatimid caliph al-Ḥākim constructed the *Dār al-ʿilm* (House of knowledge) in Cairo, in which mathematics and physics were taught, and which had a library that, by some accounts, had over a million books. Other Shiite institutions of this same name, and following it as a model, began to be established in many cities during the following century.

The institutions of higher learning, or universities, reached the climax of their development in the latter half of the fifth/eleventh century, when the Seljuq vizier, Niẓām al-Mulk, established a chain of colleges or *madāris* (sing., *madrasah*) in Baghdad, Naishapur and other cities. That of Baghdad, which is justly the most famous of the group, was founded in 459/1067 for the celebrated teacher of jurisprudence, Abū Isḥāq al-Shīrāzī; later, its most important teaching post was held by the famous al-Ghazzālī. The *madrasah* was henceforth extended, with some modification, to other parts of the Islamic world; for example, in 585/1189, Saladin introduced it to Jerusalem; the Almohads, at about the same period, built *madāris* in North Africa; finally, a large *madrasah* was constructed in Granada in 750/1349, and shortly after the beautiful al-ʿAṭṭārīn mosque of Fez was founded across the straits in Morocco.

In the East, great schools continued to be constructed—such as the recently renovated al-Mustanṣarīyah of Baghdad, which stands on the banks of the Tigris, and the *madāris* of Central Asia, especially that of Samarkand, built by Tamerlane and his descendants. Shiite institutions flourished, and many well-known schools were founded by the Safavids in Isfahan, Meshed and Shiraz—such as the Chahār Bāgh of Isfahan, whose building is one of the masterpieces of Islamic art, and the Khān school of Shiraz, where the outstanding Persian sage, Mullā Ṣadrā, was among the teachers, and where, during the eleventh/seventeenth century, European travelers witnessed a very active and comprehensive academic life.

The institutions of higher learning have continued to flourish from the early medieval period to the present, some having preserved a continuous tradition of learning over the centuries. The Qarawīyīn of Fez in Morocco is eleven centuries old, and is very likely the oldest university in the world; the al-Azhar, which was originally a Shiite institution, but later became the center of Sunni learning, recently celebrated its first millennium of existence. Likewise, the Shiite center of learning founded in Najaf in the fifth/eleventh century continues to function today as one of the largest religious universities in the Muslim world.

As far as the teaching personnel of the *madāris* is concerned, in both the Shiite and the Sunni schools, the pattern has been more or less the same. The classes are directed by a *mudarris* who is comparable to a professor, who has a *nā᾿ib* (substitute professor) and also a *mu῾īd* who acts as a "drill master," the latter repeating the teachings of the professor, like the *répétiteur* of Western universities. In the question of curriculum, however, there is a definite difference between the Sunni and Shiite institutions of learning. The Sunni *madrasah* was established essentially for the purpose of training students in the sacred law and other religious sciences; its program consisted primarily of the Quran, Ḥadīth, exegesis, Arabic grammar and literature, law, theology and oratory (to which the study of philosophy and history, and a small amount of mathematics, were occasionally added). The Shiite schools, however, showed an affinity toward the *awā᾿il* sciences, placing a much greater emphasis in their program on these subjects.

Certain schools of Greek philosophy and science, especially the more esoteric schools connected with Neopythagoreanism and Hermeticism, became integrated into the Shiite perspective at an early period, and some of the Shiite imams legitimized the study of the *awā᾿il* sciences and even encouraged it. The Sunni lawyers and jurisprudents, however, for the most part remained aloof from these sciences and, in fact, often opposed them. They usually accepted only Aristotelian logic, which thereby became an accredited discipline and aided discussions—on questions of law and theology, and even grammar. The early opposition between the rival grammatical schools of Basra and Kufa—of which the former were more "Aristotelian" and the latter more "Hermetic" and "Stoic"—was a sign of this difference in attitude, which became more marked during later centuries. The Sunni schools were in general more inclined toward the study of law and theology, and the Shiite to the sciences of Nature and mathematics, although many Sunni rulers and princes also cultivated these sciences on their own.

Logic was always part of the program of al-Azhar University, and until a few years ago the students of the Qarawīyīn in Fez studied some Islamic philosophy. But the tendency toward differentiation was present, as can be seen from the fact that the fourth/tenth century, during which political power in the Islamic world rested mainly in the hands of the Shiah, marks the height of activity in the intellectual sciences. After Islamic philosophy came to an end in the Sunni world with Averroes, it found a new life in the Shiah world, especially in Persia, and has continued as a living tradition in that country to the present day. Even today, many students from the traditional Shiite religious schools, after completing their studies in philology and the religious sciences, undertake a study of the complete cycle of Islamic philosophy and theosophy (consisting of logic, natural philosophy and metaphysics), in which they read the books of Avicenna, such as *Salvation* and *The Book of Healing,* and the *Spiritual Journeys* of Mullā Ṣadrā. Some also continue the traditional course of mathematics, which runs from simple treatises on arithmetic, through the commentary of Naṣīr al-Dīn al-Tūsī on the *Elements* of Euclid, plane and solid trigonometry, algebra, and the *Optics* of Euclid, and ends with the study of Naṣīr al-Dīn al-Ṭūsī's commentary upon the *Almagest* of Ptolemy, followed usually by a summary study of modern astronomy.

Whatever the differences may have been in the subject matter taught in the Sunni and Shiite schools, the general atmosphere of the *madrasah* has been the same throughout the Islamic world. The transmission of knowledge has always had a highly personal aspect, in that the student has sought a particular master rather than an institution, and has submitted himself to that chosen teacher wholeheartedly. The relation that has always existed between the teacher and the student has been a highly intimate one, in which the student reveres the teacher as a father and obeys him, even in personal matters not connected with his formal studies. The atmosphere of these schools has been very relaxed and informal, without there being any great academic or financial pressure upon the student. All religious education has been free; in fact, the student receives his room and board from the religious endowment of the institution in which he studies. Nor has there ever been the strong incentive to receive a diploma and then seek to benefit from its social and economic advantages, prevalent in so many modern educational institutions.

That is why a person may often remain a student all his life, mastering one subject after another and going from one teacher to the next. Usually, when he has mastered a subject to his teacher's satisfaction, he receives from him a permit *(ijāzah),* stating the student's competence in that subject. If the student is well qualified, then there is a likelihood of his becoming a teacher in turn and giving a student of his an *ijāzah*. In even the most formal type of learning, oral teaching accompanies the written texts and the importance of actually hearing a teacher and receiving an *ijāzah* from him personally keeps alive a chain *(isnād)* of transmission which is of paramount importance in preserving and perpetuating the Islamic educational tradition. In this process the intimate contact between teacher and student, and the many years of living together, often in the same quarters, has much to do with making possible the transmission of the spirit as well as the letter of the various branches of knowledge, which have always been instrumental in the normal functioning of Islamic society.

Although the curriculum of the *madrasah* has not been the same during all periods of Islamic history, and in all parts of the Islamic world, there has been a general ideal order, which has always remained in the background, and has often been followed, especially in the schools where the philosophic or *awāʾil* sciences have been taught. Early in Islamic history, the famous philosopher al-Fārābī, whose classification of the sciences we have just discussed, had already turned to a consideration of the order in which the study of the sciences should be undertaken, and the disciplines that should be mastered. In his *Attainment of Happiness* he writes:

> The first genus of beings into which one should inquire is that which is easier for man and in which perplexity and mental confusion are less likely to occur. This is the genus of numbers and magnitudes. . . .
>
> It is characteristic of this science that inquires into numbers and magnitudes that the principles of instruction in it are identical with the principles of being. Hence all demonstrations proceeding from its principles combine the two things—I mean they give an account of the thing's existence and of why it exists: all of them are demonstrations of both *that* the thing is and *why* it is. Of the principles of being, it employs [only the formal, that is] *what* the thing is and *by what* and *how* it is, to the exclusion of the other three. For numbers and magnitudes, in the mind and stripped from the material, have no principles related to their genus apart from the principles of their being just mentioned. They possess the other principles only on account of their coming into being by nature or the will, that is, when they are assumed to be in materials. Since this science does not inquire into them as being in materials, it does not

deal with what is extraneous to them so far as they are not in materials.

One begins, then, first with numbers [that is, arithmetic], proceeds next to magnitudes [that is, geometry], and then to all things in which number and magnitude are inherent essentially (such as optics, and the magnitudes in motion, which are the heavenly bodies), music, the study of weights, and mechanics. In this way one begins with things that may be comprehended and conceived irrespective of any material. He then proceeds to things that can be comprehended, conceived, and intellected by only slight reference to a material. Next, the things that can only be comprehended, conceived, and intellected with slightly more reference to a material. He continues thus toward the things wherein number and magnitude inhere, yet that which can be intellected in them does not become intelligible except by progressively greater reference to the material. This will lead him to the heavenly bodies, then music, then the study of weights and mechanics, where he is forced to deal with things that become intelligible only with difficulty, or that cannot exist, except when they are in materials. One is now forced to include principles other than *what, by what* and *how*. He has come to the borderline between the genus that does not have any other principle of being apart from *what* it is, and the genus whose species possess the four principles. It is at this point that the natural principles come into view.

At this juncture one ought to set out to know the beings that possess the four principles of being: that is, the genus comprising the things that can be perceived by the intellect only when they are in materials. (Indeed the materials are called [by some] *the* natural things.) The inquirer ought to seize upon all the principles of instruction—that is, the first premises—relative to the genus consisting of *particular* things. He also should look into the primary knowledge he has and adopt from it whatever he recognizes as appropriate for being made into principles of instruction in this science.

He then should begin to inquire into bodies and into things that are in bodies. The genera of bodies constitute the world and the things comprised by the world. In general, they are the genera of sensible bodies or of such bodies that possess sensible qualities: that is, the heavenly bodies; then earth, water, air and things of this kind (fire, vapor, etc.); then the stony and mineral bodies on the surface of the earth and inside it; and finally, plants, irrational animals, and rational animals. He should give an account of (*a*) the fact of the being, and (*b*) all the principles of being of every one of these genera, and of every one of the species of every genus: that is, in every problem relative to them, he should give an account of (*a*) the fact *that* the thing is, and (*b*) *what, by what,* and *how* it is, *from what* it is, and *for what* it is. In none of them is he to confine himself to its proximate principles. Instead he should give an account of the principles of its principles and of the principles of the principles of its principles, until he arrives at its ultimate corporeal principle.

The principles of instruction in most of what this science comprises are distinct from the principles of being, and it is through the principles of instruction that one comes to know the principles of being. For in every genus of natural things the principles of instruction are inferior to the principles of being, since the principles of being in such a genus are the grounds to which the principles of instruction owe their existence. Hence the ascent toward knowledge of the principles of being of every genus or species can be made only through things that originate in these principles. If these happen to be proximate principles *A* that in turn have other principles *B*, the proximate principles *A* should be employed as principles of instruction from which to ascend to knowledge of their principles *B*. Then, when these principles *B* become known, one proceeds from them to the principles of these principles, *C*, until he arrives at the ultimate principles of being in the genus. If, after ascending from the principles of instruction to the principles of being and the knowledge of the principles of being, there are (in addition to the primary cognitions from which we ascended to the principles) other things originating from these principles, and which are still unknown, then we proceed to use these principles of being as principles of instruction and so come to know the other, inferior things. In relation to the other things, our principles are now both principles of instruction and principles of being. We follow this procedure in every genus of sensible bodies and in each of the species of every genus.

When one finally comes to inquire into the heavenly bodies and investigate the principles of their being, this inquiry into the principles of their being will force him to look for principles that are not natures or natural things, but beings more perfect than nature and natural things. They are also not bodies or in bodies. Therefore one needs another kind of investigation here and another science that inquires exclusively into beings that are metaphysical. At this point he is again standing between two sciences: the science of nature and [metaphysics or] the science of what is *beyond* natural things in the order of investigation and instruction and *above* them in the order of being.

When his inquiry finally reaches the stage of investigating the principles of the being of animals, he will be forced to inquire into the soul and learn about psychical [or animate] principles, and from there ascend to the inquiry into the rational animal. As he investigates the principles of the latter, he will be forced to inquire into (1) *what, by what,* and *how,* (2–3) *from what,* and (4) *for what* it is. It is here that he acquaints himself with the intellect and things intelligible. He needs to investigate (1) *what* the intellect is and *by what* and *how* it is, and (2–3) *from what* and (4) *for what* it is. This investigation will force him to look for other principles that are not bodies or in bodies, and that never were or ever will be in bodies. This inquiry into the rational animal will thus lead him to the same conclusion as the inquiry into the heavenly bodies. Now he acquaints himself with incorporeal principles that are to the beings below the heavenly bodies as those incorporeal principles (with which he became acquainted when investigating the heavenly bodies) are to the heavenly bodies. He will acquaint himself with the principles for the sake of which the soul and the intellect are made, and with the ends and the ultimate perfection for the sake of which man is made. He will know that the natural principles in man and in the world are not sufficient for man's coming to that perfection for the sake of whose achievement he is made. It will become evident that man needs some rational, intellectual principles with which to work toward that perfection.

At this point the inquirer will have sighted another genus of things, different from the metaphysical. It is incumbent on man to investigate what is included in this genus: that is, the things that realize for man his objective through the intellectual principles that are in him, and by which he achieves that perfection that became known in natural science. It will become evident concomitantly that these rational principles are not mere *causes* by which man attains the perfection for which he is made. Moreover, he will know that these rational principles also supply many things to natural being other than those supplied by nature. Indeed man arrives at the ultimate perfection (whereby he attains that which renders him truly substantial) only when he labors with these principles toward achieving this perfection. Moreover, he cannot labor toward this perfection except by exploiting a large number of natural beings and until he manipulates them to render them useful to him for arriving at the ultimate perfection he should achieve. Furthermore, it will become evident to him in this science that each man achieves only a portion of that perfection, and what he achieves of this portion varies in its extent, for an isolated individual cannot achieve all the perfections by himself and without the aid of many other individuals. It is the innate disposition of every man to join another human being or other men in the labor he ought to perform: this is the condition of every single man. Therefore, to achieve what he can of that perfection, every man needs to stay in the neighborhood of others and associate with them. It is also the innate nature of this animal to seek shelter and to dwell in the neighborhood of those who belong to the same species, which is why he is called the *social* and *political* animal. There emerges now another science and another inquiry that investigates these intellectual principles and the acts and states of character with which man labors toward this perfection. From this, in turn, emerge the science of man and political science.

He should begin to inquire into the metaphysical beings and, in treating them, use the methods he used in treating natural things. He should use as their principles of instruction the first premises that happen to be available and are appropriate to this genus, and in addition, the demonstrations of natural science that fit as principles of instruction in this genus. These should be arranged according to the order mentioned above, until one covers every being in this genus. It will become evident to whoever investigates these things that none of them can possess any material at all; one ought to investigate every one of them only as to (1) *what* and *how* it is, (2–3) *from what* agent and (4) *for what* it is. He should continue this investigation until he finally reaches a being that cannot possess any of these principles at all (either *what* it is or *from what* it is or *for what* it is) but is itself the first principle of all the aforementioned beings: it is itself that *by* which, *from* which, and *for* which they are, in the most perfect modes in which a thing can be a principle for the beings, modes free from all defects. Having understood this, he should investigate next what properties the other beings possess as a consequence of their having *this* being as their principle and the cause of their being. He should begin with the being whose rank is higher than the rest (that is, the one nearest to the first principle), until he terminates in the being whose rank is inferior to the rest (that is, the one furthest from the first principle). He will thus come to know the ultimate causes of the beings. This is the divine inquiry into them. For the first principle is the divinity, and the principles that come after it—and are not bodies or in bodies—are the divine principles.

Then he should set out next upon the science of man and investigate the *what* and the *how* of the purpose for which man is made, that is, the perfection that man must achieve. Then he should investigate all the things by which man achieves this perfection or that are useful to him in achieving it. These are the good, virtuous, and noble things. He should distinguish them from things that obstruct his achieving this perfection. These are the evils, the vices, and the base things. He should

> make known *what* and *how* every one of them is, and *from what* and *for what* it is, until all of them become known, intelligible and distinguished from each other. This is political science. It consists of knowing the things by which the citizens of cities attain happiness through political association in the measure that innate disposition equips each of them for it. It will become evident to him that political association and the totality that results from the association of citizens in cities correspond to the association of the bodies that constitute the totality of the world. He will come to see in what are included in the totality constituted by the city and the nation the likenesses of what are included in the total world. Just as in the world there is a first principle, then other principles subordinate to it, beings that proceed from these principles, other beings subordinate to these beings, until they terminate in the beings with the lowest rank in the order of being, the nation or the city includes a supreme commander, followed by other commanders, followed by other citizens, who in turn are followed by other citizens, until they terminate in the citizens with the lowest rank as citizens and as human beings. Thus the city includes the likenesses of the things included in the total world.
>
> This, then, is theoretical perfection. As you see, it comprises knowledge of the four kinds of things by which the citizens of cities and nations attain supreme happiness. What still remains is that these four be realized and have actual existence in nations and cities while conforming to the account of them given by the theoretical sciences.[4]

Even if the whole field of theoretical knowledge discussed by al-Fārābī has not always been taught in every *madrasah* in Islam, there have always been those who have been competent to teach some aspect of it. Thus, the seeker after knowledge, or the real student who characteristically is called *ṭalabah* in Arabic (i.e., "one who seeks") has perhaps had to wander from one school to another, from one master to the next, but he has always found the knowledge he has sought if he has searched hard enough. The institutions of learning, although weakened in many parts of the Muslim world after the eighth/fourteenth and ninth/fifteenth centuries, have nevertheless continued to preserve that tradition of learning which is known so well by the fruit it bore during the medieval period.

4 *Alfarabi's Philosophy of Plato and Aristotle,* translated and with an introduction by M. Mahdi (New York: Free Press of Glencoe, 1962), pp. 19–25. Copyright © The Free Press of Glencoe, a division of the Macmillan Company, 1932. Reprinted by permission of The Macmillan Company.

D. The Observatories

The construction of observatories as distinct scientific institutions, in which observation is carried out, and also as centers for teaching astronomy and allied subjects, owes its origin to Islam. The first Islamic observatory was the Shammāsīyah, which al-Ma᾽mūn had built in Baghdad around 213/828, and which was headed by two famous astronomers, Faḍl ibn al-Naubakht and Muḥammad ibn Mūsā al-Khwārazmī. This was soon followed by a series of observatories, each connected with the name of an individual astronomer, such as that of al-Battānī at Raqqa, and ῾Abd al-Raḥmān al-Ṣūfī in Shiraz. However, after the fourth/tenth century, the observatory began to acquire a more general nature and was usually supported by the ruler—for example, the observatory at Hamadan was built by the Persian prince ῾Alā᾽ al-Daulah for Avicenna around 414/1023. Less than a century later, the Seljuq ruler, Malikshāh, constructed the first royal observatory to have had a fairly long life, and in which several astronomers, including ῾Umar Khayyām, devised the Jalālī calendar.

In the western lands of Islam there were fewer observatories in general than in the East. Nevertheless, one finds an observatory in Toledo, where in the fifth/eleventh century al-Zarqālī (the Latin "Arzachel") worked on the *Toledan Zīj*,[5] which was to play such an important role in the history of European astronomy. Moreover, the beautiful Giralda tower of Seville, which is now part of the cathedral, was used by Jābir ibn Aflaḥ as an observatory. Some of the astronomers, such as Avempace (Ibn Bājjah), also had private observatories of their own.

The development of the observatory reached new heights with that at Maragha, begun in 657/1261 by the order of Hulagu, the grandson of Genghis Khan, and supported by religious endowment. To it was joined a library of 400,000 books, and (as the research of several modern scholars espe-

[5] The word *zīj*, which is of Sanskrit origin and which has entered into Arabic and Persian by way of Pahlavi, means astronomical tables. But actually most *zīj*'s contain not only tables but also theoretical astronomical discussions, chapters on chronology, elaborate treatment of mathematical astronomy and other related subjects. The *zīj's* which constitute one of the most important parts of Islamic astronomical literature are usually named either after their compiler, patron, or city in which they were compiled although occasionally other means of naming have been used.

cially A. Sayili in his *The Observatory in Islam* has shown), it was well equipped with astronomical instruments—including a mural quadrant with a radius of about 430 cm., armillary spheres, solsticial armilla, equinoctial armilla and azimuth rings. Here, in 670/1274, the *Ilkhānid Zīj* were completed. But the observatory at Maragha was not just a place for astronomical observation. It was a complex scientific institution, in which nearly every branch of science was taught, and where some of the most famous scientists of the medieval period were assembled.

The institution was headed by Naṣīr al-Dīn al-Ṭūsī, and included Quṭb al-Dīn al-Shīrāzī, who is credited with the discovery of the true cause of the rainbow, Muhyī al-Dīn al-Maghribī, Najm al-Dīn Dabīrān al-Qazwīnī and Athīr al-Dīn al-Abharī, most of whom were famous philosophers, as well as astronomers. There was also on the staff a Chinese scientist named Fao-Mun-Jī, inasmuch as this was the period of exchange of astronomical ideas between Persia and China. Also at Maragha the famous Christian encyclopedist and philosopher Barhebraeus lectured on Euclid's *Elements* and Ptolemy's *Almagest.*

The peak period of the observatory as a scientific institution was reached in the ninth/fifteenth century when Ulugh Beg, the grandson of Tamerlane, built his observatory at Samarkand—which, along with the observatory at Istanbul, must be regarded as the link of transmission of this institution to the Western world. Himself a competent astronomer, Ulugh Beg assembled the best mathematicians of his day in the new observatory, which was equipped with the finest instruments possible, including a meridian arc about 50 meters high. The greatest scientists at Samarkand, besides Ulugh Beg himself were Qāḍīzādah, ʿAlī Qūshjī, and especially Ghiyāth al-Dīn al-Kāshānī whose mastery of the theory of numbers and techniques of computation was unmatched until fairly recent times.

Al-Kāshānī, who was brought specifically to Samarkand by Ulugh Beg's request, described the scientific activities of the observatory in a candid letter to his father, in which he also mentioned the difficulties he encountered in establishing himself there, difficulties which were soon overcome by his unrivaled mastery of mathematics. In this intimate document he wrote:

> We now come to the subject of the Observatory. His Majesty, may God keep his realm and preserve *his* sovereignty, had

seen the constructions at the Marāgha observatory in his childhood, but he had said that he had not seen them with a discerning eye. Before the arrival of this servant they had told His Majesty that the observatory was the place underneath the top (of the observatory hill) where people live (sit).

Two brass rings of six *gaz* diameter had been cast, for the measurement of the obliquity and solar observations, in accordance with Ptolemy's directions, unaware of the fact that, as that instrument was not free from defects, astronomers had brought about many refinements after Ptolemy's time and that they had deviated from the ring constructed by him.

No one knew either what the *geometrical pulpit* standing in the middle of the building (or, constructions) of the Marāgha Observatory was and for what purpose it was constructed. This servant brought the matter to His Majesty's knowledge and explained the divergences which may arise from their abovementioned instrument. I also pointed out that in ʿAdud al Dawla's time a ring was constructed the diameter of which was ten *gaz* and that the present one was smaller than that ring, adding that at the Marāgha Observatory they had constructed a *geometrical pulpit* instead, which is called *suds-i Fakhrī,* and that this had a diameter of six *gaz.*

His Majesty ordered the ring to be broken, and they made it into another instrument which this obedient servant had described. The construction of the building of the observatory too was ordered to be carried out in accordance with the explanations given by this servant. All these circumstances and other similar matters were made known to the notables of the country.

In like manner, every day and every week something new comes up, and through the felicity of your Lordship's magnanimity, this servant extracts it from the sphere of difficulty, with the mallet of preparedness, with the greatest ease.

One day His Majesty, may God preserve his realm and sovereignty, was busy studying, and Qāḍīzāda-i Rūmī was among those present. A proof had been referred to [al-Bīrūnī's] *Qānūn-i Masʿūdī,* and the *Qānūn* had been made ready. As the required proof could not be ascertained at the meeting, however, Qāḍīzāda had taken the *Qānūn* to his lodge in order to study it. After two days he brought it back and said that in the passage in question there was a lacuna. He believed this to be the reason why the problem could not be clarified and said that another copy of the book should be found for comparison. This servant had not left his house during the previous two days because of feverish lassitude and had at this juncture joined the meeting. Qāḍīzāda was still there. His Majesty chanced to look at this servant, and he said "Let our Mawlā solve this problem," passing the *Qānūn-i Masʿūdī* on to me. As soon as this servant read through five or six lines from that problem, he explained the whole matter, and the particular copy contained no lacunas.

Such things have happened many times since my arrival here. It will take too long to relate them all. Suffice it to say that in such a gathering and in the presence of so many authorities, one's knowledge is appraised neither through reliance upon other people's opinions nor merely on the basis of the claims made by that person himself.

Shortly after the arrival of this servant here and in a meeting in which His Majesty took part, this servant was speaking about a few problems on which there was agreement between the *Tuḥfa* [*Present*], the *Nihāya al Idrāk* [*On the Highest Understanding*], Mawlānā Niẓām al Dīn-i Nīshābūrī's *Commentary of the Tadhkira,* as well as the commentary of the *Tadhkira* [*Treasury*] by Sayyid Sharīf, may God bless his soul, but which were nevertheless wrong. My contention reached the ears of all the learned people by word of mouth. They were excited and busy speaking behind my back. "When a person objects to a thing on which so many authorities are in agreement," they declared, "he should prove his statement."

One day, at a gathering where the majority was present, I spoke on one of these controversial topics which I have thoroughly investigated, and I explained it both in a descriptive way and by geometrical proof in such a manner that it was accepted unanimously. As His Majesty is a scientist himself and well-versed in the subject, and as scientists are present here in large numbers, when a question becomes settled, no one who has previously spoken in another vein can demur, pretending to find faults, so as to make those who are not familiar with the topic believe in him. For the most distinguished scientists are present here.

One of the problems in question is this. It has been said that the maximum equation for the moon's anomaly on its epicycle takes place at a point of the eccentric region such that when this point is joined to the prosneusis center, the line joining these two points will be perpendicular to the diameter passing through the apogee. This is the assertion made in all the books written on the subject up to our day, but it is wrong. For if the line in question passes through a point seven degrees and fifty seconds underneath the prosneusis center it is perpendicular and otherwise not. The same sort of mistake has been made in the case of the planets also, and the source of the error of them all is that in the case of the sun the point of maximum equation occurs at a place such that when a line is drawn from it to the center of the universe the line is perpendicular to the said diameter. Ptolemy has given the proof for this in the *Almagest* and has referred to this proof in the cases of the moon and other planets. People have never realized that the cases of these latter cannot be referred to that of the sun. . . .[6]

As to the inquiry of those who ask why observations are not completed in one year but require ten or fifteen years, the situation is such that there are certain conditions suited to the determination of matters pertaining to the planets, and it is necessary to observe them when these conditions obtain. It is necessary, e.g., to have two eclipses in both of which the eclipsed parts are equal and to the same side, and both these eclipses have to take place near the same node. Likewise, another pair of eclipses conforming to other specifications is needed, and still other cases of a similar nature are required. It is necessary to observe Mercury at a time when it is at its maximum morning elongation and once at its evening elongation, with the addition of certain other conditions, and a similar situation exists for the other planets.

Now, all these circumstances do not obtain within a single year, so that observations cannot be made in one year. It is necessary to wait until the required circumstances obtain and then if there is cloud at the awaited time, the opportunity will be lost and gone for another year or two until the like of it occurs once more. In this manner, there is need for ten or fifteen years.

Those people who do not know the nature of this activity and who have not witnessed others do it, are surprised when they see anyone occupy himself with it. But when someone knows how to do a thing, it becomes easy. It is to be hoped that God, he is exalted and high, will grant long life and give his help, so that with the felicity of the King of Islam, may God preserve his realm and sovereignty, this activity of observation will reach the stage of completion in a happy and successful manner.

At the present the greater part of the observatory building has been constructed. Nearly five hundred *tūmāns* worth of brick and lime have been used; one armillary sphere has been completed and another one is in the process of construction. Still other instruments, such as azimuthal quadrant and the instrument with movable sights and others, are being attended to and have been half constructed.

6 A. Sayili, *Uluğ Bey ve Semerkanddeki İlim Faaliyeti Hakkinda Giyasüd-din-i Kāşīʾnin Mektubu* (Ghiyāth al-Dīn al-Kāshī's Letter on Ulugh Bey and the Scientific Activity in Samarqand) (Ankara: Türk Tarīh Kurumu Basimevi, 1960), pp. 98–100. This work includes the original letter in Persian with the Turkish and English translations and commentary by Sayili.

As to your query concerning whether the task to be accomplished at the observatory is entrusted to this servant or whether he has a partner for the work, it is a strange coincidence that your Lordship should ask this question after my achieving such fame here. The situation is that although people who are conversant with the mathematical sciences exist in large numbers here, none of them is such that he is acquainted with both the theoretical ("scientific") and applied ("practical") sides of observations (of the work done in an observatory). For none of them knows the *Almagest*.

One of them is Qāḍizāda who possesses the theoretical knowledge contained in the *Almagest* but not its applied side. He has not done anything that pertains to the practical. He is the most learned among them, but even he is only a beginner in theoretical astronomy. For every topic which is put forward by His Majesty, this servant finds the correct approach and supplies the well-rounded and complete answer, as was previously mentioned on the occasion of the problem connected with the *Qānūn-i Mas'ūdī* and the like; and I am skilled in all aspects of the applied branch of this science.

Applied astronomy too is divided into scientific and practical branches. The practical branch of applied astronomy may be illustrated with the following example. Suppose, e.g., that two stars have reached the first vertical at a certain condition. Elevation is measured with an instrument, and the longitude and latitude of one of these stars is known. It is required to derive the longitude and latitude of the other from these data. The knowledge of how to derive these, i.e., to know to multiply which quantity with which and to divide by what, and how to proceed in order to obtain the desired result, constitutes the scientific side of this operation (the scientific side of applied astronomy). The scientific side of theoretical astronomy ("the absolutely scientific") is the knowledge of the science itself.

The absolutely practical side of such a problem is the carrying out of the multiplications and divisions and the calculation of the longitudes of celestial bodies in terms of signs, degrees, and minutes, and the determination of their latitudes, giving their actual numerical values.

Qāḍīzāda is weak in the scientific side of applied astronomy, and he cannot point out what pertains to the absolutely practical (the practical side of applied astronomy) except by performing multiplications and divisions with the help of the lattices of multiplication and division. And this is such that when he wishes to set up a lattice, he cannot do it without consulting a book. They read line by line and complete the operation step by step with the help of instructions. If something unusual is being sought this is not of much use(?).

I am not boasting. Your Lordship himself knows that with God's assistance I have confidence in myself to accomplish the purely theoretical, the applied side of the theoretical, and the scientific side of the practical as well as the purely practical, without consulting a book, so that if I were without any books at the observatory I could do everything necessary from the beginning of the period of work to the end and produce the astronomical tables. The only exception would occur in dealing with the results obtained concerning mean positions in previous observations performed on a given date, which is a matter pertaining to the factual realm, as well as the date of the given day. In observational work there is need for such data. For the difference between the mean positions resulting from the present observations and those of the earlier date is found and is divided by the time between the two observations so as to obtain the quantity of motion. All these calculations can be done on two sheets of paper.

Let your Lordship keep his blessed mind at ease. For recourse to books for such an investigation is not indicative of a serious shortcoming and is not the same as the kind of recourse to books practiced at the present by others.

What I have related concerning Qādīzāda should not make people think that there is ill-will and lack of understanding between the two of us. There is a strong feeling of friendship and attachment between Qādīzāda and myself, and he acknowledges my superiority. He is not of such a disposition as to deny what is true or to be unfair. He himself asserts in the presence of others what this obedient servant has just said concerning him. He speaks and says so when he knows a thing, and he readily confesses it when he does not know.

The developments to date in the activity pertaining to the observatory have been in accordance with what this servant proposed to His Majesty, may God preserve his realm and sovereignty. This was what happened, e.g., in the case of the nature of the observatory building and the nature of each instrument. His Majesty reflected upon the recommendations with lucid mind and prompt understanding. Whatever he approved he ordered to be carried out, and as to other cases, he enriched them with new ideas and inferences and ordered the adoption of the modified versions.

The truth is that his inferences are very apt and do not contain the slightest error. If in certain cases there happens to be anything concerning which we, his servants, have some doubt, the point is discussed; and no matter from what side the clarification of the mistake comes, His Majesty will at once accept it without the least hesitation. For it is his aim to see that everything is thoroughly investigated and to have the work at the observatory accomplished in the best possible manner.

Your Lordship may infer herefrom the degree of liberality and benevolence of that personage. And there is no need to expand upon this matter. He is, indeed, good-natured to the utmost degree of kindness and charity, so that, at times, there goes on, at the madrasa, between His Majesty and the students of the seekers of knowledge so much arguing back and forth on problems pertaining to any of the sciences that it would be difficult to describe it. He has ordered, in fact, that this should be the procedure, and he has allowed that in scientific questions there should be no agreeing until the matter is thoroughly understood and that people should not pretend to understand in order to be pleasing. Occasionally, when someone assented to His Majesty's view out of submission to his authority, His Majesty reprimanded him by saying "you are imputing ignorance to me." He also poses a false question, so that if anyone accepts it out of politeness he will reintroduce the matter and put the man to shame.

When the said instrument (armillary sphere?) was completed it was brought to the side of the observatory. Every once in a while, when there is something to be done at the site of the observatory, such as the determination of the meridian line, Qāḍīzāda too comes there. If there is any problem, he too speaks in an approving or disapproving manner, as mentioned earlier apropos of the leveling of the observatory grounds wherein they disapproved, and I explained the matter to him.

The rest of the professors too present themselves to the observatory grounds and try to be obliging. The time for the difficult parts of the work has not come yet. For at the present the building is being constructed. When it is brought to completion and the instruments are completed and set up in their places, then observation, which consists of watching the stellar bodies through sights, will be made and measurements will be ascertained, and after that the eccentricities, the radii of epicycles, the degrees of inclination of the apse lines, the mean motions, and the distances of centers of constant speed to centers of eccentricity, etc., will have to be determined from these observations. It is then that work really starts.

It is not appropriate to be too lengthy. May your exalted shadow be unceasing and perpetual.

The least of your slaves,
Ghiyāth[7]

[7] *Ibid.*, pp. 106–110.

After Samarkand, the only other notable observatories in Islam were those of Istanbul in the tenth/sixteenth century, and the series of observatories constructed by the Hindu prince Jai Singh in Delhi, Jaipur, Ujjain and other Indian cities, in which the traditions of Indian and Islamic astronomy were combined. The Istanbul observatory was constructed in the tenth/sixteenth century by the Ottoman sultan Murād III for his court astronomer Taqī al-Dīn. It was contemporaneous with the observatories of Tycho Brahe and may very well have exercised some influence on them, since there is a similarity between many of their instruments. But the observatory at Istanbul had a short life and, as can be seen from the following poem written at that time by the poet ʿAlāʾ al-Dīn al-Mansūr, its destruction was ordered by the sultan because of political intrigue:

At this time, all of a sudden, the Potentate, who is the defender of the Religion,
Spoke thus to his astronomer Taqī al Dīn:
"People of learning have made inquiries concerning this:
Oh you learned man of conscientiousness and perfection,
Inform me once more on the progress and the results of the observations.
Have you untangled knots from the firmament in a hair-splitting manner?"
Taqī al Dīn answered, "In the Zīj of Ulugh Bey
There were many doubtful points, oh exalted king;
Now through observations the tables have been corrected,
And out of grief the heart of the foe has withered and twisted into coils.
From now on, order the abolishment of the Observatory,
To the consternation of the ill-wishers and the jealous."
The King of Kings summoned the Head of the Halberdiers of his body guard
And gave him instructions concerning the demolition and the abolishment of the Observatory.
Orders were given that the Admiral
Should immediately rush to the Marine Ordnance Division
And that they should at once wreck the Observatory
And pull it down from its apogee to the perigee.[8]

[8] This poem by ʿAlāʾ al-Dīn al-Manṣūr is quoted by A. Sayili in his *The Observatory in Islam* (Ankara: Türk Tarih Kurumu Basimevi, 1960), pp. 292–293, from his own English translation of the same poem in *Türk Tarih Kurumu Belleten,* Vol. XX, No. 79 (1956), pp. 481–482.

E. The Hospitals

The hospital was also of importance as an institution of learning, inasmuch as most of the teaching of clinical medicine was done in hospitals. While the theoretical aspect of medicine continued to be dealt with in both mosque and *madrasah,* the practical side was usually taught in the hospitals, many of which had libraries and schools especially designed for that purpose. The earliest hospital in Islam was that built in 88/707 by the Umayyad caliph Walīd ibn ʿAbd al-Malik in Damascus. Very likely he was influenced by the model hospitals of the pre-Islamic period, such as that of Jundishapur, which was quite elaborate, even for that time.

The Abbasid caliphs organized medical education so that students, after undergoing both theoretical and practical training, wrote a treatise—like the modern thesis—and upon its acceptance received a permit or diploma from their professor, giving them permission to practice medicine. They also had to take the Hippocratic oath.

Many great hospitals were built either by rulers or by private individuals throughout the Islamic world, such as the Mansūrī hospital in Cairo, which is still standing, or the Nūrī hospital of Damascus of the sixth/twelfth century, one of the largest hospitals ever to be built in the Islamic world. Hospitals were either constructed for a particular physician, or later put under the direction of a particularly eminent doctor. For example, Rhazes was placed in charge of a hospital, in which he worked and also taught his students. The hospital thus served as an institution of learning as well, and became an auxiliary of the mosque schools in which the theoretical principles of natural philosophy and its branches, including medicine, were taught.

F. The Sufi Centers

Finally, among the institutions of learning, we must consider the Sufi centers, which in singular form are called either *zāwiyah* or *khānaqāh.* In the earlier centuries of Islam, these centers served, as was to be expected, as the meeting place of the Sufis, where they performed their various spiritual exercises (especially the invocation) and where those who were ready were able to receive initiation into the Divine Mysteries. Here, those who had not been satisfied with formal learning alone, but had searched after the light of certainty and sought a direct vision of the truth, left the talk and discussion *(qīl* and *qāl)* of the schools to discover the ecstasies of contemplation *(ḥāl),* under the direction of a spiritual master. That is why the gnostics and the "rationalists" (or the possessors of the esoteric and the exoteric sciences) are often called the people of *hāl* and *qāl,* respectively. In this manner, the Sufi centers served as a center of learning, but a learning which was not to be found in books, and for the discovery of which it was not sufficient to train the mental faculties alone. They served as centers in which the qualified could realize the highest form of knowledge (gnosis), the attainment of which requires purification of the soul as well as of the mind.

After the Mongol invasion, however, the Sufi centers became in an ever more outward manner, institutions of learning. In the Eastern lands of Islam, with the destruction of the external institutions of society which resulted from that invasion, there was no organization capable of beginning the process of rebuilding, except that "society within society" which the Sufi orders may be said to be. Just as, for some time, the task of preserving law and order and helping justice to prevail over brute force fell to the Sufi orders, so also the Sufi centers became institutions of learning, in which in addition to the esoteric sciences and gnosis, the branches of the arts and sciences that had previously been taught in the mosque schools now found a refuge. The *khānaqāh* must thus be considered as one of the essential institutions of learning in Islam, not only because from the beginning it was the place in which instruction in the highest form of science or gnosis was given, but also because during the later period of Islamic history, it began to fulfill also the function of the mosque schools in many parts of the Islamic world. The Sufi center thus played its role—along with the mosque school, the observatory and the hospital—as one of the major institutions responsible for the cultivation and propagation of the sciences in Islam.

CHAPTER THREE

COSMOLOGY, COSMOGRAPHY, GEOGRAPHY, AND NATURAL HISTORY

A. Cosmology and Cosmography

THE STUDY OF THE COSMOS and its parts takes in a vast panorama which is covered by many scientific disciplines. In classical Islamic civilization, it was of interest to the natural scientist, the geographer, and the historian as well as to the theologian, the philosopher and the gnostic. All such studies, dealing with various parts of the cosmos—what must be considered technically as the cosmological sciences—took place within the framework of Islamic cosmology, whose basic tenets are derived from the Quran. One can hardly avoid the conclusion that not only did the law of Muslim society become that which had been promulgated in the Islamic revelation, but also that the cosmic environment in which Islamic civilization flourished became to a large extent Islamized.

There were many forms of cosmology developed in Islam by various schools; we shall refer to some of these in succeeding chapters. In all these cosmologies, a certain number of forms and symbols from the world of Nature are chosen to depict the cosmos—not in any *ad hoc* manner, however, but in the particular way that is in conformance with the Islamic world view. Traditional cosmology, whether Islamic or belonging to other traditions, is thus like sacred art which, out of many possible forms, chooses a certain number, in order to paint an icon with a definite and particular meaning, designed more for contemplation than for analysis.

The basic principles of all the cosmologies developed in Islam are the same; they can be found in the background of most cosmologies and cosmographies—whether these be by the natural historians and cosmographers or the philosophers or, for that matter, by the Sufis who, in their writings, have given the clearest exposition of them. These principles concern themselves essentially with the unity and gradation of being—with the assertion that, metaphysically, reality is ultimately one and not many, and yet cosmologically the sensible world is only one of many states of being, all of which are, to use the Sufi expression, so many "Divine Presences." Following the terminology derived from the Quran, Muslim authors usually speak of five states of being or "presences," which are: the world of Divine Essence or "Ipseity" *(hāhūt);* the world of the Divine Names and Qualities, or Universal Intellect, also identified with Pure Being *(lāhūt);* the intelligible world, or the world of angelic substances *(jabarūt);* the world of psychic and "subtle" manifestation *(malakūt);* finally, the terrestrial or physical domain, dominated by man *(nāsūt).* Sometimes a sixth state of being is added—that of the Universal Man *(al-insān al-kāmil),* in which these states are contained.

Each state of being is the principle of that which stands below it. Moreover, according to the Quranic statement that God is the First and the Last, the Hidden and the Manifested, these states of being have been conceptualized in two different but complementary ways. To the two Divine Attributes—the First and Last—corresponds the reliance in time of the world upon its Divine Origin. "God is the First" implies that the cosmos begins from Him; "He is the Last" implies that it returns unto Him.

The two different interpretations which arise from the consideration of God as the Hidden and the Manifested pertain to "space"—to "qualified" and "sacred" space—just as the first two were concerned with time. Taken as Manifested, God becomes the reality that englobes all, that "covers" and "encompasses" the cosmos. In this view, physical manifestation may be regarded as the innermost circle of a set of five concentric circles, followed by the other states of being respectively, with the outermost circle symbolizing the Divine Essence—a view which resembles the cosmological schemes of Avicenna, Dante, and others, for whom the journey through the cosmos, from the earth to the *primum mobile,* symbolized the gradual and successive realization of the various states of being, finally resulting in the state of contemplation of the Divine Itself.

As for the other view of God as the Hidden, the cosmological scheme becomes there reversed, in the sense that, if we consider once again a set of concentric circles, it is the physical or gross manifestation that is the outermost circle, and the Divine Essence that is the innermost one. This latter scheme, moreover, is more in conformity with the microcosmic point of view than is the former. It can be regarded as a symbol of the microcosm, of man, in whom the physical is the most outwardly manifested aspect and his spiritual nature the most hidden. The former scheme also conforms more closely to the macrocosmic view, in which the physical world, for all its vastness, is but a small portion of the cosmos in its totality, and is enveloped and contained by it. The two schemes, the microcosmic and the macrocosmic, are thus analogous; they correspond to each other, at the same time that one is the reverse of the other. They thus present a further instance of the principle of reverse analogy, so essential to the interpretation of symbols.

These general cosmological principles are present in all phases of the Islamic sciences. One can hardly overestimate their importance in determining the framework within which Muslim scientists studied the world of Nature. They are to the Islamic sciences what the rationalistic philosophy of the seventeenth century, whether consciously understood so or not, is to modern science. For example, the fundamental difference between the interpretations of Muslim natural historians and of modern biologists with regard to fossils and older forms of life arises from the fact that, for the former, the world of physical nature is dominated by a higher level of reality, which transcends it, while for the nineteenth-century natural historians and their modern followers such a conception does not exist. As a result, the same "data" and "observations" have been interpreted in different lights, and the "spatial" and "vertical" gradation of the medieval scientists converted into a purely temporal and "horizontal" evolution which now, in such theories as those of Teilhard de Chardin, even seeks to make the higher states of being a kind of sublimation of the physical domain which has resulted from the very process of "horizontal" evolution. However, the idea of evolution, as usually interpreted, is metaphysically and theologically unacceptable and Teilhard de Chardin did no more than try the impossible, namely to correlate the theological teachings of the Church with the concept of evolution understood in its purely "horizontal" sense. The rise of this conception of evolution—truly a parody of the medieval conception of gradation and of the hierarchy of the states of being—shows clearly how significant the cosmological background is to the cultivation of the sciences of Nature, which cannot escape having a world-view, or a general view about the cosmos, derived from sources other than the natural sciences themselves.

Islamic cosmology depends upon the particular spirit and form of the Islamic revelation, not only in its general principles, but also in its formulations and terminology. There is the germ of a complete cosmology and cosmography in the Quran; on this, the later Sufis, philosophers and scientists elaborated. The Quran speaks of the seven earths and seven heavens, of the Divine Pedestal *(kursī)* and Throne *(ʿarsh),* of the cosmic mountain *Qāf,* and of the cosmic tree all of which became important elements of Islamic cosmology. The most important verses of the Quran on this subject, commentaries on which have developed into some of the basic Islamic cosmological treatises, are the Throne verse and the Light verse. The first of these asserts majestically the dependence of all things upon God; the second outlines, in a set of important symbols, both a cosmology and a spiritual psychology. The Throne verse is as follows:

> Allah! There is no God save Him, the Alive, the Eternal. Neither slumber nor sleep overtaketh Him. Unto Him belongeth whatsoever is in the heavens and whatsoever is in the earth. Who is he that intercedeth with Him save by His leave? He knoweth that which is in front of them and that which is behind them, while they encompass nothing of His knowledge save what He will. His throne includeth the heavens and the earth, and He is never weary of preserving them. He is the Sublime, the Tremendous. [2:255.]

As for the Light verse, it practically created an obligation for the learned men to write a commentary upon it. There are, therefore, dozens of commentaries on this verse, by such famous philosophers and scientists as al-Fārābī, Avicenna, al-Ghazzālī and Mullā Ṣadrā, each of which drew a certain meaning from the many levels of interpretation to which the sacred text lends itself.

The text of the verse is as follows:

> Allah is the Light of the heavens and the earth. His Light is as a niche, wherein is a lamp. The lamp is in a glass. The glass is, as it were, a shining star. (This lamp is) kindled from a blessed tree, an olive neither of the East nor of the West, whose oil would almost glow forth (of itself) though no fire touched it. Light upon light, Allah guideth into His light whom He will. And Allah speaketh to mankind in allegories, for Allah is Knower of all things. [24:35.]

Avicenna, in his commentary upon this verse interprets it in a microcosmic sense. This commentary is contained in the third chapter of his last philosophical masterpiece, *The Book of Directives and Remarks:*

> Among the faculties of the soul, there are those that the soul possesses inasmuch as it is in need of growth and perfection, so that it can reach the state of intellect in act. The first faculty is that which prepares the soul for receiving the intelligibles, some call it the *intellectus materialis;* it is the *niche.* Above this is another faculty which the soul possesses when it has received the first intelligibles, and is prepared to receive the second. The second intelligibles can be acquired either by reflection, or by intention (which is stronger). The first is symbolized by the olive tree, the second by the olive oil itself. In both instances, the soul at this stage is called *intellectus in habitu,* and is like the glass. As for the noble soul that possesses the saintly faculty, the phrase *whose oil would almost glow forth* holds true for it. It is after this stage that the soul possesses a faculty and a perfection; and this perfection is that it "sees" the intelligibles themselves in act, in an intuition which represents them in the mind so that they are manifested to it. The impinging of the intelligibles upon the mind is like *light upon light.* After this is a faculty which can bring forth and contemplate intelligibles which had been previously acquired by the soul, without its having to acquire them anew. This faculty, which is as though illuminated by itself, is like the *lamp.* That perfection is called *intellectus in habitu* and the faculty *intellectus in actu.* And that which causes the soul to pass through these stages from the *intellectus in habitu* to the *intellectus in actu,* and from the *intellectus materialis* to the *intellectus in habitu,* is the active intellect, which is like the fire.[1]

[1] Avicenna, *Al-Ishārāt waʾl-tanbīhāt (The Book of Directives and Remarks)* (Cairo: Dār al-maʿārif, 1959), pp. 364–367. Translated by S. H. Nasr.

Islamic cosmology and cosmography are also based upon the angelology derived from Quranic sources. The description of the cosmos always takes into account not only the corporeal and terrestrial domains, but also all formal manifestations, and thus includes the angelic world as well. In fact, the Quranic angelology was developed into an elaborate system by Muslim authors, although certain philosophers and sages, such as Suhrawardī also made use of the symbolism of Mazdaean angelology. The popular treatises on cosmography, which treat of the structure of the heavens, as well as of geography and natural history—for example, *The Wonders of Creation* of Abū Yaḥyā al-Qazwīnī (the so-called Pliny of the Arabs)—are based essentially upon a study of the angels who act as the moving and guiding forces of the world of Nature, and also as the model after which man should seek to strive.

The writing of large treatises on cosmography, which sought to describe the entire universe, with special emphasis upon natural history, and with the aim of displaying God's wisdom in creation, came into vogue during the later period of Islamic history, especially from the sixth/twelfth century onward. Many of these works were called *The Wonders of Creation,* among them being that of the sixth/twelfth century Muḥammad al-Ṭūsī, and the more famous work of the above-mentioned Abū Yaḥyā al-Qazwīnī, which appeared a century later and is also known as *The Cosmography.* Likewise during the eighth/fourteenth century, there are several well-known cosmographies, such as *Selections of the Age on the Wonders of Land and Sea* by Shams al-Dīn al-Dimashqī (which became well known in the Western world during the nineteenth century through a French translation by the Danish orientalist, A. F. von Mehren), and *The Delights of the Heart,* by the Persian historian and naturalist Ḥamdallāh al-Mustaufī al-Qazwīnī, which contains a detailed study of geography, mineralogy, botany, zoology, and anthropology. These works, which are in reality scientific encyclopedias—along with such universal histories as those of al-Ṭabarī and al-Masʿūdī—serve as valuable sources for an understanding of the general Muslim vision of the world, as well as for surveying the knowledge that the Muslim scientists and scholars had of geography and natural history.

B. Geography

Geography is one of the sciences most cultivated by the Muslims. In it, they left behind a very large number of writings, mainly in Arabic, but also in Persian and Turkish. The possibility of traveling from the Atlantic to the Pacific without having to cross any real frontiers—as well as the annual pilgrimage to Mecca in which an opportunity was provided both for a long journey and for the exchange of ideas with scholars from nearly every part of the known world of that time—both these helped to enrich Islamic geography beyond what was known to the Greeks and Romans, or to the medieval Latin authors. Al-Bīrūnī, after discussing the difficulty of gaining geographic knowledge in ancient times, writes in *The Book of the Demarkation of the Limits of Areas:*

> But now (the circumstances are quite different). Islam has already penetrated from the eastern countries of the earth to the western; it spreads westward to Spain (Andalus), eastward to the borderland of China and to the middle of India, southward to Abyssinia and the countries of Zanj (i.e., South Africa, the Malay Archipelago and Java), northward to the countries of the Turks and Slavs. Thus the different peoples are brought together in mutual understanding, which only God's own Art can bring to pass. And of those (who could be obstructive to cultural relations) only common vagabonds and highway robbers are left. The remaining obstinate unbelievers have become timid and tame; they now respect the followers of Islam and seek peace with them.
>
> To obtain information concerning places of the earth has now become incomparably easier and safer (than it was before). Now we find a crowd of places, which in the (Ptolemaic) "Geography" are indicated as lying to the east of other places, actually situated to the west of the others named, and *vice versa*. The reasons (of such errors) are either confusion of the data as to the distance on which the longitude and latitude were estimated, or that the populations have changed their former places.[2]

[2] From al-Bīrūnī's *The Book of the Demarkation of the Limits of Areas,* in N. Ahmad, *Muslim Contributions to Geography* (Lahore: M. Ashraf, 1947), p. 35.

Geographical studies among the Muslims included not only the lands of Andalusia, North Africa, South Europe, and the Asiatic land mass, but also the Indian Ocean and all the adjacent seas. The Muslims were able to sail over the high seas, improving the means of navigation and the art of cartography, which was closely connected with it. Astrolabes were also perfected for sailing.

Geography in Islam was also closely tied to astronomy; observatories carried out geographic measurements, such as the determination of latitudes and longitudes, and the degree of arc, for which several different methods were employed. In fact, al-Bīrūnī has often been regarded as the founder of the science of geodesy, because of the detailed and systematized studies he made of the measurements of the features of the earth's surface. Geographical problems also included the question of the possible motion of the earth, which was treated by such authors as al-Bīrūnī in several of his works, as well as by Quṭb al-Dīn al-Shīrāzī in his *On the Highest Understanding of the Knowledge of the Spheres.*

In Islamic geographical texts, descriptive and symbolic geography are often combined, so that there is no sharp distinction between scientific geography, as it is understood in the modern sense, and the sacred geography in which directions, mountains, rivers, islands, etc., become symbols of the celestial world. The Muslim conception of the earth has been always dominated by the central cosmic mountain, *Qāf,* and the seven climates, which are the terrestrial image of the celestial order, and have their correspondence with the heavens. This is expressed through an astrological symbolism in which each climate is connected to a planet and a zodiacal sign. The climates, which are the counterparts of the seven heavens, were known to the Babylonians and the Greeks, as well as to the ancient Iranians, who had a concentric rather than longitudinal conception of it. The Quran also speaks of the seven earths, which the Muslim geographers interpreted as the seven traditional climates, and within whose matrix they made their detailed study of various regions.

The geographers in Islam made much use of the *Geography* of Ptolemy, which became the foundation stone of this science among the Muslims. The first noted Muslim figure in this field was Hishām al-Kalbī, who flourished early in the third/ninth century, and who is particularly known for his study of Arabia. He was followed, during this period, which marks the real beginning of scientific activity among the Muslims, by several well-known geographers, of whom the earliest is Muḥammad ibn Mūsā al-Khwārazmī, the famed mathematician and astronomer, whom we shall discuss in greater detail in future chapters. In geography, al-Khwārazmī helped lay the foundation of this science among the Muslims with his *Shape of the Earth,* which was an improvement upon Ptolemy's work, in its texts as well as in the maps which it provided.

Also writing in the third/ninth century were al-Kindī, the celebrated philosopher and author of the *Description of the Inhabited Parts of the Earth,* and al-Yaʿqūbī, whose *Book of Countries* is particularly noted for its topographical studies. During that century, as the result of the establishment of a regular postal system and of the need for studying the routes of various provinces closely, there appeared a series of works entitled *Routes and Kingdoms* by such figures as al-Kindī's students, Aḥmad al-Sarakhsī and Ibn Khurdādhbih. These were followed, during the next century, by the works of Abū Zaid al-Balkhī, al-Istakhrī and Ibn Ḥauqal, all of which bear the same title. The series of geographical works bearing this name are among the most important contributions to Islamic geography.

The third/ninth and fourth/tenth century also mark the rise of navigation in the Indian Ocean by Muslim sailors, and the discovery of the Far East. The first description of China, in fact, dates from this period, when Sulaimān the Merchant wrote of his sea voyages to that country. It was these and similar travels that finally produced the legend of Sindbad the Sailor in the *Thousand and One Nights,* as well as all the other similar but less well-known stories of the adventurers of the high seas. These voyages also contributed to the geographical knowledge of those regions, which became incorporated into later compendia.

In the fourth/tenth century, in addition to the several books of *Routes and Kingdoms* already noted, there appeared such important geographical writings as the large encyclopedia of Ibn Rustah, the accounts of the travels of Ibn Faḍlān, one of the first of the traveling geographers in Islam who journeyed through the Volga and Caspian regions, and the *Figures of the Climes* of the above-mentioned Abū Zaid al-Balkhī, who was one of the early mapmakers. Also belonging in this period is the *Best Division for the Knowledge of the Climes* of al-Maqdisī who, starting from

Jerusalem, visited nearly every part of the Islamic world, and the anonymous *Boundaries of the World,* the first notable geographical treatise in Persian.

The most important geographer, historian, and naturalist of this period was Abūʾl-Ḥasan al-Masʿūdī, who must be regarded as among the greatest of Muslim historians and scientists, although many of his works—such as his thirty-volume universal history—have been lost. But his *Meadows of Gold and Mines of Gems,* which contains a wealth of material on geography, geology and natural history (as well as the first written description of the windmill), and *The Book of Indication and Revision,* written at the end of his life as a summary of his general world view and philosophy, are sufficient to warrant his great reputation.

In the fifth/eleventh century, Nāṣir-i Khusrau, a leading Ismaili philosopher and Persian poet wrote his *Diary,* which contains a good many descriptions of the geography of the Middle East. At the same time, al-Bakrī, the oldest of the Andalusian geographers, composed his book of *Routes and Kingdoms,* as well as his *Geographical Dictionary,* beginning a tradition in geographical studies that was continued during the next century. Al-Bīrūnī, with whom we shall deal more fully in later chapters, composed several geographical works, of which *The Book of the Demarkation of the Limits of Areas* is perhaps the most important. He devised a new method for measuring latitudes and longitudes, and carried out his own measurements to determine the antipodes and the roundness of the earth, as well as the elevation and other geographical characteristics of many cities. He also made a study of the geography of India, contained in his *India.*

The sixth/twelfth century was marked by a series of sea-voyages and route-books, written by several famous sailors, such as Sahl ibn Abān. Several local geographies also appeared, of which one of the best known is al-Zamakhsharī's *The Book of Fars,* dealing with the southern Persian province of Fars, which has given its name to the whole country and its language. The most important geographers of this period were from the Western lands of Islam, especially Andalusia. Al-Zuhrī of Granada wrote his *Geography* at this time; his compatriot, al-Māzinī, who also flourished during this period, traveled widely throughout the Near East, the Balkans and Persia and wrote a treatise called *The Collection of Singularities Relative to some of the Marvels of the Maghrib.* Ibn Jubair, one of the best known of Muslim travelers, who was a contemporary of these figures, also came from Spain, having been born in Valencia, and wrote an account of his journeys which contains much of geographic interest.

The best-known geographer of this century, and perhaps the most outstanding figure in this science during the entire Middle Ages, was Abū ʿAbdallāh al-Idrīsī, who was born in Ceuta in 494/1101 and flourished at the Norman court at Palermo. Here he composed *The Book of Roger,* for Roger II—a work which contains the most elaborate description of the world made in medieval times. He later wrote an even larger geographical encyclopedia entitled *Pleasures of Men and Delights of Souls,* the integral text of which has however been lost. Al-Idrīsī was also a natural historian, and his botanical studies (which were along Aristotelian lines but independent of those by Theophrastus) are of interest. Moreover, he constructed a celestial sphere, and a model of the known world of that time in the form of a disc, which made him one of the outstanding Muslim cartographers.

In the seventh/thirteenth century numerous geographical manuscripts appeared. Of these, Yāqūt al-Ḥamawī's *Geographical Dictionary* is the best. Yāqūt, who was of Greek extraction, and had been sold as a slave in Baghdad, traveled widely over the Islamic world; he composed this work, which has always been very highly regarded in the Islamic world, from both personal observation and knowledge derived from earlier sources. Meanwhile, his contemporary, Ibn Saʿīd of Granada, who became a guest of Hulagu in the East, wrote *The Extent of the Earth in Length and Breadth;* somewhat later, the Egyptian Abuʾl-Fidāʾ, besides writing a universal history, composed a text on geography called *Valuation of Countries* which became well known in the West.

The most important works of geography during the eighth/fourteenth century are the cosmographical treatises, such as that of the above-mentioned Shams al-Dīn al-Dimashqī, which contains much geographical knowledge, along with cosmography and natural history. There were also several travelers of note who wrote on geography, of whom the most famous is Ibn Baṭṭūṭah.

After the eighth/fourteenth century, however, there was a gradual decline of interest in geography, as in the other natural and mathematical sciences. There are, to be sure, such works as the cosmographies of Ḥāfiẓ Abrū and ʿAbd al-Razzāq al-Samarqandī in the ninth/fifteenth century, and the *Description of Africa* by the tenth/sixteenth century John Leo the African, who, although originally a Muslim from Fez, became a Christian after he was captured by Christian corsairs and lived in Italy. Yet there was an unmistakable decline in the production of first-rate geographical studies after the eighth/fourteenth century, the only exception to this rule being the Indian geographers, many of Persian origin, at the Mogul court, who composed valuable works, like the *Āʾīn-i akbarī* of ʿAllāmī, dedicated to the Emperor Akbar, and the *Seven Climates* of Aḥmad al-Rāzī, along with the Turks, who made significant geographical studies at this time. *Descriptions of the World* by Muḥammad al-ʿĀshiq and the geographical encyclopedia of Ḥājjī Khalīfah, which includes the first attempt to compare European and Islamic geography, contain much new material, especially in the field of oceanography and the geography of the islands of the Indian Ocean. Under the Turks, who had by now become a world power, a series of sea voyages took place, which resulted in Ibn Mājid's *Book of Instructions on Nautical Principles and Regulations*, Sulaimān al-Mahrī's several works on the Indian Ocean and the Malay Archipelago, the *Oceanography* of the Turkish admiral Sīdī ʿAlī and the cartographical studies of Pīri Raʾīs, another admiral, who made use of the last map of Columbus. In this field, at least, we see the penetration of Renaissance science into the Islamic world at a time when the Muslim tradition in geography was still flourishing, albeit its activity had decreased after reaching its height during the period from the sixth/tenth through the eighth/fourteenth century.

To gain a first-hand acquaintance with some of the more important geographic ideas in Islam, we turn first to Yāqūt's unequaled *Geographical Dictionary*. In the opening section of the introduction, Yāqūt describes the spirit in which Muslim geographers usually approached the study of this field:

PRAISE BE to God who has made the earth like unto an expanse and the mountains like unto stakes, and spread therefrom peaks and gorges, deserts and towns; who has caused rivers to gush forth through the land, and streams and seas to flow; and who has guided His creatures to take dwellings unto themselves and to construct well-made buildings and homes. Whereupon they have raised edifices and founded cities, carved habitations out of mountains, and contrived wells and cisterns. He has made their eagerness to raise that which they have raised and to build that which they have built, a warning to the heedless and an example to following generations. He said, and He is the most truthful of sayers:

> "Have they not journeyed through the land and beheld the end of those before them who were more numerous than they and mightier in strength, and who left a greater mark upon the earth? Yet all that of which they possessed themselves availed them not." [Qur'ān, XL, 82.]

I give praise unto Him for that which He has given and bestowed, for inspiring rectitude and guiding to it, for imparting understanding and making wisdom manifest. May God bless Muḥammad—the elect among His prophets and apostles, the most favored among the pious and those beloved of Him, he who was sent with guidance and with the perspicuous religion, of whom it is written, "We sent thee not, save as a mercy to all creatures," [Qur'ān, XXI, 107]—and the noble and saintly members of his household and the select and righteous Companions. May God save and preserve them all.

This is a book on the names of countries; on mountains, valleys, and plains; on villages, post-houses, and dwellings; on seas, rivers, and lakes; on idols, graven images, and objects of heathen worship. I have not undertaken to write this book, nor dedicated myself to composing it, in a spirit of frolic or diversion. Nor have I been impelled to do so by dread or desire; nor moved by longing for my native land; nor prompted by yearning for one who is loving and compassionate. Rather, I considered it my duty to address myself to this task, and, being capable of performing it, I regarded responding to its challenge as an inescapable obligation.

I was made aware of it by the great and glorious Book, and was guided to it by the Great Tidings, wherein God said, glory and majesty to Him, when He wanted to manifest to His creatures His signs and warnings and establish their guilt by visiting upon them His painful wrath:

> "Have they not journeyed through the land? And have they not hearts to understand with, or ears to hear with? Surely as to these things their eyes are not blind, but the hearts which are within their breasts are blind." [Qur'ān, XXII, 45.]

This is a reproof to him who has journeyed through the world and has not heeded the warning, and to him who has contemplated the departed centuries and has not been deterred.

> "God said, and He is the most truthful of sayers: 'Say:

Journey through the land and behold the manner in which the disbelievers have met their end.' " [Qur'ān, VI, 11.]

In other words, consider how their dwelling places were razed, all traces of them obliterated, and their lights extinguished in punishment for disregarding His commandments and transgressing against His prohibitions. This message is found in other unabrogated verses setting forth irrevocable commandments and prohibitions.

The first verse is a reprimand, clearly set forth, because of previous prohibition of the offense. The second is a commandment manifestly prescribing an obligation. This is from the Book of God, which "shall remain untouched by falsehood, in the future as in the past," [Qur'ān, XLI, 42] and which shall never suffer impairment as to its composition or form.

In traditions concerning righteous men of the past, ʿIsa ibn Maryam (Jesus Son of Mary) is quoted as saying:

> "The world is a place of visitation and an abode of transition. Be you then travelers in it, and take warning from what remains of the traces of the early ones."

Quss ibn Sāʿidah, who the Prophet declared would be resurrected as an *ummah* [leader] by himself, said:

> "The most eloquent of sermons is journeying through the wilderness and contemplating the resting places of the dead."

Poets have praised caliphs, kings, and princes for journeying through the land and for braving high peaks and precipitous gorges. One of them has said in praise of al-Muʿtaṣim:

> "You ranged with power through all the land,
> As though you sought al-Khiḍr's trail."

The means for seeing [various places] may prove impossible of attainment, whereupon it becomes necessary to seek information pertaining thereto. It is therefore incumbent upon us to inform the Muslims of that which we know, and to come to their aid with that which God, in His beneficence, has bestowed upon us. Though the need for this particular knowledge is shared by everyone who has a measure of learning, has acquired a part or parcel thereof, or who is known by it and bears the impress or the traces of one of its branches, yet I have not come upon anyone who has emended the faulty nomenclature [of geography] or who has felt himself equal to the task of rectifying information concerning the routes and regions pertaining to it. Rather I have found that the majority of the transmitters of the *akhbār* (usages of the Prophet) and the eminent narrators of poetry and the *āthār* (usages of the Companions), who have devoted all their time to these studies and exhausted their lives and efforts in such endeavors, have persevered with success in doing what is right; entering the gardens of wisdom through the gateways of every pursuit, excelling in the various fields of the letters and the sciences; in the recitation of the *sunan* (practices of the Prophet) and the *āthār*, and in the narration of the *ḥadīth* (traditions of the Prophet) and the *akhbār*. For they attain to a knowledge of the meaning of these studies, whereby they deduce the significance of preceding words from those which follow. For words, as it were, are like links in a chain, the end leading to the beginning and the beginning leading to the end.[3]

The Muslim geographers, besides dividing the earth into seven climates, also made several other divisions. For example, al-Masʿūdī in his *Meadows of Gold and Mines of Gems* writes:

. . . the mathematicians have divided the earth into four quarters, the east, west, north, and south. Another division is into the inhabited and uninhabited, cultivated and uncultivated world. They say the earth is round, its centre falls in the midst of the heaven, and the air surrounds it from all sides. It is the dot (centre) in reference to the zodiac.

The cultivated land is considered to begin from the Eternal Islands (Fortunate Islands) . . . in the Western Ocean, which is a group of six flourishing islands, and to extend as far as the extremity of China. . . . They found that this is a space of twelve hours (of the daily revolution of the sun); for they know that when the sun sets in the extremity of China, it rises again in the cultivated islands of the Western Ocean; and when it sets in these islands, it rises in the extremity of China. This is half the circumference of the earth, and the length of the cultivated parts of the globe, which, if reduced into miles, amounts to thirteen thousand five hundred geographical miles.

The researches into the breadth of the cultivated land have shown that it extends from the equator as far north as the Isle of Thule . . . which belongs to Britannia . . . and where the longest day has twenty hours.

They state that there is a point of the equator of the earth between east and west, which falls in an island between India and Habesh (Abyssinia), somewhat south of these two coun-

[3] *The Introductory Chapters of Yāqūt's Muʿjam al-Buldān*, translated and annotated by Wadie Jwaideh (Leiden: E. J. Brill, 1959), pp. 1–4.

tries; and as it is in the middle, between north and south, so it is in the middle between the Fortunate Islands and the utmost cultivated districts of China; and this is known by the name of the *Dome of the Earth* . . . and defined by the description which we have just given.

Al-Masʿūdī then turns to a consideration of the shape of lands and seas about which he writes:

The philosophers are at variance about the form of the seas. Most of the ancients, such as the mathematicians of the Hindus and Greeks, believe that they are convex . . . (round). This hypothesis, however, is rejected by those who follow strictly the revelation. The former bring forward many arguments in proof of their statement. If you sail on the sea, land and mountains disappear gradually, until you lose even the sight of highest summits of the mountains, and, on the contrary, if you approach the coast, you gradually perceive, first, the mountains, and, when you come nearer, you see the trees and plains.

This is the case with the mountain of Damāwand[4]. . . between er-Raï and Taberistān. It is to be seen at a distance of one hundred farsangs, on account of its height: from the summit rises a smoke; and it is covered with eternal snow, owing to its elevation. From the foot of the mountain gushes forth a copious river, the water of which is impregnated with sulphur, and of a yellow hue like the colour of gold. The mountain is so high that about three days and nights are required to ascend it. When on the top, a platform is discovered, of about a thousand cubits square; but as seen from below, it appears as if terminating in a cone. This platform is covered with red sand (scoriae?), into which the feet sink. No animal can reach the summit, not even a bird, on account of the height, the wind, and the cold. On the top are about thirty holes, from whence issue clouds of sulphurous smoke, which is seen from the sea. From the same wind-holes . . . proceeds, sometimes, a noise to be compared with the loudest thunder, which is accompanied with flames. It frequently happens that a man who exposes himself to danger, by climbing up to the highest mouths of these holes, brings a yellow sulphur back like gold, which is used in different arts, in alchemy, and for other purposes. From the top the mountains all around appear like hillocks, however high they may be. This mountain is about

4 An 18,600-foot volcanic peak about fifty miles northeast of Tehran, from the top of which one can see the Caspian Sea to the north on a clear day. (S. H. Nasr)

> twenty farsangs from the Caspian. If ships sail in this sea, and are very distant, they will not see it; but when they go towards the mountains of Taberistān, and are within a distance of one hundred farsangs, they perceive the north side of this mountain of Damāwand; and the nearer they come to the shore the more is seen of it. This is an evident proof of the spherical form of the water of the sea, which has the shape of a segment of a ball.
>
> In the same way if a man sails on the sea of er-Rūm (Mediterranean), which is the same as that of Egypt and of Syria, he loses sight of the mount el-Akraʾ . . . which has a height beyond measure, and is near Antākiyah (Antioch) . . . and of the mountains of el-Lādikīyah (Laodicea), Atrābolos . . . (Tripolis), and those of the Isle of Kobros (Cyprus), . . . and other places in the Byzantine empire; and he does not see these places although nothing is between him and them.[5]

These selections from the works of Yāqūt and al-Masʿūdī are far from sufficient to give a fair sample of the writings of the Muslim geographers, but they at least demonstrate the concern of the Muslim authors with the general principles of geography, within whose matrix they made their descriptive studies of various parts of the surface of the earth, as well as their particular observations.

C. Natural History

The study of natural history in medieval times, in Islam as well as in Christianity, included a large number of topics, ranging from geography, geology, botany, zoology, and anthropology to sacred history, mythology, and cosmogony. The Muslim universal historians, such as al-Ṭabarī and al-Masʿūdī, began their history of mankind from the time

[5] *El Masʿudi's Historical Encyclopedia Entitled "Meadows of Gold and Mines of Gems,"* translated by A. Sprenger (London: Oriental Translation Fund, 1841), pp. 195–196; 211–214.

of creation, and considered the state of man's social existence in relation to his cosmic environment. Natural history in Islam has, in fact, usually been cultivated within the matrix of sacred history, just as in the Jewish tradition, in which authors like Philo wrote universal histories as commentaries upon the Old Testament, and particularly Genesis. In this tradition of writing natural history, no distinction is made between the sacred and the profane; all beings in the world are ultimately studied with respect to their Divine origin.

The relatively rapid consolidation of the Islamic world, from Andalusia and Morocco to India, into one vast domain, in which a common religion, way of life and language were dominant, provided a special opportunity for the development of a tradition of natural history, just as it had for geography. The Muslim natural historians were able to acquire far greater knowledge of the various parts of the earth than can be found in such classical sources as the *Historia Naturalis* of Pliny. Many a traveler like Ibn Jubair or Ibn Baṭṭūṭah was able to journey from the Atlantic all the way to the heart of Asia and to record along the way his observations of the flora and fauna, and other natural features.

In Islam, the works which are concerned with natural history fall into several categories. There are, first of all, the universal histories, some of which, like those of al-Ṭabarī and Ibn Miskawaih, are more than anything else historical, while others, like the works of al-Bīrūnī and al-Suyūṭī, combine history with the sciences of nature. There are also geographical texts, such as those of al-Idrīsī, which treat of questions of natural history. Another category of significance in this field is that of cosmographies, like *The Wonders of Creation* of Abū Yaḥyā al-Qazwīnī, which often deal with cosmography in a mythological language, but also give descriptions based on the direct observation of phenomena and events, with a view toward highlighting the wonders of creation.

Aside from these large treatises, in which many subjects appear, there are texts in the domain of natural history which are devoted chiefly to a single subject—such as the *Nabaṭaean Agriculture* of Ibn Waḥshīyah, the *Book of Agriculture* of Ibn al-ʿAwwām, the *Book of Animals* of al-Jāḥiẓ, which deals with zoology from both a scientific and a theological standpoint, and *The Book of the Multitude of Knowledge of Precious Stones* of al-Bīrūnī, which deals with minerals. Nearly all these works were written to show the wisdom of the Creator in His creation. Most Muslim natural historians, like the medieval Christians, sought to study natural history not for "curiosity" but in order to observe the "signs of God," the *Vestigia Dei,* so that they were continually drawing spiritual and moral lessons from the study of the kingdoms of Nature, and saw in the world of Nature a unified domain in which God's wisdom is everywhere manifested.

Most of the Greek texts on natural history, especially the works of Aristotle and Theophrastus, as well as some Indian and Persian works, were known to the Muslims. Already in the second/eighth century, the entourage of the sixth Shiite imam, Jaʿfar al-Ṣādiq, included several scholars and scientists who were interested in this subject, and the imam himself left behind certain teachings connected with the various branches of natural history. Moreover, the corpus attributed to Jābir ibn Ḥayyān also contains many treatises on various branches of natural history. One of the figures of the second/eighth century is al-Aṣmaʿī, who is one of the great literary figures of the Arabic language, and wrote several zoological treatises on the camel, the sheep, the horse, and many other animals, as well as on human anatomy. Although his interests were as much literary as well as scientific, al-Aṣmaʿī is generally regarded as the first Muslim authority in zoology, beginning a tradition of writing about the lives of animals, in which the literary considerations play as great a role as the zoological ones.

Early in the third/ninth century, there appeared two works, falsely attributed to Aristotle, which were widely read by later authors of natural histories. The first of these was the *Secretum Secretorum,* which is of Arabic, possibly of Syriac origin, and deals with physiognomy and other occult descriptions of Nature. This work was also well known in the West, in its Latin translation by Roger Bacon, as well as in its translation into such diverse languages as Catalan and Flemish. The second is *The Lapidary of Aristotle,* compiled from Persian and also Syriac sources, and differing from the mineralogy of Theophrastus.

In the second half of the third/ninth century, al-Jāḥiẓ, Muʿtazilite scholar and man of letters, wrote his *Book of Animals,* which is the most famous Arabic work on zoology. Al-Jāḥiẓ, like al-Âṣmaʿī, combined philology with zoology, and the Greek and Arabic traditions of animal lore. His *Book of Animals* had a marked influence upon all later writers on this subject, and in fact on Arabic literature in general, because al-Jāḥiẓ is one of the foremost Arabic prose writers.

In this work, traditions from many sources are accumulated, and scientific, literary, moral and religious studies of animals are combined. It set a standard for writing in natural history which was to be emulated by later authorities in the field.

Another treatise, which became nearly as famous as that of al-Jāhiz, was the *Nabataean Agriculture* of Ibn Wahshīyah, which appeared shortly after al-Jāhiz's work but differs greatly from it in character. This work is not only a treatise on agriculture, as its name indicates, but also concerns itself with the occult properties of things. The author maintains that he is bringing to light the esoteric teachings of the ancient Babylonians; more likely, he was expounding certain beliefs of his own time in Mesopotamia, which probably contained elements of the doctrines of the Nabataeans, who were descendants of the old Chaldeans and spoke Aramaic. In any case the *Nabataean Agriculture,* along with many other treatises attributed to Ibn Waḥshīyah, became among the most widely read works on that branch of natural history which sought to deal with the hidden properties of things. Moreover, Ibn Wahshīyah has always been regarded as one of the authorities in such domains as astrology, magic, numerology, and other branches of the occult sciences. There are many well-known figures such as Shams al-Dīn al-Būnī, who wrote numerous treatises on this branch of the history of science, a field that is of far greater significance for the understanding of the medieval sciences than is usually recognized.

During the fourth/tenth and fifth/eleventh centuries, the *Epistles* of the Brethren of Purity appeared, in which all the sciences were treated, unified by a Pythagorean philosophy of numbers, which runs throughout the whole of this large work. The *Epistles* also treat in detail of geology, mineralogy, botany, zoology, etc., and present a summary of the Islamic sciences during this period, which marks their apogee. Of special interest from the point of view of natural history is the *Dispute between Man and the Animals,* a part of the epistle on zoology which discusses the animal kingdom in a manner more reminiscent of the Indian and Persian traditions of natural history than of the Greek. In this treatise, more attention is paid to the qualities and virtues of each animal species, and to the moral and spiritual lessons that can be learned from the animal kingdom as a whole, rather than to sheer zoological description.

Contemporary with the *Epistles* of the Brethren of Purity, there appeared the *Book of the Guide* on *materia medica,* containing much about botany and mineralogy, by the Palestinian author al-Tamīmī, as well as the works of al-Bīrūnī and Avicenna. Al-Bīrūnī wrote some of the most notable pages on geology, which are contained in his geographical treatises, as well as in his *India.* As already mentioned, he is also the author of *The Book of the Multitude of Knowledge of Precious Stones,* which is the best text on mineralogy in Islam, and contains detailed descriptions of many minerals, as well as the specific weights for some of them, as will be shown later in the chapter on physics. As for Avicenna, *The Book of Healing* contains an elaborate discussion of geology, botany, and zoology as well as of mineralogy, the section on mineralogy having become famous in the West independently as *On Mineralogy (De Mineralibus)* (for a long time attributed to Aristotle).

From the fifth/eleventh century onward, there began to appear a series of works on agriculture and botany by authors from Andalusia, who soon became the foremost authorities in this field. The Arabs built elaborate water-systems in Spain; even the Persian garden found a new home in this land, becoming modified into a new form, which has survived to this day as the Spanish garden. The varied flora of Andalusia and Morocco, made possible through the ingenious irrigation system which has remained in certain regions until now, provided the background for the botanical works for which the Spanish authors were particularly famous. During the fifth/eleventh century, Abū ᶜUbaid al-Bakrī composed a work on the plants and trees of Andalusia, and his compatriot, Ibn Ḥajjāj, in his *Sufficient,* dealt with botany, which he combined with grammatical considerations.

In the sixth/twelfth century, basic treatises on botany were written, beginning with the treatise on simples by Ibn Sarābī (in Latin, Serapion Junior). Later in the century, there appeared the Andalusian al-Ghāfiqī's work on drugs and plants, the most exact in Islamic annals, and his compatriot Ibn al-ᶜAwwām's *Book of Agriculture,* the most important medieval treatise on this subject, which in thirty-four chapters deals with agriculture and animal husbandry. In zoology, there were several famous treatises—such as that of Ibn Jawālīqī on horses, Avempace's treatise on hunting, al-Marwazī's *The Natures of Animals,* and several works on falconry, in both Arabic and Persian, some of which are studied to the present day.

During the next century, ᶜAbd al-Latīf al-Baghdādī wrote over one hundred fifty treatises on nearly every subject, including an *Account of Egypt,* which contains detailed botanical observations. At the same time, Ibn al-Ṣūrī made the first known effort to paint plants at the different stages of their growth, while Abuʾl-ʿAbbās al-Nabatī, another Spanish authority on botany, wrote several works on plants, highly regarded among Muslims. There was also a well-known work on mineralogy at this time, by the Egyptian al-Tīfāshī, called *Flower of Thoughts on Precious Stones.* As for zoology, Ibn al-Mundhir's treatise on hippology, the best work of its kind in medieval times, is of particular significance.

The writing of treatises on animals continued into the eighth/fourteenth century, which also marks the appearance of the greatest Muslim treatises on zoology. *The Wonders of Creation* of Abū Yaḥyā al-Qazwīnī, mentioned above, the *Collected Stories* of al-ʿAufī, the *Description of Animals and their Uses* of Ibn al-Bukhtyishūʿ, the *Uses of Animals* of Ibn al-Duraihim and the *Lives of Animals* by Kamāl al-Dīn al-Damīrī—all of which are major zoological texts—were all written within the space of nearly a century, from the second half of the seventh/thirteenth to the second half of the eighth/fourteenth century. The work of al-Damīrī is, in fact, the most complete source for the knowledge of zoology in Islam, and one of the best sources of its folklore. This work also had influence in modern zoology, through the poem which al-Suyūṭī, the Egyptian scholar and encyclopedist, wrote about it. The poem was translated into Latin during the seventeenth century, being incorporated into the *Hierozoicon,* written in 1663, which involved a study of the animals mentioned in the Bible, just as al-Damīrī's *Lives of Animals* included a study of the animals mentioned in the Quran.

Besides these major studies on animals, the eighth/fourteenth century also witnessed the writings of several works on botany, of which the most notable is the treatise on agriculture by the sixth Rasūlī sultan of the Yemen. But, just as with other branches of the natural and mathematical sciences, so in natural history from this time on the writings of new and serious studies diminished considerably, even though a Safavid sage, Mīr Dāmād, made an observational study of bees, or scholars in the Mogul court wrote treatises on horses or falcons, or composed scientific encyclopedias containing much material on natural history.

Of the geological studies by Muslim authors, few are as exact and penetrating as those of al-Bīrūnī, who made acute observations of land forms and mountain structures, during his many journeys over the lands of Western Asia. For example, he discovered the sedimentary nature of the Ganges Basin, about which he writes:

> One of these plains is India, limited in the south by the above-mentioned Indian Ocean, and on all three other sides by the lofty mountains, the waters of which flow down to it. But if you have seen the soil of India with your own eyes and meditate on its nature—if you consider the rounded stones found in the earth however deeply you dig, stones that are huge near the mountains and where the rivers have a violent current; stones that are of smaller size at greater distance from the mountains, and where the streams flow more slowly; stones that appear pulverised in the shape of sand where the streams begin to stagnate near their mouths and near the sea—if you consider all this, you could scarcely help thinking that India has once been a sea which by degrees has been filled up by the alluvium of the streams.[6]

Al-Bīrūnī was fully cognizant of the great geologic upheavals that took place in the past, and the gradual process by which such changes were brought about:

> In a similar way, sea has turned into land and land into sea; which changes, if they happened before the existence of man, are not known and if they took place later they are not remembered because with the length of time the record of events breaks off especially if this happens gradually. This only a few can realize.
>
> This steppe of Arabia was at one time sea, then was upturned so that the traces are still visible when wells or ponds are dug; for they begin with layers of dust, sand and pebbles, then there are found in the soil shells, glass and bones which cannot possibly be said to have been buried there on purpose. Nay, even stones are brought up in which are embedded shells, cowries and what is called "fish-ears," sometimes well-preserved or the hollows are there of their shape while the animal has decayed. The same are found at the Bāb al-Abwāb on the shores of the Caspian Sea. But there is no memory of a known time nor any history about it for the Arabs have inhabited the land since their ancestor Yoqtān. Of course, they may have lived in the mountains of Yaman while the lowland was sea. These were the ʿArab al-ʿAriba of antiquity. They cultivated the land from a spring between two mountains, the waters rising to the

6 From *Alberuni's India,* translated by E. C. Sachau (London: Kegan Paul, Trench, Trubner & Co., Ltd., 1910), I, p. 198.

top, and two gardens flourished right and left till the dam break of al-ʿArim ruined them because the water sank and cultivation ceased and in place of the two gardens there were two waste lands with bitter herbs, tamarisks and a few willows.

We find similar stones in the centre of which are enclosed "fish-ears" in the sandy desert between Jurjān and Khwārazm which must have been a lake in the past, because the river Jaihūm (Oxus), I mean the river of Balkh, ran through them to the Caspian Sea past a district known as Balkhān. Thus Ptolomaios mentions in the book *Geographaia* that the river flows into the sea of Hyrcania, i.e. Jurjān. Now between to-day and the time of Ptolomaios are nearly eight hundred years. The Oxus used to flow in those days through those plains which to-day are desert from a place between Zam and Āmūya and irrigate the lands and villages which were there round Balkhān and shed into the sea between Jurjān and al-Khazar. Then happened some silting which diverted the waters to the land of the Ghuzz Turks, where its course was interrupted by a mountain known to-day by the name of *famʾal-Asad* (the lion's mouth) and among the people of Khwārazm as *Sikr ash-Shaiṭān* (Devil's Dam). There the water accumulated and rose so that the traces of the dashing of the waves are on the heights thereof. Then when the weight (of the water) and the pressure on those porous stones became excessive, it broke through and burrowed about one day's journey, then turned to the right towards Fārāb on a course known to-day as *al-Faḥmī*. The people cultivated the land on both sides of its bank, in about three hundred towns and villages, the ruins of which are remaining to this day. Then happened to this water-course after a lapse of time what happened to the first and the water turned to the left to the land of the Pajnākis and took the water-course known as *Wādī Mazdubast* in the desert between Khwārazm and Jurjān and irrigated numerous localities for a long time till they too fell into decay. So the inhabitants moved to the coast of the Caspian Sea. They are folk of the kind of the Allān and al-Uss and their language to-day is a mixture of Khwārazmī and Pajnākī. After this all the water flowed towards Khwārazm after seepings had flown there before and it purified itself at a place barred by rocks, which to-day is at the beginning of the plain of Khwārazm, and burst through it overflowing the district and making a small lake and on account of its abundance of water and the strong current it became muddy from the clay the water carried. This used to sink as the water spread with the mud it carried and harden gradually where it broke through and became dry and the lake moved further till it surrounded all Khwārazm and the lake reached the sand-dune which lay across its course and as it was not able to press it

> further it turned towards the north to the land inhabited by the Turkumān to-day. Between this lake and that which was in the Wādī Mazdubast is no great distance. It has become a muddy salt-swamp which cannot be forded and is known in Turkish as *Khīz-Tanqizi,* i.e. the Maiden's Sea.[7]

As for mineralogy, it was usually studied in connection with geology, so far as the question of the genesis of minerals was concerned. Here, the sulfur-mercury theory of metals (which we shall discuss in the chapter on alchemy) was combined with the mineralogical theories of Aristotle and Theophrastus. But there were also studies devoted to the physical, chemical and also occult aspects of minerals, such as that of al-Bīrūnī already cited. There came into being also a whole literature on precious stones, which dealt with their quality and value, as well as with their medical, theurgical and magical powers, in this way continuing a tradition which had already been well developed in Persia and India, before the rise of Islam.

Botanical studies were also combined with medical considerations, and a literature developed on the properties and uses of plants—and, in certain cases, minerals—as poisons. On this latter subject, such well-known works as the *Book of Shānāq* were based mainly on works translated from the Sanskrit and Jābir's *Book of Poisons,* the most elaborate work on this subject in Arabic, bears the imprint of Indian and Iranian influences. One of the best illustrations of the plant studies in which botany and medicine are combined is the *Book of Simple Drugs* of al-Ghāfiqī, which was later abridged and summarized by Barhebraeus. Regarding cinnamon, which reached the Islamic world from China and was therefore called "Chinese wood" (yet which was unknown in exactly this form in the drug trade of the Ancients), al-Ghāfiqī writes:

> **Dâr Sînî** CINNAMON, (Bark of Cinnamomum ceylanicum Nees., Cinnamomum Cassia Bl. and others).
>
> Its explanation in Persian is "the China tree."
>
> ISḤĀQ IBN SULAIMĀN: Cinnamon is of different kinds: one, which is the real kind, is called Chinese cinnamon *(dār sīnī as-Sīn);* another one is inferior, *i.e.* cassia bark *(dār sūs* of *Cinnamomum Cassia Bl.).* Other kinds are known as "the real bark" and "clove bark."

[7] From al-Bīrūnī, *Kitāb al-taḥdīd,* translated by F. Krenkow in *Al-Biruni Commemoration Volume* (Calcutta: Iran Society, 1951), pp. 199–200.

As to the "real cinnamon" its substance is richer, thicker and more porous than that of the "bark." Usually its substance is as thick as a little finger, and an oily exudate is produced when the bark is chewed or pounded. Its colour is intermediate between the redness of the "bark" and the blackness of "clove," but more inclined to that of the first, for its redness is more pronounced and apparent than its blackness. Its outside colour is more like that of the red cassia-bark. Its flavour causes at first a sensation of pungency with a little astringency, then is followed by sweetness and ends in bitterness, and a saffronlike flavour with a slightly oily taste. Its smell is like that of Ceylon-bark, and when chewed there is a taste like that of saffron with a trace of lotus-odour.

Concerning the "inferior cinnamon," it closely resembles the substance of the "bark" in its lightness, porosity (loose texture) and its red colour, except that its redness is more pronounced, its coloration more intense and its substance thinner and harder. Its twigs are twisted, thin and contracted, resembling the tubes of the common reed, except that they are split up longitudinally and are neither united nor coherent. Its smell and taste are similar to those of the "bark" as is also their aroma (spicy odour) and astringency, except that the cinnamon is possessed of more heat and less sweetness and astringency.

The "real bark" is sometimes thick and sometimes thin; both kinds are red, smooth and inclined to be shiny. On the outside they are rough and of whitish-red colour, a little like that of cassia-bark. It is of a fragrant aroma, and in its taste (flavour) there is pungency and acridity with a little sweetness.

As to that kind which is known as clove bark, it is thin, hard, blackish and not porous. Its smell and taste are like those of cloves, except that the latter are a little stronger.

DIOSC. [Dioscorides] I (14): *(kinámômon),* i.e. the cinnamon. The best kind is that which is called *(Mósylon),* resembling a little the cassia bark called (Mosylîtis). The best sample of this kind is the fresh, dark, inclined to ash-red colour and of very aromatic smell but free from any odour of rue, or lesser cardamom, filling the nose with its smell.

There is another kind, from the mountains, which is thick, short and of hyacinth-red colour. A third kind, still nearer to the first, is dark, smooth, brittle and with few knots.

A fourth kind is white, soft, rough grown, and has a root which is easily broken when rubbed between the fingers.

A fifth kind has an odour like that of cassia bark, is of penetrating smell, hyacinth-red colour, with a bark like that of cassia, not very brittle and with a thick root.

Any one of the above-mentioned kinds which has an odour

resembling that of frankincense, myrtle or cassia bark and whose aroma is somewhat greasy, is not good (or: inferior to the good). Refuse the white, scabbed, with wrinkled wood, and that which is (not) smooth or ligneous. Throw away the root, as it is useless.

There is another drug like cinnamon, called "false cinnamon," of rough structure and weak smell and strength. There is, moreover, a bark of cinnamon which is called *(zingíberi)* resembling, in aspect, the cinnamon, but of a rancid smell.

As to that which is called *(xylokinámômon)* and known as "bark," it is like cinnamon as to its root and the number of its knots. It is a wood with long and resistant twigs and its aromatic odour is much less than that of cinnamon. It is said that the "bark" is a different kind and not of the same nature as cinnamon.[8]

Interest in pure zoology was similarly rather rare. Usually, the study of animals was combined with interest in their medical and pharmacological uses, and even more often in deriving moral and spiritual lessons from them, and in witnessing God's wisdom in Nature. The Muslim zoologists combined many quaint beliefs, especially as to the origins of certain species, with accurate observations of their lives and habits. For example, al-Jāḥiẓ and Abū Yaḥyā al-Qazwīnī regarded the giraffe as a hybrid of a wild she-camel and a male hyena, while al-Masʿūdī believed it to be a hybrid of the camel and the panther. Buzūrg ibn Shahriyār in his *Book of the Marvels of India* considers the "ape-man" (called in Arabic *nasnās*), and also certain forms of monkeys, to be the result of the union of man with the hyena and other wild beasts. Al-Damīrī follows a general belief among the Muslims that the rhinoceros, whose description was first given by al-Bīrūnī in his *India,* is a cross between a horse and an elephant.

As an example of a zoological text in which zoology is combined with philology and also popular medicine, let us consider the beginning of the third part of the first chapter of Ḥamdallāh al-Mustaufī al-Qazwīnī's cosmographical encyclopedia, *The Delights of the Heart,* which is one of the well-known zoological works that appeared during the hun-

[8] *The Abridged Version of "The Book of Simple Drugs" of Aḥmad ibn Muḥammad al-Ghāfiqī by Gregorius Abuʾl-Farag* (*Barhebraeus*), edited with an English translation, commentary and indices by M. Meyerhof and G. P. Sobhy. Vol. I, Fasc. III (The Egyptian University, The Faculty of Medicine Publication No. 4. Cairo: Government Press, 1938), pp. 468–470.

dred years stretching from the seventh/thirteenth to the eighth/fourteenth century, a time when the best zoological texts in Islam were being written.

Concerning Animals

The decree of Eternal Wisdom has contrived the natural form of animals for the warding off of the pernicious and deadly evils which may ensue from the infections of the air, that so there might be ease for the constitution of man, the perfected of perfections. For if there had been no animal life, these evils would have brought disasters on man's constitution, and kept him from rising to the attainment of perfection.

He gave to animals sensation and motion, that they may seek their food . . . and that by reason of their movement those infections and harms may be the more readily averted from mankind. And some He made the enemies of others, so that this might be the cause of a more abundant movement in them; and He bestowed on every one, according to their necessity, the means for the preservation of their lives, and for drawing to themselves advantages, and for averting the injury an enemy might do, that thus they might be preserved. *And praise be to Him who has bestowed everything of which there is need, without redundancy and without falling short.* And since He created them as instruments for man, some He created in their nature pacific, and gave them no instruments for inflicting injury, so that by nature they are submissive to man; some are for riding, and some are for food, as God *(may He be praised and exalted!)* has said: *Have they not seen that we have created for them, amongst the things our hands have made, cattle—and they are the owners thereof? And we have tamed them for them, and of them some are to ride, and of them are what they eat.* [Quran XXXVI, 71–72.] And to some He gave the quality of teachableness, so that, although they were not naturally submissive, through teaching they became obedient, and [fit] instruments [for man]; and as to some, that resisted and rebelled against man, He directed man that he so got the upper hand of them as to overthrow them all and to share in their utilities.

And to set a limit to and enumerate the species of animals is beyond what a far-sighted intelligence and a meditative understanding can compass: God *(may He be exalted!)* has said: *And none knows the hosts of the Lord except Himself;* [Quran, LXXIV, 34] but of what our understanding can reach to, we shall make mention under three classes—of the land, of the water, and of the air.

And it has been said that every animal that goes on two legs takes a single mate, and while mated is jealous, and all those which go on four legs become enamoured of numerous mates; and those whose ears project from their heads bring forth their young, and those whose ears do not project lay eggs; and every animal that has horns is without upper front teeth. And in regard to the lawfulness and unlawfulness of their flesh, although I shall state (the ruling) according to fatwā under the name of every animal in succession still, summarily, what the Prophet *(may God pour blessings on him and preserve him!)* said has proved a felicitous guide, viz.: *All wild beasts with canine teeth are forbidden, and all birds with tearing claws.*

THE FIRST CLASS

Concerning Terrestrial Animals

And that comprises five sections.

THE FIRST SECTION

Concerning Domestic Animals

Of these I shall enumerate ten kinds in alphabetical order. **Ibl,** the Camel, is called in Arabic *baʿīr,* in Turkish *dèvé,* and in Mongolian *tamkun.* The Arabs call the male *jamal,* and the female *nāqat,* and a young camel *bakr,* and an old one *nāb* and *ʿaud,* and a two-humped camel *fālij;* a superior camel they call *najīb,* a one-year-old *ibn mukhāḍ,* a two-year-old *ibn labūn,* a three-year-old *ḥiqq,* a four-year-old *jadhaʿ,* a five- and a six-year-old *thanīy,* a seven-year-old *rabāʿī, an eight-*year-old *sadīs,* a nine-year-old *bāzil,* a ten-year-old *mukhlif;* a pregnant camel is *khalifat,* and its progeny *ḥuwār* and *faṣīl,* a baggage animal *ḥamūlat,* a milch camel *laqūḥ.* And in Turkish the male is called *baqar,* the female *īnkān.* The Arabs of the desert own large numbers of them.

The camel is an animal of a strange make, large-bodied, eating little, bearing burdens, obedient to command. God *(may He be exalted!)* said: *Do they not look then at the camel how she is created.* [Quran, LXXXVIII, 17.] It is susceptible to ecstasy and gladness; and Shaikh Saʿdī of Shirāz says (verse): The camel becomes ecstastic and dances at the Arab's song; if thou rejoicest not, thou art a cross-grained beast.

Its flesh is allowed to be eaten by all the sects; it is warm and dry in the first degree, and furnishes an atrabilious and coarse diet. The camel is intelligent, hence when it is sick it eats oak-leaves and recovers; and when a poisonous snake bites it, it eats a crab and the poison takes no effect.

Its liver averts cataract and gives clearness of vision. Wherever its fat is put down snakes flee from thence; and its fat is beneficial in piles. If its hair be tied round the left thigh it arrests diabetes.

Camels are of several kinds: the *lōk,* the *bēsurāk,* and the *bukhtī;* and the best as regards appearance and price is the *bukhtī,* and for bearing burdens the *bēsurāk,* and for enduring thirst the *lōk.*

Baghl, the Mule, is called *qāṭir* by the Turks and *lāʾūsa* by the Mongols. It is begotten of a horse and an ass; that which has the ass for its father is better than that which has the ass for its mother; its qualities are more those of the horse than of the ass, and in appearance, too, it has a greater resemblance to its mother. That which is begotten of a horse and a wild ass is the better; and the mule of the East is better than that of other countries. It is the longest lived of domestic animals, because of its seldom copulating, just as the sparrow is the shortest lived of birds through much copulating. And mules have no offspring, because the foetal membranes are not strong enough to protect the young, and the birth passage is narrow and the egress of the young difficult. And if ever a mule should become pregnant, it dies at the time of the birth and cannot bring forth.

And inasmuch as the unlawful prevails over the lawful, and the mule is born of the unlawful and the lawful, the eating of it is also unlawful. And as to that which is born of the wild ass and the horse, although the two parents are lawful to eat, yet this kind of mule is exceptional, and a rule is not to be founded on an exceptional occurrence; hence this also is ruled to be unlawful.

Its Properties.—Any woman who eats the heart of a mule will not become pregnant. Five drachms of a mule's hoof mixed with oil of myrtle, if rubbed on any place, will cause hair to grow there, and will cure ringworm of the scalp. The smoke of its hoofs, its hair, and its dung will drive away rats. If a pregnant woman drinks its urine she will bring forth a dead child. The stinging flies in the sores on its back ward off piles. If a pregnant woman ties its skin round her arm the offspring will perish, and if the woman is not pregnant she will not become so.

Baqar, the Ox, is called *saqar* (?) by the Turks and *hōkar* by the Mongols. The Arabs call the male *thaur* and the female *baqarat,* and its young they call *ʿjl.* It is an animal of great strength, and of many uses; and the world's welfare turns on it as a centre. Its flesh is lawful to eat; but a cow that eats dung they call *jallāla,* and to eat her flesh is disapproved, inasmuch as nature turns against such an action.

The ashes of the cow's horn cure fever, and increase sexual power, giving great stiffness to the male organ; and if put in the nose they check bleeding [at the nose]; and mixed with vinegar and used as an ointment on a leprous patch (of the maculo-anaesthetic type) before the rising of the sun, it restores to health. If its bile be rubbed on a tree, grubs will not attack the fruit; and if it be boiled with cottonseed and the seeds of radish, and used as an ointment on chloasma, it will cure it; incorporated with the dung of rats and given to one who has colic, it immediately gives relief; and when the ox's bile is mixed with honey, it will cure diphtheria. Its kidney daubed over the neck cures tuberculous glands.

Its flesh is cold and dry in the first degree, but the male is less cold, and the female less dry; and the flesh of the calf is better than either, though none are free from harm, causing morphoea, cancer, rash, tubercular leprosy, and elephantiasis.

The penis and testicle of a calf rubbed up will increase sexual power and the stiffness of the male organ. If its blood be burnt in the presence of a number of people, discord will break out among them. The horn of a black cow incorporated with barley meal and spread on piles, fistulas, and tuberculous glands cures them; its urine mixed with human urine and used to wash hands and feet will cure a long-standing quartan ague. The smoke of dried cow's dung gives relief in difficult labour; and if the dung be rubbed on one suffering from dropsy it cures him.

Jāmūs, the Buffalo, called *ō* by the Mongols, is a strong-bodied animal, and very powerful. It has a worm in its brain which perpetually torments it, so that it sleeps little, and stays always in the water. It is an enemy of the lion and the crocodile, and mostly gets the better of them, but it is helpless against gnats. It is lawful food in all sects, but its flesh is not free from harm.

Its Properties.—The worm of its brain causes sleeplessness. Its fat pounded up with brine cures chloasma, leprosy (maculo-anaesthetic), and the itch (scabies). Eating its flesh will get rid of lice from the clothes.

Ḥimār, the Ass, called *ʿair* by some of the Arabs, *īshak* by the Turks, *īlchakan* by the Mongols. The Arabs call its colt *jaḥsh*. It is an animal of sluggish limbs and from its excessive stupidity copulates with its own mother; no other animal has this habit—it is only rarely they mount their mothers. The quality of the ass is extremely cold; and it is unlawful to eat it.

Its Properties.—When one who has been bitten by a scorpion rides facing backwards on an ass, and the ass trots, the pain will be relieved. Its brain mixed with olive oil will make the hair grow long. Its tooth put beneath the pillow will bring sleep. Its liver cures quartan fever and epilepsy,—better if taken on an empty stomach. Its spleen causes an increase in the quantity of milk. Its hoof cures epilepsy and (maculo-anaesthetic) leprosy; and mixed with olive oil cures tubercular glands in the neck, and pains in the joints and fistula. Eating its flesh is a remedy against poison and tubercular leprosy. Its fat melted heals wounds and ulcers. A watery extract of its fresh dung, if dropped into the nose, checks nose-bleeding. If its urine be rubbed on a boat, fish will gather round it. Its blood cures piles, and will change a child of bad disposition into one of good disposition. Its milk used as a gargle will allay toothache, and if drunk will take away a long-standing cough. The hair of its tail put in wine will bring about a drunken brawl.

The ass is terrified by the lion, to such a degree that when it sees the lion it stands stock still, and the lion comes up and eats it. And in the back of the neck of some asses is a kind of stone, the account of which has been given under "Stones."

Sinnaur, the Cat, called *hirr* by some of the Arabs, *jatak* by the Turks, *malghūn* by the Mongols. It is a greedy animal, of various colours, and to eat it is unlawful and to kill it forbidden. When angry it becomes so enraged as to be beside itself; hence infidels used to bring up a devotee on the flesh of cats, so that he might overcome his antagonist. The cat is the enemy of the rat; and the elephant dreads the cat. In the *Mujmalu-t-Tawārīkh* it is said that the cat does not breed in China.

Those who apply its bile to their eyes become keen-sighted in the night; and half a drachm of it mixed with olive oil is beneficial to one with facial paralysis; and pounded up with cumin seed and salt it heals old wounds. The spleen of a black cat tied on a woman with excessive menstruation will check the flow, and until it is taken off the menses will not reappear. Its flesh boiled and used as a poultice to the gout allays the pain; and if eaten, magic will take no effect against the eater. If its blood is applied to tubercular leprosy, (the disease) will disappear. Its flesh, dried and rubbed up, and placed over the wound where a thorn or an arrow-head has entered, will extract (the foreign body).

Ghanam, Sheep and Goats, are called by the Turks *qòyun;* and the sheep is called by the Arabs *ḍaʿn* and *naʿjat;* and the lamb they call *ḥamal;* and a one-year-old sheep or goat the Arabs call *jadhaʿ*. And to eat it is lawful in all religions and sects, and is sālutary. And it is a wholesome animal, and confers prosperity; and the Prophet *(may God pour blessings on him, and preserve him!)* said, of the blessings it confers: *The sheep is affluence.* Once every year it brings forth one young one, and now and then two, and then no more for a year; and men eat of them incalculable and uncountable numbers, and [yet] the face of the earth is full of them—unlike other and predaceous animals, which bring forth several times every year and several young at a birth, and of which men eat none, whose numbers [nevertheless] are small. *And praise be to Him whose* *wisdom has decreed the fewness of the noxious and the abundance of the serviceable, in kindness and mercy towards His servants—verily He is powerful to do what He wills.* And the relation of goods lawful and unlawful is similar.

In the *ʿAjāʾibu-l-Makhlūqāt* it is related that there is a kind of sheep in India that has a tail on its breast, two on its back, two on the thigh, and one as usual at its hinder end like other sheep; and though these are not the proper places for a tail, the white flesh is in such amount because of the presence of fat that it looks like a tail. And in Fārs there is a sheep the tail-fat of which is greater in amount than [the whole of] its flesh. And in these provinces [i.e. the region round Qazwīn] there is a kind of sheep which has no tail, which they call *jarī*, and its flesh is more delicate than that of sheep with tails.

And sheep are as terrified of a wolf as asses of a lion.

The Properties of the Sheep.—The horn of a ram together with its bile mixed with honey will retard the formation of cataract, and remove corneal opacities. If a woman carries some of its wool about her she will not become pregnant. Its flesh has many virtues, and is the best of foods—particularly a yearling which has been castrated. The sheep's flesh is hot in the second degree and moist in the first; the flesh of ram and ewe is not free from harm. The milk of the sheep is salutary at most times; and the curds, and butter and cheese, and the boiled and thickened milk, and the dried sour milk, and whatever they make from it—everything is characterized by a number of properties, but it would be tedious to expound them all.

Faras, the Horse, is called *khail* and *kurāʿ* in Arabic, *āt* in Turkish, and *mūrī* in Mongolian. A stallion is called *ḥiṣān* in Arabic, and *aighir* in Turkish, and *ahraʿa* in Mongolian; a mare, *ramakat* in Arabic, *qisrāq* in Turkish, *kūn* in Mongolian; a colt in Arabic *muhrat,* in Turkish *qūlūn,* and in Mongolian *ūtghān.* A gelding in Turkish *akhtā;* in Persian the term for it is well known. A slow horse the Turks call *nāshiqa,* a swift ambling horse they call *yūrqa,* a racehorse *qūrdūna,* and a horse going quick with a jolting trot they call *qātarāk.* The eating of its flesh is allowed in the sect of the Imām Shāfiʿī *(may God be well pleased with him!),* and disapproved in the other sects; it is warm and dry in the second degree. And the horse is the most beautiful in form and colour, and the swiftest of animals, outstripping all others; it is of all colours, and along with beauty of form it has also excellent qualities, such as obedience, and intelligence, and fortitude and endurance in battle. And God most high has shown His favour by making him a riding beast for man; the Most High has said: *And horses and mules and asses, for you to ride upon, and for an ornament:*

[Quran, XVI, 8] and the Most High has said: *And prepare ye against them what force and companies of horse ye can, to make the enemies of God, and your enemies, in dread thereof.* [Quran, XVIII, 62] And the Prophet *(may God pour blessings on him, and preserve him!)* said: *Prosperity is tied to the forelock of the horse till the day of judgment.*

In the *Mujmalu-t-Tawārīkh* it is said that the horse does not bring forth young in Hindūstān; and in the *Tārikh-i-Fanākatī* that horses are in greater number among the Turks, but of greater value among the Arabs—hence the Arabs attach importance to their horses' lineage.

Its Properties.—If a horse's tooth is tied on a child its teething will be quick and painless; if its hair be hung at the door of a house, gnats will not enter. If its hoof be buried in a house, rats will leave it. If its sweat be rubbed on a child's pubes, it will grow no hair there; and if rubbed on piles it will cure them. The smoke of its dung quickly gives relief in difficult labour; the water of its dung will check bleeding at the nose. Its blood dropped in the ear will take away earache.[9]

The Muslim mind has always lived at the level of wonder vis-à-vis the world of Nature. While he has derived benefits from it, Nature has never for the Muslim become emptied of its animating spirit nor devoid of the fragrance of the terrestrial paradise. Whether as virgin Nature whose domains the works on natural history sought to describe or as gardens—especially the Persian and Andalusian ones, in which nature was "controlled" according to a deliberate plan—natural forms have presented to the Muslim eye the tranquillity and peace as well as the wonder and awe characteristic of the Islamic conception of paradise. They have evoked in the Muslim mind a sense of equilibrium and repose, repeated in the art and architecture of Islam. Nature thus did not play the negative and dark role that it did in medieval Christianity. Rather, it was a fountain of joy and beatitude, as can be seen both in the scientific and literary studies of Nature, and in the art that was created and cultivated in Islamic civilization.

[9] *The Zoological Section of the Nuzhatu-l-Qulub*, edited, translated, and annotated by J. Stephenson (Oriental Translation Fund, New Series, Vol. XXX. London: The Royal Asiatic Society, 1926), pp. 1–9.

CHAPTER FOUR

PHYSICS

PHYSICS IN MEDIEVAL SCIENCE, as among the Greeks, included the study of "all things that change," or to use Aristotelian terminology, of all things in the world of generation and corruption. In the Islamic world, the study of physics *(ṭabīʿīyāt),* more than any other science, followed the teachings of Aristotle in its basic outlines. Most of the problems posed by Muslim philosophers and scientists in this field were set within the framework of the doctrines of form and matter, potentiality and actuality, the four causes, and teleology. Aristotle was not, of course, followed in every detail, especially on the question of motion. Many Muslim writers, following the example of John Philoponus, were severely critical of Aristotle, and formulated several new concepts, such as that of impetus, which played an important role in the changes that were to occur later in the whole structure of physics in the West.

There were also anti-Aristotelian philosophers, such as Rhazes, whose approach to the study of Nature differed essentially from that of the Stagirite. Since such critics, however, usually adopted the Hermetical and alchemical perspective, we cannot classify their doctrines as physics, in the sense in which the term is understood in either the Peripatetic or modern science. There were also the Illuminatists, who like Plotinus constructed a physics based upon the symbolism of light; they also do not belong, strictly speaking, with the physicists so much as with the "theosophers" and gnostics, whose perspectives they generally shared.

Many of the "new" ideas regarding time, space, the nature of matter, light, and other basic elements of medieval physics came, not from the philosophers, who were mostly bound by the ideas of their Greek predecessors, but rather from the theologians, who usually opposed the Peripatetics. In the writings of such theologians as Abuʾl-Barakāt al-Baghdādī, Fakhr al-Dīn al-Rāzī, and Muḥammad al-Bāqillānī, who may be regarded as the "philosopher of Nature" of the dominant Ashʿarite school of Sunni theology, one finds doctrines of much interest. The theologians departed from the path of the Peripatetics and became the founders of a distinct world view. Although they were bound as theologians to those problems connected with the faith, they were not restricted to the premises of the Peripatetic philosophy, and were therefore among the severest critics of Aristotelian physics, much of which they rejected in favor of a different conception of time, space, and causality.

The study of physics among both the philosophers and the theologians was based on ratiocination, and was usually not dependent upon direct observation. In contrast with later centuries, therefore, it was not the rationalists in medieval times, but the gnostics and alchemists, who appealed to the direct observation of Nature. Yet, for the latter group, the outward and physical aspects of things did not serve as data for rational analysis, but rather as the occasion for intellection and "recollection"; the phenomena of Nature were for them symbols, not merely facts.

There was also a third group who did observe and perform experiments, and in that way sought to analyze the meaning of the sensible aspects of Nature. There were, among this group, several important students of optics, such as Quṭb al-Dīn al-Shīrāzī, and the most famous of all Muslim physicists, Alhazen, as well as al-Bīrūnī, who measured the specific weights of minerals, and Abuʾl-Fatḥ ʿAbd al-Rahmān al-Khāzinī,[1] who also dealt with the measurement of densities and gravity. This sort of physics, which resembles the works of Archimedes—at least in approach, if not always in techniques and results—is of much interest from the point of view of modern science, whose unilateral approach to Nature is based upon a somewhat similar perspective. But from the point of view of Islamic civilization, such studies, as well as those dealing with automata and various types of machines, occupy a secondary and peripheral role in the total scheme of knowledge. They should always be so regarded, therefore, if medieval Islamic civilization is to be seen in its own perspective. To make the periphery the center, and the center the

[1] See below, pp. 133 ff.

periphery, would be to destroy the fundamental relationships upon which the harmony of the sciences of the medieval world was based. Such studies as the optics of Alhazen, which from the modern standpoint of the "progressive growth of science" may seem to be of the utmost importance, have never stood at the heart of Islamic intellectual life, which has focused its interest on the unchanging rather than on the changing aspects of cosmic manifestation. These studies are, to be sure, of much interest to Islamic science, but they should never be regarded as synonymous with it.

A. Alhazen (Ibn al-Haitham)

Alhazen is undoubtedly the greatest student of optics between Ptolemy and Witelo. He was an outstanding mathematician and astronomer and even a philosopher, in addition to being a physicist whose attainments have led certain modern authorities to place him as the greatest of the medieval students of physics.

Alhazen made significant contributions to the study of motion in which he discovered the principle of inertia, to celestial physics and to the science of statics, but he transformed the study of optics and made it into a new science. Before him Muslim scientists had been acquainted with the *Optics* of Euclid, with Theon's recension, the works of Heron and Archimedes, the studies on curved mirrors of Anthenios, and the remarkable studies on refraction by Ptolemy. Euclid's *Optics* in fact became known in the West through the recension of al-Kindī as *De Aspectibus*. Also Muslim physicians such as Ḥunain ibn Isḥāq and Rhazes studied the eye independently, but in general the Greek sources were more or less followed.

Of course, Alhazen also depended on these sources, on Euclid and Ptolemy, on Aristotle's *Meteorology* and on the

Conics of Apollonius, but he transformed the basis of the study of optics and made it a well-ordered and defined discipline. He combined elaborate mathematical treatment with well-conceived physical models and careful experimentation. Like Archimedes he was both a theoretical and experimental physicist. He made experiments to determine the rectilinear motion of light, the properties of shadows, the use of the lens, the *camera obscura,* that he studied mathematically for the first time, and many other essential optical phenomena. He even had a lathe on which he made curved lenses and mirrors for his experiments.

In catoptrics, in which the Greeks had already made important discoveries, Alhazen's notable contribution was in the study of spherical and parabolical mirrors. He studied spherical aberration and realized that in a parabolical mirror all the rays are concentrated at one point so that it is the best type of burning mirror. Alhazen's problem in optics is in fact connected with reflection from a spherical surface: From two points in a plane of a circle to draw lines meeting at a point at the circumference and making equal angles with the normal at that point. This leads to a fourth-degree equation, which he solved by the intersection of a hyperbole and circle.

In refraction his contributions are more outstanding. He applied the rectangle of velocities at the surface of refraction centuries before Newton and believed in the principle of "least time." He made careful experiments by placing a graduated cylinder in water to measure the angle of refraction. Although acquainted with sine function, Alhazen preferred to work with chords. Otherwise he would most likely have discovered Snell's Law which he did discover for small angles where the angle itself can be substituted approximately for the sine. He also studied refraction through glass cylinders and spheres and sought to determine the magnifying effect of the plano-convex lens.

The third field of optics in which Alhazen made significant discoveries was that of atmospheric phenomena. There, he determined the amount of atmospheric refraction by measuring the distance of a fixed star from the pole at the time of rising and at zenith with the help of an armilla. The phenomena of dawn and twilight and the apparent change in size of the Sun and Moon on the horizon were also of much interest to him and he explained them after making a thorough analysis. He determined that twilight ends when the Sun is 19° below the horizon. Rainbows also interested him, and although he did not apply refraction to them, he explained the rainbow on the principle of reflection more completely than Ptolemy.

Finally among his contributions one must mention his study of the physiology of the eye and the problem of vision. Like his contemporaries Avicenna and al-Bīrūnī, Alhazen believed that in the process of vision light travels from the object to the eye. Moreover, he analyzed the role of the eye as a lens and tried to unravel the mystery of how one sees by combining his knowledge of physics and medicine. His study of the physiology and diseases of the eye belong as much to the history of Islamic medicine as to optics itself.

After Alhazen there was a decline in the study of optics in the Muslim world to such an extent that by the sixth/twelfth century even such a great scientist as Naṣīr al-Dīn al-Ṭūsī was not acquainted with his contributions. Only in the seventh/thirteenth century, most likely as a result of the influence of Suhrawardī's philosophy of Illumination, the study of optics became once again popular and in fact a new branch of science called the science of the rainbow came into being in Persia. Quṭb al-Dīn al-Shīrāzī, who was also a commentator of Suhrawardī, gave the first correct qualitative explanation of the rainbow by stating that it is caused by both reflection and refraction. His student, Kamāl al-Dīn al-Fārsī, wrote a commentary upon Alhazen's masterpiece in optics, *Optics* (*Kitāb al-manāẓir*), and brought the study of optics to its last brilliant period in the Muslim world. Meanwhile, Alhazen's writings were becoming well-known in the West, and his *Optics* especially left a profound effect on every student of this subject. His magnum opus, the *Opticae Thesaurus,* in Latin, was printed in the tenth/sixteenth century and his influence is to be seen in the optical studies of Kepler.

The following selection from *A Discourse on the Concave Spherical Mirror* is an excellent example of how Alhazen approached the subject of optics.

A Discourse by Al-Hasan Bin Al-Hasan Bin Al-Haitham on Burning Mirrors of Circular Shape

The sun's rays proceed from the sun along straight lines and are reflected from every polished object at equal angles, i.e. the reflected ray subtends, together with the line tangential to the polished object which is in the plane of the reflected ray, two equal angles. Hence it follows that the ray reflected from the spherical surface, together with the circumference of the circle which is in the plane of the ray, subtends two equal angles. From this it also follows that the reflected ray, together with the diameter of the circle, subtends two equal angles. And every ray which is reflected from a polished object to a point produces a certain heating at that point, so that if numerous rays are collected at one point, the heating at that point is multiplied: and if the number of rays increases, the effect of the heat increases accordingly.

(a) In the case of every concave mirror of spherical concavity, which is less than a hemisphere, placed opposite to the sun so that its axis if produced would end at the body of the sun, the rays which proceed from the body of the sun along lines parallel to the axis of the mirror are reflected from the surface of the mirror to its axis. And the axis of the mirror is the diameter of the sphere, which (diameter) is at right angles to the diameter of the base of the mirror.

Given a concave spherical mirror, let its axis be DB and its centre (of curvature) D (Fig. 1). Let a point Z be on the surface of the mirror, and let the line HZ be one of the rays which proceeds from the sun and parallel to the axis. I state that the line HZ is reflected to the axis.

Proof of that:—

Let us imagine the line DZ joining the points D and Z. The lines HZ, ZD, DB, lie in a plane surface. And let us imagine that that surface cuts the sphere, thus forming an arc in the surface of that mirror whose radius is DB and whose centre is D; let it be the arc ABG. We draw the line ZC at an angle equal to $\angle$ HZD, i.e. $\angle$ DZC.

Now since the arc ABG is less than a semicircle, the arc BZ is less than a quadrant. Thus $\angle$ ZDC $<$ a right angle. The line HZ is parallel to the line DC. Therefore, $\angle$ HZD $<$ a right angle. And $\angle$ DZC $=$ $\angle$ HZD, and is therefore $<$ a right angle. Similarly for $\angle$ ZDC. $\therefore$ The line ZC meets the line DB. Let it meet it at the point C, and let the ray HZ be reflected from the surface of the mirror at equal angles. $\therefore$ It is reflected along the line ZC, and meets the axis DB. Similarly every ray which proceeds parallel to the axis and ends at a point on the surface of the mirror is reflected to the axis, and this is what we wished to demonstrate.

If we keep the axis DB fixed and rotate the arc AB it generates the surface of the mirror. We draw through the point Z on the surface of the mirror a circle every point of which is equidistant from the point C. Thus the rays which proceed parallel to the axis and end at the circumference of this circle are all reflected to the point C, and so the relation of every point on the surface of the mirror, with respect to the point C on the axis, is the same as that of the whole circle which the

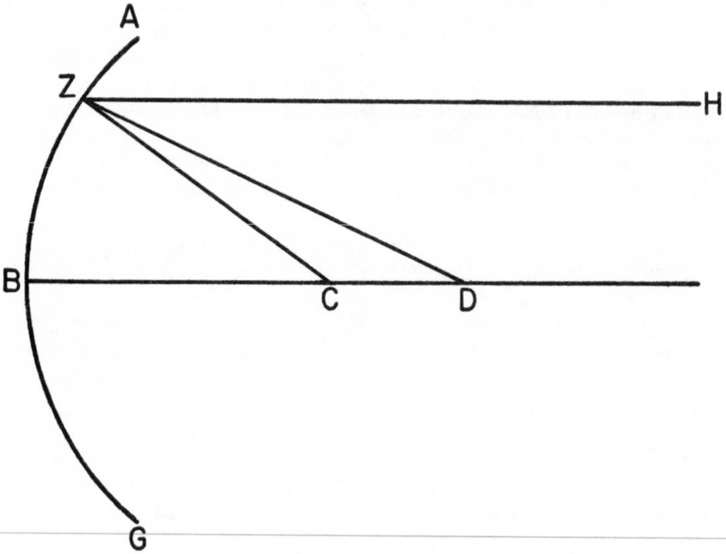

FIGURE 1.

point (Z) generates when the arc rotates. From what we have said it is clear that rays are not reflected, to a (particular) point (C) on the axis, from *within* the circumference of the circle in the surface of the mirror.

(b) If the rays from the circumference of a circle in the surface of the sphere are reflected to a (particular) point on the axis of a concave spherical mirror no other rays are reflected to it from the surface of the sphere. Let there be a spherical concave mirror and let the arc which intersects its axis be the arc ABG, and let its axis be DB, and let rays be reflected to the axis from the circumference of one of the circles which fall within the sphere (i.e.) from the point Z. Accordingly, I say that no other ray is reflected from the point Z except the rays which are reflected from that circle.[2]

2 From the translation of H. J. J. Winter and W. ʿArafat, "Discourse on the Concave Spherical Mirror," *Journal of the Royal Asiatic Society of Bengal,* Vol. XVI, No. 1 (1950), pp. 2–3. Reprinted by permission of the Asiatic Society.

B. Al-Bīrūnī

A contemporary of Alhazen, but from the other side of the Islamic world, in Eastern Persia, al-Bīrūnī was perhaps the greatest compiler and scholar in this fruitful period of Islamic history, and had a knowledge of geography, chronology and comparative religion never since surpassed in the Islamic world.

He was also the most outstanding astronomer and mathematician of his day: his *Elements of Astrology* remained a textbook in the teaching of the *Quadrivium* for centuries, while his major astronomical opus, the *Qānūn al-Masʿūdī* is undoubtedly the most comprehensive text of Islamic astronomy. Certain of his other astronomical works contain parameters of Babylonian astronomy not seen in the extant Greek texts.

Al-Bīrūnī also made a deep study of philosophy and physics. Although most of his philosophical works are lost, there is little doubt that he opposed the Peripatetic school on many points. In his letters to Avicenna, which have fortunately survived, al-Bīrūnī discusses and questions, with his usual lucidity, some of the basic tenets of the Peripatetic physics which was dominant in the teaching of most of the schools of his time. He shows considerable independence with respect to Aristotelian philosophy, and is severely critical of several points in the Peripatetic physics, such as the question of motion and place, which he attacks, not only by an appeal to reason, but also by the use of observation.

The following selections drawn from a series of correspondence exchanged between al-Bīrūnī and Avicenna show his characteristic modes of thought and inquiry in scientific problems.

Questions Asked of Avicenna by Al-Bīrūnī

Question 1. On the possible gravity of the heavens, their circular motion and the denial of the natural place of things.

Since the heavens have no motion toward or away from the center, Aristotle has not accepted the idea of the gravity of the heavens. However, such reasoning by Aristotle does not really aim at the desired end. It is possible to imagine that the heavens do possess a gravity which, however, does not cause them to move toward the center, in so far as each part of the heavens is like every other part. Having hypothesized their gravity, one may then say that, whenever by nature they are moved toward the center, their connected forms prevent them from moving so. It is because of their forms, therefore, that they remain stationary about the center. It is also conceivable that the heavens should possess levity, and that that levity could not cause them, nevertheless, to move away from the center, because motion could only take place when the parts of the heavens became separated from each other, or when a vacuum existed outside the heavens, so that the parts either moved or became fixed in that vacuum. Because it has been ascertained and proven that the dispersing of the parts of the heavens is impossible and the existence of a vacuum absurd, it follows that the heavens are themselves a hot fire assembled and confined in a place from which departure is impossible. Consequently, the levity or gravity of the heavens is not dependent upon the absurd ideas of [Aristotle].

As to only circular motion being possible for the heavens, it may be that the heavens are by essence and nature the source of rectilinear motion, and only by force and accident the source of circular motion, as is the case with the stars, which move by nature from East to West, and by force from West to East.

The presence of each element in its natural place is not certain. The natural place of gravity (i.e., the downward direction) is at the center, and the natural place of levity (i.e., the upward direction) is at the circumference. Yet the center is nothing but a point; and a part of the earth, no matter how small we conceive it to be, cannot fit at the center. As for the circumference, neither can it hold any body in such a way that a light body may ascend to it, since it is an imagined surface area. Furthermore, if we allow water to flow freely, taking away any obstacles in its path, undoubtedly it will reach the center; therefore, the assertion that the natural place of water is above the earth is without any basis. Consequently, there is no "natural place" for any body. On such a basis, he who says that the heavens are indeed heavy, but that it is their being attached that prevents their falling does not appear absurd.

• • • •

Question 4. On the continuity and discontinuity of matter and space.

Why has Aristotle rejected the assertion of the theologians that a body consists of indivisible parts, and why has he chosen instead the assertion of the philosophers that bodies are infinitely divisible, even though the wickedness of the philosophers' beliefs is greater than the disgracefulness of the theologians' opinions? According to the philosophers, who consider bodies to be connected and infinitely divisible, it is necessary that a rapidly moving body not touch a preceding but more slowly moving body. The touching of a preceding body by a succeeding one is inevitable, if the succeeding body traverses the intermediate distance, but the traversing of that distance requires the traversing of its parts. Since the parts of that distance are infinite in number, how can one imagine that the distance can be crossed? Therefore, no succeeding body can reach a preceding one. It is necessary to give an example to prove this point. If there is a definite distance assumed between the Moon and the Sun, and both bodies are moving at that distance, it should be impossible for the Moon to reach the Sun, even though the motion of the Moon is much faster than that of the Sun. However, such is not the case; by observation it is found that the Moon does in fact overtake the Sun, though such an event brings disgrace and shame upon those who hold to the view of infinite divisibility so well-known and well-established among the geometers. What happens to the philosophers is thus more disgraceful than what happens to the theologians. How then can one escape what has befallen these two groups?

To this argument, Avicenna answered that, according to Aristotle, infinite division cannot always be performed actually, but may sometimes exist only potentially; al-Bīrūnī's criticism, however, applies only to division in actuality.

This is how al-Bīrūnī replied:

Abū ʿAlī [Avicenna] has learned this answer from Muḥammad ibn Zakarīyā al-Rāzī. Muḥammad ibn Zakarīyā has said that, if for each of these objects, i.e., parts of a body, there be two sides and a middle, division can be carried out indefinitely, which is impossible. When you say "actually," I do not understand the meaning of that expression. For no matter how finely you grind collyrite, you will never actually reach that part of which you speak, because the actual division will come to a halt before you reach it. In any case, potentiality remains in its place. Also, according to your view, it becomes necessary that the side of the square be equal to its diagonal; if you deny it, you have opposed your own principles. Or you may say that between the parts there is a separation; in this case, I ask if the separation is greater or smaller than the indivisible parts. [What al-Bīrūnī means is that if a square consists of indivisible parts, the number of parts on the side and in the diagonal must be equal, as in the figure shown.

If the indivisible parts were to be connected, side and diagonal would be equal, which is impossible. And if the parts were to be connected on the sides, but remain separated on the diagonal, there would have to be space between them. If these spaces were equal to the indivisible parts, the diagonal would be twice the side, a conclusion which is also impossible. Therefore, the spaces must be smaller or larger than the indivisible parts, thus indicating that the indivisible parts possess quantity, and can therefore be divided.]

• • • •

Question 6. On the possible elliptical shape of the heavens.

Aristotle has mentioned in his second article that elliptical or lentil-shaped figures need a vacuum in order to have circular motion, while a sphere has no need of a vacuum. Such, however, is not the case, for the elliptical figure is formed by the rotation of the ellipse about its major axis, and the lentil-shaped figure by the rotation of that same ellipse about its minor axis. Therefore, if in the process of the revolution of the ellipses which form these figures, there be contradiction or infraction, what Aristotle has claimed does not hold true. There remains no necessary condition for those figures different from those for the sphere, because if we make the axis of rotation of the ellipse the major axis and the axis of rotation of the lentil-shaped figure the minor axis, they will revolve like a sphere, and have no need of a void. The objection by Aristotle and his statement become true in the instance where we make the minor axis the axis of the ellipse and the axis of rotation of the lentil-shaped figure. Still it is possible for the ellipse to move about the minor axis and the lentil-shaped figure about the major axis, and thus to have no need of a vacuum. In fact, they become capable of following one another in succession, like the bodies located in the heavens, where there is no vacuum, according to the majority of the people. I am not saying that according to my belief the shape of the great heavens is not spherical, but elliptical or lentil-shaped. I have made numerous studies to reject this view, but I do wonder at the logicians![3]

[3] Dekhodā, ʿAlī Akbar, *Sharḥ-i ḥāl-i nābighih-i shahīr-i Īrān Abū Raiḥān Muḥammad ibn Aḥmad Khwārazmī-i Bīrūnī* (Tehran: Entishārāt-i Edāreh-i Koll-i Negāresh. Vezārat-i Farhang, 1324/1945), 29ff. Translated by S. H. Nasr.

Al-Bīrūnī was also much interested in the question of the possible motion of the earth around the sun, and even wrote a book about it, which is now lost. As an astronomer, he realized that this question was a problem not for astronomy but for physics. He therefore directed the attention of students of physics to the problem, and he himself studied the physical implications of the heliocentric system. At the end of his life, after many years of neutrality on this question, he finally decided in favor of the geocentric scheme, not for astronomical reasons, but because the physics of heliocentricity seemed to him impossible.

On the question of Motion of the Earth, he wrote:

> I have seen the astrolabe called Zūraqī invented by Abu Saʿīd Sijzī. I liked it very much and praised him a great deal, as it is based on the idea entertained by some to the effect that the motion we see is due to the Earth's movement and not to that of the sky. By my life it is a problem difficult of solution and refutation . . .
>
> It is the same whether you take it that the Earth is in motion or the sky. In both cases it does not affect the astronomical sciences. It is just for the physicist to see if it is possible to refute it.[4]
>
> As regards the resting of the earth, one of the elementary problems of astronomy, which offers many and great difficulties, this, too, is a dogma with the Hindu astronomers. Brahmagupta says in the *Brahmasiddhānta:* "Some people maintain that the *first* motion (from east to west) does not lie in the meridian, but belongs to the earth. But Varāhamihira refutes them by saying: 'If that were the case, a bird would not return to its nest as soon as it had flown away from it toward the west.' And, in fact, it is precisely as Varāhamihira says."
>
> Brahmagupta says in another place of the same book: "The followers of Āryabhaṭa maintain that the earth is moving and heaven resting. People have tried to refute them by saying that, if such were the case, stones and trees would fall from the earth."
>
> But Brahmagupta does not agree with them, and says that that would not necessarily follow from their theory, apparently because he thought that all heavy things are attracted towards the centre of the earth. He says: "On the contrary, if that were the case, *the earth would not vie in keeping an even and uniform pace with the minutes of heaven, the prāṇas of the times.*"
>
> There seems to be some confusion in this chapter, perhaps

4 Al-Bīrūnī, *Istīʿāb,* translated by S. H. Barani in "Al-Biruni's Scientific Achievements," *Indo-Iranica,* Vol. V, No. 4 (1952).

by the fault of the translator. For the *minutes of heaven* are 21,600 and are called *prāṇa, i.e.*, breaths, because according to them each minute of the meridian revolves in *the time of an ordinary human breath*.

Supposing this to be true, and that the earth makes a complete rotation eastward in so many breaths as heaven does according to his (Brahmagupta's) view, we cannot see what should prevent the earth from keeping an even and uniform pace with heaven.

Besides, the rotation of the earth does in no way impair the value of astronomy, as all appearances of an astronomic character can be quite as well explained according to this theory as to the other. There are, however, other reasons which make it impossible. This question is most difficult to solve.[5]

C. Al-Khāzinī

A series of noteworthy physicists followed Alhazen and al-Bīrūnī and continued their study especially in mechanics, hydrostatics, and related branches of physics. Also the criticism of the theory of projectile motion of Aristotle was followed along lines established by Avicenna leading to the important studies of Avempace and other later Muslim philosophers and scientists who exercised much influence upon Latin medieval mechanics. In this domain the Muslim scientists developed the theory of "inclination" and founded the basis of the impetus theory and the concept of momentum which were further elaborated by late medieval scientists in the West. Moreover, Avempace's attempt to quantify projectile motion by considering the velocity as proportional to the difference between the force and the resistance rather than to their ratio is of much significance in the light of the later attempt of Bradwardine and the Mertonian school to describe motion quantitatively.

Of the later Muslim physicists, one of the most important is Abuʾl-Fatḥ ʿAbd al-Raḥmān al-Khāzinī, originally a Greek

[5] *Alberuni's India*, I, pp. 276–277.

slave who flourished in Merv at the beginning of the sixth/twelfth century, and who continued the study of mechanics and hydrostatics in the tradition of al-Bīrūnī and the earlier scientists. He also wrote several works on astronomy and physics, among which is *The Book of the Balance of Wisdom,* which is perhaps the most essential Muslim work on mechanics and hydrostatics, and especially the study of centers of gravity. Muslim scientists had been acquainted from the beginning with Heron's *On the Lifting of Heavy Things,* which itself reflects some influence of Archimedes. And, although no evidence exists as yet of the Arabic translation of the pseudo-Aristotelian *Mechanica* or the *Equilibrium of Planes* of Archimedes, the influence of both works and both schools in statics is found among Muslim physicists. The early *Liber Karatonis* of Thābit ibn Qurrah already shows the presence of the influence of these Greek schools, and it is of much interest that in this work Thābit ibn Qurrah tries to derive the law of the lever from rules of dynamics following the pseudo-Aristotelian tradition, with the emphasis on dynamics and center of gravity that was contrary to the approach of Archimedes.

The preoccupation with mechanics and especially with laws of simple machines is also to be seen in the writings of the Banū Mūsā and some of the apocryphal treatises attributed to Avicenna, while the study of hydrostatics was carried out with much success by al-Bīrūnī and also by ʿUmar Khayyām. Al-Khāzinī marks a further development in this school. He combined an interest in hydrostatics with mechanics and concentrated especially on the concept of the center of gravity as applied to balance. In his efforts he was followed a century later by Abuʾl-ʿIzz al-Jazarī, whose *Book of Knowledge of Ingenious Geometrical Contrivances* is the definitive work on mechanics in the Islamic world. He was in turn followed by Qayṣar al-Ḥanafī, who was especially expert on the mechanics of the water wheel. It was he who constructed the famous celestial globe that survives today in the national museum of Naples.

Just as the Muslims made the study of the rainbow into a separate science so did they create a separate science of the balance in which al-Khāzinī was the undisputed master. His *Book of the Balance of Wisdom* is the outstanding work in this science in which he also discussed the view of earlier scholars including Rhazes, Khayyām and al-Bīrūnī. It is particularly of interest that al-Khāzinī describes an instrument that, according to him, al-Bīrūnī used in his famous measurements of specific weights of different substances, for al-Bīrūnī himself never revealed the method by which he arrived at his results.

A. Mieli, the Italian historian of science, has compared the determination of specific weights by al-Bīrūnī and al-Khāzinī with modern results as follows:[6]

Substance	*According to al-Bīrūnī based on the fixed value for[7]* *Gold*	*Mercury*	*According to al-Khāzinī*	*Modern values*
GOLD	(19.26)	19.05	19.05	19.26
MERCURY	13.74	(13.59)	13.56	13.59
COPPER	8.92	8.83	8.66	8.85
BRASS	8.67	8.58	8.57	8.4
IRON	7.82	7.74	7.74	7.79
TIN	7.22	7.15	7.32	7.29
LEAD	11.40	11.29	11.32	11.35
	Emerald	*Quartz*		
SAPPHIRE	3.91	3.76	3.96	3.90
RUBY	3.75	3.60	3.58	3.52
EMERALD	(2.73)	2.62	2.60	2.73
PEARL	2.73	2.62	2.60	2.75
QUARTZ	2.53	(2.58)	—	2.58

6 Based on the more comprehensive table that A. Mieli published in his *La science arabe et son rôle dans l'évolution scientifique mondiale*, Leiden, E. J. Brill, 1939, p. 101, where a somewhat more complete form of the table is given. The table compiled by Mieli is, in turn, based on a series of pioneering studies by E. Wiedemann, a leading German historian of Islamic science, who wrote numerous articles on Islamic science, particularly physics, and is originally responsible for the tabulation of this table. Some of the more notable articles of Wiedemann upon which the table of Mieli and most other later studies are based include, "Über der Verbreitung der Bestimmungen des Spezifischen Gewichtes nach Bīrūnī," *Beiträge zur Geschichte der Naturwissenschaften. Sitzungsberichte der Physikalisch-medicinischen Societät in Erlangen*, XXXI, vol. 45, 1913, pp. 31–34; "Über das al-Bērūnīsche Gefäss zur spezifischen Gewichtsbestimmung," *Verhandlungen der Deutschen Physikalischen Gesellschaft*, 1908, no. 8/9, pp. 339–343; "Über die Kenntnisse der Muslime auf dem Gebiet der Mechanik und Hydrostatik," *Archiv für Geschichte der Naturwissenschaften*, 1910, vol. II, pp. 394–398.

7 The method of al-Bīrūnī is based on measuring the values of different substances by taking a particular substance with a fixed value. The values for gold, mercury, emerald, and quartz fixed in each column are given in parentheses, and in each case the other values are given based on these fixed values.

Al-Khāzinī gives a detailed statement of the theory of the balance, of centers of gravity and of the general way of applying the balance, in order to measure the specific weight of bodies made of either one or two substances. The selections presented below from *The Book of the Balance of Wisdom*—whose very title is reminiscent of the cosmic balance of Jābirian alchemy, but is here applied specifically to physical problems—demonstrate the delicacy that the use of the balance had reached among Muslim physicists. More specifically, they afford an indication of the method employed by al-Khāzinī in making his measurements of specific weights:

SEC. 1. ENUMERATION OF THE ADVANTAGES AND USES OF THE BALANCE OF WISDOM

Says al-Khāzinī, after speaking of the balance in general,—The balance of wisdom is something worked out by human intellect, and perfected by experiment and trial, of great importance on account of its advantages, and because it supplies the place of ingenious mechanicians. Among these [advantages] are: 1. exactness in weighing: this balance shows variation to the extent of a mithḳāl; provided the maker has a delicate hand, attends to the minute details of the mechanism, and understands it; 2. that it distinguishes pure metal from its counterfeit, each being recognized by itself, without any refining; 3. that it leads to a knowledge of the constituents of a metallic body composed of any two metals, without separation of one from another, either by melting, or refining, or change of form, and that in the shortest time and with the least trouble. . . .

SEC. 2. THEORY OF THE BALANCE OF WISDOM

This just balance is founded upon geometrical demonstrations, and deduced from physical causes, in two points of view: 1. as it implies centres of gravity, which constitute the most elevated and noble department of the exact sciences, namely, the knowledge that the weights of heavy bodies vary according to difference of distance from a point in common—the foundation of the steelyard; 2. as it implies a knowledge that the weights of heavy bodies vary according to difference in rarity or density of the liquids in which the body weighed is immersed—the foundation of the balance of wisdom.

To these two principles the ancients directed attention in a vague way, after their manner, which was to bring out things abstruse, and to declare dark things, in relation to the great philosophies and the precious sciences. We have, therefore, seen fit to bring together, on this subject, whatever useful suggestions their works, and the works of later philosophers, have afforded us, in connection with those discoveries which our own meditation, with the help of God and His aid, has yielded. . . .

SEC. 3. FUNDAMENTAL PRINCIPLES OF THE ART OF CONSTRUCTING THIS BALANCE

Every art we say, has its fundamental principles, upon which it is based, and its preliminaries to rest upon, which one who would discuss it must not be ignorant of. These fundamental principles and preliminaries class themselves under three heads: 1. those which rise up [in the mind] from early childhood and youth, after one sensation or several sensations, spontaneously; which are called first principles, and common familiar perceptions; 2. demonstrated principles, belonging to other departments of knowledge; 3. those which are obtained by experiment and elaborate contrivance.

SEC. 4. INSTITUTION OF THE WATER-BALANCE; NAMES OF THOSE WHO HAVE DISCUSSED IT, IN THE ORDER OF THEIR SUCCESSION; AND SPECIFIC FORMS OF BALANCES USED IN WATER, WITH THEIR SHAPES AND NAMES

It is said that the [Greek] philosophers were first led to think of setting up this balance, and moved thereto, by the book of Menelaus addressed to Domitian, in which he says: "O King, there was brought one day to Hiero King of Sicily a crown of great price, presented to him on the part of several provinces, which was strongly made and of solid workmanship. Now it occurred to Hiero that this crown was not of pure gold, but alloyed with some silver; so he inquired into the matter of the crown, and clearly made out that it was composed of gold and silver together. He therefore wished to ascertain the proportion of each metal contained in it; while at the same time he was averse to breaking the crown, on account of its solid workmanship. So he questioned the geometricians and mechanicians on the subject. But no one sufficiently skillful was found among them, except Archimedes the geometrician, one of the courtiers of Hiero. Accordingly, he devised a piece of mechanism which, by delicate contrivance, enabled him to inform the King Hiero how much gold and how much silver was in the crown, while yet it retained its form." That was before the time of Alexander. Afterwards, Menelaus [himself] thought about the water-balance, and brought out certain universal arithmetical methods to be applied to it; and there exists a treatise by him on the subject. It was then four hundred years after Alexander. Subsequently, in the days of Māmūn, the water-balance was taken into consideration by the modern philosophers. . . .

Some one of the philosophers who have been mentioned added to the balance a third bowl, connected with one of the two bowls in order to ascertain the measure, in weight, of the rising of one of the two bowls in the water: and by that addition somewhat facilitated operations. . . .

SEC. 5. FORMS AND SHAPES OF THE WATER-BALANCE

. . . Balances used in water are of three varieties of shape: 1. one with two bowls arranged in the ordinary way, called "the general simple balance"; to the beam of which are frequently added round-point numbers; 2. one with three bowls for the extreme ends, one of which is suspended below another, and is the water-bowl; which is called "the satisfactory balance," or "the balance without movable bowl"; 3. one with five bowls, called "the comprehensive balance," the same as the balance of wisdom; three of the bowls of which are a water-bowl and two movable bowls. The knowledge of the relations of one metal to another depends upon that perfecting of the balance, by delicate contrivance, which has been accomplished by the united labors of all those who have made a study of it, or prepared it by fixing upon it [points indicating] the specific gravities of metals, relatively to a determined sort of water. . . .[8]

These passages from al-Khāzinī's study on the balance show that the Muslim physicists by this time were able to measure the absolute and specific weights of bodies made of two simple substances as well as of one substance, although for the former task very large balances were needed. If we consider $A =$ the absolute weight of the body in question, $S =$ the specific gravity, d_1 and d_2 the densities of its two components, and $x =$ the absolute weight of the latter component, then

[8] From N. Khanikoff, "Analysis and Extracts of the Book of the Balance of Wisdom, in Arabic and English," *Journal of the American Oriental Society*, Vol. VI (1859), pp. 8–14.

$$x = A \frac{\frac{1}{d_1} - \frac{1}{S}}{\frac{1}{d_1} - \frac{1}{d_2}}$$

Through this formula the absolute weight and consequently specific gravity of bodies composed of two simple components can be determined.

The modern reader may wonder, in connection with men like Alhazen, al-Bīrūnī or al-Khāzinī, what their reactions would be to modern science. Would they regard this type of science as the continuation and perfection of what they had started, or—as modern historians usually express it—as an example of the "progress of ideas"? The difficulty with answering this question in modern terms is that today historic time has taken on a quantitative meaning, while the qualitative nature of history itself has been nearly forgotten. Actually, even a physicist like Alhazen lived in a spiritual and psychological milieu completely different from that of the modern expert on optics. In the world in which he lived, the phenomena of Nature had not as yet become completely divorced from their archetypes: light still reminded man of the Divine Intellect, even if he did perform quantitative experiments with it. It may also be asked whether Alhazen would not have become a modern physicist if he were living in this century. The answer is that, since there is something "definite" and "absolute" regarding time—that is, the fifth/eleventh century differs qualitatively from this century—historical time is not the reversible time of classical physics, and the Alhazen of the fifth/eleventh century could not metaphysically be the same being with the same powers and faculties if he were suddenly placed in the twentieth century.

If, however, the idea of bringing Alhazen or al-Bīrūnī into the twentieth century could be realized, then the most probable reaction of these men to modern science would be that of surprise at the position that quantitative science has come to occupy today. Alhazen and al-Bīrūnī were able to practice a kind of science which may be called "progressive," while still remaining within a "nonprogressive" world view, because for them all *scientia* was subordinated to *sapientia*. Their quantitative science was only *one* interpretation of a segment of Nature, not *the* interpretation of all of it. The matrix of their world view remained immutable, even while they were pursuing their study of the world of becoming and change. The surprise felt by medieval Muslim natural scientists, if faced with modern science, would not arise from recognizing the "progress" of ideas which they had begun, but from seeing the complete reversal of relations. They would see the center of their perspective made peripheral, and the periphery made central; they would be astonished to learn that the "progressive" science, which in the Islamic world has always remained secondary, has now in the West become nearly everything, while the immutable and "non-progressive" science or wisdom which was then primary has now been reduced to almost nothing.

CHAPTER FIVE

MATHEMATICS

MATHEMATICS IN THE ISLAMIC PERSPECTIVE is regarded as the gateway leading from the sensible to the intelligible world, the ladder between the world of change and the heaven of archetypes. Unity, the central idea of Islam, is an abstraction from the human point of view, even though in itself it is concrete. With respect to the world of the senses, mathematics is similarly an abstraction; but considered from the standpoint of the intelligible world, the "world of ideas" of Plato, it is a guide to the eternal essences, which are themselves concrete. Just as all figures are generated from the point, and all numbers from unity, so does all multiplicity come from the Creator, who is One. Numbers and figures, if considered in the Pythagorean sense—that is, as ontological aspects of Unity, and not merely as pure quantity—become vehicles for the expression of Unity in multiplicity. The Muslim mind has therefore always been drawn toward mathematics, as may be seen not only in the great activity of the Muslims in the mathematical sciences, but in Islamic art as well.

The Pythagorean number, which is the traditional conception of number, is the projection of Unity, an aspect of the Origin and Center which somehow never leaves its source. In its quantitative aspect, a number may divide and separate; in its qualitative and symbolic aspect, however, it integrates multiplicity back into Unity. It is also, by virtue of its close connection with geometric figures, a "personality": for example, three corresponds to the triangle, and symbolizes harmony, while four, which is connected with the square, symbolizes stability. Numbers, viewed from this perspective, are like so many concentric circles, echoing in so many different ways their mutual and immutable center. They do not "progress" outwardly, but remain united to their source by the ontological relation which they always preserve with Unity. So too with geometrical figures, each of which symbolizes an aspect of Being. The majority of Muslim mathematicians, like the Pythagoreans, never cultivated the science of mathematics as a purely quantitative subject, nor did they ever separate numbers from geometric figures, which conceptualize their "personalities." They knew only too well that mathematics, by its inner polarity, was the "Jacob's ladder" which, under the guidance of metaphysics, could lead to the world of the archetypes and to Being itself, but, divorced from its source, would become instead the means of descent to the world of quantity, to the pole which is as far away as the conditions of cosmic manifestation permit from the luminous source of all existence. There can be no "neutrality" on the part of man with respect to numbers: either he climbs to the world of Being through knowledge of their qualitative and symbolic aspects, or he descends through them, as mere numbers, to the world of quantity. As mathematics was studied in the Middle Ages, it was usually the first role that was envisaged. The science of numbers was, as the Brethren of Purity wrote, "the first support of the soul by the Intellect, and the generous effusion of the Intellect upon the soul"; moreover, it was regarded as "the tongue which speaks of Unity and transcendence."

The study of the mathematical sciences in Islam included almost the same subjects as the Latin *Quadrivium,* with the addition of optics and a few secondary subjects. The main elements of it remain—as in the *Quadrivium*—arithmetic, geometry, astronomy, and music. Most Islamic scientists and philosophers were learned in all of these sciences; some, like Avicenna, al-Fārābī and al-Ghazzālī, wrote important treatises on music and its effect on the soul.

Astronomy, and its sister astrology, with which it was nearly always associated (in Arabic, as in Greek, the same word denotes both subjects), was cultivated for a multiplicity of reasons. There were problems of chronology and the calendar; the necessity of finding the direction of Mecca, and the time of day for the daily prayers; the task of drawing horoscopes for princes and rulers, who nearly always consulted an astrologer with regard to their activities; and, of course, the desire to perfect the science of motion of the heavenly bodies, and to overcome its inconsistencies, so as to attain perfection of knowledge.

The main tradition of astronomy came down to the Muslims from the Greeks through the *Almagest* of Ptolemy.

There was, however, also the Indian school, whose doctrines concerning astronomy, as well as arithmetic, algebra, and geometry, were embodied in the *Siddhāntas* translated from the Sanskrit into Arabic. There were moreover some Chaldean and Persian texts most of whose originals have been lost, as well as a pre-Islamic Arabic astronomical lore. The Muslim astronomers, as we already have seen, made many observations, whose results were compiled in a number of *zīj*'s more comprehensive than those of the ancients, and used until modern times. They also continued the school of mathematical astronomy of Ptolemy, applying their own perfected science of spherical trigonometry to the more exact calculation of the motion of the heavens, within the context of the epicyclic theory. They usually followed a geocentric theory, although they were aware, as al-Bīrūnī shows, of the existence of the heliocentric system. And as al-Bīrūnī reports Abū Saʿīd al-Sijzī had even made an astrolabe based on the heliocentric theory.

The influence of Indian ideas was also to result in the development and systematization of the science of algebra. Although the Muslims were acquainted with the work of Diophantos, there is little doubt that algebra as cultivated by Muslims had its roots in Indian mathematics which they synthesized with Greek methods. The genius of the Greeks was evidenced in their expression of finite order, of the cosmos, and therefore of numbers and figures; the perspective of Oriental wisdom is based upon the Infinite, whose "horizontal image" corresponds to the "indefinity" of mathematics. Algebra, which is integrally associated with this perspective based on the Infinite, was born of Indian speculation and raised to maturity in the Islamic world where it was always related to geometry, and where it preserved its metaphysical basis. Along with the use of Indian numerals—today known as "the Arabic numerals"—algebra may be regarded as the most important science which the Muslims added to the corpus of ancient mathematics. In Islam, the traditions of Indian and Greek mathematics met and became unified into a structure in which algebra, geometry, and arithmetic were to possess a contemplative, spiritual, and intellectual aspect, as well as that practical and purely rational aspect, which was the only part of medieval mathematics to be inherited and developed by the later Western science, known by the same name.

The history of mathematics in Islam begins properly speaking with Muḥammad ibn Mūsā al-Khwārazmī, in whose writings the Greek and Indian traditions of mathematics became united. This third/ninth-century mathematician left behind several works, of which *The Book of Summary in the Process of Calculation for Compulsion and Equation,* discussed later, is the most important. It was translated into Latin several times, under the title of *Liber Algorismi,* namely the "book of al-Khwārazmī"; it became the source of the word "algorism."

Al-Khwārazmī was followed during the same century by al-Kindī, the first well-known Islamic philosopher who was also a competent mathematician, writing treatises in nearly every branch of the subject, and his student, Aḥmad al-Sarakhsī, best known for his works on geography, music and astrology. Also of this period was al-Māhānī, who continued the development of algebra, and became particularly famous for his study of Archimedes' problem, and the three sons of Shākir ibn Mūsā—Muḥammad, Aḥmad, and Ḥasan—who are also called the "Banū Mūsā." They were all well-known mathematicians, Aḥmad being in addition a competent physicist.

The beginning of the fourth/tenth century marks the appearance of several great translators, who were also mathematicians of note. Outstanding among them was Thābit ibn Qurrah, who translated the *Conics* of Apollonius, several treatises of Archimedes, and the *Introduction to Arithmetic* of Nicomachus, and was himself one of the foremost Muslim mathematicians. He was responsible for calculating the volume of a paraboloid, and for giving a geometrical solution to some third-degree figures. His contemporary, Qusṭā ibn Lūqā, who became famous in later Islamic history as a personification of the wisdom of the ancients, was also a competent translator, and rendered the works of Diophantos and Heron into Arabic.

Among other mathematicians of note of the fourth/tenth century, one must include Abuʾl-Wafāʾ al-Buzjānī, the commentator on al-Khwārazmī's *The Book of Summary in the Process of Calculation for Compulsion and Equation,* who solved the fourth degree equation $x^4 + px^3 = q$, by means of the intersection of a parabola and a hyperbola. Also of this century were Alhazen, whom we have already discussed, and the "Brethren of Purity," to whom we shall turn shortly. They were followed by Abū Sahl al-Kūhī, another of the outstanding Muslim algebraists, and the author of *Additions to the Book of Archimedes,* who made a thorough study of trinomial equations.

One might also refer to Avicenna as one of the mathematicians flourishing at this time, although his reputation is far greater as a philosopher and physician than as a mathematician. Avicenna, like al-Fārābī before him, elaborated the theory of the Persian music of his period, a music which has survived as a living tradition down to the present day. It is incorrect to refer to their works as contributing to the theory of "Arabic music," since Persian music belongs essentially to a different musical family. It is very much akin to the music of the ancient Greeks—to the music heard by Pythagoras and Plato—although it has exercised some influence upon Arabic music as well as a strong influence upon Flamenco, and has in turn been affected by the rhythm and melody of Arabic music. It was this tradition of Persian music that Avicenna, and before him al-Fārābī, theorized in the form of study then regarded as a branch of mathematics.

Avicenna was contemporary with the celebrated al-Bīrūnī, who has left us some of the most important mathematical and astronomical writings of the medieval period, and who made a special study of such problems as numerical series and the determination of the radius of the earth. His contemporary, Abū Bakr al-Karkhī,[1] also left behind two basic works on Islamic mathematics, *The Book Dedicated to Fakhr al-Dīn* on algebra and *The Requisite for Arithmetic.*

The fifth/eleventh century, which marks the rise of the Seljuqs to power, was characterized by a certain lack of interest in mathematics in the official schools, although a number of great mathematicians appeared during this period. They were headed by ʿUmar Khayyām and a host of other astronomers and mathematicians, who worked with him in revising the Persian calendar. The work of these mathematicians finally led to the fruitful activity of the seventh/thirteenth century—when, following the Mongol invasion, the study of mathematical sciences was rejuvenated. The foremost figure of this period was Naṣīr al-Dīn al-Ṭūsī. It was under his direction, as we saw earlier, that many scientists, especially mathematicians, were assembled in the observatory at Maragha.

Although, after the seventh/thirteenth century, interest in the study of mathematics gradually diminished, important

[1] In some manuscripts the name appears as al-Karajī and some modern scholars believe this to be the correct form. In later Islamic history, however, he has usually been known as al-Karakhī.

mathematicians continued to flourish, who solved new problems and discovered new methods and techniques. Ibn Bannāʾ al-Marrākushī in the eighth/fourteenth century made a new approach to the study of numbers, to be followed a century later by Ghiyāth al-Dīn al-Kāshānī. The latter was the greatest Muslim mathematician in the field of computation and number theory. He was the real discoverer of decimal fractions and made a very exact determination of the value of pi (π), as well as discovering many new methods and contrivances for computation. His *The Key of Arithmetic (Miftaḥ al-ḥisāb)* is the most fundamental work of its kind in Arabic. Meanwhile, a contemporary of al-Kāshānī, Abūʾl-Ḥasan al-Bustī, who lived in Morocco, at the other extreme of the Islamic world, was also treading new paths in the field of the study of numbers, and the Egyptian Badr al-Dīn al-Māridīnī was composing significant mathematical and astronomical treatises.

The Safavid renaissance in Persia marks the last period of relatively extensive activity in the field of mathematics, although little of it is known to the outside world. The architects of the beautiful mosques, schools and bridges of this time were all competent mathematicians. The most famous of these tenth/sixteenth century figures in the field of mathematics is Bahāʾ al-Dīn al-ʿĀmilī. In mathematics, his writings were mostly a survey and a summary of the works of the earlier masters; they became the standard texts in the various branches of that science from the time when, in the official schools, the study of mathematics became limited to a summary treatment, leaving more serious study to personal initiative.

A contemporary of Bahāʾ al-Dīn al-ʿĀmilī, Mullā Muḥammad Bāqin Yazdī, who flourished at the beginning of the tenth/sixteenth century, made original studies in mathematics. It is even claimed by some later mathematicians that he made an independent discovery of the logarithm, but this claim has not yet been fully investigated and substantiated. After Yazdī, mathematics remained chiefly bound to the framework that had been established by the medieval masters of that science. There were occasional figures, such as the twelfth/eighteenth century Narāqī family of Kashan, who wrote several original treatises, or the thirteenth/nineteenth century Mullā ʿAlī Muḥammad Iṣfahānī, who gave numerical solutions for third degree equations. There were also a few Indian mathematicians of note. Generally speaking, however, the speculative power of Islamic society turned almost wholly to questions of metaphysics and gnosis; mathematics, except for its use in daily life, served essentially as the ladder to the intelligible world of metaphysics. It thus fulfilled the function that the Brethren of Purity and many other earlier authorities had regarded as being its very *raison d'être*.

To summarize the achievements of Islamic mathematics, it can be said that the Muslims first of all developed number theory in both its mathematical and metaphysical aspects. They generalized the concept of number beyond what was known to the Greeks. They also devised powerful new methods of numerical computation that reached their height rather late with Ghiyāth al-Dīn al-Kāshānī in the eighth/fourteenth and ninth/fifteenth centuries. They also dealt with decimal fractions, numerical series, and similar branches of mathematics connected with numbers. They developed and systematized the science of algebra, though always preserving its link with geometry. They continued the work of the Greeks in plane and solid geometry. Finally, they developed trigonometry, both plane and solid, working up accurate tables for the functions and discovering many trigonometric relations. Furthermore, although this science was from the beginning cultivated in conjunction with astronomy, it was perfected and made into an independent science for the first time by Naṣīr al-Dīn al-Ṭūsī in his famous *Figure of the Sector*, which represents a major achievement in medieval mathematics.

A. The Brethren of Purity

The Brethren of Purity, whose historic identity still remains in doubt, were a group of scholars, probably from Basra, who in the fourth/tenth century produced a compendium of the arts and sciences in fifty-two epistles. In addition there is the *Risālat al-jāmiʿah*, which summarizes the teachings of the *Epistles*. Their clear style and their effective simplification of difficult ideas succeeded in making their *Epistles* very popular, and thus in arousing much interest in the philosophical and natural sciences. The sympathies of the Brethren of Purity were definitely with the Pythagorean-Hermetic aspect of the Greek heritage, as is especially evident in their mathematical theories, which exercised a great influence during later centuries, particularly among Shiite circles. Like the Pythagoreans they emphasized the symbolic and metaphysical aspect of arithmetic and geometry, as can be gathered from the following selections from their writings.

The Meaning of Number

The form of the numbers in the soul corresponds to the form of beings in matter (or the *hylē*). It [number] is a sample from the superior world, and through knowledge of it the disciple is led to the other mathematical sciences, and to physics and metaphysics. The science of number is the "root" of the sciences, the foundation of wisdom, the source of knowledge, and the pillar of meaning. It is the First Elixir and the great alchemy. . . .[2]

The Science of Number

Know, oh Brother, experienced and merciful, that because this has been the way of our exalted brethren (may God assist them in the knowledge of all things in the world, from substance and accident, simple bodies and separate substances, elements and compounds to its structure and order as it is now, and how that came about and that it issued forth from one cause and one source and from one designer, may His Glory Be Exalted), and because they bring as witness to their clarification numerical symbols and geometrical evidence, just as do the Pythagoreans, therefore it is incumbent upon us to introduce this treatise before all other treatises, and to mention in it the science of numbers and of their properties, known as arithmetic. This is like a preface, or like the prolegomena which would make the road more easy for those who seek that knowledge and wisdom which is called philosophy, and would also make it more accessible to beginners just looking into the mathematical sciences.

2 Ikhwān al-Ṣafā', *Risālat al-Jāmi'ah* (Damascus: al-Taraqqī Press, 1949), I, p. 9. Translated by S. H. Nasr.

The beginning of philosophy is the love of science; its midpoint, such knowledge of the reality of created things as is within human capacity; its end, words and deeds in conformity with such knowledge. The philosophical sciences are of four kinds: 1) Mathematics; 2) Logic; 3) Natural philosophy (physics); 4) Divine science (metaphysics). And mathematics is of four kinds: 1) Arithmetic; 2) Geometry; 3) Astronomy; 4) Music. Music is the knowledge of the harmony of sound, and through it the elaboration of the principles of melody; astronomy is the science of the stars, based on the evidence brought forth in the *Almagest;* just as the science of geometry is based on the evidence brought forth in Euclid; arithmetic is the science of the properties of numbers, and of the meanings that correspond with them, concerning the inner reality of created things, as has been stated by Pythagoras and Nicomachus. . . .

UNITY AND MULTIPLICITY

Expressions indicate meaning; meaning is that which is named, and expressions are names. The commonest of expressions is "thing" and the "thing" is either one or more than one. The one can be shown in two ways—either as reality or as symbol. The one as reality is the "thing" that has no parts, and cannot be divided: everything indivisible is one; it is by reason of its oneness that it is indivisible. (If you want, you can say that the one as reality is that which does not have in it anything outside of itself.) But the one as symbol is every assemblage which is called one: one may say that 10 is a unit, or 100 is a unit, or 1000 is a unit. And one is one by its oneness, just as black is black by its blackness. As for multiplicity, it is an assemblage of units. The first multiplicity is two, and then 3, 4, 5, and so on, indefinitely. Multiplicity is of two kinds: either a number or a "numbered"; the difference between the two is that the number is the quantity of the forms of things in the soul of him who numbers, while the "numbered" are the things themselves. . . .

Know that there is no number that does not have either one or several properties. And the meaning of a property of anything is that it is an attribute, pertaining especially to that thing which it does not share with anything else. The property of one is that it is the principle and origin of numbers, as we have mentioned before; by it, all things are numbered, both the odd and the even. And the property of two is that, speaking absolutely, it is the first number: by it, one counts one-half of all numbers—i.e., the even, but not the odds. The property of three is that it is the first of the odd numbers; by it, one can measure one-third of all numbers, which are odd and sometimes even. The property of four is that it is the first square number. The property of five is that it is the first circular number; it is called spherical. The property of six is that it is the first complete number [equal to the sum of its divisors], while the property of seven is that it is the first perfect number. The property of eight is that it is the first cubic number. The property of nine is that it is the first odd square, and the last of the single digits. The property of ten is that it is the first of the two-digit numbers. The property of eleven is that it is the first mute number. The property of twelve is that it is the first exceeding number [the sum of its divisors is greater than the number itself.]

Metaphysical Significance of Unity and Multiplicity

Know, oh Brother (may God assist thee and us by His Spirit), that Pythagoras was a unique sage, a Harranaean [from the community of Harran in Mesopotamia; they asserted that their prophet was Idrīs or Enoch, who is usually identified with Hermes Trismegistus], who had a great interest in the study of the science of numbers and their origin, and discussed in great detail their properties, classification and order. He used to say: "The knowledge of numbers, and of their origin from unity (which is before two), is the knowledge of the Unity of God, May He Be Exalted; and the knowledge of the properties of numbers, their classification and order is the knowledge of the beings created by the Exalted Creator, and of His handiwork, its order and classification. The science of numbers is centered in the soul, and needs little contemplation and little recollection before it becomes clear and is known without evidence. . . ."

Know, oh Brother (May God assist thee and us by the Spirit from Him) that God, Exalted Be His Praise, when He created all creatures and brought all things into being, arranged them and brought them into existence by a process similar to the process of generation of numbers from one, so that the multiplicity [of numbers] should be a witness to His Oneness, and their classification and order an indication of the perfection of His wisdom in creation. And this would be a witness to the fact, too, that they [creatures] are related to Him who created them, in the same way as the numbers are related to the One which is prior to two, and which is the principle, origin and source of numbers, as we have shown in our treatise on arithmetic. Since God (May His Praise Be Exalted) is One in Reality, and in every aspect and sense, it is impossible that the creature, His handiwork, should be in reality one. Instead, it would be necessary that there should be multiplicity in unity, duality, "coupled"—because it is the Creator (Exalted Be His Praise) who first began, with a single action, upon a unified single recipient of His action, which is indeed the Cause of causes; thus, this action was in reality not unity, but rather duality. That is why it is said that He brought into being and created things in duality, in pairs, and made [duality] the law of creatures and the principle of beings.

And that is why the philosophers and sages have said: *hylē* [matter] and form; and some of them have said: light and darkness; and others substance and accident; and others, good and evil; and others, affirmation and negation; and others, positive and negative; and others, spiritual and corporeal; and others, the Guarded Tablet and the Pen; and others, effusion and intellect; and others, love and hatred; and others, motion and rest; and others, existence and non-existence; and others, soul and spirit; and others, generation and corruption; and others, this world and the next; and others, cause and effect; and others, the beginning and the end; and others, contraction and expansion.

Similarly, we find many dualities or opposites in Nature, such as: moving and stationary bodies; the manifest and the hidden; the high and the low; the outside and the inside; the subtle and the gross; the hot and the cold; the moist and the dry; the excessive and the deficient; the inanimate and the animate; the articulate and the inarticulate; the male and the female, and all opposites which form a pair.

This is the necessary condition of all beings, whether animal or plant. [Duality is] life and death; sleep and awakening; illness and health; pleasure and pain; scarcity and plenty; joy and sorrow; happiness and sadness; well-being and decay; harmful and beneficial; good and evil; good luck and evil omen; going and coming.

Such too are the basic characteristics of the institutions of sacred law, and of social and religious matters; command and restraint; promise and threat; attraction and repulsion; submission and revolt; praise and blame; punishment and reward; the permissible and the forbidden; limits and licenses; right and wrong; good and bad; truth and falsehood, justice and injustice. . . .

Know, oh Brother, that since it is not wise to have all beings in pairs, some things were also made in threes, fours, fives, sixes, and sevens, and so on, indefinitely. . . .

Know, oh Brother, that all beings are of two kinds, no more, no less: the universals and the particulars. The universals are of nine levels, whose order is: the Creator (May His Praise Be Exalted); then the Intellect, having two powers; then the Soul, having three attributes; then the *materia prima,* having four expansions; then Nature, having five elements [ether, fire, air, water, earth]; then the Body, with six directions; then the Heavens, having seven levels [of planets]; then the elements, having eight mixtures; then the compounds [animals, plants and minerals], having nine kinds.

Geometry

As we have mentioned, sensible [as opposed to intelligible] geometry is the beginning and the introduction. We want to say something about intellectual geometry, because it was one of the goals sought by the sages deeply learned in the divine sciences, and disciplined in philosophical mathematics. Their objective in classifying geometry after the science of number, was to show the order by which the disciples are led from the sensible to the intelligible domain, and students and the young raised up from physical matters to spiritual ones.

Know, oh Brother (May God assist thee, and assist us by the Spirit which comes from Him), that the study of sensible geometry leads to skill in all the practical arts while the study of intelligible geometry leads to skill in the intellectual arts, because this science is one of the gates through which we move to the knowledge of the essence of the soul, and that is the root of all knowledge, and the element of wisdom, and the principle of all practical and intellectual arts. . . .[3]

B. Al-Khwārazmī

The science of algebra may be said to have had its origin in the celebrated work of Muḥammad ibn Mūsā al-

[3] Ikhwān al-Ṣafā', *Rasā'il* (Cairo: 'Arabīyah Press, 1928). From the epistles on arithmetic and geometry. Translated by S. H. Nasr.

Khwārazmī entitled *The Book of Summary in the Process of Calculation for Compulsion and Equation (Kitāb al-mukhtaṣar fī ḥisāb al-jabr waʾl-muqābalah)* where for the first time the Arabic word *al-jabr*, meaning "compulsion" and also "restoration," was used. It is from this word that, according to some authorities, the English word "algebra" is derived. Moreover, al-Khwārazmī's book on arithmetic, which was later translated into Latin along with his work on algebra, was responsible more than any other single text for spreading the Indian system of numeration both in the Islamic world and in the West.

The following excerpts are from Chapter I of the *Algebra*, and from a series of problems, appended to the six-chapter work, as illustrations to each chapter.

The Book of Algebra and Almucabola Containing Demonstrations of the Rules of the Equations of Algebra.

(WRITTEN SOME TIME AGO IN ARABIC, BY AN UNKNOWN AUTHOR, AND AFTERWARDS, ACCORDING TO TRADITION IN 1183, PUT INTO LATIN BY ROBERT OF CHESTER, IN THE CITY OF SEGOVIA.)

In the name of God, tender and compassionate, begins the book of Restoration and Opposition of number put forth by Mohammed al-Khowarizmi, the son of Moses. Mohammed said, Praise God the creator who has bestowed upon man the power to discover the significance of numbers. Indeed, reflecting that all things which men need require computation, I discovered that all things involve number and I discovered that number is nothing other than that which is composed of units. Unity therefore is implied in every number. Moreover I discovered all numbers to be so arranged that they proceed from unity up to ten. The number ten is treated in the same manner as the unit, and for this reason doubled and tripled just as in the case of unity. Out of its duplication arises 20, and from its triplication 30. And so multiplying the number ten you arrive at one-hundred. Again the number one-hundred is doubled and tripled like the number ten. So by doubling and tripling etc. the number one-hundred grows to one-thousand. In this way multiplying the number one-thousand according to the various denominations of numbers you come even to the investigation of number to infinity.

Furthermore I discovered that the numbers of restoration and opposition are composed of these three kinds: namely, roots, squares and numbers. However number alone is connected neither with roots nor with squares by any ratio. Of these then the root is anything composed of units which can be multiplied by itself, or any number greater than unity multiplied by itself: or that which is found to be diminished below unity when multiplied by itself. The square is that which results from the multiplication of a root by itself.

Of these three forms, then, two may be equal to each other, as for example:

Squares equal to roots
Squares equal to numbers, and
Roots equal to numbers

CHAPTER I. CONCERNING SQUARES EQUAL TO ROOTS

The following is an example of squares equal to roots: a square is equal to 5 roots. The root of the square then is 5, and 25 forms its square which, of course, equals five of its roots.

Another example: the third part of a square equals four roots. Then the root of the square is 12 and 144 designates its square. And similarly, five squares equal 10 roots. Therefore one square equals two roots and the root of the square is 2. Four represents the square.

In the same manner then that which involves more than one square, or is less than one, is reduced to one square. Likewise you perform the same operation upon the roots which accompany the squares.

SIXTH PROBLEM, ILLUSTRATING THE SIXTH CHAPTER

I multiply $\frac{1}{3}x$ and $\frac{1}{4}x$ in such a way as to give x itself plus 24 units.

Explanation: first you observe that when you multiply $\frac{1}{3}x$ by $\frac{1}{4}x$ you obtain $\frac{1}{2}$ of $\frac{1}{6}x^2$ equal to $x + 24$ units. The multiplication of $\frac{1}{2}$ of $\frac{1}{6}x^2$ by 12 gives the complete square. Similarly, the multiplication of x plus 24 units gives $12x$ plus 288 which equal x^2. Therefore take one-half of the roots and multiply the half by itself. Add the product of this multiplication to 288, giving 324. Take now the root of this, *i.e.*, 18, and add it to the half of the roots. The root finally is 24. So this problem has led you to the sixth of the six chapters in which we treated the type, roots and numbers equal to a square.[4]

[4] *Robert of Chester's Latin Translation of the Algebra of al-Khowarizmi*, translated into English by L. C. Karpinski (London: The Macmillan Company, 1915), pp. 66, 69, 109.

C. ʿUmar Khayyām

The name of ʿUmar Khayyām has become very familiar in the English-speaking world through the beautiful, although sometimes free, translation of his *Rubāʿīyāt* or *Quatrains* by Fitzgerald. In his own time, however, Khayyām was known as a metaphysician and scientist rather than as a poet, and he is remembered in Persia today most of all for his mathematical works and his participation with other astronmers in devising the Jalālī solar calendar, which has been used there ever since his time.

During his own time, he was known not only as a master of the mathematical sciences and as a follower of Greek-inspired philosophy, especially the school of Avicenna, but also as a Sufi. Although he was attacked by some religious authorities, and even by certain Sufis, who wanted to present Sufism in a more exoteric dress, Khayyām must be regarded as a gnostic, behind whose apparent skepticism lies the absolute certainty of intellectual intuition. His adherence to Sufism is shown by the fact that he assigned to the Sufis the highest place in the hierarchy of possessors of knowledge.

In Khayyām several perspectives of Islam unite. He was a Sufi and poet, as well as a philosopher, an astronomer and a mathematician. Unfortunately, he apparently wrote little, and even of that little, some works have been lost. Nevertheless, his remaining works—which include, besides his poetry, treatises on existence, generation and corruption, physics, the totality of the sciences, the balance, metaphysics, as well as mathematical works consisting of research on Euclid's axioms, arithmetic, and algebra—are sufficient evidence of his universality. The *Algebra* of Khayyām is one of the most outstanding mathematical texts of the medieval period. It deals with equations through the cubic order, classifying and solving them (usually geometrically), and always preserving the relation between the unknowns, numbers and geometrical forms, thereby maintaining the link between mathematics and the metaphysical significance inherent in Euclidean geometry.

The following excerpts are from the first four sections of the *Algebra;* the very important subsequent sections, which deal with cubic and quadratic equations, are omitted, primarily because of their difficulty for the general reader.

II. The Text. *A Treatise on al-jabr by the wise the unique master Abu'l Fatḥ ʿUmar ibn Ibrahīm al-Khayyāmī, May God preserve him in his perfection. . . .*

One of the mathematical processes required in that branch of philosophy known as mathematical is the art of al-jabr and al-muqābala, designed for the extraction of numerical and areal unknowns, and there are kinds of it in which you require very hard kinds of introductions, (and which are) impossible to solve by most people who consider them. As for the Ancients we have had no discourse from them concerning it. Perhaps after searching and looking into it they failed to notice it, or they were not forced by the discussion to investigate it, or their statements about it were not translated into our language.

As for the later scholars, it occurred to Māhānī to analyze, by the methods of *al-jabr,* the introduction which Archimedes used, as given, in the fourth figure of the second essay of his Book of the Sphere and the Cylinder, and he (Māhānī) went as far as (the case of) cubes, squares, and numbers being equated. But he did not succeed in obtaining a solution even after much thought, and he came to the conclusion that it was impossible to solve, (and no one did so) until the advent of ʾAbū Jaʿfar al-Khāzin, who solved it by conic sections. And after him a number of geometricians lacked some kind of them. Now the proof of these is a discourse which is reliable except as regards two kinds, which I am going to set down.

For I have always been very anxious to investigate all its kinds and to distinguish, with proofs in the various cases of every kind, the possible from the impossible, because I know that the need for it in the difficult problems is very great. And I was unable to devote myself to the learning of this al-jabr and the continued concentration on it, because of obstacles in the vagaries of Time which hindered me; for we have been deprived of all the people of knowledge save for a group, small in number, with many troubles, whose concern in life is to snatch the opportunity, when Time is asleep, to devote themselves meanwhile to the investigation and perfection of a science; for the majority of the people who imitate philosophers confuse the true with the false, and they do nothing but deceive and pretend knowledge, and they do not use what they know of the sciences except for base and material purposes; and if they see a certain person seeking for the right and preferring the truth, doing his best to refute the false and untrue and leaving aside hypocrisy and deceit, they make a fool of him and mock him. God is the helper in every case, and in Him we take refuge.

Then God—May He be exalted—graciously allowed me to

devote myself entirely to our unique and most eminent master, the chief justice the Imām Saiyid Abū Ṭāhir—May God perpetuate his glory and suppress his envious enemies—after my despairing of ever seeing his perfect equal in every virtue theoretical and practical, he who gathered in himself the extremes of knowledge and who was firm in action and sought good for every one of his kind. My heart rejoiced in seeing him and my reputation rose high due to his patronage, and my state prospered by borrowing from his light, and I was strengthened by his gifts and favours. And I had no alternative but to endeavour to compensate for what Time had made me miss, to summarize what I ascertain of the essence of the philosophical ideas so as to bring me nearer to his high company; so that I started to enumerate these kinds of the algebraic introductions, for mathematics is most worthy of priority. And I held fast to the cord of success from God the Exalted, hoping that He would guide me to follow this by investigating the conclusions of my discussions and those of my predecessors in the more important sciences, placing my trust in God who would meet all my needs, and upon whom I depend in every circumstance.

I say, with God's help and good guidance, that the art of al-jabr and al-muqābala is a mathematical art, whose subject is pure number and mensurable quantities in as far as they are unknown, added to a known thing with the help of which they may be found; and that (known) thing is either a quantity or a ratio, so that no other (ratio) is like it, and the thing is revealed to you by thinking about it. And what is required in it (the art) are the coefficients which are attached to its subject-matter (of the equation) in the manner stated above. And the perfection of the art is knowing the mathematical methods by which one is led to the manner of extracting the numerical and mensurable unknowns.

Now these quantities are any of the four variable quantities, which are the line, the plane, the solid, and time, as was mentioned briefly in the Categories and in detail in the First Book of (his) [Aristotle's] philosophy. His followers regard place as well as a plane as sharing the genus "continuous" but investigation refutes their view and corrects it to "place is a plane with certain qualifications," but the occasion of this investigation is outside the present discussion. It is not customary to mention time among the subjects of the problems of al-jabr, but should it be mentioned it would be possible to include it. The practice of algebraists in their art is to call the unknown, which it is required to find "the thing," and the product of it with itself "a square," and its product with its square "a cube," and the product of its square with its square "the square of the square," and the product of its cube with the square "the square of the cube," and the product of its cube with itself is "the cube of the cube," and so forth, however great (a power) it may be. It is known from the Elements of Euclid that all these powers are proportional, i.e., the ratio of unity to the root is as the ratio of the root to the square and as the ratio of the square to the cube; so that the ratio of the numeric to the roots is as the ratio of the roots to the squares and as the ratio of the squares to the cubes, and as the ratio of the cubes to the squares of the squares, and so forth, however great it (the square of the square) may be. It must be realized that this treatise cannot be understood except by one who has mastered Euclid's Elements and his book called the Data and two books of Apollonius on the Conics, and anyone who does not know (any) one of these three cannot understand (the present treatise). And I have undertaken not to base myself in this treatise except on these three books.

Now the extractions of al-jabr are effected by equating, i.e., the equating of these powers to each other, as is well known; and when the algebraist uses "square of the square," respecting areas, that is only in a metaphorical way and not literally, for it is impossible for the square of the square to be in quantities. And it is the single dimension, i.e., the root, which is in quantities; when the side is taken with its square, we have the two dimensions which are the surface; and the square in quantities is the square surface; then there are the three dimensions which make the solid; and the solid cube in quantities is the solid which is surrounded by six square faces; and as there is no other dimension, there does not occur in them, i.e., quantities, the square of the square, nor anything which comes above that. And when we speak of the square of the square in quantities, we are referring to the magnitude of its parts when the area is being found, and to itself (i.e., the square of the square) after the area has been taken, for there is a difference between them. Thus the square of the square does not occur in quantities either itself, or by accident, as an even or odd number which might occur accidentally when we break it into its two parts.

The books of the algebraists contain, out of these four geometrical relations, i.e., pure numbers, edges, squares, and cubes, three equations between the numbers, the edges, and squares. For our part, we shall mention the ways by which it is possible to find the unknown by equations involving the four powers; i.e., the numbers, the thing, the square, and the cube:—and beyond which, we said, none (no power) could occur in quantities. And what may be proved by the properties of the circle, i.e., by the two books of Euclid on the Elements and on the Data we shall prove it and simplify it considerably; but what is not possible except by the properties of the conic sections, we shall prove by the two treatises on Conics. As for the proof in those cases where the subject of the problem is a pure number, we cannot solve it, neither can anyone who knows this art (of al-jabr). Perhaps someone else who comes after us may know it—except for the first three powers, which are the number, the thing, and the square; and I may point to numerical proofs of what can be proved in the book of Euclid. But observe that the proof of these methods by geometry is not a substitute for a proof by numbers (al-jabr) if the subject is a number and not a mensurable quantity. Do you not see that Euclid proved (the theorems about) proportional quantitative unknowns when their subject is a number, in Book VII? Equations between these four are either simple or compound.

The simple equations are of six kinds; (a) a number equals a root; (b) a number equals a square; (c) a number equals a cube; (d) (so many) roots equal a square; (e) (so many) squares equal a cube; (f) (so many) roots equal a cube. Three of these six kinds are mentioned in the books of algebraists. They said that the ratio of the things to the square is as the ratio of the square to the cube, whence it follows that equating the square to the cube is the same as equating the thing to the square; and also the ratio of the number to the square is as the ratio of the root to the cube, but they did not prove it geometrically. As for the case of the number equal to the cube, there is no way of extracting its edge except by calculation; whereas in the case of the geometrical method, it cannot be solved except by conic sections.

As for the compound equations, they comprise either three or four terms. Those having three terms are of 12 kinds:—the first three (of these kinds) are: (a) square plus root equal to a number, (b) square plus the number equal to a root, (c) root plus number equal to a square. These three are mentioned in the books of the algebraists and are proved geometrically, but not from the standpoint of numbers (algebraically). The second three are: (a) a cube plus a square equal to a root, (b) cube plus root equal to a square, (c) cube equal to root plus square.

The algebraists have said that these second three are proportional to the first three, each to its corresponding one, i.e., a cube plus a root equal to a square is equivalent to a square plus a number equal to a root; and so on, for the other two; but they gave no proof in the case where the subject of the problems was mensurable. However, when the subject of the problems is a number, that is evident from the Book of Elements, and I shall prove those of them which are geometrical. The remaining six of the 12 kinds are: (a) cube plus root equal to a number, (b) cube plus a number equal to a root, (c) a number plus root equal to cube, (d) cube plus square equal to number, (e) cube plus a number equal to square, (f) a number plus a square equal to a cube. There is nothing in their books about these six kinds except a discourse on one of them, which is incomplete, and I shall explain that one and prove it geometrically, but not algebraically. It is impossible to prove these six except by the properties of conic sections.

The compound equations having four terms are of two kinds; firstly, that in which three different powers together are equal to one, of which there are four cases—(a) cube plus square plus root equal to a number, (b) cube plus square plus number equal to a root, (c) cube plus root plus number equal to square, (d) a cube equal to root plus square plus number; secondly, that in which two powers are equal to two powers, of which are three cases—(a) cube plus square equal to root plus number, (b) cube plus root equal to square plus number, (c) cube plus number equal to root plus square. These are the seven cases of equations of four terms, and we cannot solve any of them except geometrically.

Of our predecessors, one of them lacked one case of one kind which I shall mention; and the proof of these cases is effected only by the properties of conic sections. We shall mention these twenty-five cases one by one, and prove each, asking help from God, for he who depends on Him sincerely will be guided and satisfied.

(I) In the first case of the simple equations, *a root equal to a number,* the root is necessarily known, and its application to numbers and areas is the same.

(II) In the second case, where *a number is equal to a square,* the square is known numerically, for it equals a known number (1); it is not possible to know its root numerically except by calculation, for anyone who knows that the root of 25 is 5 knows it by calculation and not by any artificial formula, and one ignores what the pedants in this art say. The Hindus have their own methods for extracting the sides of squares and cubes based on a little calculation, which is the knowledge of the squares of the 9 integers, i.e., the squares of 1, 2, and 3, etc. and of their products into each other, i.e., the product of 2 with 3, etc. I have written a book to prove the validity of those methods and to show that they lead to the required solutions, and I have supplemented it with their kinds, i.e., finding the sides of the square of the square, and the square of the cube, and the cube of the cube, however great they may be; and no one has done this before; and those proofs are only algebraic proofs based on the algebraical parts of the book of Elements.

The geometrical proof of the second case is as follows:—

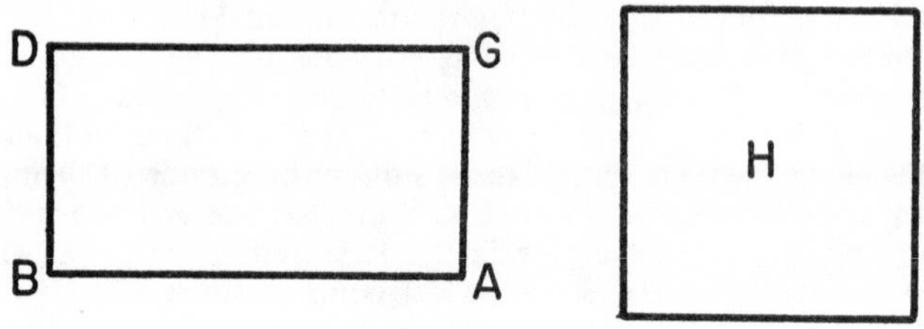

FIGURE 1.

Draw the given line *AB* (Fig. 1) equal to the given number and *AG* equal to unity and perpendicular to *AB*. Complete the rectangle *AD*. It is known that the area of the surface *AD* is equal to that given number. We construct a square surface, which is the square *H*, equal in area to *AD*, as Euclid showed in Proposition 14, Book II. The square *H* is equal to the given number, which is known, whence its side also becomes known. Cf. the proof in Euclid. Q.E.D. Whenever we state in this treatise that a number equals a surface, we mean by the number a surface with all its angles right angles and one side of unit length, the other side being equal to the given number. And each of the parts of the area is equal to the second side, i.e., the side which we assumed equal to unity.

TRINOMIAL EQUATION

The first kind is a square plus 10 times its root equal to 39 [x^2 plus $10x$ equals 39]. Multiply half (the coefficient of) the roots into itself, and add the result to the number (the 39). Subtract from the root of the number (obtained) half (the coefficient of) the roots. The remainder is the root of the square.[5] As for the number it must fulfill two conditions: (*i*) that (the coefficient of) the roots must be even to have a half (integral), and (*ii*) the square of half (of the coefficient of) the roots, and the number, when added together, must be a perfect square; otherwise the problem is impossible algebraically. Geometrically, none of its problems is impossible at all, and the algebraical proof is easy when you picture to yourself the geometrical proof.

[5] The modern algebraic explanation may be expressed as follows: x^2 plus $10x$ equals 39; ½ of 10 is 5 which squared equals 25; 25 plus 39 equals 64; $\sqrt{64}$ equals 8; x equals 8 minus 5 equals 3. The negative root is discarded in mathematics until Descartes. (S. H. Nasr)

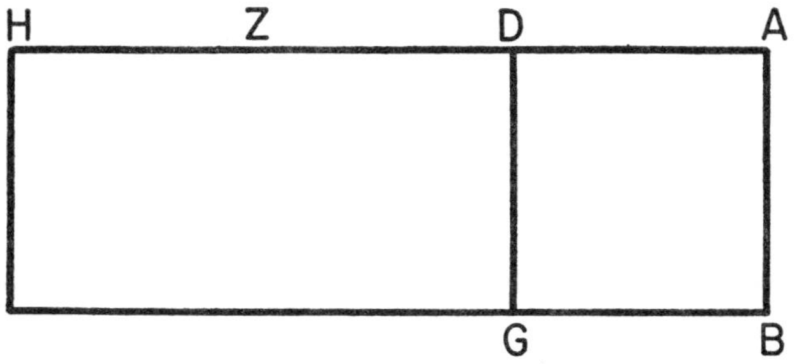

FIGURE 2.

The geometrical proof is as follows: Construct the square *AG* so that together with 10 times its root it equals the number 39. And 10 times its root is the area (rectangle) *GH,* so that the line *DH* is 10. Bisect it *(DH)* at *Z.* Since the line *DH* is bisected at *Z* and continues as *AD,* it is as if the product of *AH* with *AD,* which is equal to the area *BH,* when added to the square of *DZ,* were equal to the square of *AZ.* Now the square of *DZ,* which *(DZ)* is half (the coefficient of) the roots, is known; and the area *BH,* which is the given number, is known. Hence the square of *AZ* becomes known, and when we subtract *ZD* from *AZ,* the line *AD* is known.[6, 7]

[6] The geometrical reasoning may be formulated as follows:
AD equals *AB* equals *x*
DH equals 10
area of *BH* equals 39
DZ equals *ZH* equals *DH*/2
HA times *AD* plus $(DZ)^2$ equals $(ZA)^2$ (Euclid, Elements, II, 6)
BH plus $(DZ)^2$ equals $(ZA)^2$
BH and *DZ* are known, therefore *ZA* is known
and (*ZA* minus *ZD*) equals *AD* equals *x*. (S. H. Nasr)

[7] From the translation of H. J. J. Winter and W. ʿArafat, "The Algebra of ʿUmar Khayyām," *Journal of the Royal Asiatic Society of Bengal,* XVI, No. 1, pp. 28–35. Reprinted by permission of the Asiatic Society.

CHAPTER SIX

ASTRONOMY

In astronomy, the Muslims continued the tradition of Ptolemy, while making extensive use of the knowledge of the Persians and Indians. The first astronomers in Islam, who flourished during the second half of the second/eighth century in Baghdad, based their astronomical works essentially on Persian and Indian astronomical tables. The most important astronomical work that has survived from pre-Islamic Persia was the *Zīj-i Shāhī* or *Zīj-i Shahriyārī (The Tables of the King)*, composed around A.D. 555, during the reign of the Sassanid king, Anūshīrawān the Just, and itself based to a large extent on the astronomical theories and practices of the Indians.

This work was to Sassanid astronomy what the *Siddhāntas* were to the Indians, and the *Almagest* to the Greeks; it played the same important role in the formation of Islamic astronomy as did these latter sources. This text—which possessed several peculiar features, including the fact that it began the day at midnight, instead of at the usual noontime—was translated into Arabic by Abuʾl-Ḥasan al-Tamīmī, with a commentary by Abū Maʿshar (Albumasar), the most famous of Muslim astrologers. The *Zīj-i shāhī* was the basis of the astronomical activity of such famous astronomers as Ibn al-Naubakht and Māshāʾallāh, who flourished during the reign of al-Manṣūr, and who assisted in making preliminary calculations for the founding of the city of Baghdad. Along with a few astrological treatises, in which the distinctly Sassanid emphasis upon Jupiter-Saturn conjunctions became transmitted to the Muslims, the *Zīj-i shāhī* represents the most important astronomical heritage of Sassanid Persia, and the earliest basis for the foundation of Islamic astronomy.

With the first official astronomer of the Abbasids, Muḥammad al-Fazārī, who died around 161/777, direct Indian influence became dominant. In 155/771 an Indian mission came to Baghdad, to teach the Indian sciences and to aid in the translation of texts into Arabic. A year or two later the *zīj* of al-Fazārī appeared, based on the *Siddhānta* of Brahmagupta. Al-Fazārī also composed several astronomical poems, and was the first person in Islam to make an astrolabe, which later became the characteristic instrument of Islamic astronomy. His major work, which became known as the *Great Siddhānta,* remained the sole basis of astronomical science until the time of al-Maʾmūn, in the third/ninth century.

Also instrumental in introducing Indian astronomy into Islam was a contemporary of al-Fazārī, Yaʿqūb ibn Ṭāriq, who studied under an Indian master and became well versed in the subject. Mainly through the efforts of these two men, more than of all others, Indian astronomy and mathematics entered the stream of Islamic science. Other Sanskrit works, especially the *Siddhānta* of Āryabhata, also became disseminated at this time, remaining, along with the Persian works already cited, the authoritative source of astronomy until the time of al-Maʾmūn, when Greek works were rendered into Arabic.

During the extensive movement that took place under al-Maʾmūn to translate foreign works into Arabic, basic Greek astronomical texts also became available, to a certain extent replacing the Indian and Persian works that had monopolized the field until that time. The *Almagest* was translated several times, as were also the *Tetrabiblos* and the astronomical tables of Ptolemy, known as *Canones procheiroi.*

With these and other translations from Greek and Syriac, the background for the rise of Islamic astronomy was prepared, and in the third/ninth century some of the greatest figures in the science appeared upon the scene. The early part of the century was dominated by Ḥabash al-Ḥāsib, under whose direction the "Maʾmūnic" tables were composed; al-Khwārazmī who, besides his important mathematical writings, also left behind significant astronomical tables; and Abū Maʿshar. The latter figure is the Muslim astrologer most often quoted in the West, his *Great Introduction to Astrology* being translated and printed several times in Latin. Also of the period of al-Maʾmūn was al-Farghānī (Alfraganus), the author of the well-known *Elements of Astronomy.*

In the second half of the third/ninth century, the cultivation of astronomy continued its rapid pace. Al-Nairīzī (Anaritius) commented on the *Almagest,* and wrote the most elaborate treatise ever composed in Arabic on the spherical astrolabe. His contemporary, Thābit ibn Qurrah, also played a major role in astronomy; he is especially famous for upholding the theory of the oscillatory motion of the equinoxes. To account for this trepidation, he added a ninth sphere to the eight of Ptolemaic astronomy, a feature adopted by most of the later Muslim astronomers.

His compatriot al-Battānī, (or Albategnius), whom some authorities consider to be the greatest Muslim astronomer, soon followed Thābit ibn Qurrah, and continued his line of study, although rejecting the trepidation theory. Al-Battānī made some of the most accurate observations in the annals of Islamic astronomy. He discovered the increase of the sun's apogee since the time of Ptolemy, which led to the discovery of the motion of the solar apsides. He determined the precession as 54.5″ a year, and the inclination of the ecliptic as 23°35′. He also discovered a new method for determining the time of the vision of the new moon, and made a detailed study of solar and lunar eclipses, used as late as the eighteenth century by Dunthorn, in his determination of the gradual change in lunar motion. Al-Battānī's major astronomical work, which also contains a set of tables, became known in the West as *De scientia stellarum (On the Science of Stars);* it was one of the basic works of astronomy down to the Renaissance. It is not surprising that his works, in the edition, translation and commentary of the noted Italian scholar, C. A. Nallino, have received a more careful study than the writings of any other Muslim astronomer during modern times.

Astronomical observation was continued during the fourth/tenth century by such figures as Abū Sahl al-Kūhī and ʿAbd al-Raḥmān al-Ṣūfī. The latter is particularly well-known for his *Figures of the Stars,* which G. Sarton, the outstanding historian of Islamic science, regards, along with the *zīj*'s of Ibn Yūnus and Ulugh Beg, as one of the three greatest masterpieces of observational astronomy in Islam. This book, which gives a map of fixed stars with figures, was disseminated widely in both East and West; its manuscripts are among the most beautiful of the medieval scientific works. Also of this period is Abū Saʿīd al-Sijzī, who was particularly noted for constructing an astrolabe based on the motion of the earth around the sun, and the above-mentioned Abuʾl-Wafāʾ al-Buzjānī who, besides being one of the most notable of the Muslim mathematicians, was also an accomplished astronomer. He wrote a simplified version of the *Almagest*, to facilitate the understanding of Ptolemy's work, and spoke of the second part of the evection of the moon in such a manner as to lead the French scholar L. Am. Sédillot in the nineteenth century to begin a long controversy on Abu'l-Wafā''s supposed discovery of the third inequality of the moon. Current opinion, however, tends to discredit this thesis, and to reinstate Tycho Brahe as its discoverer.

Finally one must cite, as a contemporary of Abu'l-Wafā', the Andalusian alchemist and astronomer, Abu'l-Qāsim al-Majrīṭī, whose chief fame lies in his Hermetical and occult writings. Al-Majrīṭī was also an accomplished astronomer, and wrote commentaries on the tables of Muḥammad ibn Mūsā al-Khwārazmī and the *Planisphaerium* of Ptolemy, as well as a treatise on the astrolabe. Also, it was he and his student al-Kirmānī who made the *Epistles* of the Brethren of Purity known in Andalusia.

The fifth/eleventh century, which marks the apogee of activity in the Islamic sciences, was also witness to the activity of several important astronomers, including al-Bīrūnī, whose determination of latitudes and longitudes, geodetic measurements, and several major astronomical calculations mark him among the outstanding figures in this field. Ibn Yūnus, who was the astronomer of the Fatimid court in Cairo, completed his *Zīj* (the Hākimite Tables) in 397/1007, and thus made an enduring contribution to Islamic astronomy. These tables, in which many constants were remeasured accurately, are among the most accurate to have been composed during the Islamic period. Ibn Yūnus is for this reason considered by some historians of science, such as Sarton, to have been perhaps the most important Muslim astronomer, aside from the fact that he was an accomplished mathematician, solved problems of spherical trigonometry by means of orthogonal projections, and was probably the first to study the isometric oscillatory motion of a pendulum—an investigation which later led to the construction of mechanical clocks.

To the latter half of this century belongs the first outstanding Spanish observational astronomer, al-Zarqālī. He invented a new astronomical instrument called *ṣaḥīfah (Saphaea Arzachelis)*, which became widely known; he is also credited with the explicit proof of the motion of the apogee of the sun with respect to the fixed stars. His most important contribution, however, is the editing of the *Toledan Zīj*, composed with the aid of several other Muslim and Jewish scientists, and widely used by both the Latin and Muslim astronomers of later centuries.

Spanish astronomy after al-Zarqālī developed in an anti-Ptolemaic vein, in the sense that criticism began to be made of the epicyclic theory. In the sixth/twelfth century, Jābir ibn Aflāḥ, who was also known as "Geber" in the West and was often mistaken for the famous alchemist, began to criticize the Ptolemaic planetary system. The philosophers, Avempace and Ibn Ṭufail (known to the Occident as Abubacer) also criticized Ptolemy. Avempace, under the influence of Aristotelian cosmology, which was then becoming dominant in Andalusia, proposed a system based solely on eccentric circles; Ibn Ṭufail is regarded as the author of a theory which was more fully developed by his student, the seventh/thirteenth century al-Bitrūjī (Alpetragius). This was an elaborate system of homocentric spheres, which has also been called the "theory of spiral motion," because in its view the planets appear to perform a kind of "spiral" movement. Although this newly proposed planetary system did not have any advantage over the Ptolemaic one, and was not accepted in its place, the criticisms brought against the Ptolemaic system by al-Bitrūjī and the astronomers before him were used as effective instruments by the Renaissance astronomers against the age-old astronomy of Ptolemy.

In the East also, a certain dissatisfaction with the Ptolemaic system went hand in hand with astronomical work based on his theory. The *Sanjarī Zīj* was composed in the sixth/twelfth century by al-Khāzinī, and was followed by the *Ilkhanid Zīj* of the seventh/thirteenth century, which came as the fruit of observations at Maragha. But at the same time Naṣīr al-Dīn al-Ṭūsī, the chief astronomer at Maragha, also criticized Ptolemy severely. In his *Memorial of Astronomy*, al-Ṭūsī showed clearly his dissatisfaction with the Ptolemaic planetary theory. In fact, al-Ṭūsī proposed a new planetary model which was worked out to completion by his student, Quṭb al-Dīn al-Shīrāzī. This new model sought to be more faithful to the concept of the spherical nature of the heavens than the Ptolemaic model by placing the earth at the geometric center of the heavenly spheres rather than at a distance from the center as we find in Ptolemy. Al-Ṭūsī then conceived of two spheres rolling one within the other to explain the apparent motion of the planets. That is why the American historian of Islamic mathematics, E. S. Kennedy, who discovered this planetary model, has named it the Ṭūsī

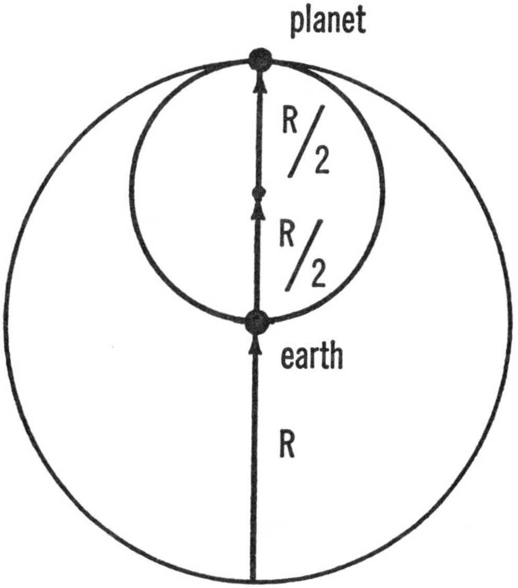

The Tūsī Couple

FIGURE 3.[1]

couple (see Figure 3), since it represents the sum of two moving vectors. Al-Ṭūsī intended to calculate the details of this model for all the planets but apparently did not complete the process. It was left to his immediate student Quṭb al-Dīn al-Shīrāzī to work out a variation of this model for Mercury, and to the eighth/fourteenth century Damascene astronomer Ibn al-Shāṭir to complete the lunar model in his *A Text of the Final Inquiry in Amending the Elements.* Ibn al-Shāṭir, going back to the Ṭūsī model, dispensed with the Ptolemaic eccentric deferent, and introduced a second epicycle in both the solar and the lunar systems. The lunar theory proposed two centuries later by Copernicus is the same as that of Ibn al-Shāṭir, and it seems that Copernicus was somehow acquainted with this late development of Islamic astronomy, perhaps through a Byzantine translation.

[1] I am indebted to Professor E. S. Kennedy for having supplied this diagram.

All that is astronomically new in Copernicus can be found essentially in the school of al-Tūsī and his students.

The tradition of Maragha was continued by al-Ṭūsī's immediate students, such as Qutb al-Dīn al-Shīrāzī and Muḥyī al-Dīn al-Maghribī as well as by the astronomers assembled by Ulugh Beg in Samarkand, such as Ghiyāth al-Dīn al-Kāshānī and Qūshchī. It even survived up to modern times in different regions of the Islamic world, such as northern India, Persia and to a certain extent Morocco. Many commentaries were written on earlier works such as the commentary on the treatise of Qūshchī on astronomy by ʿAbd al-Ḥayy Lārī in the eleventh/seventeenth century, which has been popular until modern times in Persia.

This later tradition of Islamic astronomy continued to correct the mathematical shortcomings of the Ptolemaic model, but it did not break the bounds of the closed Ptolemaic system, which was so intimately tied to the medieval world view. It is true that many of the later Muslim astronomers criticized various aspects of Ptolemaic astronomy. It is also certain that such astronomers as al-Bīrūnī knew of the possibility of the motion of the earth around the sun, and even—as al-Bīrūnī proposed, in his questions to Avicenna—the possibility of an elliptic rather than circular motion of the planets. But none of them did, nor could they, take the step to break with the traditional world view, as was to happen during the Renaissance in the West—because that would have meant not only a revolution in astronomy, but also an upheaval in the religious, philosophical and social domains. No one can overestimate the influence of the astronomical revolution upon the minds of men. And as long as the hierarchy of knowledge remained intact in Islam, and *scientia* continued to be cultivated in the bosom of *sapientia,* a certain "limitation" in the physical domain was accepted in order to preserve the freedom of expansion and realization in the spiritual domain. The wall of the cosmos was preserved, in order to guard the symbolic meaning which such a walled-in vision of the cosmos presented to most of mankind. It was as if the old scientists and scholars foresaw that the breaking of these walls would also destroy the symbolic content of the cosmos, and even obliterate the meaning of "cosmos" (literally order) for the great majority of men, for whom it is difficult to conceive of the sky as some incandescent matter whirling in space and at the same time as the throne of God. And so, despite all the technical possibility, the step toward breaking the traditional world view was not taken, and the

Muslims remained content with developing and perfecting the astronomical system that had been inherited from the Greeks, Indians, and Persians, and which had become fully integrated into the Islamic world view.

The several new features of Islamic astronomy include, besides all the refinements made in the Ptolemaic system, the star catalogue of Ulugh Beg, which was the first new catalogue since the time of Ptolemy, and the replacement of the calculus of chords by the calculus of sines and trigonometry. The Muslim astronomers also modified the general system of the Alexandrians in two important respects. The first modification was to abolish the eight spheres which Ptolemy had hypothesized to communicate the diurnal movement to each of the heavens; the Muslims substituted a single starless heaven at the confines of the Universe, above the heaven of fixed stars, which in undergoing diurnal motion carried all the heavens with it. The second modification, which had a greater significance for the philosophy of the sciences, involved a change in the nature of the heavens. Among the many problems of astronomy those that were of particular interest to Muslim astronomers were the nature of the heavenly bodies, planetary motion and the distance and size of the planets which were connected with calculations based on the mathematical models with which they worked. They were of course also interested in descriptive astronomy as seen in new star catalogues and fresh observations of the heavens.

A. The Nature of the Heavenly Spheres

It is well known that, in the *Almagest,* Ptolemy had dealt with the heavenly spheres as purely geometrical forms, hypothesized in order to "save the phenomena." He was thereby following the tradition of the Greek mathematical astronomers, who were not concerned so much with the ultimate nature of the heavens as with the means of describing their motions according to mathematical laws. The Muslims, reacting against this point of view, proceeded to "solidify" the Ptolemaic heavens, in conformity with the "realist" outlook of the Muslim mind, and following tendencies already present in the *Hypotheses of the Planets,* sometimes attributed to Ptolemy himself. The Muslims have always considered the role of natural science to be the discovery of those aspects of Reality represented in physical existence, rather than the creation of mental constructs to impose upon Nature, without their having a necessary correspondence to any aspects of Reality. The solidification of the abstract Ptolemaic heavens therefore represents a profound transformation of the meaning and role of the mathematical sciences in their dealing with Nature, an issue basic to the philosophy of the sciences.

The tendency toward the "physical" interpretation of the heavens was already evident in the writings of the third/ninth-century astronomer and mathematician, Thābit ibn Qurrah, especially in his treatise on the constitution of the heavens. Although the original of this treatise seems to have been lost, excerpts in the works of many later writers, including Maimonides and Albertus Magnus, indicate that Thābit ibn Qurrah had conceived of the heavens as solid spheres with a compressible fluid between the orbs and the eccentrics.

This process of transforming the abstract heavens of the Greeks into solid bodies was continued by Alhazen, who is more famous for his studies in optics than for those in astronomy. In his *Resumé of Astronomy* (although the original Arabic has been lost, Hebrew and Latin versions survive), Alhazen describes the motion of the planets, not only in terms of eccentrics and epicycles, but also according to a physical model, which exercised a great influence upon the Christian world up to the time of Kepler. It is curious, however, that the Muslim philosophers and scientists did not in general seem to recognize the implications of this solidification of the Ptolemaic heavens. The Andalusian Peripatetics, such as Ibn Ṭufail and Averroes, continued their attacks upon Ptolemaic astronomy in the name of Aristotelian physics, failing even to consider Alhazen's work—perhaps because, as Duhem suggests, it would have weakened their argument. However, with the translation of Alhazen's treatise into Spanish, following the directive of Alfonso the Wise, the work became instead an instrument of the Latin partisans of Ptolemy in their defense against the attacks of the Peripatetics. In the Muslim world, too, it now came to be looked upon with favor by the astronomers; three centuries later, Naṣīr al-Dīn al-Ṭūsī was to compose a treatise on the heavens based on Alhazen's *Resumé* and closely following his ideas.

In the *Resumé of Astronomy*, after criticizing those who interpret the heavens as merely abstract geometric forms, Alhazen writes:

> The movements of circles, and the fictitious point which Ptolemy has considered in a wholly abstract manner, we transfer to plane or spherical surfaces, which will be animated by the same movement. This is in fact a more exact representation; at the same time, it is more comprehensible to the intelligence. . . . Our demonstrations will be shorter than those in which use is made only of that ideal point and those fictitious circles. . . . We have examined the diverse movements produced within the heavens in such a way as to make each of these movements correspond to the simple, continuous and unending movement of a spherical body. All these bodies, assigned thus to each of these movements, can be put into action simultaneously, without this action being contrary to their given position and without their encountering anything against which they could strike or which they could compress or shatter in any way. Moreover, these bodies in their motion will remain continuous with the interposed substance . . .

In describing the heavens, Alhazen writes that, at the extremity of the Universe, there is

> the really supreme heaven, which envelops all things and which is immediately contiguous with the sphere of fixed stars. On its own poles, which are the poles of the world, it turns rapidly from East to West carrying with it, by its motion, all the heavens of the different stars. . . . It is itself starless.

As for the heaven of the fixed stars, it is

> a round globe, enclosed within two spherical surfaces, whose center is the center of this globe and of the world. The external surface of this globe is contiguous with the largest of the heavens, the one which encloses all the moving heavens, and involves them in its rapid movement; the internal surface of the same globe touches the orbit of Saturn. This heaven [of the

fixed stars] turns from the West to the East, according to the order of the signs on two fixed poles. Its movement is slow: during each hundred years it moves only one degree, while the whole circle is divided into three hundred and sixty degrees. The poles of this heaven are also the poles of the heaven of the signs [of the Zodiac], which the Sun traverses; Ptolemy, who discovered this by means of observations of the ancients and of his own, also mentions it. All the fixed stars are set in this heaven, and never change the position they occupy therein. Their mutual distances do not undergo any variations; rather, they always move together, according to the order of the signs and in accordance with the slow movement of their heavens. . . .

The spheres of the three upper planets—i.e., Saturn, Jupiter and Mars—are absolutely alike, both with regard to the number of heavens of which they are composed, and the nature of the movement which animates them. . . . Each of these planets has its own sphere, which is determined by two spherical surfaces, parallel to each other, whose common center is the center of the world; each sphere embraces the sphere immediately following it. The first heaven is that of Saturn, whose external surface is bounded by the sphere of the fixed stars, its internal surface by the sphere of Jupiter. Furthermore, the upper surface of the sphere of Jupiter touches the orb of Saturn; its inferior surface, the orb of Mars. Finally, the external surface of the sphere of Mars is contiguous with the sphere of Jupiter, while its internal surface touches the orbit of the Sun. Each of these heavens moves with the same slow movement around poles placed on the same axis as the poles of the heaven of the signs.

In each heaven there is contained an eccentric sphere, encompassed by two surfaces with the same center as this sphere, which turns with a regular movement around two fixed poles in the direction in which the signs follow one another. This sphere is called the *deferent orb*.

Between the two surfaces which form the boundary of this orb, there is enclosed a sphere . . . ; this sphere is named, in the case of each planet, for the epicycle of that planet. It moves in a circular path around its own center and two particular poles.

Finally, the substance of each of the three upper planets is set in the substance of its epicycle, and moves with its motion. When the deferent orb is in its motion, the sphere of the epicycle moves at the same time, and its center describes a fictitious circle, which also bears the name of deferent.[2]

[2] Pierre Duhem, *Le système du monde II* (Paris: Hermann, 1914), pp. 122–124. Translated from the French by S. H. Nasr.

B. Planetary Motion

Nearly every Muslim astronomer, especially those concerned with mathematical astronomy, dealt with the problem of planetary motion. Few, however, treated it with such thoroughness and rigor as al-Bīrūnī. We have already had occasion to mention the name of al-Bīrūnī as one of the most universal Muslim scientists and scholars. In astronomy, as well as in physics and history, he made many major contributions. His *Canon of al-Masʿūdī* is the most important Muslim astronomical encyclopedia; it deals with astronomy, astronomical geography, and cartography, and with several branches of mathematics, drawing upon the writings of the Greeks, Indians, Babylonians, and Persians, as well as of earlier Muslim authors, and also upon his own observations and measurements. Had this work been translated into Latin, it would surely have become as famous as the *Canon* of Avicenna. Writing during nearly the same period as Alhazen, al-Bīrūnī described the motion of the planets in the manner of Ptolemy, putting the eccentric and epicyclic system into that very complex form for which medieval astronomy has become famous. This astronomical encyclopedia is the best evidence of the mental processes of the Muslim astronomical scientist, as he was trying to decipher the complex planetary motions in terms of the circles of the Pythagoreans—on the one hand, transforming the abstract geometric figures of the Greeks into concrete spheres, on the other hand preserving the idea of celestial harmony which had profoundly penetrated the spirit of the Greek gnostics, especially those of the school of Pythagoras. Here is al-Bīrūnī's description of the motion of Mercury (Figure 4).

> In order to form a conception of [the motion of] Mercury in terms of what is like it, we place the deferent upon the center *D*, find the diameter *ADHJ*, and divide *DH* into three equal parts by *KṬ*. We draw the circle *DḤṬ* upon the center *K* with the radius *KṬ*, this circle being the deferent for the center of the deferent circle. We say that the motion of Mercury is like that of the Moon in that it [the deferent] has no permanent position but moves discontinuously by reason of the motion of its center upon the circumference of the circle *DḤṬ*, thus making a complete revolution in one year.

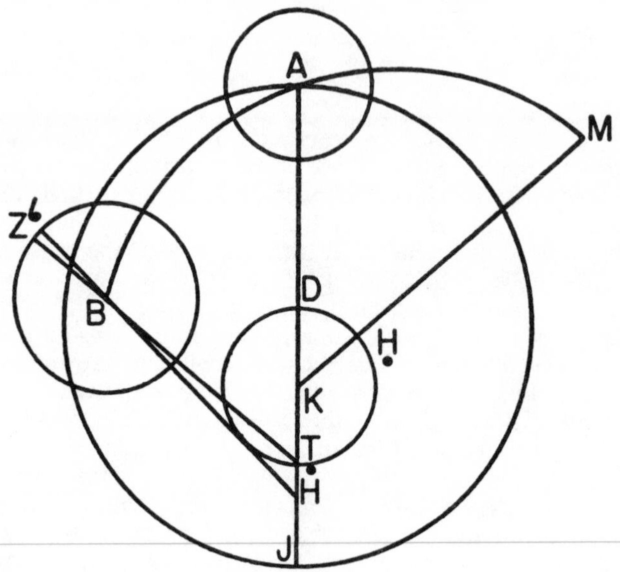

FIGURE 4.

Let us suppose that the center of the epicycle is at *A*, when the center of the deferent is at *D*. Then, as the center moves through *ḤD*, the location of the deferent goes through *MB*. The center of the epicycle moves about it [the deferent] continuously in a motion equal to its motion, so that they both make their revolution in the same period of time. During this time, while the center of the deferent has gone through the arc *DḤ*, the center of the epicycle has reached point *B*. It is clear that it reaches the apogee *M* when line *KM* coincides with line *KḤ*, which event occurs in half a year. To reach the perigee, half of each half of *AJ* and *JA* is needed, so that the center of the epicycle of the Moon reaches the apogee of the deferent in twice the ratio. The epicyclic motion of Mercury, however, is not at the middle of the center of the deferent, but rather at point *Ṭ* which is between points *K* and *H*.

We find the line *ṬBZ* and *HB*ʿ so that the mean is at *Z* and the point of vision at ʿ. In order for the above-mentioned motions to be equal, angles *DKḤ* and *AṬB* must be equal. These two angles are the mean longitude, the angle *AHB* is the average longitude and the angle *ṬBH* the adjustment of the longitude, more specifically the angle to be shared between them [the above angles]. The point *Ṭ*, which is to keep the orbit of Mercury even, is located between *H*, the center of the heaven of the signs of the Zodiac [the heaven of fixed stars], and *K*, the center of the [circle which is itself the] deferent for the center of the deferent circle, just as the center of the deferent for the four planets [Mars, Jupiter, Saturn and Venus] is located between *H* the center of the heaven of the signs of the Zodiac, and the point where the orbit is even.

From what we have said it becomes clear from the existence of this characteristic motion of the planets with regard to the motion of the Sun, that the center of the epicycle of each one of the inferior planets accompanies the Sun, and that they [the planets] cannot move farther away from the Sun, in any direction, than the radius of their epicycles. It has also become clear that the motion of each of the upper planets about its epicycle is equal to the sum of two motions—that of its own epicycle and that of the Sun—so that this motion forces their constant immersion [of these planets] behind the apex [the disappearance of the superior planets because of their nearness to the Sun]. It is possible for the planet to be located at any spherical dimension with respect to the Sun, because of the closeness of the motion of the center of the epicycle to the motion of the Sun, until it reaches the Sun, passes it by and then returns toward it. It is this motion [of the planets] in the heavens that brings about the harmony of the cosmos, without its Sustainer being evident.

This motion appears to be accidental, because of our own vision of it. And it is for this reason that if it were to happen [by accident] that the center of the heaven of the apogee of the Sun *Z* were to be placed upon a line crossing *H*, the center of the heaven of the signs of the Zodiac, and *Ṭ*, the point of the evenness of the orbit, and then the center of the epicycle were to be placed at *A* (the apogee) or *J* (the perigee), the planet would become immersed at the apex *K* upon reaching the line which is the limit of the position of the mean Sun with regard to it. Likewise, for one of the lower planets, the point *M* would become the place of immersion, while for one of the upper planets, it would be the place of opposition to the position of the mean Sun. The apogee of the Sun, however, does not coincide with the apogee of any of the planets.[3]

[3] Al-Bīrūnī, *Qānūn al-Masʿūdī* (Hyderabad: Dairat ʾul-Maʿarif-il-Osmānia, 1956), III, pp. 1163–1166. Translated by S. H. Nasr.

C. The Distance and Size of the Planets

Another question which occupied a central position in Muslim astronomy was the size of the cosmos and the planets. Of the several attempts made by Muslim astronomers to give the distance and size of the planets, none became as well known as that of al-Farghānī, the third/ninth-century astronomer from Transoxiana. His *Elements of Astronomy* was translated into Latin, and the distances given in it became universally accepted in the West up to the time of Copernicus. In determining the distances of the planets, al-Farghānī followed the theory that there is no "wasted space" in the universe—that is, that the apogee of one planet is tangent to the perigee of the next. As al-Farghānī writes, in the *Elements of Astronomy:*

> After having enumerated the stars according to their diverse orders, we now give the measurements of their distances to the Earth. In his book, Ptolemy has given us only the distances of the Sun and the Moon to the Earth; we do not find him speaking, however, about the distance of the other stars. He was satisfied with saying what we have already said, regarding the distances from the centers of the orbits to the center of the Earth, and the magnitudes of the orders of revolution (of the epicycles). Having assumed that the greatest distance from the Earth to the two circles of the Moon—i.e., to the eccentric and the epicycle—was equal to the least distance from Mercury to the Earth, we used the relation that we had determined, and went on to repeat the same operation for Venus and Mercury. We found that the greatest distance from the Earth to the two orbits of Venus coincided with the shortest distance from the Sun, as determined by Ptolemy. We have determined in that way that there is no void between the heavens. We have subsequently performed the same operation for the other stars until we reached the heaven of the fixed stars, whose center is the center of the Earth.[4]

We outline below the table of planetary distances and sizes given by al-Farghānī and compare them with those calculated by modern astronomers, so as to give an idea of the dimensions of the finite and limited cosmos of the medieval world, by comparison with those found in the modern conception of the planetary system. The distances which al-

[4] Duhem, *op. cit.*, p. 45.

Farghānī gives for the apogee and perigee of each planet in the epicyclic system correspond to the eccentricities of the ellipses in modern astronomy.

	Al-Farghānī's determination in millions of English miles[5]			Modern determination in millions of English miles		
Planet	*perigee*	*apogee*	*volume in ratio to Earth's*	*closest*	*farthest*	*volume in ratio to Earth's*
MOON	.134	.256	.026	.221	.252	.0204
MERCURY	.256	.666	.000031	50.	136.	.055
VENUS	.666	4.47	.027	26.	160.	.87
SUN	4.47	4.47	166.	91.4	94.4	1300000.
MARS	4.47	35.4	1.63	35.	234.	.14
JUPITER	35.4	57.5	95.	370.	580.	1355.
SATURN	57.5	80.2	90.	744.	1028.	800.

5 *Ibid.*, p. 49. Duhem has followed al-Farghānī and given distances in terms of the Earth's radii. For the value of the radius of the Earth, he gives 3,250 Arabic miles—which, according to Nallino, the foremost Western authority on Islamic astronomy, is equal to about 6,410,000 meters or 3,990 English miles. Here, they have been converted into miles.

CHAPTER SEVEN

MEDICINE

ISLAMIC MEDICINE is one of the most famous and best known facets of Islamic civilization, being one of the branches of science in which the Muslims most excelled. Not only during the Middle Ages were the Muslim physicians studied seriously in the West, but even during the Renaissance and the eleventh/seventeenth century their teachings continued to carry weight in Western medical circles. It was in fact only a century ago that the study of Islamic medicine was completely omitted from the curriculum of medical schools throughout the Occidental world. In the East, despite the rapid spread of Western medical education, Islamic medicine continues to be studied and practiced, and is far from being merely of historical interest.

This school of medicine, which came into being early in the history of Islam, is of great significance not only for its intrinsic value, but also because it has always been closely allied with the other sciences, and especially with philosophy. The wise man or *ḥakīm,* who has been throughout Islam's history the central figure in the propagation and transmission of the sciences, has usually also been a physician. The relationship between the two is in fact so close that both the sage and the physician are called *ḥakīm;* many of the best-known philosophers and scientists in Islam, such as Avicenna and Averroes, were also physicians, and made their livelihood through the practice of the medical art. (The same thing holds true, incidentally, for the Jewish philosophers, such as Maimonides who, besides being a great thinker, was also the physician to Saladin.)

This close relationship between the philosopher-sage and the physician had much influence upon the position which the practitioner of the medical art occupied in Islamic society, and the conception that the community had of him. The physician was in general expected to be a man of virtuous character, who combined scientific acumen with moral qualities, and whose intellectual power was never divorced from deep religious faith and reliance upon God. In his *Four Discourses,* which is one of the most reliable sources for the scientific and literary activities in medieval Islam, Niẓāmī-i ʿArūḍī of Samarkand, who flourished in the sixth/twelfth century, describes what was expected of the physician in the following terms:

> The physician should be of tender disposition and wise nature, excelling in acumen, this being a nimbleness of mind in forming correct views, that is to say a rapid transition to the unknown from the known. And no physician can be of tender disposition if he fails to recognize the nobility of the human soul; nor of wise nature unless he is acquainted with Logic, nor can he excel in acumen unless he be strengthened by God's aid; and he who is not acute in conjecture will not arrive at a correct understanding of any ailment, for he must derive his indications from the pulse, which has a systole, a diastole, and a pause intervening between these two movements.
>
> Now here there is a difference of opinion amongst physicians, one school maintaining that it is impossible by palpation to gauge the movement of contraction; but that most accomplished of the moderns, that Proof of the Truth Abū ʿAli al-Ḥusayn ibn ʿAbduʾllāh ibn Sīnā (Avicenna), says in his book the *Qānūn* that the movement of contraction also can be gauged, though with difficulty, in thin subjects. Moreover the pulse is of ten sorts, each of which is divided into three subordinate varieties, namely its two extremes and its mean; but, unless the Divine guidance assist the physician in his search for the truth, his thought will not hit the mark. So also in the inspection of the urine, the observing of its colours and sediments, and the deducing of some special condition from each colour are no easy matters; for all these indications depend on Divine help and Royal patronage. This quality [of discernment] is that which we have indicated under the name of acumen. And unless the physician knows Logic, and understands the meaning of genus and species, he cannot discriminate between that which appertains to the category, that which is peculiar to the individual, and that which is accidental, and so will not recognize the cause [of the disease]. And, failing to recognize the cause, he cannot succeed in his treatment. But let us now give an illustration, so that it may be known that it is as we say. Disease is the genus; fever, headache, cold,

delirium, measles and jaundice are the species, each of which is distinguished from the others by a diagnostic sign, and in turn itself constitutes a genus. For example, "Fever" is the genus, wherein quotidian, tertian, double tertian and quartan are the species, each of which is distinguished from the other by a special diagnostic sign. Thus, for instance, quotidian is distinguished from other fevers by the fact that the longest period thereof is a day and a night, and that in it there is no languor, heaviness, lassitude, nor pain. Again inflammatory fever is distinguished from other fevers by the fact that when it attacks it does not abate for several days; while tertian is distinguished by the fact that it comes one day and not the next; and double tertian by this, that one day it comes with a higher temperature and a shorter interval, and another day in a milder form with a longer interval; while lastly quartan is distinguished by the fact that it attacks one day, does not recur on the second and third days, but comes again on the fourth. Each of these in turn becomes a genus comprising several species; and if the physician be versed in Logic and possessed of acumen and knows which fever it is, what the *materies morbi* is, and whether it is simple or compound, he can then at once proceed to treat it. But if he fail to recognize the disease, then let him turn to God and seek help from Him; and so likewise, if he fail in his treatment, let him have recourse to God and seek help from Him, seeing that all issues are in His hands.[1]

Despite the high position that the physician occupied, and the dignity in which his office was held, it must not be thought that everyone in the Islamic world had complete faith in the medical art. Many, especially among the Arabs, continued to be distrustful of this art (which had been, after all, adopted from foreign sources), and remained skeptical of the power of the physician to cure the illnesses of the body. The following poem, composed in 243/857 upon the death of Yuḥannā ibn Māsawaih who was one of the most famous among the early physicians in Islam, bears testimony to the skepticism of many who refused to take the claims of the doctors seriously:

Verily the physician, with his physic and his drugs,
Cannot avert a summons that hath come.

[1] From Niẓāmī-i ʿArūḍī, *Chahār Maqāla,* translated by E. G. Browne (E. J. W. Gibb Memorial Series, Vol. XI, 2. London: Luzac and Co., 1921), pp. 76–77.

What ails the physician that he dies of the disease
Which he used to cure in time gone by?
There died alike he who administered the drug, and he who took the drug,
And he who imported and sold the drug, and he who bought it.[2]

In opposition to such a skeptical view, however, there were also those who eagerly accepted the claims of the medical art, and had respect for its practitioners. Even among the Arabs themselves, who during the early centuries were usually less favorably inclined toward this art than were the Persians, Christians, or Jews, medicine became integrated into the texture of their language. They began to speak of it in their daily life, and soon created an excellent technical vocabulary for terms of Greek, and also of Pahlavi and Sanskrit origin, which greatly facilitated the study of medicine in Arabic. The concern with various medical questions in daily life became in fact so great that many Arab poets wrote verses about medical subjects. The beautiful poem on fever by al-Mutanabbī, the celebrated Arab poet, who was attacked by fever in Egypt in 348/960, bears testimony to the penetration of medical ideas into Islamic culture. Comparing fever to a young woman who visits the poet only under the cover of night, al-Mutanabbī writes:

And it is as though she who visits me were filled with modesty,
For she does not pay her visits save under cover of darkness.
I freely offered her my linen and my pillows,
But she refused them, and spent the night in my bones.
My skin is too contracted to contain both my breath and her,
So she relaxes it with all sorts of sickness.
When she leaves me, she washes me [with perspiration]
As though we had retired apart for some forbidden action.
It is as though the morning drives her away,
And her lachrymal ducts are flooded in their four channels.
I watch for her time [of arrival] without desire,
Yet with the watchfulness of the eager lover.
And she is ever faithful to her appointed time, but faithfulness is an evil
When it casts thee into grievous sufferings.[3]

[2] E. G. Browne, *Arabian Medicine* (London: Cambridge University Press, 1921), p. 8.
[3] *Ibid.*, p. 31.

A. The Historical Background of Islamic Medicine

Islamic medicine came into being as a result of the integration of the Hippocratic and Galenic traditions of Greek medicine with the theories and practices of the Persians and Indians, within the general context of Islam. It is therefore synthetic in nature, combining the observational and concrete approach of the Hippocratic school with the theoretical and philosophical method of Galen, and adding to the already vast storehouse of Greek medical knowledge the theories and experiences of the Persian and Indian physicians, especially in pharmacology. Furthermore, Islamic medicine remained for the most part closely allied to alchemy, seeking—as did Hermetic and Stoic physics—the concrete causes for individual phenomena rather than the general causes sought by the Peripatetic "natural philosophy." In this manner, it also retained its ties with numerical and astrological symbolism, which had already become an important element of Alexandrian Hermeticism before the rise of Islam.

1. JUNDISHAPUR

The link between Islamic medicine and the older schools is to be found in the school of Jundishapur, which must be regarded as the most vital organic connection between the Islamic and earlier traditions of medicine. Jundishapur, whose site lies near the present Persian city of Ahwaz, has an ancient history, reaching back to prehistoric times when it was called Genta Shapirta, or "The Beautiful Garden." The city was refounded at the end of the third century by Shāpūr I, the second Sassanid king, shortly after he defeated the Byzantine emperor Valerian and conquered Antioch. The Persian monarch sought to make the city a center of learning to rival and even surpass Antioch, and therefore named it *Veh-az-Andev-i Shāpūr,* that is, "Shāpūr's better than Antioch." The name "Jundishapur," by which the city became famous during the Islamic period, is most likely a simplification of the name given to it by Shāpūr, while at the same time it resembles the earlier name mentioned above.

Jundishapur rapidly became a major center of learning, especially of Hippocratic medicine. It became further strengthened after A.D. 489, when the school of Edessa was closed by order of the Byzantine emperor, and its physicians took refuge in that city. Shāpūr II enlarged Jundishapur and founded a regular university there, in which several schools of medicine met. It was here that Nestorian physicians taught and practiced Greek medicine, while Zoroastrian ideas and the local Persian medical practice continued to exert much influence; it was also here that the last philosophers and scientists of Athens took refuge when, in A.D. 529, Justinian ordered the school of Athens to be closed.

Moreover, the influence of Indian medicine gradually began to make itself felt in Jundishapur, especially during the sixth century, under the reign of Anūshīrawān the Just, who sent his vizier Burzūyah (or "Perzoes") to India to learn the sciences of the Indians. Burzūyah brought back to Persia not only the *Fables of Bidpai,* but also a knowledge of Indian medicine, along with several Indian physicians. A book titled *Wisdom of the Indians,* translated from Arabic into Greek by Simeon of Antioch in 462/1070, is ascribed to him.

The interest of Burzūyah in Indian medicine, which was to play such an important role in its introduction into Persia, is mentioned in the preface to the *Fables of Bidpai,* which contains the autobiography of this Sassanid vizier.

> My father [writes Burzūyah] belonged to the soldier class; my mother was the daughter of a family of distinguished priests. One of the first favours that God gave to me was that I was the favourite child and that I received a better education than my brothers. My parents sent me when I was seven to an elementary school. As soon as I could write well, I returned thanks to my parents. Then I took up science. The first branch of science that attracted me was Medicine. It interested me so much because I knew how excellent it was. The more I learnt of it, the more I liked it and the more eagerly I studied it. As soon as I had reached such a degree of proficiency that I could think of treating patients, I began to deliberate within myself. For I observed that there were four things to which men aspire. Which of these ought I to aim at—money, prosperity, fame, or a heavenly reward? What decided my choice was the observation that all intelligent persons praise Medicine and that no Religion condemns it. I also used to read in medical books that the best doctor is the one who gives himself over to his profession and only seeks a reward in the hereafter. So I determined to follow this lead and to aim at no earthly gain lest

I be like a merchant who sells for a valueless bauble a ruby by which he might have gained all the riches of the world.

I also read in the works of the ancients that if a physician aspire to gain through his art a reward in the hereafter, he will nevertheless not lose his share in this world's goods. Thus he resembles a sower who carefully scatters his barley grain in his field and for whom there springs up together with the barley all sorts of useful herbs.

So then, with the hope of a reward in the hereafter I set to work to treat the sick. I exerted myself in the treatment of patients whom I expected to cure. And no less did I strive in those cases where I could not hope to effect a cure. In such cases I tried at the least to make their sufferings more bearable. Whenever I could I used to attend in person to my cases. When this was impossible, I would write out for them the necessary prescriptions and give them medicines. From no one whom I treated did I demand any fee or any sort of reward. And none of my colleagues did I envy who equalled me in knowledge and surpassed me in fame or fortune, if he was lax in his standards of honesty or in word or deed.[4]

The school of Jundishapur thus became the meeting ground for Greek, Persian and Indian medicine. Its activities continued to expand, and there, in a cosmopolitan and free atmosphere, a new school came into being, which was a synthesis of the various medical traditions. The school of Jundishapur was at the height of its career at the beginning of the Islamic era, and flourished well into the Abbasid period, when its physicians were slowly brought to Baghdad. As late as the eighth/fourteenth century, Muslim travelers and geographers spoke of the city as a prosperous one, even though its scientific activity had already been transferred elsewhere. And today, on the site of the old city, there stands the village of Shahabad, which bears testimony to the existence of a once thriving metropolis, the seat for several centuries of the most important medical center of Western Asia, and the most direct bridge between Islamic and pre-Islamic medicine.

[4] From the *Fables of Bidpai* in C. E. Elgood, *A Medical History of Persia and the Eastern Caliphate from the Earliest Times to the Year A.D. 1932* (London: Cambridge University Press, 1951), pp. 52–53. This book contains an excellent history of medicine in the eastern lands of Islam, and especially of the school of Jundishapur, which I have used extensively in writing this section.

2. THE ALEXANDRIAN SCHOOL

At the beginning of the Islamic period, Greek medicine continued to be practiced in Alexandria, once the greatest center of Hellenistic science. This school, which combined Egyptian theories and practices with those of the Greeks, had ceased to produce any outstanding medical figures for some time before the advent of Islam; as far as practice was concerned, however, there seems to be every indication that Hellenistic medicine was still alive when the Muslims conquered Egypt in the first/seventh century. In this connection, traditional Islamic sources speak particularly of John the Grammarian, a Jacobite bishop of Alexandria, who was held in high esteem by ʿAmr ibn al-ʿĀṣ, the conqueror of Egypt. (This John must not, however, be confused with the philosopher John Philoponus, who is also called "the Grammarian." The latter, whose criticism of certain theses of the Aristotelian theory of motion was well known to the Muslim philosophers, flourished a century earlier; he is not particularly famous for medical knowledge.)

Whatever may have been the extent of the vitality of Graeco-Egyptian medical practice in Alexandria, there is no doubt that, through the physicians of that city, and also through the medical works, which still survived in its libraries, the Muslims made some acquaintance with Greek medicine. Many of the most frequently cited Greek authorities—such as Hippocrates, Galen, Rufus of Ephesus, Paul of Aegina, and Dioscorides—as far as *materia medica* was concerned—probably became first known to the Muslims through Alexandria. Moreover, the well-authenticated accounts of the Umayyad prince, Khālid ibn Yazīd, who went to Alexandria to master alchemy, and who was responsible for the first translations of Greek texts into Arabic, bear witness to the existence of some kind of tradition of learning in Alexandria at that time, although it is certain that whatever survived in that period could not in any way compare with the school of a few centuries earlier. Similarly, the famous library of Alexandria whose burning has been erroneously attributed by many Western scholars to the caliph, ʿUmar, had been for the most part destroyed long before the advent of Islam. In any case, there is little doubt that the Muslims made some kind of contact with Greek medicine in Alexandria, although this contact was of much less significance than that made at Jundishapur, where the medical school was at the height of its activity during the early Islamic period.

3. MEDICINE OF THE PROPHET

The Arabs who, under the banner of Islam, conquered both Alexandria and Jundishapur and thus gained mastery over the main centers of science and medicine, also had a simple medicine of their own, which did not undergo any immediate change with the coming of Islam, but had to wait until the second/eighth century to become transformed by Greek medicine. The first Arab physician whose name is recorded by later chronicles is al-Ḥārith ibn Kaladah, who was a contemporary of the Prophet, and had studied medicine at Jundishapur. The Arabs of his day, however, remained for the most part skeptical about this foreign form of medicine. Of much greater significance to them were the sayings of the Prophet with regard to medicine, hygiene, diet, etc., which they heartily accepted and followed, with all the ardent faith that characterized the early Muslim generations.

Islam, as a guide for all facets of human life, had also to concern itself with the more general principles of medicine and hygiene. There are several verses of the Quran in which medical questions of a very general order are discussed; there are also many sayings of the Prophet dealing with health, sickness, hygiene, and other questions pertaining to the field of medicine. Such diseases as leprosy, pleurisy, and ophthalmia are mentioned; remedies such as cupping, cautery and the use of honey are proposed. This body of sayings on medical questions was systematized by later Muslim writers, and became known as *Medicine of the Prophet (Ṭibb al-Nabī).* The beginning of the fourth volume of the collection of prophetic traditions of Bukhārī which is one of the most authoritative sources of its kind, consists of two books in which are collected, in 80 chapters, the sayings about illness, its treatment, the sick, etc. There are also other medical books of a religious nature, especially the medical work attributed to the sixth Shiite imam, Jaʿfar al-Ṣādiq.

Since all the sayings of the Prophet are guideposts for the life of the devout Muslim, these latter sayings, even though they do not contain an explicit system of medicine, have played a major role in determining the general atmosphere in which Islamic medicine has come to be practiced. Their guidance has been followed over the centuries by every succeeding generation of Muslims; they have determined many of the Muslims' dietary and hygienic habits. Moreover, *The Medicine of the Prophet* became the first book to be studied by a medical student, before he undertook the task of mastering the usual compendia of medical science. It has thus always played an important role in creating the frame of mind with which the future physician has undertaken the study of medicine.

THE TRANSLATORS AND THE BEGINNINGS OF ISLAMIC MEDICINE

The first direct influence of Jundishapur in Islamic circles occurred in 148/765, when the second Abbasid caliph, the founder of the city of Baghdad, al-Manṣūr, who had been suffering from dyspepsia for many years, sought the aid of the physicians of Jundishapur. For some time, the hospital and medical center of that city had been headed by Jirjīs Bukhtyishūʿ (a Syriac name, meaning "Jesus has saved"), the first famous physician of a family which was to become one of the most important medical families in the Muslim world, whose members continued to be prominent physicians as late as the fifth/eleventh century. The reputation of Jirjīs as a competent doctor had already reached the ears of the caliph, who asked that this Christian physician be brought to his court. The successful treatment of the caliph by Jirjīs was the beginning of a process which eventually transferred the medical center of Jundishapur to Baghdad, and laid the groundwork for the appearance of the first well-known Muslim physicians. Toward the end of his life, Jirjīs returned to Jundishapur to die in the native city of his ancestors. His students, as well as his descendants, however, went back to Baghdad, thus forming the organic link between this school and the first medical centers in the Abbasid capital.

Another medical family which originated in Jundishapur and later came to Baghdad, and which matches the Bukhtyishūʿ family in importance, is that of Māsawaih (or Māsūyah, in its Persian pronunciation). The head of this family, Māsawaih, was an uneducated physician and pharmacologist, who spent thirty years gaining medical experience in the dispensary of the hospital at Jundishapur. When he was forced to resign, he went to Baghdad to seek his fortune in that thriving capital. Here, he became a celebrated ophthalmologist, and the private physician of the vizier of Hārūn al-

Rashīd. His three sons became physicians also; among them, Yuḥannā ibn Māsawaih (the Latin "Mesue Senior" or "Janus Damascus") must be regarded as one of the important physicians of this period. Ibn Māsawaih, the author of the first ophthalmological treatise in Arabic, became the most celebrated physician of his day. His sharp tongue, rebellious nature, and skepticism toward Christianity—to which he formally adhered—created many enemies against him, but he succeeded, through his unrivaled mastery of the medical art, in preserving his eminent position until his death in 243/857.

The medieval West also knew another figure by the name of Mesue (called "Junior," to distinguish him from the older Mesue). Although the pharmacological and medical works attributed to Mesue Junior—such as the *Grabadin*—were among the most widely read works of their kind in the Latin world, little is known of the real identity of this figure, whom the medieval Latinists referred to as *pharmacopoeorum evangelista.* John Leo the African writes that he was born in a village in Iraq called Marind, and is therefore named Māsawaih al-Mārindī. Some modern scholars have even doubted his existence; others, such as C. Elgood, whose masterly study of Islamic medicine marks him as one of the most competent authorities in this field, believe that he may have been the same person as Mesue Senior. Whatever the origin of this figure, his work at least, added to those of Mesue Senior, have helped to make the name of Mesue among the most famous in the Western image of Islamic medicine.

The early translators of medical texts into Arabic, like the early physicians, were mostly Christians and Jews. The first translation known to be made into Arabic appears in the *Pandects* of an Alexandrian priest named Ahrūn; it was made by a Jewish scholar from Basra known to the Occident as Masarjoyah, who lived during the Umayyad period. This work has been held in high esteem by most of the later medical authorities, and the name of this first translator of medical texts became famous in later works on medical history.

The interest in Greek learning, which had been gradually rising during the latter part of the Umayyad rule, assumed unprecedented proportions during the Abbasid period when, as we have seen in a previous chapter, a concerted effort was made on the part of the government and of influential individuals to have translations made into Arabic. During the early years of Abbasid rule, Ibn Muqaffaʿ began his translations of medical texts from Pahlavi into Arabic, to be followed a generation later by Mesue Senior. Especially important among the private patrons of this movement were the members of the Barmacid family, who were the viziers of the Abbasids. It was Yaḥyā, the Barmacid, who engaged the Indian physician Mikna to translate works on Indian medicine into Arabic; one of them, named *Sarat,* still survives.

The greatest of all the translators of this period, however, was Ḥunain ibn Isḥāq, or Johannitus Onan, as the medieval West knew him. Ḥunain was not only a very competent translator; he was also one of the outstanding physicians of his day. His medical pursuits took him to Jundishapur, where he studied with Ibn Māsawaih. The latter was, however, disappointed with him, and tried to discourage him from continuing his medical studies. Without losing heart, he went on to master the subject, and to become one of the important figures in the formation of the Islamic sciences at this time.

Aided by his nephew Ḥubaish and his son Isḥāq, Ḥunain often translated texts from Greek into Syriac, leaving the translation from Syriac into Arabic to his students, and especially to Ḥubaish. At those times, he would check the final translation, and compare it with the original Greek himself. At other times, he would translate directly from Greek into Arabic. In this way, Ḥunain and his school made a large number of excellent translations, including 95 works of Galen into Syriac, and 99 into Arabic. There were other famous translators, such as Thābit ibn Qurrah, mathematician from Harran or Hellenopolis, who also translated and wrote several medical works, of which the *Treasury* is the best known. Yet none of these figures can match Ḥunain, whose mastery as both translator and physician entitles him to be regarded as one of the basic figures of the history of Islamic medicine.

B. *Medicine during the Early Centuries*

With medical texts of Greek, Pahlavi, and Sanskrit origin translated into Arabic, and a sound technical vocabulary firmly established, the ground was prepared for the appearance of those few giants whose works have dominated Islamic medicine ever since. The author of the first major work of Islamic medicine was ʿAlī ibn Rabbān al-Ṭabarī, a convert to Islam, who wrote his *Paradise of Wisdom (Firdaus al-ḥikmah)* in 236/850. The author, who was also the teacher of Rhazes, drew mainly upon the teachings of Hippocrates and Galen, and also upon Ibn Māsawaih and Ḥunain. In 360 chapters, he summarized the various branches of medicine, devoting the last discourse, which consists of 36 chapters, to a study of Indian medicine. The work, the first large compendium of its kind in Islam, is of particular value in the fields of pathology, pharmacology, and diet, and clearly displays the synthetic nature of this new school of medicine, now coming into being.

Al-Ṭabarī's student, Rhazes, was without doubt the greatest clinical and observational physician of Islam, and along with Avicenna, the most influential, both East and West. We shall have occasion to discuss him further in the later chapter on alchemy; here we concern ourselves with his medical achievements, the major cause for his fame. Attracted late in life to medicine, Rhazes became the director of the hospital in his native city of Rai, and later the director-in-chief of the main hospital at Baghdad. He thus gained much practical experience, which played no small part in making him the greatest clinician of the medieval period.

The skill of Rhazes in prognosis, and his analysis of the symptoms of a disease, its manner of treatment and cure, have made his case studies celebrated among later physicians. Rhazes himself recorded some of the more unusual cases he encountered during his medical practice; of these, the following is one example:

> Abduʾllāh ibn Sawāda used to suffer from attacks of mixed fever, sometimes quotidian, sometimes tertian, sometimes quartan, and sometimes recurring once in six days. These attacks were preceded by a slight rigor, and micturition was very frequent. I gave it as my opinion that either these accesses of fever would turn into quartan, or that there was ulceration of the kidneys. Only a short time elapsed ere the patient passed pus in his urine. I thereupon informed him that these feverish attacks would not recur, and so it was.
>
> The only thing which prevented me at first from giving it as my definite opinion that the patient was suffering from ulceration of the kidneys was that he had previously suffered

from tertian and other mixed types of fever, and this to some extent confirmed my suspicion that this mixed fever might be from inflammatory processes which would tend to become quartan when they waxed stronger.

Moreover the patient did not complain to me that his loins felt like a weight depending from him when he stood up; and I neglected to ask him about this. The frequent micturition also should have strengthened my suspicion of ulceration of the kidneys, but I did not know that his father suffered from weakness of the bladder and was subject to this complaint, and it used likewise to come upon him when he was healthy, and it ought not to be the case henceforth, till the end of his life, if God will.

So when he passed the pus I administered to him diuretics until the urine became free from pus, after which I treated him with terra sigillata, *Boswellia thurifera,* and Dragon's Blood, and his sickness departed from him, and he was quickly and completely cured in about two months. That the ulceration was slight was indicated to me by the fact that he did not complain to me at first of weight in the loins. After he had passed pus, however, I enquired of him whether he had experienced this symptom, and he replied in the affirmative. Had the ulceration been extensive, he would of his own accord have complained of this symptom. And that the pus was evacuated quickly indicated a limited ulceration. The other physicians whom he consulted besides myself, however, did not understand the case at all, even after the patient had passed pus in his urine.[5]

Another case, in which Rhazes' mastery of treatment by means of psychological shock is well displayed, is described in the *Four Discourses* of Niẓāmī-i ʿArūḍī, and has become famous among later students of medicine. To quote:

Another of the House of Sāmān, Amīr Manṣūr ibn Nūḥ ibn Naṣr, became afflicted with an ailment which grew chronic, and remained established, and the physicians were unable to cure it. So the Amīr Manṣūr sent messengers to summon Muḥammad ibn Zakariyyā ar-Rāzī to treat him. Muḥammad ibn Zakariyyā came as far as the Oxus, but, when he reached its shores and saw it, he said, "I will not embark in the boat, for God Most High saith—*'Do not cast yourselves into peril with your own hands';* and again it is surely a thing remote from wisdom voluntarily to place one's self in so hazardous a position." Ere the Amīr's messenger had gone to Bukhārā

[5] Browne, *Arabian Medicine,* pp. 52–53.

and returned, he had composed the *Kitāb-i-Manṣūrī,* which he sent by the hand of that person, saying, "I am this book, and by this book thou canst attain thine object, so that there is no need of me."

When the book reached the Amīr he was grievously afflicted, wherefore he sent a thousand *dīnārs* and one of his own private horses fully caparisoned, saying, "Show him every kindness, but, if this proves fruitless, bind his hands and feet, place him in the boat, and fetch him across." They did so, but their entreaties moved him not at all. Then they bound his hands and feet, placed him in the boat, and, when they had ferried him across the river released his limbs. Then they brought the led-horse, fully caparisoned, before him, and he mounted in the best of humours, and set out for Bukhārā. So they enquired of him saying, "We feared lest, when we should cross the water and set thee free, thou wouldst cherish enmity against us, but thou didst not so, nor do we see thee annoyed or vexed in heart." He replied, "I know that every year twenty thousand persons cross the Oxus without being drowned, and that I too should probably not be drowned; still, it was possible that I might perish, and if this had happened they would have continued till the Resurrection to say, 'A foolish fellow was Muḥammad ibn Zakariyyā, in that, of his own free will he embarked in a boat and so was drowned.' So should I be one of those who deserve blame, not of those who are held excused."

When he reached Bukhārā, the Amīr came in and they saw one another and he began to treat him, exerting his powers to the utmost, but without relief to the patient. One day he came in before the Amīr and said, "To-morrow I am going to try another method of treatment, but for the carrying out of it you will have to sacrifice such-and-such a horse and such-and-such a mule," the two being animals noted for their speed, so that in one night they would go forty parasangs.

So next day he took the Amīr to the hot bath of Jū-yi-Mūliyān, outside the palace, leaving that horse and mule ready equipped and tightly girt in the charge of his own servant at the door of the bath; while of the King's retinue and attendants he suffered not one to enter the bath. Then he brought the King into the middle chamber of the hot bath, and poured over him tepid water, after which he prepared a draught, tasted it, and gave it to him to drink. And he kept him there till such time as the humours in his joints had undergone coction.

Then he himself went out and put on his clothes, and, [taking a knife in his hand], came in, and stood for a while reviling the King, saying, "O such-and-such, thou didst order thy people to bind and cast me into the boat and to threaten my life. If I do not destroy thee as a punishment for this, I am no true son of [my father] Zakariyyā!"

The Amīr was furious and rose from his place to his knees. Muḥammad ibn Zakariyyā drew a knife and threatened him yet more, until the Amīr, partly from anger, partly from fear, completely rose to his feet. When Muḥammad ibn Zakariyyā saw the Amīr on his feet, he turned round and went out from the bath, and both he and his servant mounted, the one the horse, the other the mule, and turned their faces towards the Oxus. At the time of the afternoon prayer they crossed the river, and halted nowhere till they reached Merv. When Muḥammad ibn Zakariyyā alighted at Merv, he wrote a letter to the Amīr, saying, "May the life of the King be prolonged in health of body and effective command! I your servant undertook the treatment and did all that was possible. There was, however, an extreme failure in the natural caloric, and the treatment of the disease by ordinary means would have been a protracted affair. I therefore abandoned it in favour of psychical treatment, carried you to the hot bath, administered a draught, and left you so long as to bring about a coction of the humours. Then I angered the King, so as to aid the natural caloric, and it gained strength until those humours, already softened, were dissolved. But henceforth it is not expedient that a meeting should take place between myself and the King."

Now after the Amīr had risen to his feet and Muḥammad ibn Zakariyyā had gone out and ridden off, the Amīr at once fainted. When he came to himself he went forth from the bath and called to his servants, saying, "Where has the physician gone?" They answered, "He came out from the bath, and mounted the horse, while his attendant mounted the mule, and went off."

Then the Amīr knew what object he had had in view. So he came forth on his own feet from the hot bath; and tidings of this ran through the city. Then he gave audience, and his servants and retainers and people rejoiced greatly, and gave alms, and offered sacrifices, and held high festival. But they could not find the physician, seek him as they might. And on the seventh day Muḥammad ibn Zakariyyā's servant arrived, riding the mule and leading the horse, and presented the letter. The Amīr read it, and was astonished, and excused him, and sent him an honorarium consisting of a horse fully caparisoned, a cloak, turban and arms, and a slave-boy and a handmaiden; and further commanded that there should be assigned to him in Ray from the estates of al-Maʾmūn a yearly allowance of two thousand *dīnārs* in gold and two hundred ass-loads of corn. This honorarium and pension-warrant he forwarded to him at

Merv by the hand of a man of note. So the Amīr completely regained his health, and Muḥammad ibn Zakariyyā attained his object.[6]

Rhazes was also well versed in anatomy in which he, like other Muslim physicians, continued the tradition of Galen. The following passages from *The Book of al-Manṣūr* give a fair picture of anatomical knowledge among Muslim physicians.

CHAPTER FIVE
ON VEINS

All the veins commence from the convex side of the liver, the liver being concave from the inner side and convex from the outer. From the convex side a large vein rises up. When this vein in rising has traversed only a short distance, it becomes divided into two portions, of which the one that is larger turns toward the lower parts of the body in order to water all the members of the body it encounters there. The other portion heads for the higher parts in order to water the upper members of the body.

This upper portion follows its course until it comes close to the diaphragm. There, two veins are detached from it which are distributed in the diaphragm in order to nourish it. Then it passes by the diaphragm; when it has passed it, slender veins are detached from it which reach the membrane that divides the thorax into two parts, and also the envelope of the heart and the gland called "mulberry," and are there distributed. We shall speak of these members later. Then a long branch is detached from it which comes to the right auricle of the heart. This branch is divided into three parts, one of which enters into the right cavity of the heart and is the largest of these parts. The second encircles the heart on the outside and spreads throughout the heart. The third part reaches the lower regions of the thorax and nourishes the members which are found there.

When it has passed the heart, it follows its course in a straight direction until it reaches the level of the clavicles. During this passage, small branches separate from it on each side, which water what is situated near and before them, and from which there issue small branches extending to the outside in order to water the external muscles situated before these internal members. When the vein has reached the level of the arm-pit, a large branch separates from it, which reaches the upper part from the side of the arm-pit. This is called the Basilical vein.

6 Niẓāmī ʿArūḍī, *Chahār Maqāla*, pp. 83–85.

When the vein is at the level of the middle of the two clavicles, at the place of the jugular dimple, it is divided into two parts, one going to the right and the other to the left. Each of these portions is in turn divided into two parts, one of which goes up the shoulder and comes to the upper member from the outside; it is the vein that is called Cephalic. The other is divided into two parts on each side, one of which passes into the depths, rising by the neck until it enters the skull and waters the parts of the brain found there and its membranes. During the passage from the neck until it enters the brain, small branches give off from it which water the interior parts of the neck; this is called the internal jugular vein. The other continues on, rising near the surface to become divided in the face, the head, the eye and the nose and in order to water all these members. It is called the external jugular vein.

During the passage of the shoulder vein in the arm, small branches separate from it to water the external parts of the arm, and from the vein of the arm-pit small branches are detached which water the internal parts of the arm. When the Cephalic and Basilic veins reach near the articulation of the elbow, they become divided; one of the branches of the Cephalic vein joins with one of the branches of the Basilic vein and from these two there forms near the fold of the elbow the vein called the black vein. The second branch of the shoulder vein extends to the external part of the fore-arm and passes after that above the upper *zand* (Radius); it is the vein called the ligament of the fore-arm. One branch of the vein of the arm-pit, the branch that is lowest of all, passes by the interior side of the fore-arm until it reaches the extremity of the lower *zand* (Cubital). From some of these branches the vein is formed which is found between the small finger and the ring-finger and it is the vein called the small salutary vein. . . .

Chapter Six
On Arteries

Arteries originate in the left cavity of the heart. From this cavity there come forth two arteries one of which is smaller than the other. This has only one membrane which besides is thinner than any one of the two membranes of the other arteries. This artery enters into the lungs and is there divided. The other artery [aorta] is much bigger. As soon as this artery shows itself, two branches [the coronaries] separate from it, of which one goes to the right cavity of the two cavities of the heart and is the smaller of the two branches. The other encircles the entire heart, then enters the partition-wall of the heart and spreads there. After that the rest of the artery which originates in the left cavity of the heart, once these two branches are detached from it, is divided into two parts, of which the bigger is directed toward the lower members of the body, while the other is directed toward the upper members.

From the portion that goes toward the upper parts of the body there separate off, during its ascent, on both sides, branches which reach the parts situated before them in order to give them natural heat. When this portion comes to the arm-pit, there issues from it a branch which, accompanying the vein of the arm-pit, goes to the upper members and there becomes divided in the same manner as this vein. Small branches of this artery arrive at the internal and external muscles of the arm. At the same time it passes into the depths and remains hidden, until it comes near the elbow, when it rises in such a way that its beating is perceptible at this point in the case of most bodies. It remains under the vein of the arm-pit, to which it is joined, until in descending it is separated from the elbow. Then it thrusts deeply again and from it five branches become detached and come to the muscles of the fore-arm. Thereupon, it divides into two branches, one of which goes to the wrist, passing by the Radius; that is the tube that physicians feel. The other is directed also toward the wrist, passing by the Cubitus; it is the smaller of the two. The two branches are distributed in the hand and sometimes their beating is perceptible at the dorsal side of the hand.

When this upper portion has reached the jugular dimple, it is divided into two parts, each of which is further divided into two other parts. One of these parts accompanies the internal jugular vein, and it rises upward until it enters the skull. During its passage, branches are detached from it which reach the deep parts found at this point, as we have described in speaking of the veins. Upon entering the skull it becomes divided in a marvellous manner, and forms something called the network, which is extended under the brain. It is a body like that of several networks thrown one upon another. Then, after this artery becomes divided in this network, the divisions become reunited and return [to their previous disposition]. From this network two arteries of equal size come forth, as they were before their division in the network. Then they enter into the substance of the brain and become distributed there. The other of these two parts, which is the smaller, rises to the exterior parts of the face and head, and becomes distributed among the external parts of the face in the same manner as the external jugular vein. The beating of this part is perceptible behind the ear and at the temple, whereas the beating that is perceptible near the two jugular veins is that of the considerable portion that accompanies the deep jugular vein. These two arteries are called the soporific arteries.

Chapter Fourteen
On the Disposition of the Heart

The form of the heart resembles that of a reversed fir-cone whose tip in the form of a cone is turned toward the lower part of the body and whose base is turned toward the upper part. It has an envelope formed of a thick membrane that surrounds it, not attached to the whole heart but only near its base. The heart is placed at the center of the thorax but its point in the form of a cone inclines toward the left side and the great artery originates from the left side. For this reason the beating is perceptible at the left side of the heart. [In the heart there are two ventricles of which one is found] at the right side and the other at the left side. Near its base and its origin there is found something which resembles a cartilage and which is the base for the entire heart and there are passages which lead from the right to the left ventricle. The right ventricle has two orifices. One of these orifices is that by which the vein that originates in the liver enters, and by this orifice it pours the blood into the right ventricle of the heart. On this orifice are found three membranes which close from the [outside to the inside], in order to allow themselves to push back and to yield to what enters the heart. The second orifice is that of the vein which from this cavity comes to the lung. It is a non-beating vein but its walls are thick and heavy. For this reason the anatomists call it the arterial vein [pulmonary artery] because the arteries have a heavier, thicker and harder wall than the veins—and with reason, since they move perpetually during the whole life of man and the rupture of an artery is more dangerous than that of a vein.

On the orifice by which this vein leaves there are found [three] membranes, but they close from the inside to the outside in order to allow themselves to push back and to yield to what leaves the heart. In the left ventricle there are two orifices, one of which is that of the great artery [aorta], from which the arteries of the whole body originate. On its orifice there are [three] membranes which close from the inside to the outside, in order to allow themselves to push back and to yield to the pneuma and the blood that leave the heart. The second orifice is that of the artery which comes to the lungs and by which the air passes from the lungs to the heart. On this orifice there are found two membranes which close from the outside to the inside in order to open up and

> to yield to the air which enters the heart. The heart has two accessory parts similar to ears, one to the right and the other to the left. The lungs cover the heart in order to prevent the bones of the chest from having contact with it from the front.[7]

The work of Rhazes best known in the Western world is his treatise on measles and smallpox which was published in Europe many times, as late as the eighteenth century. Besides this, and many other short treatises on various diseases, Rhazes also composed several large medical works, including his *Compendium, Sufficient,* the greater and the lesser *Introduction, The Guide,* the *Royal* and the *Splendid* books of medicine, as well as *The Book of al-Manṣūr* and *Kitāb al-Ḥāwī (Continens),* which are his two greatest masterpieces.

The *Continens* is the most voluminous medical work ever written in Arabic. It must be regarded as the most basic source for the study of the clinical aspects of Islamic medicine. It was studied avidly in the Western world from the sixth/twelfth to the eleventh/seventeenth century, when Rhazes and Avicenna were held in higher esteem than even Hippocrates and Galen, and it constitutes one of the mainstays of the traditional curriculum of medicine in the Islamic world. The criticism by ʿAlī ibn al-ʿAbbās al-Majūsī, a famous physician of the next generation, affords a fair picture of the strengths and weaknesses of this lengthy masterpiece of Islamic medicine:

> As to his book which is known as *al-Ḥāwī,* I found that he mentions in it everything the knowledge of which is necessary to the medical man, concerning hygiene and medical and dietetical treatment of diseases and their symptoms. He did not neglect the smallest thing required by the student of this art concerning treatment of diseases and illnesses. But he made no mention at all of natural matters, such as the elements, the temperaments and the mixtures of the humours. Nor did he speak of anatomy and surgery. He wrote, moreover, without order and method, neglecting the side of scholastic learning. He omitted to subdivide his book into discourses, sections and chapters, as might have been expected from his vast knowledge of the medical art and from his talent as a writer. Far be it from me to contest his excellence or to deny his knowledge of the medical art or his eminence as an author. Considering this condition or imagining the causes of it by comparison with

[7] From Rhazes, *The Book of al-Manṣūr*. The translation is by S. H. Nasr based on that of P. de Koning in *Trois traités d'anatomies arabes* (Leiden: E. J. Brill, 1903), pp. 37–41; 43–45; 63–65.

> the vast knowledge shown in this book, I think there are two possibilities; either he composed it and collected in it the entire field of Medicine as a special memorandum of reference for himself, comprising hygiene and therapeutics, for his old age and time of forgetfulness: or being afraid of damage which might occur to his library, which was to be made good in this case by the book in question. Likewise in order to relieve his writing from bulkiness and in order to be useful to the people and to create for himself a good memorial for coming generations, he provided reference notes for his entire text, put them in order and compared each one with its like and fitted it in its chapter according to his knowledge of appropriateness in this art. In this way the book should be complete and perfect.
>
> He was, however, prevented from continuing it by hindrances, and death befell him before its completion. If such was his aim, he treated his subject at too great length and made his book too voluminous without any urgent necessity to claim in his favour. This was the reason why most scholars were not able to order and purchase copies of the book, except a few wealthy literary men, and so copies are scarce. He proceeded in such a manner that for every disease, its causes, symptoms and treatment, he mentioned the sayings of every ancient and modern physician on the disease in question from Hippocrates and Galen down to Isḥāq bin Ḥunayn, and all the physicians, ancient and modern, who lived in between them, without omitting the sayings of any one of them and reference to them in this book, so that the entirety of medical literature was comprised in this book. You must know, however, that skilful and experienced physicians agree about the nature of diseases, their causes, symptoms and medical treatment, and that there exists no marked difference between their opinions, except that they treat more or less of the matter and that they speak in different terms, because the rules and the schools they follow in the knowledge of diseases, their causes and treatment, are obviously the same. If this is so, it was not necessary to record the sayings of all the ancient and modern physicians and the reiteration of their utterances, since they all repeat the same things.[8]

As a master of psychosomatic medicine and psychology, Rhazes treated the maladies of the soul along with those of the body and never separated the two completely. He in fact composed a work on the medicine of the soul in which he sought to demonstrate the way to overcome those moral and psychological illnesses which ruin the mind and the body and

[8] From *Continens* in Elgood, *A Medical History of Persia*, pp. 199–201.

upset that total state of health that the physician seeks to preserve. In this book, named *Spiritual Physick* in its English translation, Rhazes devotes twenty chapters to the various ailments that beset the soul and body of man. For example, in the fourteenth chapter he writes:

OF DRUNKENNESS

Chronic and habitual drunkenness is one of the evil dispositions that bring those indulging it to ruin, calamity and all kinds of sickness. This is because the excessive drinker is imminently liable to apoplexy and asphyxia, that filling of the inner heart which induces sudden death, rupture of the arteries of the brain, and stumbling and falling into crevices and wells; not to mention various fevers, bloody clots and bilious swellings in the intestines and principal parts, and delirium tremens and palsy especially if there be a natural weakness of the nerves. Besides all this, drunkenness leads to loss of reason, immodesty, divulging of secrets, and a general incapacity to grasp even the most important mundane and spiritual matters; so that a man will hardly hold on to any cherished purpose or achieve any lasting happiness, but on the contrary he will go on slipping and sliding downwards. It was of such a situation that the poet wrote:

When shall it be within thy power
To grasp the good things God doth shower
Though they be but a span from thee,
If all thy nights in revelry
Be passed, and in the morn thou rise
With fumes of drinking in thine eyes
And, heavy with its wind, ere noon
Returnest to thy drunkard's boon?

In short, drink is one of the most serious constituents of passion, and one of the greatest disorders of the reason. That is because it strengthens the appetitive and choleric souls and sharpens their powers, so that they demand urgently and insistently that the drinker shall embark precipitately upon their favourite course. Drink also weakens the rational soul and stultifies its powers, so that it is scarcely able to undertake careful thought and deliberation but rushes headlong to a decision and liberates action before its energy is firmly established. Hence the rational soul is led on easily and smoothly by the appetitive soul, until it is scarcely able to resist it or deny it anything. This is the sign of a departure from rationality, and of enrolment in the order of beasts.

It therefore behoves the intelligent man to beware of drink, and to keep it in its proper place, namely that which is here indicated, fearing it as he would fear one who aims to rob him of his most prized and precious possessions. If he touches drink at all, he should do so only when anxiety and care oppress and overwhelm him. Moreover his purpose and intention should be not to seek pleasure for its own sake and to follow it wherever it may lead, but to reject superfluous pleasure and to indulge only so much as he is confident will not mischief him and upset his constitution. He should call to mind in this and similar situations our remarks on the suppression of passion, keeping before him a picture of these overall observations and general principles so that he may not need to remember them again and repeat them. In particular he should recall our statement that the constant and assiduous indulgence of pleasure diminishes our enjoyment thereof, reducing that to the position of something necessary for the maintenance of life.

This idea is almost more valid when applied to the pleasure of drunkenness than in the case of any other pleasure; that is because the drunkard reaches a stage where he cannot conceive of living without drink, while sobriety is to him just like the state of a man beset by pressing cares. Moreover drunkenness is not less insatiable than greed; indeed it is even very much more insatiable; one must accordingly be equally swift to grapple with it and equally strenuous in reining and denying it.[9]

The contributions of Rhazes to medicine and pharmacology as contained in his many medical writings—of which al-Bīrūnī mentions 56—are numerous. He was the first to identify several important diseases, such as smallpox, and to treat them successfully. To him is generally credited the isolation and use of alcohol as an antiseptic, and the first use of mercury as a purgative, which became known in the Middle Ages as "Album Rhasis." Although criticized vehemently by both Sunni and Shia alike for his "anti-prophetic" philosophy, his medical views became the undisputed authority wherever medicine was studied and taught; he came to exercise more influence upon Latin science than any of the Muslim thinkers, if we exclude Avicenna and Averroes, whose great influence, however, was in the field of philosophy.

9 Rhazes, *The Spiritual Physick of Rhazes*, translated by A. J. Arberry in the Wisdom of the East Series (London: John Murray, 1950), pp. 78–80.

After Rhazes, the most outstanding physician, whose writings have been of universal import, was ʿAlī ibn al-ʿAbbās al-Majūsī (the Latin "Haly Abbas"). As his name indicates, he was of Zoroastrian descent (Majūsī meaning "Zoroastrian"), but was himself a Muslim. Although little is known of his life, one can conclude from the dates of some of his contemporaries that he flourished during the second half of the fourth/tenth century, dying around 385/995, and that he hailed from Ahwaz near Jundishapur. Haly Abbas is best known for his *Kāmil al-ṣināʿah (The Perfection of the Art)* or *Kitāb al-malikī (The Royal Book* or *Liber Regius),* which is one of the best-written medical works in Arabic, and remained a standard text until the works of Avicenna appeared. The *Liber Regius* is of particular interest in that in it Haly Abbas discusses the Greek and Islamic physicians who preceded him, making a frank judgment of their virtues and shortcomings. Haly Abbas has always been regarded as one of the chief authorities on Islamic medicine, and many stories have been recorded, revealing his acumen in treating various diseases. The following is a well-known example:

> The author of the *Kāmiluʾṣ-Ṣināʿat* was physician to ʿAḍuduʾd-Dawla in Pārs, in the city of Shīrāz. Now in that city there was a porter who used to carry loads of four hundred and five hundred maunds on his back. And every five or six months he would be attacked by headache, and become restless, remaining so for ten days or a fortnight. One time he was attacked by this headache, and when seven or eight days had elapsed, and he had several times determined to destroy himself, it finally happened that one day this great physician passed by the door of his house. The porter's brothers ran to meet him, did reverence to him, and, conjuring him by God Most High, told him about their brother's condition and headache. "Show him to me," said the physician. So they brought him before the physician, who saw that he was a big man, of bulky frame, wearing on his feet a pair of shoes each of which weighed a maund and a half. Then the physician felt his pulse and asked for and examined his urine; after which, "Bring him with me into the open country," said he. They did so, and on their arrival there, he bade his servants take the porter's turban from his head, cast it round his neck, and twist it tight. Then he ordered another servant to take the shoes off the porter's feet and strike him twenty blows on the head, which he accordingly did. The porter's sons lamented loudly, but the physician was a man of consequence and consideration, so that they could do nothing. Then the physician ordered his

servant to take hold of the turban which he had twisted round his neck, to mount his horse, and to drag the porter after him round the plain. The servant did as he was bid, and made him run far afield, so that blood began to flow from his nostrils. "Now," said the physician, "let him be." So he was let alone, and there continued to flow from him blood stinking worse than carrion. The man fell asleep amidst the blood which flowed from his nose, and three hundred *dirhams*' weight of blood escaped from his nostrils ere the haemorrhage ceased. They then lifted him up and bore him thence to his house, and he never woke, but slept for a day and a night and his headache passed away and never again returned or required treatment.

Then ʿAḍuduʾd-Dawla questioned the physician as to the rationale of this treatment. "O King," he replied, "that blood in his brain was not a matter which could be eliminated by an aperient of aloes, and there was no other method of treatment than that which I adopted."[10]

The works of Haly Abbas, as well as those of most of the other early physicians in Islam, were overshadowed by those of Avicenna, the most influential of all Muslim physicians and philosophers, who for many centuries held the title of "Prince of Physicians" in the Occident, and who dominates Islamic medicine to this day in the East. The name of Avicenna and his influence can be seen wherever and whenever the sciences have been studied and cultivated in the Muslim world, and not least of all in medicine, in which the perfection and lucidity of his works put in the shade many previously written treatises. Like many of the other celebrated philosophers and scientists of Islam, Avicenna practiced medicine in order to gain a livelihood, while his love for knowledge took him to all branches of the philosophy and the sciences of his day. In many of these, he became peerless, especially in Peripatetic philosophy which reached its apogee with him. Yet this intense devotion to philosophy did not make him in any way a worse physician. On the contrary, his intellectual powers enabled him to unify and systematize all the medical theories and practices of the earlier centuries into a vast synthesis which clearly bears the imprint of his genius.

Avicenna wrote a large number of medical works in Arabic, and also a few in Persian, including treatises on particular diseases, as well as poems summarizing the basic prin-

10 Niẓāmī-i ʿArūḍī, *Chahār Maqāla*, pp. 90–91.

ciples of medicine. His masterpiece, however, is the *Canon of Medicine,* which is certainly the most widely read and influential work of Islamic medicine. This vast opus, which was one of the books most often printed in Europe during the Renaissance, in the Latin translation of Gerard of Cremona, comprises five books: general principles, simple drugs, diseases of particular organs, local diseases that have the tendency to spread over the body, such as fever, and compound drugs. In these books, Avicenna summarized medical theory and practice in such fashion that the *Canon* became once and for all *the* authoritative source of Islamic medicine. Of its value, the author of the *Four Discourses,* Niẓāmī-i ʿArūḍī, writes:

> The Lord of the two worlds and the Guide of the two Grosser Races says: "Every kind of game is in the belly of the wild ass": all this of which I have spoken is to be found in the *Qānūn,* with much in addition thereto; and whoever has mastered the first volume of the *Qānūn,* to him nothing will be hidden of the general and fundamental principles of Medicine, for could Hippocrates and Galen return to life, it were meet that they should do reverence to this book. Yet have I heard a wonderful thing, to wit that one hath taken exception to Abū ʿAlī [ibn Sīnā] in respect of this work, and hath embodied his objections in a book, which he hath named "the Rectification of the *Qānūn*"; and it is as though I looked at both, and perceived what a fool the author was, and how detestable is the book which he has composed! For what right has anyone to find fault with so great a man when the very first question which he meets with in a book of his which he comes across is difficult to his comprehension? For four thousand years the wise men of antiquity travailed in spirit and melted their very souls in order to reduce the Science of Philosophy to some fixed order, yet could not effect this, until, after the lapse of this period, that incomparable philosopher and most powerful thinker Aristotle weighed this coin in the balance of Logic, assayed it with the touchstone of definitions, and measured it by the scale of analogy, so that all doubt and ambiguity departed from it, and it became established on a sure and critical basis. And during these fifteen centuries which have elapsed since his time, no philosopher hath won to the inmost essence of his doctrine, nor travelled the high road of his method, save that most excellent of the moderns, the Philosopher of the East, the Proof of God unto His creatures, Abū ʿAlī al-Ḥusayn ibn ʿAbduʾllāh ibn Sīnā (Avicenna). He who finds fault with these two great men will have cut himself off from the company of the wise, placed himself in the category

of madmen, and exhibited himself in the ranks of the feeble-minded. May God (blessed and exalted is He!) keep us from such stumblings and vain desires, by His Favour and His Grace!

So, if the physician hath mastered the first volume of the *Qānūn,* and hath attained to forty years of age, he will be worthy of confidence; yet even if he hath attained to this degree, he should keep ever with him some of the smaller treatises composed by proved masters, such as the "Gift of Kings" *(Tuḥfatu'l-Mulūk)* of Muḥammad ibn Zakariyyā [ar-Rāzī], or the *Kifāya* of Ibn Mandūya of Iṣfahān, or the "Provision against all sorts of errors in Medical Treatment" *(Tadāruku anwāʿi'l-khaṭā fi't-tadbīri'ṭ-ṭibbī)* of which Abū ʿAlī (Avicenna) is the author; or the *Khuffiyy-i ʿAlā'ī,* or the "Memoranda" *(Yādigār)* of Sayyid Ismāʿīl Jurjānī. For no reliance can be placed on the Memory, which is located in the most posterior part of the brain, and when it is slow in its operation these books may prove helpful.

Therefore every King who would choose a physician must see that these conditions which have been enumerated are found in him; for it is no light matter to commit one's life and soul into the hands of any ignorant quack, or to entrust the care of one's health to any reckless charlatan.[11]

Avicenna possessed much clinical insight, and is given credit for the first description of several drugs and diseases, such as meningitis, which he was the first to describe correctly. But it is essentially for his penetration and his understanding of the philosophical principles of medicine, on the one hand, and his mastery of the psychological treatment of physical ailments, or of "psychosomatic medicine" as it is called today, on the other hand, that he is celebrated.

Many case histories are attributed to Avicenna that have become part and parcel of Persian and Arabic literature and have transcended the bounds of medical science. Some of these stories have become so commonly known that they have been adopted and transformed into gnostic tales by the Sufis, while others have entered into the folklore of the Islamic people.

With Rhazes and Avicenna, Islamic medicine reached its apogee, becoming incorporated into the writings of these men in the definitive form that it was to take for later generations of students and practitioners. The medical student

[11] *Ibid.,* pp. 79–80.

usually began his formal studies with the *Aphorisms* of Hippocrates, the *Questions* of Ḥunain ibn Isḥāq and the *Guide* of Rhazes; then he passed on to the *Treasury* of Thābit ibn Qurrah, and *The Book of al-Manṣūr* of Rhazes; finally, he undertook the study of the *Sixteen Treatises* of Galen, the *Continens* and the *Canon*. The *Canon* of Avicenna thus became the final authority in the medical profession, its study and comprehension being the aim toward which the whole medical curriculum was directed. Even during later centuries, when many other important medical encyclopedias were written in both Arabic and Persian, the *Canon* continued to preserve its exalted position. Its author, along with Rhazes, has reigned as the supreme medical authority, in the West until the seventeenth century, and in the East to the present day.

C. *Medicine after Avicenna*

1. EGYPT AND SYRIA

The medical tradition, basing itself upon the works of Avicenna, Rhazes and the other early masters, continued to flourish in Egypt and Syria, in the Maghrib and Andalusia, and in Persia and the other Eastern lands of Islam. In Egypt, where eye diseases have always been prevalent, it was ophthalmology that was especially developed, even leaving a profound impression on the West, as can be seen in such Arabic words as retina and cataract. Even in the pre-Islamic days, Egyptian ophthalmologists, such as Antyllos and Demosthenes Philalethes, were well known. During the Islamic period, likewise, intense study continued in this branch. The first important treatise on the eye was the *Note-Book of the Oculists* of ʿAlī ibn ʿĪsā (Jesu Haly) of Baghdad, composed at the end of the fourth/tenth century, and followed shortly by the *Book of Selections on the Treatment of the Eye* of Canamusali who was the physician to the Egyptian ruler al-Ḥākim. These works remained authoritative in their field in the Occident, until the dioptrics of Kepler was published; they continued to be consulted until the eighteenth century, when the study of this branch of medicine was revived in France. The court of al-Ḥākim was also the scene of the activities of Alhazen who, as we have seen, was the greatest of the Muslim opticians, and who also made many studies on the structure and illnesses of the eye, especially in so far as the problem of vision was concerned.

Egypt was also the center of activity of many other famous physicians, such as the fifth/eleventh century ʿAlī ibn Riḍwān (the Latin "Haly Rodoam"), who wrote commentaries on the works of Galen, and carried on a series of bitter debates with Ibn Buṭlān, the author of *The Calendar of Health,* who had come from Baghdad to settle in Cairo. The hospitals and libraries of Cairo always drew physicians from near and far, as when, for example, two centuries later Ibn Nafīs, who was born in Damascus, finally settled in Cairo, dying there in 687/1288.

Ibn Nafīs, whose importance became known only a generation ago, was the discoverer of the lesser or pulmonary circulation, which was thought until recently to have been discovered in the sixteenth century by Michael Servetus. Ibn Nafīs made a critical study of the anatomical works of Galen and Avicenna, publishing it as *The Epitome of the Canon.* It became a popular work of medicine, and was translated into Persian. Ibn Nafīs describes the lesser circulation, which marks one of the major discoveries of Islamic medicine, as follows:

> When the blood has been refined in the Right Ventricle, it needs be that it pass to the Left Ventricle where the Vital Spirit is generated. But between these two there exists no passage. For the substance of the heart there is solid and there exists neither a visible passage, as some writers have thought, nor an invisible passage which will permit the flow of blood, as Galen believed. But on the contrary the pores of the heart are shut and its substance there is thick. But this blood, after being refined, must of necessity pass along the Pulmonary Artery

> into the lungs to spread itself out there and to mix with the air until the last drop be purified. It then passes along the Pulmonary Veins to reach the Left Ventricle of the Heart after mixing with the air in order to become fit to generate the Vital Spirit. The remainder of the blood, less refined, is used in the nutrition of the lungs. That is why there are between these two vessels (i.e., the Pulmonary Arteries and Veins) perceptible passages.[12]

Of later Egyptian physicians, one can refer to the eighth/fourteenth-century al-Akfānī and Sadaqah ibn Ibrāhīm al-Shādhilī, the author of the last important ophthalmological treatise to come from Egypt. Also of significance is Dā'ūd al-Anṭākī, who died in Cairo in 1008/1599, and whose not unoriginal *Treasury* is an indication of the state of Islamic science and medicine during the sixteenth century, at the very moment when the stream of science in Europe was beginning to move in a new direction, away from the mainstream in which it had flowed for so many centuries.

2. *SPAIN AND THE MAGHRIB*

Spain and the Maghrib, or the Western lands of Islam, which formed a cultural unit, were also the loci of many great physicians. Cordova especially was a center of medical activity; here, in the fourth/tenth century, the Jewish scholar Hasday ben Shaprūt translated the *Materia Medica* of Dioscorides, which was then corrected and commented on by Ibn Juljul, who also wrote a book on the lives of the physicians and philosophers. Also from Cordova was ʿArīb ibn Saʿd al-Kātib, who composed a well-known treatise on gynecology. He was followed in turn, during the early fifth/eleventh century, by Abu'l-Qāsim al-Zahrāwī (the Latin "Albucasis"), who is the greatest Muslim figure in surgery. Relying on the work of the Greek physicians, especially Paul of Aegina, but adding much original material of his own, Albucasis composed his famous *Concession* or *Concessio*, which Gerard of Cremona translated into Latin, and which was also studied for several centuries in Hebrew and Catalan translations.

[12] From *The Epitome of the Canon* in Elgood, *A Medical History of Persia*, p. 336.

Islamic medicine in Spain also owes a great deal to the Ibn Zuhr or Avenzoar family, which for two generations produced several famous physicians, and even a woman doctor, who gained some fame for her mastery in the art of healing. The most famous member of the family was Abū Marwān ʿAbd al-Malik, who died in Seville around 556/1161. He left several works behind, of which the *Book of Diets* is the most important. These writings mark him as the greatest Andalusian physician in the clinical aspects of medicine, second only to Rhazes in this domain.

Among Andalusian physicians, there were also several of the well-known medical philosophers. Ibn Ṭufail, the author of the philosophic romance *Living Son of the Awake,* was also a competent physician, as was his successor on the philosophical scene, Averroes. This famous philosopher, whom we shall treat more fully later in the chapter on philosophy, was officially a physician, and composed several medical works, including a medical encyclopedia entitled *The Book of Generalities on Medicine,* along with commentaries upon the medical works of Avicenna. Averroes's career was also in a sense followed by Maimonides. Born in Cordova in 530/1136, he set out early in life for the East, finally settling in Egypt. By his birth and early upbringing, however, he belongs to the Spanish scene. Maimonides wrote ten medical works, all in Arabic, of which the most famous is *The Book of Aphorisms Concerning Medicine* which, like many of his other works, was also translated into Hebrew.

The Spanish physicians and scientists are also to be remembered for their special contribution to the study of plants and their medical properties. It is true that important works on drugs had been composed in the East—such as the fourth/tenth-century *Foundations of the True Properties of Remedies* by Abū Manṣūr al-Muwaffaq, which is the first prose work in modern Persian, or the pharmacological works of Mesue Junior. But it was the Spanish and Maghribī scientists who made the greatest contributions in this field, which lies between medicine and botany. The commentary of Ibn Juljul on Dioscorides was followed in the sixth/twelfth century by the *Book of Simple Drugs* of the Tunisian physician, Abuʾl-Ṣalt. He in turn was followed a few years later by al-Ghāfiqī, the most original of the Muslim pharmacologists, who in his above-cited work, also entitled *Book of Simple Drugs,* gave the best description of plants to be found among Muslim authors.

The work of al-Ghāfiqī, as already mentioned, was completed a century later by another Andalusian, Ibn al-Baiṭār, who was born in Malaga and died in Damascus in 646/1248. Of this figure, the greatest of the Muslim botanists and pharmacologists, several works have survived, including *The Complete Book of Simple Drugs* and *The Sufficient Book of Simple Drugs,* in which all that was known to the pharmacologists, as well as three hundred drugs not previously described, was recorded alphabetically and discussed in detail. These works, among the most important fruits of Islamic science in the field of natural history, became the source for much of the later writing in this field in the East. In the West, however, they had little influence, since they came at a time when most of the translations from Arabic into Latin had already taken place, and the intellectual contact which had become established between Christianity and Islam during the fifth/eleventh and sixth/twelfth centuries was coming to an end. As far as Islamic science itself is concerned, Ibn al-Baiṭār represents the last important figure of a long line of great Spanish botanists and pharmacologists who, from that land of beautiful gardens and diverse flora, dominated this branch of learning, a part of natural history and botany, as well as of medicine.

3. THE EASTERN LANDS OF ISLAM, PERSIA, AND INDIA

In Persia itself, the scene of so much of the early medical activity, Avicenna was followed a generation later by Ismāʿīl Sharaf al-Dīn al-Jurjānī, the author of the *Treasury dedicated to the King of Khwārazm,* which is the most important medical encyclopedia in Persian. The size as well as the style of the work places it between the *Canon* and the *Continens;* it is a treasure house, not only of medieval medical theory, but also of pharmacology, for which it presents the additional interest of containing the names of plants and drugs in Persian. The *Treasury,* although still not printed, has always been very popular in Persia and India, and has been translated into Hebrew, Turkish, and Urdu.

Also of significance among those who followed Avicenna is the sixth/twelfth-century theologian Fakhr al-Dīn al-Rāzī, the author of the *Book of Sixty Sciences* mentioned earlier.

Al-Rāzī was also a competent physician and, although he wrote severe criticisms of the philosophical writings of Avicenna, he wrote a commentary on the *Canon* and explained many of its difficulties. He also commenced a large medical work, entitled the *Great Medicine*—which, however, was never completed.

The seventh/thirteenth century, despite its turbulent political life, highlighted by the Mongol invasion, and the destruction of many schools and hospitals, was nevertheless witness to the production of several important medical works. It is curious, first of all, that the four most important authorities on the history of medicine in Islam—namely, Ibn al-Qifṭī, Ibn Abī Uṣaibiʿah, Ibn Khallakān, and Barhebraeus—all flourished in the middle of that century. Secondly, it is remarkable that the Mongols, who at first did so much to destroy the institutions in which medicine was practiced and taught, soon became its patrons, so that at their courts flourished some of the best-known physicians of Islam. Quṭb al-Dīn al-Shīrāzī, the most celebrated student of Nasīr al-Dīn al-Ṭūsī, was also a physician, and wrote a commentary on the *Canon,* which he called *The Present to Saʿd.* He was followed, at the beginning of the eighth/fourteenth century, by Rashīd al-Dīn Faḍlallāh, the learned vizier of the Ilkhānids, who wrote the most authoritative history of the Mongol period, as well as a medical encyclopedia. Rashīd al-Dīn was also an ardent patron of learning and, in the capital city of Tabriz, he constructed many schools and hospitals. It is interesting to note, as a sign of the still intimate contact between the various parts of the Islamic world, that, when Rashīd al-Dīn offered prizes to anyone who wrote a book in his honor, several among those who soon responded came from Andalusia, and a few from Tunisia and Tripoli. Despite the Mongol invasion, the unity of the Islamic world was well enough preserved to permit rapid communication between the most distant lands concerning medical and scientific questions. (One doubts whether, despite all the modern facilities, there would be the same rapid response to a scholarly question from such distant parts of the Islamic world today.)

The eighth/fourteenth century also marks a new interest in veterinary medicine; several treatises on horses, one of which is attributed to Aristotle, along with a few that were translated from Sanskrit, date from this period. This was also the age of an intense interest in anatomy, which the physician and the theologian shared, and the date of the appearance of the first illustrations for anatomical texts. The first known illustrated anatomy was one composed in 798/1396 by Muḥammad ibn Aḥmad Ilyās, and named the *Illustrated Anatomy*. Also from this period is the widely read *Anatomy of al-Manṣūr,* in which embryological ideas—combining Greek and Indian with Quranic conceptions—are discussed.

The Safavid period, which marks a renaissance in Persian art and philosophy, was also the period in which Islamic medicine was thoroughly revived. The greatest physician of this age, Muḥammad Ḥusainī Nūrbakhskī, who died in 913/1507, wrote a large medical work entitled *The Quintessence of Experience,* which shows the clinical powers of the author. He was the first person to identify and treat several common diseases, among them hay fever and whooping cough. This period was also marked by the emergence of expert pharmacologists, and has been called by Elgood "the Golden Age" of pharmacology in Islam. The most important work in this field was the *Shāfiʿī Medicine,* composed in 963/1556; it served as the foundation of Fr. Angelus's *Pharmacopoeia Persica,* the first European study of Persian medicine. Also of this period, although written a century later, is the *Gift of the Two Muʾmins,* which is still widely read in the East, and shows the rising tide of Indian influence at that time.

The tenth/sixteenth and eleventh/seventeenth centuries were also the period of the spread of Islamic medicine in India, through the works of several Persians who had gone to settle there. In 1037/1629 ʿAin al-Mulk of Shiraz composed the *Vocabulary of Drugs,* dedicated to Shāh Jahān. He was probably also involved in the composition of *The Medicine of Dārā Shukūh,* which is the last great medical encyclopedia in Islam. Dārā Shukūh, the Mogul prince, who was also a Sufi and a student of the *Vedanta,* is best known for his translations of Sanskrit metaphysical works into Persian, and especially the *Upanishad,* which Anquetil-Duperron rendered into Latin from the Persian translations of Dārā Shukūh, thus making this work available for the first time in Europe. It was this version that William Blake, among many other famous figures, read in the nineteenth century—most likely without knowing of the Mogul prince who had paved the way for it. The actual translation of a vast medical encyclopedia by Dārā Shukūh seems, however, unlikely; it was more probably under his patronage and direction that the work was done by competent physicians, such as ʿAin al-Mulk.

Islamic medicine continued to flourish in India during the

twelfth/eighteenth century, when such works as the *Scales of Medicine,* by another Persian physician, Muhammad Akbar Shāh Arzānī from Shiraz, were composed. Interestingly enough, with the invasion of India by Nādir Shāh in the twelfth/eighteenth century, Islamic medicine received a new boost in that country at the very moment when it was beginning to weaken in Persia itself, under the advent of European medicine. And today it is most of all in the Indo-Pakistani sub-continent that Islamic medicine continues to thrive as a living school of medicine, competing with both *Ayurveda* and modern European medicine which, in such movements as Neo-Hippocratism, is beginning to show some interest in the medical philosophy from which it departed several centuries ago.

D. *The Philosophy and Theory of Islamic Medicine*

"Medicine," as Avicenna states at the beginning of the *Canon,* "is a branch of knowledge which deals with the states of health and disease in the human body, with the purpose of employing suitable means for preserving or restoring health." The task of medicine, is, therefore, the restoration or preservation of that state of equilibrium which is called health. Following the humoral pathology of Hippocrates, Islamic medicine considers the "elements" of the body to be blood, phlegm, yellow bile, and black bile. These four humors are to the body what the four elements—fire, air, water, and earth—are to the world of Nature. It is not, in fact, surprising to discover that Empedocles, to whom this theory of the four elements is generally attributed, was also a physician. Like the elements, each humor possesses two natures, blood being hot and moist, phlegm cold and moist, yellow bile hot and dry, and black bile cold and dry. Just as, in the world of generation and corruption, everything comes into being from the mixture of the four elements, so in the human body there is a humoral constitution, brought into being from the mixture of the four humors, which marks the state of health of that body. Moreover, the particular constitution or temperament of each person is unique; no two people can be treated medically as though they were exactly the same subject, with identical reactions to external stimuli.

The body also has the power to preserve and restore that balance which marks its state of health—that power of self-preservation being traditionally called *vis medicatrix naturae.* The role of medicine then becomes no more than to help this power function properly, and to remove any obstacles from its path. The process of regaining health is therefore accomplished by the body itself, and drugs are merely an aid to this natural force, which exists within each body and is a characteristic of life itself.

The physiology which results from this humoral theory is summarized by Avicenna as follows:

> A body-fluid or *Humor* is that fluid moist physical substance into which our aliment is transformed.
>
> That part of the aliment which has the capacity to be transformed into body-substance, either by itself or in combination with something else, is the healthy or *good* humor. It is what replaces the loss which the body-substance undergoes. The residue from the aliment, the *superfluity,* is *bad* humor, and is properly expelled.
>
> Of the fluids, some are primary, some are secondary. The primary body-fluids are: the sanguineous humor, the serous humor, the bilious humor, and the atrabilious humor. The secondary body-fluids are either nonexcrementitious, such as those located at the orifices of even the minutest channels and near the tissues, those permeating the tissues and capable of transformation into nourishment, a special almost congealed fluid, a fluid found among tissues from birth; or excrementitious.
>
> The *Sanguineous Humor* (predominant in blood) is hot and moist. It is normally red, without offensive odor, and very sweet to the taste.
>
> The *Serous Humor,* cold and moist in nature, occurs in normal and abnormal form. Normal serous humor is capable of transformation into blood by Innate Heat, and is in fact imperfectly matured blood. It is a kind of sweet fluid, not too cold compared with the body as a whole. It has no special locus

or receptacle in the body, and is like blood in that it is equally necessary to all the tissues, which receive it along with the blood. Its essential function is twofold: first, to be near tissues in case of inadequate supply of their habitual nutriment—healthy blood—and, second, to qualify sanguineous humor before the latter reaches and nourishes tissues of lymphatic temperament. Its accessory function is to lubricate joints and all tissues and organs concerned in movement.

The abnormal forms of serous humor are:

One, the *salty,* warmer, dryer, and lighter than the other forms, made salty by the mixture of oxidized earthy matters of dry temperament and bitter taste with the normal moisture of the humor;

two, the *attenuated,* insipid or slightly salty as a result of the admixture of oxidized bile, which is dry and bitter; the resultant heating fluid is called the bilious serous humor;

three, the *bitter,* due either to admixture of atrabilious humor or to over-infrigidation;

four, the *sour,* found in two forms, one sour because the humor has fermented and then gone sour, the other sour through the admixture of acrid atrabilious humor;

five, the *vitreous,* dense and glassy, the original aqueity yielding to a vitreous appearance after condensation and increase in coldness.

The *Bilious Humor,* hot and dry in nature, is in its normal form the foam of blood, bright red, light, and pungent. Formed in the liver, it either circulates with the blood or passes to the gall-bladder. That which passes into the bloodstream subserves two purposes: it enables the blood to nourish such tissues or organs as need a certain amount of dispersed bilious humor (the lung, for instance); and mechanically it attenuates the blood, enabling it to traverse the very minutest channels of the body. The part which passes to the gall-bladder also serves two purposes: first, the removal of some of the effete matter of the body and nourishment of the walls of the gall-bladder; and second, a dual function of cleansing food-residues and viscous serous humor from the bowel walls and stimulating the intestinal and anal muscles for defecation.

Besides the normal clear bilious humor in the liver and blood there are seven abnormal types, of which the first four are so by admixture of alien substance:

One, *citron-yellow* bile in the liver, due to admixture of attenuated serous humor, less hot than normal bile;

two, *vitelline-yellow* bile, the color of egg-yolk, in the liver, due to admixture of coagulated serous humor, still less hot;

three, *ruddy-yellow* oxidized bile, an opaque fluid in liver and blood due to simple admixture of atrabilious humor, and somewhat deleterious;

four, *oxidized* bile of another type, in the gall-bladder, due to spontaneous oxidation resulting in an attenuated fluid plus an ash which does not separate out; more deleterious than the last.

The three abnormal biles which result from internal change of substance are:

five, *hepatic* bile, in the liver, due to oxidation of the attenuated part of the blood, so that its denser part separates out as atrabilious humor; a moderately toxic bile;

six, *gastric leek-green* bile in the stomach, due to intense oxidation of vitelline bile; less toxic than the last; and

seven, *mildew-* or *verdigris-green* bile in the stomach, due to intense oxidation of vitelline bile and loss of all its moisture; very hot, and extremely toxic.

Of these the seventh is possibly derived from the sixth through increased oxidation resulting in total desiccation, which would account for its whitish hue. For we know that heating a moist body first blackens it, and further heating whitens it, the whiteness becoming evident when the degree of moisture is less than half-and-half. Wood, for example, first is charred black, and finally becomes white ash.

The *Atrabilious Humor,* cold and dry in nature, is in its normal form the *faex* or sediment of good blood, an effete matter, in taste between sweet and bitter. After its production in the liver it divides into two portions, of which one enters the blood and the other the spleen. The former, first, contributes to the nourishment of such members as require a trace of atrabilious humor in their temperaments, as for example the bones; and, second, gives the blood its stamina, strength, density, and consistence. The latter portion, passing to the spleen, and no longer necessary to the blood, is primarily useful in clearing the body of effete matter, the spleen being the one organ to whose nourishment it contributes. Its secondary use is that, travelling to the mouth of the stomach by a kind of milking movement, one, it tones up, tightens, and thickens it; and two, its bitterness, irritating the mouth of the stomach, stimulates the sense of hunger.

Similarly, that portion of bilious humor which passes to the gall-bladder is unnecessary to the blood, and what emerges from the gall-bladder is no longer needed by the organ. And just as the bilious humor passing to the intestine arouses peristalsis and so helps to withdraw food from the stomach, so the atrabilious humor after leaving the spleen arouses appetite and leads to the drawing-in of food to the stomach.

Wherefore thanks be to God the Best Artificer of all things, and unending His Praise.

Water is not counted one of the body-fluids because it is not a nutrient. By the word nutrient we mean something assimilable into the form of the human body; and such substances are always complex, never simple.

Galen regards the sanguineous as the only normal body-fluid, all others being excrementitious. But if sanguineous humor were the only nourisher of the various organs, it would be because the organs were all alike in temperament and nature. Actually, bone would not be harder than flesh were it not for the dryness of the atrabilious humor present in blood, nor would the brain be softer were it not for the presence in blood of the soft serous humor which nourishes it. We must conclude that in the blood are other humors than the sanguineous.

Moreover, when blood is withdrawn into a vessel, we see how it shrinks and how its various components visibly separate out: a foam (bilious), a turbid *faex* (atrabilious), an albuminous portion (serous), and a watery part such as passes in urine.

Some think that physical strength is due to abundance of blood, and weakness to its paucity. But it is not so. It is rather this: that the state of the body determines whether a nutriment will benefit it or not.[13]

The uniqueness of the temperament of each individual indicates that each microcosm is a world of its own, not identical with any other microcosm. Yet, the repetition of the same basic humors in each constitution bears out the fact that each microcosm presents a morphological resemblance to other microcosms. Moreover, there is an analogy between the human body and the cosmic order, as shown by the correspondence between the humors and elements. There is in the Hermetico-alchemical natural philosophy, which was always closely tied to medicine in Islam, a basic doctrine of the correspondence between all the various orders of reality: the intelligible hierarchy, the heavenly bodies, the order of numbers, the parts of the body, the letters of the alphabet which are the "elements" of the Sacred Book, etc. The seven cervical and the twelve dorsal vertebrae correspond to the seven planets and the twelve signs of the Zodiac, as well as to the days of the week and the months of the year; and the

[13] From Avicenna's *Canon* translated by Eric Schroeder in *Muhammad's People* (Portland, Oregon: The Bond Wheelwright Company, 1955), pp. 786–790.

total number of discs of the vertebrae, which they consider to be twenty-eight, to the letters of the Arabic alphabet and the stations of the moon. There is, therefore, both numerical and astrological symbolism connected with medicine, although the closeness of the relation has not been the same during all periods of Islamic history, nor among all the medical authorities. But the correspondence and "sympathy" (in the original sense of the word "*sympathia*") between various orders of cosmic reality form the philosophical background of Islamic medicine.

The destruction of the equilibrium of the four humors is, as we have seen, the cause of illness; its restoration is the task of the physician. The master of Islamic medicine, Avicenna, applies the four Aristotelian causes to the case of disease, as follows:

> Material cause is the physical body which is the subject of health and disease. This may be immediate as the organs of body together with their vital energies and remote as the humours and remoter than these the Elements which are the basis both for structure and change (or dynamicity). Things which thus provide a basis (for health and disease) get so thoroughly altered and integrated that from an initial diversity there emerges a holistic unity with a specific structure (or the quantitative pattern of organisation) and a specific type of temperament (the qualitative pattern).
>
> Efficient causes are those which are capable of either preventing or producing changes in the human body. These are age, sex, occupation, residence, climate and other allied factors like the seasons, habit, rest and activity, both physical and mental, sleep and wakefulness, food and drink, retention, depletion and finally things inimical or otherwise that may be in contact with the body.
>
> Formal cause is the temperament (or the pattern of constitution as a whole) and the faculties which emerge from it and the structure (the quantitative patterns).
>
> Final cause (or the purpose) is the functions which can be only understood by a knowledge of the faculties (the biological systems) and of vital energies that are ultimately responsible for them. These will be described presently.[14]

14 Avicenna in M. H. Shah, "The Constitution of Medicine," in *Theories and Philosophies of Medicine* (Delhi: Institute of History of Medicine and Medical Research, 1962), p. 96.

With the causes thus defined, Avicenna proceeds to a description of the contents of the Islamic system of medicine:

> Having disposed of the question of causes generally it may now be said that medicine deals with Elements (the units of constitution as a whole), Organs (anatomy), Faculties (biological system) like the organic, vital and nervous and the various (physiological) functions connected with them. It also includes descriptions of health and disease and the intermediate states of the body together with their exciting causes like food and drink, air, water, residence, elimination and retention, occupations, habits, physical and mental activities, age, sex and the various external influences. It, therefore, includes a discussion regarding choice of a suitable diet, air, rest, medicines and operative procedures for the preservation of health and the treatment of disease.[15]

The human body, with all its different organs and elements, and its physical, nervous and vital systems, is unified by a vital force or spirit, which resembles somewhat the basal metabolic energy of modern medicine. The three systems of the body each has its own functions, differentiated and interrelated at the same time by the vital spirit—which, however, must not be confused with the soul.

> *Physical System* has two varieties. One is concerned with preservation of the individual and as such is responsible for the functions of nutrition and growth. This is located in the Liver. The other for preserving the race is responsible for the sexual functions, the formation of the germinal fluid and the fertilization and further development of the ovum. This is located in the testicles and ovaries.
>
> *Nervous System* consists of the faculty of cognition and the faculty of (conation or) movement. The cognitive faculty functions externally [as sensation and internally (as inner) perception]. . . . Brain is the centre of the nervous system as it performs its various functions.
>
> *Vital System.* This system conditions and suitably prepares the vital Force for the sensory and motor function of the Brain. It also carries vital force right into the organs and tissues for their very life and vigour. This system is centred in the Heart and functions through it.
>
> Although the Vital Force first gets organised and differentiated into the Vital System, according to the Physicians it is

[15] *Ibid.*, p. 97.

(however) not (just) the appearance of this system which leads to the differentiation of the other systems. They are not differentiated until the Vital Forces acquire the (necessary) disposition for their own special organisation.[16]

As for the origin of the vital spirit and its function in directing the life of the body, Avicenna states:

> God made the left side of the heart hollow to serve both as reservoir for the Vital Spirit and as its producing source. He created Vital Spirit to convey the faculties of the soul or Form to the appropriate bodily members. The Vital Spirit therefore serves both as ground for the unification of the soul's faculties and secondly as vehicle of emanation into the various material members and tissues.
>
> This Vital Spirit God produces by combining the subtler particles of bodily humors with Elemental Fire; at the same time producing the body-tissues from the coarser and more Earthy particles of the same humors. The relation of the Vital Spirit to the subtler particles is precisely like the relation of the body to the grosser. Just as the mingling of the humors results in a temperamental pattern which permits the visible physical formation, inconceivable without this mixture, so the mingling of subtler particles in a temperamental compound enables the Vital Spirit to receive the powers of the soul, which it could not do were the humors not so mixed.
>
> Initially, Vital Spirit is to be conceived as a Divine emanation from potentiality to actuality proceeding without intermission or stint until the pattern is complete. Each bodily member, though substantially derived from the same set of humors, has nevertheless its own particular temperament, since both the proportions and the mode of the humoral commixture are peculiar to each member. Similarly three aspects or branches of the Vital Spirit are differently developed: the vegetative or Natural (that is, as considered with regard to vegetative process in the body, the Vital Spirit as located in the liver and associated with venous blood), the Animal or sensitive (as associated with nerve-fibers), and the Vital properly speaking (as located in the heart and associated with arterial blood). Each of these three has its own peculiar temperament, determined by the mode and proportions of the commixture of the subtler particles.
>
> The body consists of many members. As to which is the original one, there is no agreement; but the fact remains that

[16] *Ibid.*, pp. 118–119.

one must have come into existence before others could develop from it. Similarly a prime Vital Spirit must be regarded as necessarily precedent to the others; and this, according to the most authoritative philosophers, is the Spirit located in the heart. Thence passing into the main physical centers, Spirit is located in them sufficiently to be modified by their respective temperamental characters. Its location in the cerebrum tempers it for receiving the Animal faculties of sensation and movement, location in the liver for receiving the Vegetative faculties of nutrition and growth, location in the generative glands for the Reproductive faculty.

Aqueity or moisture is the material cause of growth. But moisture does not develop or construct itself; it is not a self-creating being, but only undergoes change in virtue of a formative power acting upon it. This formative power or Form—the soul in the living creature—has its existence in Divine Decree. And the Form requires, in order to work, an instrument: this instrument is the Innate Heat.

A person at the period of life when growth has reached its limit approaches as near as may be to equability of temperament so far as co-equation of his members goes, the contra-action of hot members such as the heart with cold ones such as the brain, of moist ones such as the liver with dry ones such as the bones. But as regards the Vital Spirit and main organ, temperament can never approximate to ideal equability: the temperament of Vital Spirit and vital organs is always predominantly hot and moist. Heart and Vital Spirit, which are the root of life, are both extremely hot. For life itself depends on Innate Heat referred to above, and growth depends on Innate Moisture. The Innate Heat both penetrates and feeds upon the Innate Moisture.

The Innate Heat of young creatures is derived from the sperm of their generation, which is very hot in nature. This initial heat is steadily used up. But the quantitative loss is made up, and more than made up, by the heat added as a result of progressive growth. On the other hand, the *proportional* or relative amount of Innate Moisture (on which the Innate Heat feeds) progressively diminishes, this being the mechanism by which Innate Heat remains at a constant level up to senescence. In the end, the moisture is inadequate in proportional quantity even to keep the Innate Heat constant. At life's outset, it had been adequate both to the feeding of the heat and to growth. But there comes a time when either one or the other or both must fail. It is clear that growth has to stop, for the Innate Heat cannot be the one to be sacrificed.

But at last the Innate Heat dies out. This is the death of the nature or Form to which every creature is destined, its

> APPOINTED TERM. The diversity of temperaments is what accounts for the different durations of creaturely lives, the differences in their natural terms. There are also, of course, what are called premature deaths; but these other causes exist also (like the Form) in the realm of Divine Decree.[17]

The elements and organs, and the biological systems and their functions—all serve to preserve the equilibrium of the four humors, the state of equilibrium being determined by the particular nature of each human body. There are, however, general patterns and causes for variation of the temperaments, which include such factors as race, climate, age, sex, etc. Thus an Indian and a Slav, or a man of sixty and a woman of twenty, would have quite different temperaments, while Indians or Slavs as racial groups, or people of sixty as an age group, would have a similar, although not identical, temperament.

The treatment of illnesses also depends upon these factors. In Islamic medicine, all foods and drugs are classified according to their quality—that is, hot, cold, etc.—and also according to their potency. Thus a person with a choleric temperament usually needs food and drugs with a dominance of the cold and moist qualities, to counterbalance the heat and dryness of yellow bile. The same food or drug, however, would have the opposite effect upon a person of phlegmatic temperament. In this manner, pharmacology, following the theories of medicine, divided all drugs according to their qualities. The whole range of dietary habits of the Islamic countries has become established according to this theory, so that in a normal meal the various qualities and natures are well balanced.

In its attempt to view man as a whole, as a single entity in whom body and soul are united, and in seeking to relate man to the total cosmic environment in which he lives, Islamic medicine has remained faithful to the unifying spirit of Islam. Although originating from the older medical traditions of Greece, Persia and India, Islamic medicine, like so many other pre-Islamic sciences, became profoundly Islamized, and penetrated deeply into the general structure of Islamic civilization. To this very day, its theories and ideas dominate the daily dietary habits of the Islamic people; they still serve as the framework for a unifying vision of man, as an entity in whom body and soul are closely intertwined, and

17 Avicenna in Schroeder, *Muhammad's People*, pp. 783–786.

in whom the state of health is realized through harmony and equilibrium. Since these ideas are all closely akin to the Islamic view of things, they have aided in making this tradition of medicine one of the most widespread and enduring sciences cultivated in the bosom of Islamic civilization during its history.

CHAPTER EIGHT

THE SCIENCES OF MAN

THE MUSLIM MIND occupied itself not only with the sciences of Nature, with mathematics, and with philosophy and metaphysics, but also with the sciences of man, with anthropology in the most general sense of that term. Man was studied by the Muslims in his social and political setting; his diverse activities were scrutinized with an objective eye, which sought to observe before it judged. Historians such as al-Ṭabarī and al-Masʿūdī devoted many pages to what must be regarded as a scientific study of the human state. Similarly, the authors of "The Nations and Their Beliefs" *(al-Milal waʾl-niḥal)*, who were the founders of the study of comparative religion—men like ʿAbd al-Laṭīf al-Baghdādī and al-Shahristānī—were students of an essential aspect of man's life, expressed in his cults and religious beliefs. The many manuals of social ethics, as well as the ethical poetry of men like Saʿdī, likewise reflect the science of human nature in exquisite literary forms, which have made them a lasting element in the life of every educated Muslim.

The study of human society and of history on a large scale was carried to its perfection by Ibn Khaldūn, whose classification of the sciences we have already mentioned. In the hands of this famous "philosopher of history," the rise and fall of nations and the interaction between the nomadic and sedentary elements of human society were studied in the light of the natural as well as the religious, ethnical and social factors that determine the structure of all human civilizations. Ibn Khaldūn meditated upon the human condition considered from the standpoint of the general tendencies and trends governing human society, and the effect of these dominant political and social forces on the life of man.

The scholar who studied man most objectively, and in a way provided the kind of materials upon which Ibn Khaldūn could base his general observations of human history, was al-Bīrūnī, whom we have already met as an astronomer. Al-Bīrūnī made a study of both Islamic and Indian society; it was about the latter that he wrote his memorable *India*, a work that is without question one of the most scientific and objective studies of man and his society made in medieval times, at a time when, in the Western world, such studies did not pass beyond the level of chronicles. As E. C. Sachau, who translated both the *India* and the *Chronology of Ancient Nations* into English, and who was most responsible for introducing al-Bīrūnī to the Western world, wrote:

> Apparently Alberuni felt a strong inclination towards Indian philosophy. He seems to have thought that the philosophers both in ancient Greece and India, whom he most carefully and repeatedly distinguishes from the ignorant, image-loving crowd, held in reality the very same ideas, the same as seem to have been his own, *i.e.* those of a pure monotheism; that, in fact, originally all men were alike pure and virtuous, worshipping one sole Almighty God, but that the dark passions of the crowd in the course of time had given rise to the difference of religion, of philosophical and political persuasions, and of idolatry.[1]

Al-Bīrūnī was a man of clear and determined thought, who sought with sincerity and courage after the truth, wherever he found it. To quote Sachau again:

> He is a stern judge both of himself and of others. Himself perfectly sincere, it is sincerity which he demands from others. Whenever he does not fully understand a subject, or only knows part of it, he will at once tell the reader so, either asking the reader's pardon for his ignorance, or promising, though a man of fifty-eight years, to continue his labours and to publish their results in time, as though he were acting under a moral responsibility to the public. He always sharply draws the limits of his knowledge; and although he has only a smattering of the metrical system of the Hindus, he communicates whatever little he knows, guided by the principle that the best must not be the enemy of the better, as though he were afraid that he should not live long enough to finish the study in question. He is not a friend of those who hate to avow their

1 *Alberuni's India*, I, preface, p. xviii.

ignorance by a frank *"I do not know,"* and he is roused to strong indignation whenever he meets with want of sincerity.[2]

Al-Bīrūnī himself opens his own preface to the *India* with an evaluation of the various types of evidence upon which the studies of man and his society and history are based:

No one will deny that in questions of historic authenticity *hearsay* does not equal *eye-witness;* for in the latter the eye of the observer apprehends the substance of that which is observed, both in the time when and in the place where it exists, whilst hearsay has its peculiar drawbacks. But for these, it would even be preferable to eye-witness; for the object of eye-witness can only be *actual* momentary existence, whilst hearsay comprehends alike the present, the past, and the future, so as to apply in a certain sense both to that which *is* and to that which is *not* (*i.e.* which either has ceased to exist or has not yet come into existence). Written tradition is one of the species of hearsay—we might almost say, the most preferable. How could we know the history of nations but for the everlasting monuments of the pen?

The tradition regarding an event which in itself does not contradict either logical or physical laws will invariably depend for its character as true or false upon the character of the reporters, who are moved by the divergency of interests and all kinds of animosities and antipathies between the various nations. We must distinguish different classes of reporters.

One of them tells a lie, as intending to further an interest of his own, either *by lauding* his family or nation, because he is one of them, or *by attacking* the family or nation on the opposite side, thinking that thereby he can gain his ends. In both cases he acts from motives of objectionable cupidity and animosity.

Another one tells a lie regarding a class of people whom he likes, as being under obligation to them, or whom he hates, because something disagreeable has happened between them. Such a reporter is near akin to the first-mentioned one, as he too acts from motives of personal predilection and enmity.

Another tells a lie because he is of such a base nature as to aim thereby at some profit, or because he is such a coward as to be afraid of telling the truth.

Another tells a lie because it is his nature to lie, and he cannot do otherwise, which proceeds from the essential meanness of his character and the depravity of his innermost being.

Lastly, a man may tell a lie from ignorance, blindly following others who told him.

2 *Ibid.*, I, preface, p. xx.

If, now, reporters of this kind become so numerous as to represent a certain body of tradition, or if in the course of time they even come to form a consecutive series of communities or nations, both the first reporter and his followers form the connecting links between the hearer and the inventor of the lie; and if the connecting links are eliminated, there remains the originator of the story, one of the various kinds of liars we have enumerated, as the only person with whom we have to deal.

That man only is praiseworthy who shrinks from a lie and always adheres to the truth, enjoying credit even among liars, not to mention others.

It has been said in the Koran, "*Speak the truth, even if it were against yourselves*" (Sūra, 4, 134); and the Messiah expresses himself in the Gospel to this effect: "*Do not mind the fury of kings in speaking the truth before them. They only possess your body, but they have no power over your soul*" (*cf.* St. Matt. x. 18, 19, 28; St. Luke xii. 4). In these words the Messiah orders us to exercise *moral courage*. For what the crowd calls courage—bravely dashing into the fight or plunging into an abyss of destruction—is only a *species* of courage, whilst the *genus,* far above all *species,* is *to scorn death,* whether by word or deed.

Now as justice (*i.e.* being just) is a quality liked and coveted for its own self, for its intrinsic beauty, the same applies to *truthfulness,* except perhaps in the case of such people as never tasted how sweet it is, or know the truth, but deliberately shun it, like a notorious liar who once was asked if he had ever spoken the truth, and gave the answer, "If I were not afraid to speak the truth, I should say, no." A liar will avoid the path of justice; he will, as matter of preference, side with oppression and false witness, breach of confidence, fraudulent appropriation of the wealth of others, theft, and all the vices which serve to ruin the world and mankind.[3]

As for his own competence in writing a work on the Hindus and their civilization, he is fully aware of his shortcomings, for he writes:

In order to please him [referring to a friend who had read previous works on India and was not satisfied by them] I have . . . written this book on the doctrines of the Hindus, never making any unfounded imputations against those, our religious antagonists, and at the same time not considering it inconsistent with my duties as a Muslim to quote their own

3 *Ibid.*, I, pp. 3–5.

> words at full length when I thought they would contribute to elucidate a subject. If the contents of these quotations happen to be utterly heathenish, and *the followers of the truth, i.e.* the Muslims, find them objectionable, we can only say that such is the belief of the Hindus, and that they themselves are best qualified to defend it.[4]

The author of the *India* had a great deal of difficulty making this first-hand study of Hinduism, although he sought every opportunity to do so during the long period of his stay in that country. Accompanying Maḥmūd of Ghazna in his conquest of India and spending a good many years in the northern regions of that country, al-Bīrūnī had many opportunities to study the diverse facets of the Hindu tradition from first-hand sources. But this was a time when the political situation discouraged amicable relationships, and he did not find the Hindu scholars quite as willing to teach him their sciences as he was eager to learn from them. He mentions his impressions of the Hindus with whom he came into contact, and of the sciences he acquired from them, in the course of his discussion of the causes for his difficulty in studying their civilization. In a passage which is a good example of his honest compilation and recording of observations obtained in his study of man, in another society and in a different setting, he writes:

> In the fifth place, there are other causes, the mentioning of which sounds like a satire—peculiarities of their national character, deeply rooted in them, but manifest to everybody. We can only say, folly is an illness for which there is no medicine, and the Hindus believe that there is no country but theirs, no nation like theirs, no kings like theirs, no religion like theirs, no science like theirs. They are haughty, foolishly vain, self-conceited, and stolid. They are by nature niggardly in communicating that which they know, and they take the greatest possible care to withhold it from men of another caste among their own people, still much more, of course, from any foreigner. According to their belief, there is no other country on earth but theirs, no other race of man but theirs, and no created beings besides them have any knowledge or science whatsoever. Their haughtiness is such that, if you tell them of any science or scholar in Khurāsān and Persis, they will think you to be both an ignoramus and a liar. If they travelled and mixed with other nations, they would soon change their minds, for

[4] *Ibid.*, I, p. 7.

their ancestors were not as narrow-minded as the present generation is. One of their scholars, Varāhamihira, in a passage where he calls on the people to honour the Brahmans, says: *"The Greeks, though impure, must be honoured, since they were trained in sciences, and therein excelled others. What, then, are we to say of a Brahman, if he combines with his purity the height of science?"*

In former times, the Hindus used to acknowledge that the progress of science due to the Greeks is much more important than that which is due to themselves. But from this passage of Varāhamihira alone you see what a self-lauding man he is, whilst he gives himself airs as doing justice to others. At first I stood to their astronomers in the relation of a pupil to his master, being a stranger among them and not acquainted with their peculiar national and traditional methods of science. On having made some progress, I began to show them the elements on which this science rests, to point out to them some rules of logical deduction and the scientific methods of all mathematics, and then they flocked together round me from all parts, wondering, and most eager to learn from me, asking me at the same time from what Hindu master I had learnt those things, whilst in reality I showed them what they were worth, and thought myself a great deal superior to them, disdaining to be put on a level with them. They almost thought me to be a sorcerer, and when speaking of me to their leading men in their native tongue, they spoke of me as *the sea* or as *the water which is so acid that vinegar in comparison is sweet.*

Now such is the state of things in India. I have found it very hard to work my way into the subject, although I have a great liking for it, in which respect I stand quite alone in my time, and although I do not spare either trouble or money in collecting Sanskrit books from places where I supposed they were likely to be found, and in procuring for myself, even from very remote places, Hindu scholars who understand them and are able to teach me. What scholar, however, has the same favourable opportunities of studying this subject as I have? That would be only the case with one to whom the grace of God accords, what it did not accord to me, a perfectly free disposal of his own doings and goings; for it has never fallen to my lot in my own doings and goings to be perfectly independent, nor to be invested with sufficient power to dispose and to order as I thought best. However, I thank God for that which he has bestowed upon me, and which must be considered as sufficient for the purpose.

The heathen Greeks, before the rise of Christianity, held much the same opinions as the Hindus; their educated classes thought much the same as those of the Hindus; their common people held the same idolatrous views as those of the Hindus. Therefore I like to confront the theories of the one nation with those of the other simply on account of their close relationship, not in order to correct them. For that which is not *the truth* (*i.e.* the true belief or monotheism) does not admit of any correction, and all heathenism, whether Greek or Indian, is in its pith and marrow one and the same belief, because it is only a deviation *from the truth*. The Greeks, however, had philosophers who, living in their country, discovered and worked out for them the elements of science, not of popular superstition, for it is the object of the upper classes to be guided by the results of science, whilst the common crowd will always be inclined to plunge into wrong-headed wrangling, as long as they are not kept down by fear of punishment. Think of Socrates when he opposed the crowd of his nation as to their idolatry and did not want to call the stars gods! At once eleven of the twelve judges of the Athenians agreed on a sentence of death, and Socrates died faithful to the truth.

The Hindus had no men of this stamp both capable and willing to bring the sciences to a classical perfection. Therefore you mostly find that even the so-called scientific theorems of the Hindus are in a state of utter confusion, devoid of any logical order, and in the last instance always mixed up with the silly notions of the crowd, *e.g.* immense numbers, enormous spaces of time, and all kinds of religious dogmas, which the vulgar belief does not admit of being called into question. Therefore it is a prevailing practice among the Hindus *jurare in verba magistri;* and I can only compare their mathematical and astronomical literature, as far as I know it, to a mixture of pearl shells and sour dates, or of pearls and dung, or of costly crystals and common pebbles. Both kinds of things are equal in their eyes, since they cannot raise themselves to the methods of a strictly scientific deduction.

In most parts of my work I simply relate without criticising, unless there be a special reason for doing so. I mention the necessary Sanskrit names and technical terms once where the context of our explanation demands it. If the word is an *original* one, the meaning of which can be rendered in Arabic, I only use the corresponding Arabic word; if, however, the Sanskrit word be more practical, we keep this, trying to transliterate it as accurately as possible. If the word is a secondary or *derived* one, but in general use, we also keep it, though there be a corresponding term in Arabic, but before using it we explain its signification. In this way we have tried to facilitate the understanding of the terminology.

Lastly, we observe that we cannot always in our discussions

> strictly adhere to the geometrical method, only referring to that which precedes and never to that which follows, as we must sometimes introduce in a chapter an unknown factor, the explanation of which can only be given in a later part of the book, God helping us![5]

The study of man, and of human societies other than the Islamic, was not limited to al-Bīrūnī, although his studies are unique for their penetration and conciseness. The vastness of the Islamic world, and the unity imposed upon it by a common law, sacred language and cultural elements, facilitated travel to the farthest regions by both land and sea. The accounts of these travels, which vary greatly in quality, provide a precious source for the study of many different human societies, as well as of aspects of natural history and geography. There is hardly a region which some Muslim traveler did not visit, whether in Central Africa, in northern Europe or in the farthest confines of Asia.

Among the Muslim travelers, none is as famous as Ibn Baṭṭūṭah, the eighth/fourteenth century Moroccan religious scholar from Tangiers, who set out on a piligrimage to Mecca without knowing that he was undertaking what was to be the greatest travel adventure up to the invention of modern means of communication. Ibn Baṭṭūṭah's journeys took him throughout North and East Africa, the Middle East, the Indian Ocean, India, according to his own accounts to China and the East Indies as well as to Central Africa and the neighboring Iberian peninsula. One can scarcely imagine such a vast journey taking place at that time, a Moroccan reaching Isfahan or Delhi (where he was even appointed a judge). The accounts of these travels, later recorded and assembled upon his return to Tangiers, provide what is perhaps the most vivid and colorful picture of the life of the medieval Muslim traveler, as well as considerable knowledge of the state of Islamic society at that time, and also of the life of the non-Islamic countries that he visited.

Ibn Baṭṭūṭah's account cannot be compared with those of al-Bīrūnī from a scientific point of view; but it must be asserted that it is as colorful and as useful a source as al-Bīrūnī's of the sciences of man, from the viewpoint of portraying a true-to-life image of the medieval Muslim and his world. Ibn Baṭṭūṭah also provided one of the few Muslim sources about China and Chinese civilization which, since

[5] *Ibid.*, I, pp. 22–26.

the Mongol invasion, had gained much closer contact with the Islamic world, in the arts as well as in the sciences.[6]

> The land of China is of vast extent, and abounding in produce, fruits, grain, gold and silver. In this respect there is no country in the world that can rival it. It is traversed by the river called the "Water of Life," which rises in some mountains, called the "Mountain of Apes," near the city of Khān-Bāliq [Peking] and flows through the centre of China for the space of six months' journey, until finally it reaches Sīn as-Sīn [Canton]. It is bordered by villages, fields, fruit gardens, and bazaars, just like the Egyptian Nile, only that [the country through which runs] this river is even more richly cultivated and populous, and there are many waterwheels on it. In the land of China there is abundant sugar-cane, equal, nay superior, in quality to that of Egypt, as well as grapes and plums. I used to think that the ʿOthmānī plums of Damascus had no equal, until I saw the plums in China. It has wonderful melons too, like those of Khwārism and Isfahan. All the fruits which we have in our country are to be found there, either much the same or of better quality. Wheat is very abundant in China, indeed better wheat I have never seen, and the same may be said of their lentils and chick-peas.
>
> The Chinese pottery [porcelain] is manufactured only in the towns of Zaytūn and Sīn-kalān. It is made of the soil of some mountains in that district, which takes fire like charcoal, as we shall relate subsequently. They mix this with some stones which they have, burn the whole for three days, then pour water over it. This gives a kind of clay which they cause to ferment. The best quality of [porcelain is made from] clay that has fermented for a complete month, but no more, the poorer quality [from clay] that has fermented for ten days. The price of this porcelain there is the same as, or even less than, that of ordinary pottery in our country. It is exported to India and other countries, even reaching as far as our own lands in the West, and it is the finest of all makes of pottery. . . .
>
> The Chinese themselves are infidels, who worship idols and burn their dead like the Hindus. The king of China is a Tatar, one of the descendants of Tinkiz [Chingiz] Khān. In every Chinese city there is a quarter for Muslims in which they live by themselves, and in which they have mosques both for the Friday services and for other religious purposes. The Muslims are honoured and respected. The Chinese infidels eat the flesh

6 Some Western scholars have doubted whether Ibn Baṭṭūṭah ever visited China at all. But as H. A. R. Gibb, the translator of his travels into English, has pointed out in his Introduction, these doubts raise more problems than they solve, and none of the reasons offered against them is sufficient to impugn their authenticity.

of swine and dogs, and sell it in their markets. They are wealthy folk and well-to-do, but they make no display either in their food or their clothes. You will see one of their principal merchants, a man so rich that his wealth cannot be counted, wearing a coarse cotton tunic. But there is one thing that the Chinese take a pride in, that is gold and silver plate. Every one of them carries a stick, on which they lean in walking, and which they call "the third leg." Silk is very plentiful among them, because the silk-worm attaches itself to fruits and feeds on them without requiring much care. For that reason it is so common as to be worn by even the very poorest there. Were it not for the merchants it would have no value at all, for a single piece of cotton cloth is sold in their country for the price of many pieces of silk. It is customary amongst them for a merchant to cast what gold and silver he has into ingots, each weighing a hundredweight or more or less, and to put those ingots above the door of his house.

The Chinese use neither [gold] dinars nor [silver] dirhams in their commerce. All the gold and silver that comes into their country is cast by them into ingots, as we have described. Their buying and selling is carried on exclusively by means of pieces of paper, each of the size of the palm of the hand, and stamped with the sultan's seal. Twenty-five of these pieces of paper are called a *bālisht,* which takes the place of the dinar with us [as the unit of currency]. When these notes become torn by handling, one takes them to an office corresponding to our mint, and receives their equivalent in new notes on delivering up the old ones. This transaction is made without charge and involves no expense, for those who have the duty of making the notes receive regular salaries from the sultan. Indeed the direction of that office is given to one of their principal amīrs. If anyone goes to the bazaar with a silver dirham or a dinar, intending to buy something, no one will accept it from him or pay any attention to him until he changes it for *bālisht,* and with that he may buy what he will.

All the inhabitants of China and of Cathay use in place of charcoal a kind of lumpy earth found in their country. It resembles our fuller's earth, and its colour too is the colour of fuller's earth. Elephants [are used to] carry loads of it. They break it up into pieces about the size of pieces of charcoal with us, and set it on fire and it burns like charcoal, only giving out more heat than a charcoal fire. When it is reduced to cinders, they knead it with water, dry it, and use it again for cooking, and so on over and over again until it is entirely consumed. It is from this clay that they make the Chinese porcelain ware, after adding to it some other stones, as we have related.

The Chinese are of all peoples the most skilful in the arts and possessed of the greatest mastery of them. This characteristic of theirs is well known, and has frequently been described at length in the works of various writers. In regard to portraiture there is none, whether Greek or any other, who can match them in precision, for in this art they show a marvelous talent. I myself saw an extraordinary example of this gift of theirs. I never returned to any of their cities after I had visited it a first time without finding my portrait and the portraits of my companions drawn on the walls and on sheets of paper exhibited in the bazaars. When I visited the sultan's city I passed with my companions through the painters' bazaar on my way to the sultan's palace. We were dressed after the ʿIrāqī fashion. On returning from the place in the evening, I passed through the same bazaar, and saw my portrait and those of my companions drawn on a sheet of paper which they had affixed to the wall. Each of us set to examining the other's portrait [and found that] the likeness was perfect in every respect. I was told that the sultan had ordered them to do this, and that they had come to the palace while we were there and had been observing us and drawing our portraits without our noticing it. This is a custom of theirs, I mean making portraits of all who pass through their country. In fact they have brought this to such perfection that if a stranger commits any offence that obliges him to flee from China, they send his portrait far and wide. A search is then made for him and wheresoever the [person bearing a] resemblance to that portrait is found he is arrested.

When a Muhammadan merchant enters any town in China, he is given the choice between staying with some specified merchant among the Muslims domiciled there, or going to a hostelry. If he chooses to stay with the merchant, his money is taken into custody and put under the charge of the resident merchant. The latter then pays from it all his expenses with honesty and charity. When the visitor wishes to depart, his money is examined, and if any of it is found to be missing, the resident merchant who was put in charge of it is obliged to make good the deficit. If the visitor chooses to go to the hostelry, his property is deposited under the charge of the keeper of the hostelry. The keeper buys for him whatever he desires and presents him with an account. If he desires to take a concubine, the keeper purchases a slave-girl for him and lodges him in an apartment opening out of the hostelry, and purveys for them both. Slave-girls fetch a low price; yet all the Chinese sell their sons and daughters, and consider it no disgrace. They are not compelled, however, to travel with those who buy them, nor on the other hand, are they hindered from going if they choose to do so. In the same way, if a stranger desires to marry, marry he may; but as for spending his money in debauchery, no, that he may not do. They say "We will not have it noised about amongst Muslims that their people waste their substance in our country, because it is a land of riotous living and [women of] surpassing beauty."

China is the safest and best regulated of countries for a traveller. A man may go by himself on a nine months' journey, carrying with him large sums of money, without any fear on that account. The system by which they ensure his safety is as follows. At every post-station in their country they have a hostelry controlled by an officer, who is stationed there with a company of horsemen and footsoldiers. After sunset or later in the evening the officer visits the hostelry with his clerk, registers the names of all travellers staying there for the night, seals up the list, and locks them into the hostelry. After sunrise he returns with his clerk, calls each person by name, and writes a detailed description of them on the list. He then sends a man with them to conduct them to the next post-station and bring back a clearance certificate from the controller there to the effect that all these persons have arrived at that station. If the guide does not produce this document, he is held responsible for them. This is the practice at every station in their country from Sīn as-Sīn to Khān-Bāliq. In these hostelries there is everything that the traveller requires in the way of provisions, especially fowls and geese. Sheep, on the other hand, are scarce with them. . . .[7]

7 Ibn Baṭṭūṭah, *Travels in Asia and Africa,* translated by H. A. R. Gibb (London: C. Rankedge & Sons, Ltd., 1929), pp. 282–296. Reprinted by permission of Routledge & Kegan Paul Ltd., London.

CHAPTER NINE

THE ALCHEMICAL TRADITION

ALCHEMY CONSIDERED IN ITS TOTALITY, and as it has been understood and practiced throughout its long history, has to do not only with the physical domain of existence but with the subtle or psychological and the spiritual domain as well. One must distinguish between a spiritual alchemy, whose subject matter is the soul and whose aim is its transformation, and a "physical" alchemy, which deals with various substances, especially metals, and is employed by artisans and members of craft guilds. Both, however, make use of similar symbols and a common language; moreover, they are connected by the nexus that binds together different domains of existence.

Among the famous alchemical writers, we find some who deal essentially with inner transformations, others with chemical ones; yet a third group uses external operations as a support for the inner transformations of the soul. For example, among Islamic alchemical works, al-ʿIrāqī's writings belong for the most part to the first category, Rhazes' to the second and Jābir's mostly to the third, as will be seen in the selections presented from their works later in this chapter. There are also instances of alchemical transformations performed by spiritual masters—in the Islamic world by the Sufis—which have the character of a miraculous intervention, and must therefore be considered as separate cases within the tradition of alchemy. Alchemy, therefore, is not just a prelude to chemistry, although it is in part connected with it. If we are searching solely for the origins of chemistry, we must turn as much to technological sources as to alchemical treatises, for in alchemy we find a science whose subject matter is the soul, as well as the mineral world.

Yet, while keeping in mind the overall distinction between alchemy as a science of the soul and alchemy as a prelude to chemistry, we must remember that ancient and medieval man did not separate the material order from the psychological and spiritual in the categorical manner that has become customary today. There was a "naiveness" in the mentality of premodern man which made it possible for him to "combine" the physical and psychological domains, and to see a deeper significance in physical phenomena than just plain facts. It is this belief in the multiple states of being, their interrelationships, and the possibility of moving from one level to another, that comprises the general matrix of the long tradition of alchemy whose origins extend back to prehistoric times.

The basic symbols and principles of alchemy stem from the earliest periods of human history, and convey through their very concreteness the primordial character of this point of view. Ancient man, during the millennia before recorded history, considered metals to be a special class of beings, which did not belong to the natural environment of the "Adamic race." The earliest iron probably came from meteorites which, in falling from the heavens, gave that metal special virtues and powers. Metallurgy in ancient times was seen as a kind of obstetrics, which removed from the womb of the earth the fruits that the earth had "conceived" and brought to maturation. The metallurgical guilds of Babylonia, India, and China—as among contemporary African tribes—developed special rites of initiation to protect themselves from the subtle power inherent in metals. They themselves were a group to be feared and respected by others, because of the power they had attained by virtue of their dominance over the mineral world.

Alchemy as an explicitly defined discipline emerges at a much later period of history. Neither in the West nor in the Orient was the world-view of alchemy regarded as a science and a "philosophy of Nature" until about the time of the birth of Christ. In the Western world, the birth of alchemy, as is well known, took place in Alexandria, where the cosmological doctrines of the Egyptian tradition, attributed historically to Hermes or to Thoth, became formulated in the language of Greek philosophy. In fact, one can observe two early alchemical schools—one Egyptian, the other Neoplatonic—connected, respectively, with Olympiodorus and Stephanos.

Leaving aside Chinese and Indian alchemy, each of which possesses a vast literature of its own, as well as many cosmological doctrines resembling Western and Islamic alchemy, one may divide the schools of alchemy stemming from Alexandria, and later integrated into the esoteric aspects of Islam and Christianity, into four branches: Byzantine, Arabic and Persian (Islamic), Latin and postmedieval.

The earliest texts of Alexandrian alchemy still extant are Byzantine, and written in Greek. They are usually connected with the names of Zosimus, Bolos Democritus, the monk Cosmas and Nicephorus. The Hermetic collection is named for the Egyptian god Hermes Trismegistus, who is identified by alchemical writers, and by medieval philosophy in general with the antediluvian prophet Enoch (in Hebrew) or Idrīs (in Arabic); it contains the most important sources of Byzantine as well as of Arabic and Latin alchemy, and includes such texts as the *Perfect Sermon* and the Theban Papyrus. The famous *Emerald Table,* usually attributed to Hermes, is however most likely of much later origin.

In Arabic or Islamic alchemy, which arose soon after the rise of Islam in the first/seventh century, and has had a continuous tradition until today, there is a very large number of texts, written during the past twelve centuries and dealing with all phases of the art. The most important corpus is that of Jābir ibn Ḥayyān, the alchemist, who became the greatest authority on the subject, not only in the Islamic world but also in the West, where as "Geber" he became universally accepted as the leading authority.

By the sixth/twelfth century, following the translation of alchemical texts from Arabic into Latin, interest in alchemy grew in the Latin West, continuing into the seventeenth and even eighteenth centuries. The earliest Latin text known is the *Turba Philosophorum,* which was translated from the Arabic; among the earliest students of alchemy who wrote on the subject, one may mention Roger Bacon, Albertus Magnus, Arnold of Villanova, Raymond Lully, and somewhat later, Nicolas Flamel.

Even after the end of medieval civilization, interest in alchemy continued; in fact, a great deal of what had remained secret until then began to appear in writing. During this phase, the local European languages—especially French, German, and English—became vehicles, along with Latin, for the expression of alchemical ideas, a process which continued into the seventeenth century. Among the famous alchemists of this period one may name Paracelsus, Agrippa, "Basil Valentine," and the Rosicrucians, Michael Maier and Robert Fludd. Hermeticism, of which alchemy is an "application," was connected not only with the Kabbalah, but also with the Rosicrucian movement in Germany and England.

During the seventeenth century—even after the rise of the mechanical philosophy—many of the foremost philosophers and scientists of the age took an intense interest in alchemy: one need hardly mention the extensive writings of Newton on the subject. It was also in the seventeenth century that the remarkable German cobbler and theosophist, Jakob Boehme, was to express his gnostic visions in the language of alchemy. The alchemical and Hermetical tradition continued to survive in England in the eighteenth century although by now its world view had been completely rejected in "official" scientific circles. Moreover, in the nineteenth century the few surviving students of alchemy journeyed to Fez in Morocco to renew their contact with the alchemical tradition.

During this long history, the principles of alchemy remained nearly unchanged. Considered in its most essential meaning, alchemy has always been a spiritual science, concerned primarily with the transformation of the soul, and using as its support artisanal operations for the preparation of metals, as well as the symbolism of the mineral kingdom. The fact that the transformation of base metals into silver and gold is chemically impossible is precisely what shows that the domain of the soul is not based on the same strict physical laws as those of the material order. For the soul, by its encounter with the pure spirit, can liberate itself from its own "material" conditions—a liberation which has a miraculous character, such as the production of gold would express perfectly.

It may then be asked how this spiritual science differs from mysticism, as it was understood in its medieval sense. Actually, alchemy is related to mysticism, in that it has as its end the realization of the "Adamic state," or state of Paradise, and is therefore comparable to the "small mysteries" of antiquity, while mysticism (or, in Islamic terminology, Sufism or gnosis) is comparable to the "great mysteries." All spiritual techniques seek to awaken fallen man from the dream in which he lives: he dreams continuously of his individual state of being, and of the many forms through which the external world presents itself to him; he builds for himself a paradise of illusions, so as to forget the absence of God. To recover the vision of the spiritual world, the soul of man must "die" to this dream, this ceaseless flow of images which fallen man regards as the normal, everyday state of his consciousness. Spiritual methods, therefore, seek to kill the dream, to break the flow of images either by asking—as among the followers of the Vedanta, and certain schools of Sufism—the question "Who am I?," or by the invocation of one of the Divine Names, the central technique of Sufism, which has its parallels in other traditions.

Alchemy, on the other hand, makes use of the dream itself, in order to transcend it. It enlarges the dream of the individual soul to cosmic dimensions, breaking the prison of individual existence by the love of the beauty of Nature. The dream of the individual soul becomes that of the World Soul, and the contents of this dream, hitherto merely the sensible appearances of things, becomes virgin Nature in its original purity. Man thereby recovers the relationship which existed between Adam and all of creation, before that spiritual event which, in Christianity, is symbolized by the Fall. In the end, when the base metal is transformed into gold, the alchemist realizes that it is not he but the Divine Principle of the universe that is truly dreaming the cosmos.

In a more general sense, alchemy is a science that includes other elements than the spiritual. One may in fact distinguish, in medieval times, three elements: a spiritual alchemy, which is the most essential aspect of alchemy; a sort of chemistry, which was expressed in alchemical terms, but which actually belongs to the history of chemistry and technology; and a vulgar alchemy, which really tried to make gold by purely chemical means, and whose practitioners the medieval alchemists themselves called "charcoal burners" and "blowers."

Spiritual alchemy is not, however, merely a science of the human psyche, independent of the physical domain, as has been maintained by certain scholars. To totally separate the soul or the psychic element from Nature would be to misunderstand completely the alchemical point of view. The authentic alchemy is a "sacrificial science" of the materials of this earth—a science dealing with the transmutation of earthly elements, in which the material substance is ennobled, "made sacred." It thus regards the material aspect of things not as an independent and autonomous reality, but as the "condensation" of psychic and spiritual realities belonging to the higher orders of being. The alchemist seeks to know Nature not in its own terms, but in the light of that which is superior to it. The medieval *Liber Platonis Quartorum* clearly expresses the hierarchy in terms of which the alchemist seeks knowledge of Nature:

> Know that the goal of the science of the Ancients is that from which all things proceed—the invisible and immobile

God, whose Will brings into being the Intelligence. From out of the Will and the Intelligence appears the Soul in its unity; from the Soul are born the distinct natures, which in turn generate the composed bodies. Thus one sees that a thing can be known only if one knows what is superior to it. The Soul is superior to Nature, and it is by it that Nature can be known. The Intelligence is superior to the Soul, and it is by it that the Soul can be known. Finally, the Intelligence cannot but lead back to that which is superior—that is, to the One God who envelops it and whose Essence is imperceptible.

When man penetrates the mysteries of Nature, the "facts of Nature" become transparent symbols, revealing the "divine energies" and the "angelic" state which fallen man has lost, and which he may recover only for a moment, as when he is enraptured by the beauty of music or of a lovely face. At such moments man forgets his limited self, his individualistic dream, and participates in the cosmic dream, thus becoming freed from the prison of his own carnal soul. For the alchemist, Nature becomes the body of the Logos, and the female aspect of the Divine Act. It is now a sacred, living body, an anthropos similar to the human microcosm, in which the "Divine Breath" is to be found everywhere as the animating principle. For the alchemist, correspondences—such as that between the seven planets and the seven metals engendered in the earth by them; or the seven centers of life in the human body gravitating around the solar heart, and the seven notes of the musical scale that manifest the "silent music of Nature"—are so many incorporations, both macrocosmic and microcosmic, of the same Divine Word. The alchemist discovers, in that very Nature that veils God, the Nature that manifests Him.

The work of alchemy is the spiritual integration and absorption of Nature; or, as Meister Eckhart says, the precipitation of substances in the Divine Paternity, for "the nature which is in God seeks nothing but the image of God." The possibility of this transformation for the whole of Nature is, however, at this moment of time far away, because creation has fallen away from its original condition—Paradise or the Edenic state—and the reestablishment of what in Christianity is called the "Celestial Jerusalem" is yet to come. Therefore, the transformation of Nature can occur immediately only in man's heart, which—as the instrument of gnosis—can "see" gold in the base metals. Alchemy, thus, seeks to awaken in man a sense of Divine omnipresence, even in the realm of matter, where one would least expect to look for it.

From the alchemical point of view, therefore, the transformation of base metal into gold by the alchemist may be regarded as the counterpart of the transformation of a lost soul by a saint. The alchemist who has become a master of his art "sees" in the base metal the possibility of its becoming "sanctified"—that is, of its becoming gold. Moreover, his vision is "operative," as is that of the saint, who transforms the lost soul, not only theoretically but effectively.

While the alchemical tradition was still fully alive, the alchemist played the role of one who helped Nature, which is "suffocated" by the presence of fallen man, to "breathe the Divine Presence," and thus to be purified. Moreover, he awakened in the materials of this world their real nature, making from them the elixir which gives strength to the soul. He was, therefore, the real though hidden king of Nature, and its source of grace. His role was, to use the Christian terminology, "to celebrate analogically a mass, the materials of which would not only be bread and wine but the whole of nature."[1]

For the artisan every process, such as making transparent glass out of opaque substances, which ennobled matter, served as a "mass" in which a physical substance was made "sacred" and integrated into its spiritual prototype. In the mentality of the ancient and medieval craftsman the smelting of a black ore and its transformation into a shiny metal or the formation of glass or other transparent objects as well as the making of things according to the principles of traditional art was an alchemical process in which matter was ennobled and made "sacred." It was not only the transmutation of base metal into gold which comprised alchemy but, in a more general sense, every transformation of matter which, through a "spiritual presence," ennobled and purified matter and made it a more direct and intelligible symbol of the spiritual world.

The alchemical texts, upon which most of our knowledge of alchemy depends, were meant as supplements to a tradition of oral teaching; alchemy remained always a secret art, taught only to those capable of understanding its principles

[1] M. Aniane, "Alchimie, Yoga cosmologique de chrétienté médiévale," in *Cahiers du Sud* (Paris: Loga, 1953, p. 247. Much of this introduction on alchemy is indebted to this article and to the several articles of T. Burckhardt in *Etudes Traditionnelles,* as well as to his *Alchemie, Sinn und Weltbild* (Olten: Walter-Verlag, 1960).

and worthy of being initiated into its mysteries. The texts taken by themselves, are therefore usually abstruse and often incomprehensible; the study of them alone cannot reveal the processes and methods of alchemy and much of what concerns the technical operations of this art remains unknown to us.

Alchemy, however, also has a "philosophy of Nature," which we can come to know and which remains of primary importance today, even though the alchemical procedures cannot be known exactly. All the schools of alchemy shared a particular view of the cosmos: a view which served as background for both spiritual and artisanal alchemy. Alchemy, as a cosmological science of Alexandrian origin, was like a crystal which, when brought into the light of the living esotericism of Islam and Christianity, began to glow with great brilliance. Its integration into Islam and Christianity—like that of its sister art, astrology—was to result in certain transformations of its formulations, but the principles of its spiritual vision of Nature were to persist. Alchemy was to provide first of all, a complete language for the processes of the soul's transformation from its chaotic state to its final illumination, those processes of transformation which al-Ghazzālī and Ibn ʿArabī, in fact, call the "alchemy of happiness." Secondly, the symbolism of alchemy became integrated into the craft initiations in both Islam and Christianity, enabling the medieval artisan to derive spiritual benefit from manual work: the transformation of amorphous things into objects of art became the external support for the inner transformation of the craftsman.

In the Christian world, which provided the background for Western alchemy (to be discussed later), Hermeticism, of which alchemy was a branch, became a complement of Christianity up to the Gothic period. Christianity is based on the hatred of the flesh and the world. It neglects the world because its aim is not to install man in the world but to make him leave it. Hermeticism became an application of Christianity to the "psychocosmic" domain, so that with its aid Christianity could become incarnated in a totality governing all aspects of a civilization. Hermeticism, by giving the crafts, the arts and sciences and heraldry their character of "small mysteries," integrated the various orders of society into the "greater mysteries" of Christianity. Moreover, it provided a sacred conception of Nature which was absent from Christianity—particularly from Thomistic theology which, in "secularizing Nature" eventually provided the background for the separation of the natural sciences from the context of Christianity.

Between the alchemy of the medieval period and modern chemistry there is a continuity of subject matter, and perhaps some similarity of certain techniques; as to their point of view and ultimate objective, however, there is an abyss between them. In alchemy, Nature is sacred; all the operations performed upon it therefore have an effect upon the soul of the alchemist himself, by virtue of the analogy between the microcosm and the macrocosm. Chemistry, on the contrary, could come into the foreground only after the substances with which alchemy dealt were deprived of their sacred character, so that operations upon them affected only the substances.

Like many other traditional sciences, but unlike modern chemistry, alchemy is symbolic; it is based on the adage attributed to Hermes, that "that which is lowest symbolizes that which is highest"—which means that the sensible and immediate aspects of things symbolize the highest domain, that of the Intellect, which lies above the intermediate domain of individual human faculties, such as discursive reason. Sciences based on the sensible domain are therefore capable of intellectual applications of the highest order, "intellectual" here meaning not only "rational," but "based on the universal Intellect," whose knowledge is immediate, not indirect.

In medieval times, the study of alchemy was closely allied with that of astrology. In fact, one may describe the two subjects as complementary, the one dealing with heaven, the other with the earth, as these terms are understood in their cosmic sense. Astrology is based on the Zodiac and the planets, alchemy on the elements and metals. The Zodiac is the world of archetypes, hiding and at the same time revealing that Pure Being that lies beyond it and above the cosmos. The planets are so many "material" modes of the cosmic intelligence, forming in a descending order the intermediary domains between Being and becoming; astrology is the path of descent from the essential and superior pole of the cosmos to the substantial and inferior pole. Alchemy, on the contrary, begins "from below" with the substance or *materia prima* that is the inferior pole of the cosmos, and builds by ascent toward the superior pole. It deals with the four qualities—the basic polarizations of Nature—and with the seven metals commonly used in antiquity. The metals may be called "intelligent" modes of terrestrial matter, just as the seven visible planets are "material" modes of the heavenly intelligences. Between them lie the various degrees of cosmic existence.

Seven symbols, the same for both metals and planets, provide the meeting place for the alchemical and astrological perspectives: the metals are the "signs" of the planets on earth, generated in the earth's bosom through planetary influences.

♄	♃	♂	☉	♀	☿	☽
Saturn	Jupiter	Mars	Sun	Venus	Mercury	Moon
lead	tin	iron	gold	copper	quicksilver	silver

These symbols are made up of three basic parts. The circle ○, which symbolizes the active, male principle, identified with sulfur; the semicircle ☽, which symbolizes the female, passive principle, identified with mercury; and the cross +, symbolizing the four qualities or elements, which typify all "material" differentiation. Gold, therefore, corresponds to the Essence or sulfur, and silver to the Substance, or mercury. Only in the gold symbolized by the circle is everything integrated into the archetype; all the other metals are more or less "peripheral," reflecting the transcendent model only partially and extrinsically. Gold and silver, the two noble metals, may be regarded as the "static" aspects of the sulfur and mercury principles; chemical sulfur 🜍 and quicksilver, ☿, however, are the "dynamic" aspects of these same principles, as is shown by the fiery, igneous quality of sulfur, and the slippery, gliding quality of quicksilver (or mercury).

As for the other metals, those whose signs contain the semicircle have a predominance of the mercury principle, while those with a circle have a greater amount of sulfur. The position of these symbols with respect to the cross determines the internal structure of the metal. For example, in the symbol for lead, ♄, the semicircle is dominated by the cross; this metal, therefore, is most "chaotic," because the "chaos" of a virtual differentiation has neutralized the mercurial substance. In the symbol for copper, ♀, on the other hand, the sulfur dominates the differentiation, so that copper is more stable than lead, although of course it still falls short of the inner stability of gold. As for iron, ♂, the arrow, which plays the role of the cross, dominates the sulfur principle, so that this metal is also chaotic and greatly coagulated, even though rich in sulfur.

Only in the symbol for quicksilver, ☿, are all three symbolic elements present; here the three principles coexist without absorbing one another. The semicircle or lunar principle cannot entirely dominate the cross of "material" differentiation without causing dissolution because of the "volatilizing" character of mercury. Sulfur, on the other hand, does not necessarily dissolve the contrasts in the *materia,* because of the "forming" action it exhibits, by virtue of which it gives form to things. The hierarchical position of the three symbols shows the dominance of the mercury principle over the others. Since this principle by virtue of its passivity corresponds to the receptive substance, the symbol for quicksilver becomes the logical image of the cosmic substance, which contains all forms. The use of quicksilver in crafts to assimilate other metals may be regarded as a physical application of this principle.

Sulfur and mercury, the active and passive principles, are related to the four qualities in the following manner (Figure 1):

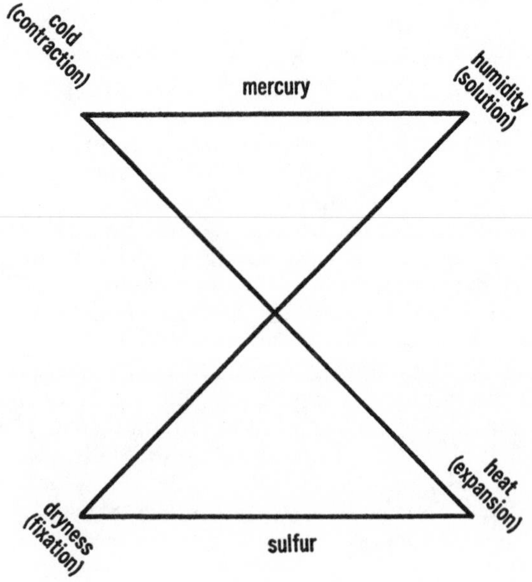

Figure 1.

Those qualities which belong to both the corporeal and the subtle or psychic domain are shared by sulfur and mercury, in such a way that there is always both repulsion and attraction between them. The elements which comprise the four basic natures possess both a contrasting character, which resists all synthesis, and a complementarity which makes this synthesis possible. Both sulfur and mercury, the male and female principles, seek to reach their common supreme archetype. They therefore tend to diverge from each other, at the same time as they are attracted to one another. The union of man and woman, sulfur and mercury, spirit and soul, of the Divine Act and Universal Nature—all of which signify the same cosmic principles, acting at various levels of existence—reconstitute the image of the transcendent model from which all cosmic polarities originate. In the mineral kingdom, gold symbolizes the perfect wedding of these principles, toward which all the other metals tend.

The alchemical work of which the texts speak so often may be regarded, both microcosmically and macrocosmically, as the effort to emulate Nature and to overcome those obstacles which negative cyclic conditions have placed in the way of that work. "Horizontally," it deals with the tension of the contraries, the attraction and repulsion, the "love" and "hate" which characterize both the human and the cosmic domains; "vertically," it integrates cosmic manifestation into its Divine Principle. Microcosmically, the alchemical work reestablishes the soul in its primordial condition, the state (in Arabic called *al-fiṭrah*) in which the soul is like gold, in perfect equilibrium, pure and incorruptible. This work, whether it be inward or outward, is achieved by dissolving things into the *materia* and then "regenerating" them, according to the order of the formal world—that is, first reducing things to the *materia prima* which symbolizes the inferior or substantial pole of the cosmos, and then transforming them into higher and more perfect states.

The *materia prima* is also the substance of the soul, which lies hidden in its bosom and must be found, before the soul can be transformed by the light of the Intellect. The "hidden" stone of alchemy is the *materia prima* which is at once negative, in as much as it is the source of multiplicity, and positive, since it is the mirror in which the Essence or Divine Principle is reflected—the only way in which the Essence can be known in the cosmic domain. The *materia prima* is given many names, each corresponding to a different aspect of its reality; for example, it is called the "sea" because it contains all forms, "tree" because it bears the fruit of the alchemical work, "virgin" because it is pure, and "prostitute" because it accepts all forms. Considered by itself, it is obscure and dark; it can be known only when it is identified with the *forma* which, by the achievement of perfection, reintegrates it into the Essence.

The Hermetic "great work" is based on the rhythm of "solution" and "coagulation" *(solve* and *coagula),* which can also be understood as expansion and contraction, or compared with the two phases of the breath. From the point of view of cosmogony, the first step is the *coagula,* which gives birth to manifestation; then follows the *solve,* which returns manifestation to the state of nonmanifestation. This process can also be discovered at any level of cosmic existence; in fact, what is condensation with respect to one pole of existence is always expansion with respect to the other pole. Every alchemical "transmutation" is designed to "dissolve" what is "coagulated," and to "coagulate" what is "dissolved," these being two aspects of the same process. As the medieval alchemists said: "Dissolution of the body is fixation of the spirit." The alchemical work means the reversal of "ordinary" relations, and the reestablishment of the natural and primordial harmony of parts; it also means bringing together the sulfur (which is the internal principle) with the mercury (which is the external, subtle ambiance), in order to give birth to the salt (which symbolizes a new individual state). The process of alchemy involves bringing together the contrary qualities of expansion and contraction, fixation and solution, in such a way that they compensate each other in perfect equilibrium. It is at the same time a "science of the balance," as explicitly set forth in Jābirian alchemy—a balance of the tendencies of the World Soul into which the individual soul seeks to integrate itself—and the art of the marriage of cosmic dualities, as symbolized by mercury and sulfur.

In many alchemical texts, the work is divided into two phases. First, there is the mortification, or descent and dissolution in the "waters," the surrender to the *Anima Mundi* —that is, the cosmos, regarded as the female principle, which devours her own son, the individual human state. This stage marks the dominance of the female over the male, of the moon over the sun, until the soul reaches that state of purity and virginity in which it begins to reveal the Spirit that is its luminous source. In the second stage, the "son" is regenerated: the Moon submits to the Sun, the female to the male. The "son," or the soul of the alchemist, which in the first stage was devoured by the cosmic "mother," now gains mastery over her, and by "philosophical incest" makes of his "mother" his "wife" and "daughter." As the *Turba Philosophorum* puts it: "The mother generates the Son, and then the Son generates the mother, and kills her." Modern psychologists have interpreted these stages only psychologically, regarding the dissolution of the soul into the state of purity as a disintegration of the mind into the "unconscious." All such interpretations are partial and incomplete, however, since they leave out of consideration the spiritual element illuminating the psyche, and standing above both the psychic and the physical domains.

In other texts, the alchemical work is divided into three steps: the work of "the black" *(nigredo),* the work of "the white *(albedo),* and the work of "the red," which itself is divided into *(citrinitas)* and *(iosis).* In the work of "the black," man detaches himself from the cosmic illusion, and plunges into the cosmic ocean, here regarded as female. This phase of the alchemical work is a kind of death, a "descent into hell." It is the preparation of the mercury, the subtle *materia* of the world. By this detaching himself from mental and physical activities, man becomes like the surface of calm water as he is absorbed into the *materia prima.* This absorption is exactly the reverse of the cosmogony of the Book of Genesis: it is the dissolution of a formal and created state into formless "waters." At this point, man perceives his body and Nature as aspects of the cosmic "play," upon which he no longer projects his own individuality. The mental state, which from the point of view of cosmogony had been a "coagulation" of the World Soul, is now reabsorbed into the Soul. Man returns to the root of matter, to the subtle mercury, in order to make it the source of his regeneration. This "descent into hell," to which reference is made in the phrase *Visita Interiora Terrae Rectificando Invenies Occultum Lapidem* ("visit the interior parts of the earth; in refining them, thou shalt find the hidden stone."),[2] is often symbolized as a nocturnal journey under the sea, like that of Jonas in his encounter with the monster. This monster is the Ouroboros, the serpent biting its own tail, who is the guardian of the latent energy present in the *materia.*

In the work of "the white," the alchemist uses the subtle aspects present potentially in the *materia,* in order to reach

2 Note that the first letters of the Latin words, taken in that order, spell out the English word "vitriol."

the light of the Intellect. By perceiving the subtle and not merely the gross aspects of Nature, he gains knowledge of the principles of the three kingdoms, and begins to understand the "language of the birds." Before him, the cosmic "matter" becomes transparent in the virgin purity of the World Soul, and he begins to see Nature "from within," in its Edenic purity. As Boehme says, in the *De Signatura Rerum,* "Paradise is still on earth, but man is far away from it, so long as he is not regenerated." The work of "the white" is conse quently an intermediary stage, as silver lies between the base metals and gold. Just as white is the synthesis of all colors, so is the work of "the white" an integration, which prepares matter for its final spiritual transformation.

The work of "the red" marks the final state of the purification of the soul, in which it is transformed into gold by the light of the Spirit shining through it. The fire in which the gold is made symbolizes the direct intervention of the transcendent Principle in the cosmic domain. This is therefore the stage of the ultimate "chemical marriage," in which sulfur "fixes" mercury, the Sun unites with the Moon, and the Spirit becomes wed to the soul.

The alchemical work is, in effect, a copy of the "mode of operation" of Nature, which is that of a Divine power and a unique principle acting in the cosmos. Just as the art of alchemy aids in the work of Nature, so too does Nature come to the aid of the art. When the sulfur and mercury principles are awakened in the "amorphous state" of matter, they first manifest their contrasts; then, as they grow, they begin to embrace and complement each other. That is why the alchemists say: "Nature disports itself with Nature; Nature contains Nature; and Nature is able to surmount Nature." Sulfur and mercury unite to form a superior state of being, in which their contrasts are integrated into a higher synthesis. Alchemy, which deals with the subtle domain as the principle of the corporeal, is an operation upon the *materia* performed in *conformity with* Nature, and not an act *against* it; the performance of this operation is in accordance with the power which governs the universe, it is based on the harmony between man and cosmos. Alchemy therefore offers a key to the understanding of that active-passive polarization which characterizes the cosmic domain at its psychic as well as at its corporeal level of existence. Moreover, its symbolism can lead to knowledge of the spiritual domain, because of this analogy, both direct and inverse, between the various states of being.

It is not possible for us to formulate explicitly the methods used in the alchemical work, because the texts remain intentionally vague on the question of methods, becoming here even more abstruse than on other aspects. What is said here regarding methods must of necessity remain general.

Alchemists used minerals not only for their physico-chemical reality, but as supports for meditation and contemplation, making use especially of such aspects of minerals as their color, transparency and other sensible characteristics—which since the time of Galileo and Descartes, have come to be known as "secondary qualities," and are usually left out of consideration altogether in modern physics and chemistry. The alchemist seeks to realize the cosmic dimensions of his own soul, as well as to purify and ennoble the cosmic "matter"; these two functions are the complementary aspects of that single, spiritual transformation through which the alchemist himself becomes the "world-egg," containing the philosopher's stone.

The major instrument for this transformation is the "imagination"—the Latin *imaginatio* and Arabic *khayāl*—which the alchemist sharply distinguishes from the fantasy with which it has become identified today. As the world is in the end nothing but the forms created by the "Divine Imagination," the "dream of the World Soul" (as Shakespeare says: "We are such stuff as dreams are made of"), so the faculty of the imagination in man is the instrument by which the alchemist "sees" the "subtle processes" of Nature and their divine archetypes. It is this faculty that perceives the symbolic aspects of space and time; it is that which the alchemists used to call "the star" in man, or which Paracelsus named *astrum*. Having penetrated the cosmic ambiance, and thus "deciphered" the cosmos, it reabsorbs it into the spiritual world. Fallen man sees the world only in its externality; the alchemist sees Nature inwardly, in the dream of the World Soul.

The alchemists—more generally speaking, the Hermeticists—consider Nature also to be the rhythm of the Divine Breath; in fact, Ibn ʿArabī calls Nature the "Breath of the Compassionate." They undoubtedly made use of the human breath so as to realize the "Divine Respiration" within themselves. It is, however, difficult to discover exactly how this use of the breath was made to correspond to the rhythm of solution and coagulation upon which the alchemical work was based. Nevertheless, the use of the breath in the techniques of *Laya-Yoga* (which, as a branch of Tantrism, resembles Hermeticism in so many ways) adds support to the belief that the cycles of the human breath did play a major role in the methods of alchemy.

In this brief statement of the general "philosophy of nature" of alchemy, we have sought to indicate some of its general principles, which pertain to both the spiritual and physical domains. Moreover, we have sought to show that alchemy in its highest meaning was a spiritual technique for liberating the soul from its material bonds by making it realize that the world is not a series of images and dreams of the individual psyche, but the dream of the Universal or World Soul, in which the human soul must participate. Alchemy was thus a way of awakening man from that illusion which he calls the "world" by means of the contemplation of the primordial beauty of Nature and participation in the dream of the World Soul through the removal of the limitative barriers of the individual psyche.

A. Jābir ibn Ḥayyān

The name of Jābir ibn Ḥayyān—more especially, in its Latin version, Geber—was, for many centuries, almost synonymous with final authority in alchemy. Yet as we have seen there is little known of the life of this remarkable author (possibly, group of authors) who was responsible for the Jābirian corpus, that group of treatises linked with his name.

Jābir was both a Shiite and a Sufi. He is in fact said to be a disciple of the sixth Shiite imam, Jaʿfar al-Ṣādiq, who was not only the founder of the Twelver-Shiite school of law called the Jaʿfarī school, but also one of the chief authorities on all esoteric knowledge. Jābir often writes that he is himself nothing but a spokesman for his master's doctrines and adopts the method of symbolic and hermeneutic interpretation *(taʾwīl)* of things so common among the Shia.

The large number of works bearing the name of Jābir has

cast some doubt upon the authenticity of some of them. Paul Kraus, the authority on Islamic science who made a special study of the Jābirian Corpus, has actually found that certain of these writings are by fourth/tenth century Ismailis.[3] By and large, most of what is not by Jābir himself is by later alchemists, who followed his teachings closely.

In fact there was very probably a kind of "society" or "fraternity," which used his name for all of its writing. The name Jābir, therefore, not only refers to a historical person, but is also (like that of Vyasa in Hinduism, or of Hermes in Hermeticism) a symbol for an intellectual function and a point of view. It is in this sense both the proper name, and the name of the "archetype," of the Muslim alchemist. Consequently, one can safely refer to a Jābirian corpus, which expounds a particular intellectual perspective of specific origin, even if all the works in it are not by Jābir himself.

The numerous works in this Jābirian corpus deal with nearly every subject—from cosmology, astrology, and alchemy, to music and the science of numbers and letters. In them, we can see the merging of certain esoteric aspects of Islam with Oriental Pythagoreanism, Hermeticism, and even elements from the Far East. They are important, both intrinsically and for the understanding of medieval science as a whole. Unfortunately, despite the commendable efforts of Kraus, Ruska, Holmyard and Stapleton, only a fraction of these texts has so far been studied.

The persons whom Jābir regarded as his authorities and sources, particularly in alchemy, are a strange mixture: Egyptian and Greek gods, such as Hermes and Agathodamon; philosophers, such as Pythagoras and Socrates; and certain other figures whose identity remains obscure. The alchemists, however, considered their wisdom to be universal and perennial, so that they did not hesitate to enlist among their sources certain persons who may seem to us to have nothing to do with alchemy. Jābir himself had definite ideas about the history of alchemy, and about the authorities who had expounded it through the ages; he writes:

> Know that successive philosophers have enabled the science of [alchemy] to profit from a long development, and have given it an extraordinary power, thus attaining their end. Arius [precursor of Hermes] was the first of those who devoted

[3] P. Kraus, *Jābir ibn Ḥayyān* (Cairo: Institut Français d'Archéologie Orientale, 1943), Vol. I.

himself to this art; starting with him, an uninterrupted tradition has come down to us, despite the distant epoch in which he lived. Pythagoras, the most ancient of the known philosophers, used to say of him: "It was my father Arius who said that"—an expression like our way of calling Adam our "father." In the same way, philosophers living in a more recent epoch have had the habit of speaking of "our father Pythagoras," conferring this title upon him because of his antiquity. This Arius was the first who spoke in an allegorical language about this art; it was he who applied to the Stone the first treatment. He asserted that this method had been taught to him by his ancestors, passed on from one man to another until it finally reached him. Following him, philosophers also applied to the Stone this first treatment, down to the time of Socrates. After Socrates came those who simplified and modified the original treatment pretending that by only repeating they could reach the end. This simplification produced, in fact, several advantages: the duration of the operation was shortened, and the operation itself made easier, and its use more general. Understand this! Then came other philosophers who, upon examining the second treatment, considered it too long. Knowing that they were able, with the aid of the subtle art, to shorten it even further, they invented an operation which is now called the third treatment. This third treatment occupies, with respect to the second, the same position as the second occupies with respect to the first. It is, therefore, the best of all the three. . . .

When these principles [the four natures] were mixed and combined, each of these accidents becoming attached to a body, someone [Arius] appeared and declared that man possesses the ability to imitate the action of Nature. He gave an example of this by reducing things to their primitive nature: he melted metals, and submitted them to perpetual coction, analogous to the perpetual and unchanging coction that Nature uses. He first constructed an instrument for melting, giving it a round shape similar to that of a sphere; then he put it in a pipe, as one does with a hydraulic wheel, and made it turn perpetually. In the ditch below the melting apparatus, he made a lasting fire; then he put some lead into the apparatus and submitted it to coction until what came out was transformed into gold. In the same manner he proceeded with tin, iron, and copper until he had transformed them all; he did the same with silver.[4] This was the first stage in the growth of the Art.

[4] Jābir is referring here, in the external meaning of his words, to the metallurgical practice of the melting of metals by means commonly used in the Middle Ages and antiquity. As for the gold, it most likely refers to the slight traces of it found in many ores.

> The first master disappeared; another made his appearance, one possessed of extraordinary abilities. It was he who [first] prepared the lofty elixir . . . then he made efforts to abridge time required for its preparation, and succeeded in reducing it to one-tenth of what it had been originally. Continuing these efforts, he finally succeeded in reducing the time for preparation to one-hundredth.[5] After that, new combinations and operations were discovered: some were legitimate; but there were likewise some without value, such as false and bad coins and all other exterior applications [this applies to the vulgar alchemy, to which reference has already been made]. By this, the later efforts of the philosophers became corrupted. Finally, the principle of the art was determined solely by the concurrences of the natures; it is by the weights, or the Balance, of the natures that one succeeds in knowing them. Therefore, he who knows their Balance, understands all the ways in which they behave, and the manner in which they are composed.[6]

As Jābir says, his method is based on the idea of the Balance, by means of which the correct proportion of elements is reached. According to him, all alchemical work involves the establishment of the correct proportion of the qualities or natures—namely, hot, cold, moist and dry.

> As for the second production, which is that of the Art: he who has acquired the knowledge of the necessary exercise . . . will choose first the Time in which he wants to compose something, and then the Place; or he will choose first the Place, and then the Time. . . . After that, he will choose, in order to add the natures to a substance, a suitable quantity and a quality. . . . Then he will fashion [with the substance] the one among the natures which is the strongest [that is, the most active], and which will occupy the interior part of the body. (Beware of beginning by fashioning [the nature which is] outside, for that would be a grave mistake.) To this, he will add its counterpart

[5] Jābir is making an allusion to the "law of contraction of time," i.e., the cosmological doctrine that, as a cosmic cycle unfolds events become more rapid.

[6] Jābir ibn Ḥayyān, *Kitāb al-Sabaʿīn* (*The Seventy Books*) in *Mukhtār rasāʾil Jābir ibn Ḥayyān,* edited by P. Kraus (Cairo: Maktabat al-Khānijī, 1354), pp. 463–464. This and several other works of Jābir's have been studies by P. Kraus in his *Jābir ibn Ḥayyān,* Vol. II (Cairo: Imprimerie de L'Institut Français d'Archéologie Orientale, 1942), pp. 58ff. Kraus's book is in French and was consulted by the author, although this and the following translations are the author's own.

> among the passive [natures]. Thus the outside is fashioned . . . conforming to the composition of the inside; in this way, the thing is produced, from non-being to being.[7]

Proportion means, of course, relations expressed in numbers; but here numbers are understood, not as pure quantity, but in the Pythagorean sense, as ontological aspects of Unity. The Balance of the qualities means the harmony of the various tendencies of the World Soul, which determines and orders the basic qualities. Jābir, like Pythagoras, relates this harmony to music; he writes:

> A certain sage decided to bring back these [relations] to the imitation of musical ratios [in order to show] that the emanation from which the things [of the sublunary world] are derived is perfect, [at least] to the degree that it corresponds to the emanation dispensed by the stars and their [numerical] relationships. . . .
>
> This imitation of which the sage speaks leads to music, but it does not reproduce the noble and sublime ratio which exists between 1½ and 1⅓, which leads to the ratio of two to one [referring to the series $1 : (1 + \frac{1}{3}) : (1 + \frac{1}{2}) : 2$]. This difference is due to the fact that the value of the first degree is doubtful. If we suppose that the second degree was four, the third six, and the fourth eight, the ratio could well have gone in this way. But the ratios could not have been perfect, since they contain four terms [degrees]: the terms of a perfect ratio are always three, that is, beginning, middle and end. This is the Trinity, which teaches us about Nature itself, and which is the sign of perfection. . . .
>
> I therefore say: Given that there are four degrees, as has been said, and that [on the other hand, the ratio] which possesses the medium with the best equilibrium is the ternary, it follows that the degrees of the natures [which imitate the musical ratio] must necessarily be [limited to] three, that is, the degrees one, two and three, so that the balanced and perfect relations, one-and-a-half to one-and-a-third to two, are based on them. These are the ratios in equilibrium of [musical] rhythm, which do not tend to go beyond the limits. He who wants to establish the ratios between the natures and the degrees of the qualities, in the image of the ratios which exist between the planets, and in the first movement (as is said by the astrologers, theurgists and philosophers), can easily do so. This is the basic principle.[8]

7 *Mukhtār rasāʾil*, p. 454; *Jābir ibn Ḥayyān*, II, p. 102 for the French.
8 *Mukhtār rasāʾil*, pp. 511–512; *Jābir ibn Ḥayyān*, II, pp. 201–202 for the French.

The use of the balance in alchemy implies the existence of correct proportions of the qualities in metals. Each metal has two exterior and two interior qualities: for example, gold is inwardly cold and dry, outwardly hot and humid; silver is just the reverse—hot and humid inwardly, cold and dry outwardly. Each quality has four degrees and seven subdivisions, or altogether twenty-eight parts. According to Jābir, everything in this world exists by the number 17, divided into the series 1:3:5:8. He assigns each of the twenty-eight parts of the qualities to one of the letters of the Arabic alphabet, and bases the four-fold division upon the series 1:3:5:8. The opposing natures of the metals are in the ratio of either 1:3 or 5:8, or vice versa.

Transmutation means the adjustment of the manifest and hidden aspects of a metal in order to reach the perfect proportion found in gold. This transmutation occurs by means of the Elixir, a substance from the mineral, plant or animal kingdom, the spiritual agent whose presence is necessary for the success of the transmutation. The numbers used by Jābir are intimately bound to the magic square shown (Figure 2), which, if divided gnomonically, gives the numbers 17 and 28 as well as the ratio 1:3:5:8. This well-known magic square—the Ming-Tang, according to which the provinces of ancient China were divided, and in whose central province (bearing the central number 5) the emperor resided—is essential to the arithmetical symbolism used by Jābir, and the numbers connected with it appear in many of his treatises.

As part of his numerical symbolism, Jābir also gives several tables in which the value of each of the Arabic letters, depending upon its position in the Arabic name for each metal, is given in terms of the quantity of each of the four natures,

4	9	2
3	5	7
8	1	6

FIGURE 2.

seven of the twenty-eight letters being assigned for each nature. For example, lead in Arabic is called *usrub;* it consists of the Arabic letters *alif* (a), *sīn* (s), *rā* (r) and *bā* (b) [the short vowels do not appear in written form]. The *alif* which appears first in the name symbolizes the heat in the lead; it is of the first degree, because of its position in the name. In the table which Jābir gives, heat in the first degree has a value of 1¼ *dirham* (the traditional Arabic unit of weight). The *sīn* comes in the second degree and, having a dry quality, has a value of one *dirham.* In the same way, Jābir gives the values of 1⅙ *dirham* for heat, 1 for dryness, 1¼ for humidity and 9⅓ for cold. A piece of lead of 12¾ *dirham* would therefore contain 1⅙ *dirham* of heat, 9⅓ of cold, 1 of dryness and 1¼ of humidity. All lead, according to the Jābirian theory, contains these same proportions of the natures, no matter what its weight or size or any other external features may be. These ratios correspond to the essential features of lead, and are the only factors that truly distinguish lead from another metal. To change the ratios of its natures would be to transmute the lead into another member of the metallic species.

The four qualities, and the masculine and feminine principles in terms of which Jābir explains the mineral domain, also form the basis of his elaborate cosmology; along with the balance and the harmony of symbolic numbers, they may be considered the principles of all Jābirian sciences. Jābirian alchemy itself is the establishment of equilibrium between the four natures and qualities, by means of the elixir symbolizing the presence of that spiritual principle that makes the harmony of the elementary natures possible.

> The four principles that act on bodies which belong to the three kingdoms, influencing them and determining their tincture, are: fire, water, air and earth. There is no action in the three kingdoms which is not produced by these elements. That is why in this art [alchemy] we rely upon operations applied to [the four elements], strengthening the one among them that is too weak, or weakening that which is too strong—in short, correcting that which is deficient. Therefore, he who succeeds in manipulating the elements in the three kingdoms succeeds, by the same act, in acquiring knowledge of all things, and in understanding the science of creation and the art of Nature. Do not let yourself be hampered by any doubt, because the nature of every elixir is derived from the elements, and is constituted by them. It is by the elixir that we introduce a

> nature which removes from the body the noxious nature existing in it. Thus, in something which possesses a surplus of the aqueous quality, one introduces fire and applies it to the degree necessary, without however allowing that thing to be consumed by the fire—which would add to its depredation. In this way, the body which is submitted to the action of fire reaches equilibrium and attains the desired state.[9]

The establishment of the equilibrium or balance of which Jābir speaks depends upon the reduction of the elements to their natures, from which the correct proportion of the qualities can be harmonized, according to the alchemical balance. For example:

> Water is poured into a cucurbit in which a substance possessing great dryness, such as sulfur, or something analogous to it, has been placed. Thus, the humidity of the water will be dried up by the dryness [of the sulfur], and by the heat [of the fire of distillation]. Humidity will be entirely burned out, and there will remain [of the water] isolated coldness. . . .
>
> As for heat and dryness, one proceeds in the same way as for humidity and cold: one takes the tincture, and extracts from it heat and dryness. The same is true for the earth, which is cold and dry: one takes it, and extracts dryness from it, and eliminates the cold.[10]

Jābir divided the materials with which alchemy deals into three classes, each having certain specific qualities, based on the predominance of one of the natures: (1) the "spirits" which become completely volatilized into fire; (2) the "metallic bodies," which may be hammered, possess a luster, produce a sound, and are not "mute," like the "spirits" and "bodies"; (3) the "bodies" [mineral substances] which cannot be hammered, but can be pulverized. Moreover, the "spirits" are five in number: sulfur, arsenic, mercury, ammoniac and camphor; the metals include: lead, tin, gold, silver, copper, iron and *khārṣīnī* ("Chinese iron").

There is little doubt that, in his classification of the minerals, Jābir is referring to substances that have real meaning in terms of the physical aspects of things. The key to the understanding of these phenomena, however, is to be found, not in terms of their physical aspects, but in the light of the balance of the qualities, and in the harmony between the

9 *Mukhtār rasā'il,* pp. 481–482; *Jābir ibn Ḥayyān,* II, p. 7 for the French.
10 *Mukhtār rasā'il,* p. 473; *Jābir ibn Ḥayyān,* II, p. 10 for the French.

inner and outer aspects of substances. Jābir, like the other alchemists, thus employs a language which applies to the psychic as well as to the physical domain. Even when considering materials in their physical aspects, he deals with them in such a way as to preserve the correspondence existing between their psychic and physical states.

An excellent example of Jābir's approach is his sulfur-mercury theory of the constitution of minerals. This theory—which, if considered only from the physical point of view—is the origin of the modern acid-base theory, was at one time attributed to the Latin Geber; it has been established, however, that the Arabic Jābir had already fully outlined it. The sulfur-mercury principles which in each domain of manifestation correspond to the active (or masculine) and passive (or feminine) principles became, from a chemical point of view, the acid and base through whose union a salt is formed. Alchemically, this theory explains the masculine-feminine duality upon which all cosmic existence depends, and in terms of which all of the medieval cosmological sciences sought to explain the phenomena of Nature.

Jābir writes, about the sulfur-mercury theory, that

> the metals are all, in essence, composed of mercury and coagulated with sulfur. . . . They differ from one another only because of the difference of their accidental qualities, and this difference is due to the difference of their varieties of sulfur, which in turn is caused by variation in the earths, and in their expositions with respect to the heat of the sun in its circular motion.[11]
>
> When mercury and sulfur combine to form one single substance, it is thought that they have changed essentially, and that an entirely new substance has been formed. The facts are otherwise, however. Both the mercury and the sulfur retain their own natures; all that has happened is that their parts have become attenuated, and placed in close approximation to one another, so that to the eye the product appears uniform.
>
> If one could devise an apparatus to separate the parts of one sort from those of the other, it would be apparent that each of them has remained in its own permanent and natural form, and has not been transmuted or changed. We say, indeed,

[11] E. J. Holmyard (ed.), *The Arabic Works of Jābir ibn Ḥayyān*, Vol. I, Part One (Paris: P. Geuthner), p. 54; Kraus, *Jābir ibn Ḥayyān*, II, p. 1 for the French.

that such transmutation is not possible for natural philosophers.[12]

There are many passages in the writings of Jābir which can be readily understood as chemical operations, without the need to unravel any complex alchemical symbolism, or to refer to the subtle domain. Besides the spiritual and psychological interpretations inherent in Jābirian alchemy, there is no doubt that Jābir also had considerable knowledge of the physical properties of things, a knowledge which he acquired through observation and experience. As an example of this aspect of Jābirian alchemy, here is his description of the preparation of cinnabar or mercuric oxide:

> To convert mercury into a red solid [mercuric sulfide]: take a round glass vessel and pour a convenient quantity of mercury into it. Then take a Syrian earthenware vessel and into it put a little powdered yellow sulfur. Place the glass vessel on the sulfur and pack it round with more sulfur up to the brim. Place the apparatus in the furnace for a night, over a gentle fire . . . after having closed the mouth of the earthenware pot. Now take it out, and you will find that the mercury has been converted into a hard red stone of the colour of blood. . . . It is the substance which the men of science call cinnabar.[13]

If the Jābirian corpus contains chemical texts which are easily understood in terms of modern chemistry, it also contains several cosmological treatises which, along with the purely alchemical writings, belong to quite another type of knowledge. In them, the various orders of cosmic reality are explained in terms of the masculine-feminine or sulfur-and-mercury principles. His scheme of cosmology is based upon the relation of a number of states of being with each other, a relation that is dependent upon the effect that a lower state derives from the action of a higher one, and in turn transmits to the state lying below it in the chain of Being. He describes the descent from the world of the Intellect, through the Soul to the world of the elements—which, as we have already seen, are composed of the four natures. The elements

12 From *One Hundred and Twelve Books*, translated by E. J. Holmyard in "Chemistry in Mediæval Islam," *Journal Society of Chemical Industry*, 1923, Vol. 42, p. 388, and in "The Identity of Geber," *Nature*, Vol. III (February 10, 1923), p. 192.

13 From Jābir ibn Ḥayyān, *The Book of Properties*, translated by E. J. Holmyard in "The Identity of Geber," *Nature*, Vol. III (February 10, 1923), p. 192.

of alchemy, therefore, form a part of the great unity which is the universe, just as the science of alchemy forms a branch of the more universal science of cosmology.

B. Rhazes

Al-Rāzī (in Latin Rhazes), as we have already seen in the chapter on medicine, was the greatest clinical physician in Islam, and enjoyed a fame in medieval and Renaissance Europe matched only by that of Avicenna. Before turning to medicine, however, Rhazes was an alchemist. In fact, it has been said that, as a result of too strenuous experimentation with alchemical processes, his eyesight began to give way and it was in desperation that he gave up the practice of alchemy.

Although most of Rhazes' philosophical works are lost, enough fragments survive to indicate some of the peculiar ideas that he held. He favored Plato over Aristotle and yet adopted an atomism similar to that of Democritus. He posited five eternal principles—the Creator, Soul, Matter, Time, and Space—in terms of which he sought to explain all things. His cosmology in fact echoes in certain ways some of the beliefs of Manichaeism. Most important of all, contrary to the rest of Muslim philosophers who accepted the "prophetic philosophy" of Islam, Rhazes openly opposed prophecy and in fact wrote against it. Furthermore, his denial of the necessity of revelation is directly connected to the transformation he brought about in the domain of alchemy.

Rhazes considered himself a disciple of Jābir and even the titles of most of his alchemical works are either identical with or resemble closely those of the Jābirian corpus. But Jābirian alchemy was based on the principle of the esoteric interpretation—"hermeneutic exegesis"—of nature as the cosmic text *(ta'wīl)* that is central to Shiism as well as to Sufism. Through the application of this method of interpreting the inner meaning of things, every Jābirian science, and especially alchemy, was concerned with both the external and symbolic or inward meaning of phenomena. Rhazes, by denying prophecy and therefore the possibility of this spiritual exegesis that is inseparable from it, also negated the symbolic dimension of alchemy and transformed it into chemistry. His alchemical works are in reality the first treatises of chemistry. His careful classification of substances is an important achievement from the point of view of chemistry, not alchemy. His *Secret of Secrets,* the Latin *Liber secretorum bubacaris,* which is the most famous of his alchemical works, is a text of chemistry which has preserved the alchemical language. It describes the chemical processes and experiments which Rhazes himself performed and which can be identified in their modern equivalent form of distillation, calcination, crystallization, etc. Rhazes in this and other works gives also a description of a large number of chemical apparatuses, such as beakers, flasks, phials, casseroles, naphtha lamps, smelting furnaces, shears, tongues, alembics, pestles, mortars and many others that have in part survived to the present day.

Even if later Muslim alchemical sources considered Rhazes as belonging to the Jābirian tradition of alchemy, a study of his works reveals that he belongs to quite another school. The symbolic and metaphysical dimensions of Jābir are no longer to be seen in Rhazes' writings. He is describing chemical and medical properties of substances, and he is in fact credited with major discoveries in this domain including that of alcohol and of certain acids. But the world-view of alchemy is absent in his works. In denying prophecy and the possibility of an esoteric interpretation of things, Rhazes also eliminated the symbolic dimension of alchemy leaving a science that was concerned with external properties alone, namely chemistry. The few examples given below from *The Secret of Secrets* reveal clearly that Rhazes was writing about chemical processes albeit in an alchemical language and that he himself had little interest in the alchemical world-view that existed before him and continued to survive long after his works had seen the light of day.

[The Smelting of Metals]

The hardest of the "Bodies" to melt is Iron. It does not become as fluid as water, except after treatment and (the use of) Medicines. The process of melting it is this. Take filings of iron, as much as you want, and having thrown on them one-quarter their weight of powdered red [arsenic sulfide], stir (the mixture) up. Then put it in a bag, and after luting it with good clay, place it in a hot (oven). Afterwards take it out, and weigh it. Then throw upon it one-sixth of its weight of [hydrated sodium carbonate], and add olive oil to the mixture. Next it is placed in a perforated crucible, fitted on to another. What comes down is received, and (again) melted. Then Sal-ammoniac and Syrian vitriol—both powdered, and mixed with olive oil—are taken and made into small balls, and it (the fused product) is fed with these. It may be melted as many times as you choose, for that adds to its fusibility and whiteness. If this (process) is repeated, the mass becomes so soft that it may be beaten out, and it will be as easily melted as silver.

Next (comes) copper. The method of melting copper is this. Cut it into small pieces and place them in a crucible in a (furnace). The furnace is filled with charcoal, and air is blown in until the copper melts. Then you sprinkle over it a little Goldsmiths' Borax. This is called, in their phraseology, ("feeding"). They say "He fed it with *būraq* [fusible salt], so that its eye might be opened" which means "you see that it is altered (in appearance)."

This process will also melt Gold, and Silver. The tins *Raṣāṣ* (i.e. Tin and Lead) melt more easily, being fused (even) in an iron ladle.[14]

SUBLIMATION

There are two methods of subliming Mercury, one for the "Red" and one for the "White." In subliming it there are two secrets, one the removal of its moistness, and the other to make it dry, so that it may be absorbent. The removal of its moistness is by either of two processes. After triturating it with what you wish to sublime it, you heat it over a gentle fire in a phial luted with clay, and then triturate and (again) heat it, doing this 7 times till it completely dries. Then sublime it with whatever you wish to sublime it, and heat it gently and place it in the aludel. Over the aludel there should be an alembic of green pottery, or glass, with a short wide spout, for the purpose

[14] Rhazes, *Instructive Introduction,* translated by H. E. Stapleton, R. F. Azo, and M. Hidāyat Ḥusain in "Chemistry in ʿIrāq and Persia in the Tenth Century A.D.," *Memoires of the Royal Asiatic Society of Bengal,* Vol. VIII, No. 6 (1927), pp. 354–355. Reprinted by permission of the Asiatic Society. (This study consists of translations from a variety of scientific texts by a number of different authors interspersed with critical comments on the texts.)

of distilling all the moisture that is in the mercury. Under (the spout) is placed a dish.

In place of this alembic, we may have a cover properly adjusted on the head of the aludel. It should have a hole large enough for the head of a large needle to enter. In this (hole) is placed a woollen lamp-wick, with one end of the wick hanging down into the dish, so that all the moisture that is in the mercury may be distilled.

Then you remove it (the alembic or cover), and replace it by the cover which covers its top completely, and lute the joint.

A better way (than using an alembic) is to have a hole in the cover of the aludel large enough for the little finger to enter. This hole is kept open until the substance appears in the form of dust, either white or black, by which you learn that the moisture has come to an end. Then the hole is closed with a properly-fashioned stick bound round with a rag, in accordance with the direction of our Master (Jābir) ibn Ḥayyān.

The substances with which Mercury is sublimed are Alum, Vitriol, Salt, Sulphur, Lime, (powdered) Brick, Glass, Ashes of Gallnuts, Oak Ashes, . . . ; and, of Waters, Vinegar, Water of Vitriol, "Water of Sal-ammoniac," "Water of Alum," and the "Water of Quicklime" [and sulphur, . . .].[15]

Sublimation of Mercury for the "White"

Take of Mercury that has been coagulated 1 *raṭl* (lb), and bruise it with an equal quantity of white Alum, the like quantity of Salt, and the like quantity of Ashes. Next sprinkle Vinegar over it, after placing it on a [flat stone mortar], and triturate it thoroughly for three hours a day, one hour in the morning, one hour at noon, and one hour in the evening. Then place it in a phial covered with clay. Close the head of the phial, and place it on hot ashes in an oven which has just been used for bread making. Leave it there for one night, and in the morning transfer the substance to the pot of the aludel, after (again) triturating it. Place powered salt at the bottom of the aludel. Adjust the alembic previously mentioned above the aludel, and (thus, by heating), remove the moisture from the substance. Then replace the alembic by a cover; and lute the

15 This and the succeeding selections are from the *Secret of Secrets* in the translation of Stapleton et al., *op. cit.*, pp. 385–393. In a recent Russian edition of the *Secret of Secrets* it is claimed that the work known until now by this name is actually Rhazes' *Book of Secrets* while the *Secret of Secrets* is an independent text also by him. In any case the work is one of Rhazes' authentic writings. See U. I. Karimov, *An Unknown Work of al-Rāzī "The Book of the Secret of Secrets"* (Tashkent, 1947).

joint; but first light a small fire beneath it, till its moisture has been removed by the gentle fire. Fit the cover to it and heat it (the aludel) for one hour with a gentle fire. Then increase the fire to a moderate degree. Keep the fire burning 12 hours for each *raṭl* (of the substance); and, whenever the ring of the cover gets heated, stop the fire, lest the substance that is on the shelf be spoilt and burnt. (This is continued) until the whole has sublimed. Then bring back the sublimate to the residue, triturate, and again sublime it. This is done thrice.

Then take burnt bones, which are procured from furnaces, pound them thoroughly, and triturate the sublimate with an equal quantity of these burnt bones for an hour. Sublime it in this way thrice, adding fresh bones each time. It will come out the third time white, dead, and absorbent. At one end of the cover there should be a hole, large enough for a large needle to enter, in which you insert a stick, bound round with cotton. Take this out once an hour, and drop the sublimate that is on it (onto the shelf). When, on removing it, you see no more sublimate on it, stop the fire, and let it (the apparatus) cool. Then collect what is on the shelf after gently breaking the joint. Moisten and soften what has collected with castor oil, and place it in a luted phial. Place this in a pot of ashes and close the mouth of the phial with (a piece of) wool. Burn a fire under the pot, in order to remove the moisture. When this has occurred, seal up the mouth of the phial and heap ashes over it. Over the ashes small pieces of charcoal are placed, by which a fire is lit on the top. In this way the substance will coagulate in the phial like (the metal used to make) a Chinese mirror. When this is attained, project 1 *dirham* of it on to 20 *dirhams* of Copper. Then it will penetrate into it, and function most effectively.

SOLUTION IN DUNG

This solution is carried out as follows: Dig, in a place in which the wind does not blow, two trenches, the depth of each of them being two cubits, and their breadth one cubit, and lute them with the droppings of house pigeons, mixed with turnip juice.

Take one part of fresh horse dung, produced that very day, and an equal part of the droppings of house pigeons, and after making the mixture into a thick paste with turnip juice, fill up one of the trenches to the depth of one cubit.

Place the thing which you desire to dissolve in a square bottle with a broad base. There should also be with you a mould of the same size as the bottle in which the substance has been placed. Press the mould down into the paste and shake it (so that it fits loosely). Then take the mould away and put in its place the bottle after closing its mouth with plaster. Put over the bottle a moistened basket and cover it with dung up to its top. Place over (the whole) a (large) pitcher and fill up the joint. Remove the pitcher every day, and sprinkle hot water over the dung, and renew the dung once a week.

Next, fill up to the middle with pigeon droppings the other luted trench, and add more of the prepared dung, and insert the mould, and place over it the pitcher for a night, and do not close the joint. When the morning dawns, uncover the buried bottle, remove the mould, take the bottle quickly and having buried it (in the depression on the second trench), place the basket over it and cover the basket with dung. Then cover everything with the pitcher, and close the joint. You will act in this fashion until the substance has (completely) dissolved; and this (process) will bring about the solution of most refractory substances, viz. Stones, "Bodies," etc.

On Animal Preparations

PREPARATION OF SAL-AMMONIAC FROM HAIR

Take washed black Hair, and put it in an iron pan with a cover, and close the joint, and cover the pan with small pieces of charcoal, and ignite them, and let them burn until they are extinguished. Then pour upon it (i.e., the calcined residue of hair), after placing it in an iron (pot), 20 times (its weight) of distilled water of Hair—and it is Spirit—and let it (the mixture) undergo coction for one hour. Then filter it, and coagulate with it the Spirits which whiten by means of coction, if you so desire. But if you need Sal-ammoniac, coagulate the solution, and it will turn into solid Sal-ammoniac.

ANOTHER (METHOD)

If you distil Hair, and take its water and oil separately, and place over it (the residue) an alembic with a wide spout, and light a fire, and fit below the spout a receiver wrapped in moistened felt, then the best (sort of) Sal-ammoniac will be coagulated in the receiver, if it please Allāh!

ANOTHER (METHOD)

Take washed Hair, and distil its water, placing under (the spout of) the alembic a receiver, whose bottom has holes fitted with tubes, and, below (each of) these, another receiver. The oil will then drop into the lower receiver, and the Sal-ammoniac will remain in a crystalline form in the upper one.

ANOTHER (METHOD)

If you dissolve Hair and distil off its white, yellow and red water, and, if then, you place over it an alembic with a broad spout, and distil off its tar and blackness, and finally transfer it (the dregs) to the Blind Alembic, and kindle a fire, then Sal-ammoniac will rise up, according to your desire, if it please Allāh!

[SODIUM CARBONATE, OR MILD ALKALI]
CALCINATION OF [SODA]

Take pieces of [Soda] and put them in a luted pot in an oven. Take it out when it becomes cold. Do this without trituration, until it (the salt) is whitened.

[SOLUTION OF THE SAME]
WATER OF STRONG [SODA]

Take 1 *raṭl* of white [Soda], and after pouring over it 12 *raṭls* of pure water, leave it for a day and a night. Then boil and filter it, and add another *raṭl* of [Soda], and leave it (again) for a day and night. Boil it (again) and filter it. Do this 7 times. Then decant and keep it, because it will dissolve [Amianthus] and Gypsum as we have said previously in our book.

[PREPARATION OF CAUSTIC SODA]

SECTION ON SALT OF [SODA] AND LIME

Take 1 *mann* of white [Soda] and an equal quantity of Lime and pour over it (the mixture) 7 times its amount of water, and boil it until it is reduced to one half. Purify it (by filtration or decantation) 10 times. Then place it in thin evaporating cups and hang them in (heated) beakers. Return what separates out (to the cup) and raise it (the cup) gradually, and protect from dust whatever drops from the cups into the beakers, and coagulate it into salt.

[Solution of Calcium Polysulphide]

Take 2 parts of Lime that has not been slaked, and 1 part of Yellow Sulphur, and digest them with 4 times (their weight) of pure water until it becomes red. Filter it, and repeat the process until it becomes red. Then collect all the water, and cook it until it is decreased to half, and use it. And Allāh knows (what is best!).

[Solution of Sodium and Ammonium Sulphide and Arsenide]

SECTION ON A SHARP WATER

Take 20 *raṭls* of pure water, and after adding to it 2½ *raṭls* of white [Soda] and unslaked Lime, leave for 3 days. Filter it, and repeat the process 7 times, each time adding one-eighth of pure water. Then add to it about one-tenth of (copper acetate) and yellow Arsenic Sulphide, and leave for 3 days. Filter it, and add half its amount of dissolved Sal-ammoniac. Leave it several days. Dissolve with it anything you like. It will dissolve [Amianthus] immediately.

[Solution of Caustic Soda and Ammonia]

WATER OF [SODA] AND QUICK LIME

Take equal parts of calcined [Soda] and unslaked lime, and pour over them 4 times their amount of water and leave it for 3 days. Filter the mixture, and again add [Soda] and lime to the extent of one-fourth of the filtered solution. Do this 7 times. Pour into it half (the volume) of dissolved Sal-ammoniac. Then keep it; for, verily, it is the strongest Sharp Water. It will dissolve [Amianthus] immediately.

[IMPURE SOLUTION OF AMMONIA]

A POISONOUS WATER

Take equal parts of pounded Sal-ammoniac and Copper oxide, and distil it. Then pour upon that which has been distilled, a similar quantity of Sal-ammoniac and Copper Oxide, and distil them. Do this 7 times. While distillation is going on, put a plug of cotton moistened with the oil of violets, or the oil of roses, in your nose, and put aside what has been distilled. Mix the dregs with a similar quantity of Sal-ammoniac and one-fourth of Colocynth pulp, and sublime it. Take what sublimes, and cerate it, and dissolve it, and mix with it that which has been put aside and bury it several days. It will be turned into a Sharp Water.

[USE OF MERCURY AMMONIUM CHLORIDE SOLUTION AS A DISSOLVING REAGENT]

Take volatilized Mercury and drench it with dissolved Sal-ammoniac. Cause it (the mixture) to perspire 10 times in a luted cup and dissolve it. If anything of it (the Mercury) remains, drench it (again) with Sal-ammoniac, and cause it to perspire several times. Then dissolve it till everything is dissolved. Do not be annoyed with the (length of time necessary for the) dissolving, for it is one of the most important of the substances, because it is a very strong water, dissolving all calcined substances and filings.

[USE OF SAL-AMMONIAC AS A DISSOLVING REAGENT]

ANOTHER (PROCESS)

Take the Calx of whichever you like (of Lead or Tin), and drench it with the water of Sal-ammoniac and the water of distilled Alum on the [flat stone mortar], and rub it for 8 hours. Then cause it to perspire in a rose-water bottle, until its smoke comes out. Do this 7 times. Then cause it to perspire 3 times with the water of Sal-ammoniac, until it becomes a salt which will melt.

[Saponification of Olive Oil to Soap]

CERATION OF SALTS WITH OILS

Take food Salt, and make it into a paste with Olive Oil and heat it for one night with a Dung fire in a luted pot which has its head closed. Do this 7 times. It will melt and flow.

[Preparation of Glycerine from Olive Oil]

DISTILLATION OF OLIVE OIL

Take as much as you like of fresh Olive Oil, and heat it with a similar quantity of water containing a little pure white clay, until two-thirds of the water has disappeared. Then filter it. Repeat the process with water and clay thrice. Then place it in a cucurbit, and after scattering over it Lime until it becomes like a thin paste, distil it. Do this several times. When you will test it, fire will not be ignited in it.[16]

These selections demonstrate fully Rhazes' concern with chemical reactions while at the same time he was faithful to the alchemical theory of transmutation of one metal into another. However, Rhazes makes no reference to the Jābirian mercury-sulfur theory.[17] In its place Rhazes believes that bodies are composed of potentially active matter, "spirit" and "soul." Since all things possess essentially the same substance, Rhazes believes that transmutation can be brought about by changing the proportions of the constituent ingredients of any substance, which in modern language means the removal of impurities.

As for the alchemical process itself Rhazes thinks that it consists of five stages: purifying of the substances to be used, their fusion, disintegration through solution, combination of the solutions of the different substances, and finally the coagulation of the product. In this matter he does not differ profoundly from Jābir who had a similar conception of the

16 Rhazes, *Secret of Secrets, ibid.*, pp. 385–393.
17 This fact has been pointed out by Stapleton and his colleagues in the above-mentioned study.

alchemical process but with certain alterations. Rhazes differs from Jābir in that, while Jābir is an alchemist who also deals with chemistry, Rhazes is a chemist who preserves the alchemical belief in the transmutation of one substance into another and employs an alchemical language to explain chemical processes.

C. Al-ʿIrāqī

The seventh/thirteenth century alchemist, Abuʾl-Qāsim al-ʿIrāqī, who was the author of one of the best-known Islamic alchemical tracts, the *Cultivation of Gold,* was also a disciple of Jābir. Unlike Rhazes, who had confined himself chiefly to the chemical properties of things, al-ʿIrāqī remained faithful to the teachings of Jābir, studying the external and physical properties of materials in conjunction with their symbolic significance, and in relation to the psychological and spiritual domains. His book is for the most part a summary of some of the teachings of Jābir; like other alchemists, he aimed not to innovate but to continue faithfully the doctrines of the masters of the art.

Alchemists such as al-ʿIrāqī regarded alchemy as of divine origin; they always sought therefore to preserve its original principles. This lack of "development" did not mean mere repetition, or an abandonment of intellectual activity on their part. For them, intellectual activity was not the creation of new ideas, but the "organic" assimilation of the principles of the Art. The beauty and freshness still to be found in the writings of some of the great alchemists arise from the fact that, having assimilated the principles of alchemy themselves, they were now able to express these same ideas in a fresh language, which did not depend merely upon the use of others' texts, but also upon their own direct and intimate experience. It is this freshness of language and beauty of symbolism that truly distinguishes the great alchemists from those who merely put together bits of the older texts. The intellectual activity of these alchemists, therefore, consisted of their piercing through the many veils of symbolism, in order to reach the immutable principles of the alchemical art, rather than of any "thinking about" the mineral kingdom, with the hope of "explaining" it according to new theories.

For example, al-ʿIrāqī follows Jābir in regarding metals as a single species, differing only in accidents, a species which he readily compares with plant and animal species; he expresses these ideas, however, in a manner which reveals his own mastery of alchemy, rather than by the simple repetition of Jābir's ideas. Likewise he has a similar conception of the all-embracing prime matter which he however describes in a particular manner.

Prime Matter

This prime matter which is proper for the form of the Elixir is taken from a single tree which grows in the lands of the West. It has two branches, which are too high for whoso seeks to eat the fruit thereof to reach them without labour and trouble; and two other branches, but the fruit of these is drier and more tanned than that of the two preceding. The blossom of one of the two is red [corresponding to gold] and the blossom of the second is between white and black [corresponding to silver]. Then there are two other branches weaker and softer than the four preceding, and the blossom of one of them is black [referring to iron] and the other between white and yellow [probably tin]. And this tree grows on the surface of the ocean [the *materia prima* from which all metals are formed] as plants grow on the surface of the earth. This is the tree of which whosoever eats, man and jinn obey him; it is also the tree of which Adam (peace be upon him!) was forbidden to eat, and when he ate thereof he was transformed from his angelic form to human form. And this tree may be changed into every animal shape.

This prime matter is also found in a bird, whose body is that of a man but its wings the wings of a bird. It has four feet and two hands, but its feet are despised [the opacity of matter], while its hands [form] are honoured on account of the benefit to be derived from them. But if ignorant man knew that the hands have no power save by the feet [since all things consist

> of form and matter], he would be more watchful of the feet than of the hands.[18]

Al-ʿIrāqī also explains the manner of writing the alchemical texts, and the symbolism of some of the terms found in them. He thus provides in his own text a sample of the way in which alchemical texts must be interpreted in order to make sense. But even then, he stops at a particular level, without giving the ultimate metaphysical significance of his terms, and asks us not to try to proceed beyond what he has chosen to expose.

> *Know* (May *Allāh* the Exalted have mercy on thee!) that complete phrases are divided into three classes: (1) a phrase of exact agreement which perfectly describes the allusion; this is the plainest form of speech and is not used in an allegorical sense at all; it is, rather, straightforward; (2) a phrase of inclusion; this indicates a part only of the meaning and is more obscure than the first, in contrast to which it may be used in an allegorical sense; (3) a phrase of necessary association; this is more obscure than the first two and is simple allegory. . . .
>
> An example of the third is the description of a man as a lion, in order to convey the idea of bravery by metaphor and simile. Most of the allegories of the Sages are constructed on this plan, that is, they describe the thing meant by indicating the necessary characteristics of it.
>
> As for the way of "inclusion," this is little used, in contrast to the way of "necessary association," since it is more obvious. As for the way of "exact agreement," this is not called allegory at all. Allegory must be either absolute, that is, indication by "necessary association," or relative, that is (a) indicating by necessary association coupled with "inclusion," or (b) indicating by "inclusion" coupled with "exact agreement" or (c) indicating by "inclusion" alone, or (d) indicating by "exact agreement" coupled with "necessary association."
>
> Of their description by "necessary association" we have an example in their phrase "Eastern Mercury." They mean by this the mercury extracted from their stones, and this is a phrase of "necessary association," for the Eastern Mercury is extracted from rocks, in contrast to the Western Mercury which is extracted from soft earth. Now if any characteristic of Eastern Mercury is found in their mercury they know it by this name. Understand that, therefore.

18 Al-ʿIrāqī, *The Cultivation of Gold,* translated by E. J. Holmyard (Paris: Paul Geuthner, 1923), pp. 23–24.

And they often indicate by their phrase "Eastern" a substance which is hot and dry as is the nature of the region of the East, and as is also the nature of the sun which appears from the East. Similarly by the "West" and by "Egypt" they mean the moistness extracted from their stone, as the West is related to moisture. "The River Nile" means the same.

The term "Land of India" is also employed by them to mean a substance in proper equilibrium, resembling the land of India in the equableness of its climate. The terms "heaven" and "earth" are intended by them to mean two substances, one of them volatile like the heaven and the other stable like the earth. By "animal" they mean an animal characteristic, that is, a substance which, when it goes into the fire, acquires movement like the movement of an animal, the cause of which movement is heat. They mean also by it a durable and equable substance, as an animal is durable and equable. By "death" and "life" they refer to a substance from which it is possible by suitable treatment to remove its lightness, or to do away with its movement in the fire, so much so that when it is placed therein it shows no movement. Such are the limes and other "dead" stones; they contain a characteristic of death as it is found in animals, a characteristic necessarily associated with these substances.

By "life" they mean the opposite of this, just as it is reported in stories that the spirits returned to their bodies and they arose; now this is a necessary characteristic of their stone, and so therefore they describe the latter thus.

They also use the term "marriage" meaning thereby a substance to which this name is necessarily appropriate, since it will join with a substance female in relation to itself, its lightness being transferred to the latter as the sperm is transferred from the male to the female; they therefore describe it by this characteristic of it. From this thou mayst judge of the rest of the analogies and allegories of the Sages. Therefore be grateful to him who has favored thee with this explanation, and have compassion on him, and do thou likewise that which it is meet for thee to do. But do not explain this matter except to its followers. . . .

Labour not to expose our secret more than we have exposed it unto thee, or thy exposure thereof will expose thyself; and leave the world and its pleasures to those whose only aim is enjoyment and sport and amusement. And let not doubt assail thee concerning that which I have spoken, for there is no disagreement among us in all I have said.[19]

The tradition of alchemy represented by Jābir, al-ʿIrāqī

[19] *Ibid.*, pp. 55–57.

and others has been a continuous one in the Islamic world, having lasted over the centuries to modern times. Its language and symbolism became integrated in part into that of Sufism, while at the other end its world view gave a spiritual dimension to the work of the craftsmen. Alchemy thus became tied to gnosis and, at the same time, came to provide a contemplative dimension for the creativity of the artisan.

CHAPTER TEN

ISLAMIC ALCHEMY AND ITS INFLUENCE IN THE WESTERN WORLD

INTEREST IN ALCHEMY in the Western world began with the translation of texts from the Arabic during the sixth/twelfth century. Perhaps the earliest, and certainly one of the most important Latin texts is the *Turba Philosophorum,* which was to be quoted as an unimpeachable authority by many succeeding generations of alchemists. The work is the account of a conference, in which nine "Greek" philosophers—Iximidrus, Exumdrus, Anaxagoras, Pandulfus, Arisleus, Lucas, Locustor, Pitagoras and Eximenus—describe the principles of alchemy, partly in terms of cosmology, and then proceed to describe the various phases of this art. The *Turba* is unquestionably a translation from the Arabic, although the original text has not been found. Martin Plessner, the contemporary specialist in the history of alchemy, argued quite convincingly that the *Turba* is a translation of the *Book of the Controversies and Conferences of Philosophers* by the third/ninth-century Egyptian alchemist, ʿUthmān ibn al-Suwaid. By transliterating the Latin names of the philosophers back into the Arabic, he has been able to identify the group of philosophers as Anaximander, Anaximenes, Anaxagoras, Empedocles, Archelaus, Leucippus, Ecphantus, Pythagoras and Xenophanes. These pre-Socratic philosophers are seen discussing the elements, the void and plenum in cosmological terms, before proceeding to purely alchemical discussions; their views, however, do not correspond to what is known about the pre-Socratics from other sources. Much of the *Turba* bears a resemblance to the *Refutation of All Heresies* by Hippolytus, so that the Arabic text may itself have been an adaptation from the earlier Greek text.

The use of Greek authorities in the *Turba* demonstrates the desire to show a unanimity of views among various philosophers on the subject of alchemy. These philosophers, who, during the Renaissance and later centuries, were to become pivots of controversy, meet in the *Turba* in a spirit of agreement, affirming a single point of view. Obviously, the medieval alchemists who quoted them, unlike the Renaissance authors, were not interested in polemics, but in the establishment of a universal agreement within their doctrines.

Another early source of Western alchemy was the corpus of the Latin "Geber," including the famous *Sum of Perfection,* for which no Arabic original has been found. The works of Geber follow the principles of Islamic alchemy, but some of their basic character differs from that of Jābir's writings. The texts attributed to Geber lack the numerical and alphabetical symbolism and the concept of the balance, both of which are basic to Jābirian alchemy. In these texts, as in those of Rhazes, interest in the symbolism of alchemy has already become less central, and is displaced by an interest in the physical properties of things. The author of those texts of Geber which are not translated from Arabic was probably a Spanish alchemist who used the name of the acknowledged master of the art. He displays a much more empirical and less contemplative attitude than the Arabic Jābir, without however deviating basically from the established principles of alchemy. Interest in the physical aspects of things became increasingly primary among the alchemists, to the extent that the contemplative spirit was weakened, and transparent symbols replaced in their thinking by opaque facts.

It may be unfair, however, to characterize Geber in this manner, because in the *Sum of Perfection* he reveals that he was forced to use the language of chemistry in order to hide the doctrines of spiritual alchemy. It may be that he actually differs from the Arabic Jābir only in his manner of expression, rather than because of any change in his point of view, from alchemy toward chemistry. Up to the seventeenth century, alchemy in the West was essentially the same science as its Islamic counterpart, except for the change of language from that of the Muslim to that of the Christian revelation. There is no historical reason whatsoever for making Western alchemy an intermediate stage between Islamic alchemy and modern chemistry.

Nicolas Flamel

Nowhere is the integration of the tradition of alchemy learned from Islamic sources into Latin Christianity better exemplified than in the writings of Nicolas Flamel. The traditional account of his life can itself be regarded both as a symbolic narrative and as a historical account. As Flamel himself tells us, he was born at Pontoise near Paris around 1330, and led a normal life as a skillful scribe and successful bookseller until one evening, when he saw an angel in a dream, showing him a book containing mysterious pictures. In 1357 the same book, called *The Book of Abraham the Jew,* was sold to him by an old dealer. From that moment on, the life of Flamel became transformed from that of a bookseller into that of an ardent student of alchemy. He spent many long days and nights in studying the book, revealing its existence only to his wife Pernelle. All his efforts were negated, however, by his lack of knowledge of Hermeticism and of the Jewish Kabbalah.

Determined to find a clue to the meaning of his book, Flamel set out to make the pilgrimage to the tomb of Saint James of Compostella in Spain. There he frequented the synagogue, in hope of finding a guide; yet, even there, his search was in vain. In despair, he started back to France. On this return journey, he was introduced to a converted Jew, Maître Conches, a Kabbalist, who was at last able to explain to him the inner meaning of this precious book, which even the Kabbalists had considered lost. Maître Conches died soon thereafter, after giving him enough instruction to permit Flamel to continue the Great Work by himself. In 1382, he finally succeeded in making the Great Elixir and as he himself writes, in converting lead into gold. An extremely devout man, Flamel is said to have used up the gold he had made to endow churches and hospitals all over Paris. Having lost his wife and companion in 1397, he spent the rest of his days in devotion, charity and writing on alchemy. He died in 1417 and was buried at a place chosen by himself and covered with a marble stone, bearing alchemical symbolism in a Christian setting.

The life of Flamel, a devout Christian who, through alchemy, had acquired the means to perform many acts of charity, seized the imagination of his contemporaries; he became the prototype of the alchemical sage. His indisputably devout life also saved him from outright condemnation by Christian authors of later centuries who no longer had any interest in cosmological sciences. The Abbé Villain, for example, embarrassed by Flamel's alchemical activity, tried in his biography to prove that Flamel was not an alchemist at all. Historical as well as doctrinal elements prove, however, that Flamel was both a devout Christian and an alchemist. His works are, in fact, among the best illustrations of the integration of the alchemical perspective into Christianity and the interpretation of alchemical symbolism in Christian terminology.

The *Book of the Hieroglyphical Figures* by Flamel is an example of Christian Hermeticism. It also deals with a universal aspect of alchemy, namely, the relation of alchemical elements to animal symbolism. This relation can be found expressed in different forms in many civilizations. Flamel's dragon or serpent, for example, appears not only in Islamic alchemy, but also—and with nearly the same meaning—in Hindu Tantrism, Taoism and, greatly elaborated, among the Mayas. Likewise, the unicorn, a symbol of the active aspects of mercury, is found with minor variations in nearly every tradition. The universality of these ties between alchemy and the serpent may be accounted for, in part, by the geometric form of this creature. The relation of the Divine Act to the cosmos is symbolized geometrically by a vertical axis, while Nature as a process is symbolized by a spiral revolving around the axis, as it traverses the various domains of existence. The primordial symbol of the serpent coiled around the world tree therefore signifies this relationship between the Divine Act and Nature. The serpent is always the symbol of cosmic power: Nature as potentiality is symbolized by the dragon biting its tail, the *Ouroboros,* which forms a circle; Nature as actuality is symbolized by two serpents forming the caduceus. These two serpents symbolize the basic polarity upon which the rhythm of the cosmos is based—the *solve* and *coagula* of alchemy; the ascending and descending phases of solar motion in astrology; or, from another point of view, the alchemical sulfur and mercury.

The Hermetic myth of the origin of the caduceus is that Hermes, finding a pair of serpents fighting each other, struck them with his baton, upon which the serpents wrapped themselves around it, thus giving him the theurgic power of "binding" and "loosening." This act symbolizes the transformation of chaos into cosmos by the intervention of a spiritual agent. The transformation of Moses' rod into the serpent may similarly be interpreted as the *solve* and *coagula* of the alchemical work.

The dragon, a form of serpent, may be regarded as symbolizing the fixed sulfur, so long as it remains without wings; the winged dragon, however, symbolizes "volatile" mercury. The dragon can have several meanings, symbolizing all phases of the work: it can have either feet or wings; it can live on earth, in water or in air, and as a salamander—even in the fire. It then resembles the Chinese dragon which begins as a fish in water and ends as a winged creature flying to the heavens. Another common animal symbol, the lion knocking down or eating the dragon, refers to the "fixing" of mercury by sulfur; a winged lion may symbolize both the masculine and feminine natures, or the androgyne.

In his *Book of the Hieroglyphical Figures,* from which we quote below, Flamel explains the symbolism of several of these animals and the colors used to paint them. While thus underlining the universality of the alchemical perspective, he expresses his formulations in the specific language of the Christian Revelation, within whose bosom alchemy found its metaphysical complement during the medieval period in the Western world.

Of the Theological Interpretations, which may be given to these Hieroglyphics, according to the sense of me the Author.

I have given to this *Church-yard,* a *Charnel-house,* which is right over against this fourth *Arch,* in the midst of the *Church-yard,* and against one of the Pillars of this *Charnel-house,* I have made be drawn with a coal, and grossly painted, a *man all black,* who looks straight upon these *Hieroglyphics,* about whom there is written in *French; I see a marvel, whereat I am much amazed.* This, as also three plates of *Iron* and *Copper* gilt, on the *East, West,* and *South* of the *Arch,* where these *Hieroglyphics* are, in the midst of the *Church-yard,* representing the holy *Passion* and *Resurrection* of the *Son* of *God;* this ought not to be otherwise interpreted, than according to the common *Theological* sense, saving that this *black man,* may as well proclaim it a wonder to see the admirable works of God in the *transmutation* of *Metals,* which is figured in these *Hieroglyphics* which he so attentively looks upon, as to see buried so many *bodies,* which shall rise again out of their Tombs at the fearful day of *Judgment.* . . .

The two *Dragons* united together, the one within the other, of colour *black* and *blue* in a field of *sable,* that is to say, *black,* whereof the one hath the *wings* gilded, and the other hath none at all, are the *sins* which naturally are interchained, for the one hath his *original* and birth from another. Of them some may be easily *chased* away, as they *come* easily, for they fly towards us every hour; and those which have no *wings* can never be chased away, such as is the sin against the *Holy Ghost.* The *gold* which is in the *wings,* signifieth that the greatest part of sins cometh from the *unholy hunger* after *gold;* which makes so many people diligently to hearken from whence they may have it; and the colour *black* and *blue* showeth that these are the desires that come out of the dark pits of hell, which we ought wholly to fly from. These two *Dragons* may also morally represent unto us the Legions of *evil spirits* which are always about us, and which will accuse us before the just Judge, at the fearful day of Judgment, which do ask, nor seek nothing else but to sift us. . . .

The two Dragons of colour yellowish, blue, and black like the field.

Look well upon these *two Dragons,* for they are the true principles or beginnings of this *Philosophy,* which the *sages* have not dared to show to their own children. He which is undermost without wings, he is the *fixed* or the *male,* that which is uppermost is the *volatile,* or the *female, black* and *obscure,* which goes about to get the domination for many months. The first is called *Sulphur,* or heat and dryness; and the lattar [sic] *Argent vive,* or cold and moisture, these are the *Sun* and the *Moon* of the *Mercurial* source, and *sulphurous original,* which by continual fire, are adorned with *royal* habilaments [sic]; that being united and afterwards changed into a *quintessence,* they may overcome everything *Metallic,* how solid, hard and strong soever it be. These are the *Serpents* and *Dragons* which the ancient *Egyptians* have painted in a *Circle,* the *head* biting the *tail,* to signify that they proceed from one and the same thing, and that it alone was sufficient, and that in the turning and *circulation* thereof, it made itself perfect. These are the *Dragons,* which the ancient Poets have feigned did without sleeping keep and watch the Golden Apples of the Virgins *Hesperides.* These are they upon whom *Jason* in his adventure for the Golden Fleece, poured the broth or liquor prepared by the fair *Medea,* of the discourse of whom the Books of the *Philosophers* are so full, that there is no Philosopher that ever was, but he hath written of it, from the time of the truth; telling *Hermes Trismegistus, Orpheus, Pythagorus* [sic], *Artephius, Morienus,* and the other following, even unto myself. These are the *two Serpents,* given and sent by *Juno* (that is the nature Metallic) the which the strong *Hercules,* that is to say, the sage and wise man must *strangle* in his *cradle;* that is, overcome and kill them, to make them putrify, corrupt and engender at the beginning of his work. These are the *two Serpents* wrapped and twisted about the *Caduceus,* or *rod* of *Mercury,* with the which he exerciseth his great power, and transformeth himself as he listeth. He, saith *Haly,* that shall kill the one, shall also kill the other, because the one cannot die but with his brother. These two then, (which *Avicen* calleth the *Corussene bitch* and the *Armenian dog,*) these two, I say, being put together in the vessel of the *Sepulchre,* do bite one another cruelly, and by their great poison, and furious rage, they never leave one another from the moment that they have seized on one another (if the *cold* hinder them not) till both of them by their slavouring [sic] venom, and mortal hurts, be all of a gore blood, over all the parts of their bodies, and finally, killing one another, be stewed in their proper *venom,* which after their death, changeth them into living and *permanent water;* before which time, they lose in their corruption and putrefaction, their first natural forms, to take afterwards, one only new, more noble and better form. These are the two *Sperms, masculine* and *feminine,* described at the begining [sic] of my *Abridgment of Philosophy,* which are engendered (say *Kasis, Avicen,* and *Abraham* the *Jew*) within the reins and entrails, and of the operations of the four *Elements.* These are the radical moisture of Metals, *Sulphur* and *Argent vive,* not vulgar, and such as are sold by the Merchants and Apothecaries, but those which give us those two fair and dear bodies which we love so much. These two sperms, saith *Democritus,* are not found upon the *earth* of the *living,* the same saith *Avicen,* but he addeth, that they gather them from the dung, odour and rottenness of the *Sun* and *Moon.* O happy are they that know how to gather them, for of them they afterwards make a *treacle,* which hath power over all grief, maladies, sorrows, infirmities, and weaknesses, and which fighteth puissantly against *death,* lengthening the life, according to the permission of *God,* even to the time determined, triumphing over the miseries of this world, and filling a man with the riches thereof. Of these two *Dragons* or Principles *Metallic,* I have said in my fore-alledged *Summary,* that the Enemy would by his heat inflame his enemy, and that then if they take not heed, they should see in the air a venomous fume and a stinking, worse in flame, and in poison, than the envenomed head of a *Serpent* and *Babylonian Dragon.* The cause why I have painted these two *sperms* in the form of *Dragons,* is because their stink is exceedingly great, and like the stink of them, and the *exhalations* which arise with the glass are dark *black, blue,* and *yellowish,* (like as these two *Dragons* are painted) the force of which, and of the *bodies* dissolved, is so venomous, that truly there is not in the world a ranker *poison:* for it is able by the force and stench thereof, to mortify and kill everything living. The *Philosopher* never feels this *stench,* if he breaks not his vessels, but only he judgeth it to be such, by the sight, and the changing of colours, proceeding from the rottenness of his confections.

These colours signify the *putrefaction* and *generation* which is given us, by the biting and dissolution of our *perfect bodies,* which dissolution proceedeth from external heat aiding, and from the *Pontique fieriness,* and admirable sharp virtue of the poison of our *Mercury,* which maketh and resolveth into a pure cloud, that is, into impalpable powder, all that which it finds to resist it. So the heat working upon and against the *radical metallic viscous,* or *oily* moisture, engendereth upon the subject *blackness.* For at the same time, the Matter is dissolved, is corrupted, groweth black and conceiveth to engender; for all *corruption* is *generation,* and therefore ought *blackness* to be much desired; for that is the *black sail* with which the *Ship of Theseus* came back victorious from *Crete,* which was the cause, of the death of his *Father,* so must this father die, to the intent that from the ashes of this *Phoenix,* another may spring, and that the *son* may be *King.* Assuredly he that seeth not this *blackness,* at the beginning of his operations, during the days of the *Stone;* what other colour soever he see, he shall altogether fail in the *Mastery,* and can do no more with that *Chaos:* for he works not well, if he *putrify* not, because if he do not *putrify,* he doth not *corrupt,* nor *engender,* and by consequent, the *Stone* cannot take *vegetative* life to increase and multiply. And in all truth, I tell thee again, that though thou work upon the true matter, if at the beginning, after thou hast put thy *Confections* in the *Philosophic Egg;* that is to say, some time after the fire has stirred them up, if then I say, thou seest not this *head of the Crow,* the black of the *blackest black,* thou must begin again, for this fault is irreparable, and not to be amended; especially the *Orange colour,* or *half red,* is to be feared, for if at the beginning thou see that in thine *Egg,* without doubt, thou burnest, or hast burnt the *verdure* and liveliness of thy *Stone.* The colour which thou must have ought to be entirely perfected in *blackness,* like to that of these *Dragons,* in the space of *forty days.* Let them therefore which shall not have these essential marks, retire themselves betimes from their operations, that they may redeem themselves from assured loss. Know also, and note it well, that in this Art it is but nothing to have this *blackness*, there is nothing more easy to come by: for from almost all things in the world, mixed with *moisture*, thou mayest have a *blackness* by the fire; but thou must have a *blackness* which comes of the perfect *Metallic bodies*, which lasts a long space of time, and is not destroyed in less than *five months*, after the which followeth immediately the desired *whiteness*. If thou hast this, thou hast enough, but not all. As for the colour *blueish* and *yellowish*, that signifieth that *Solution* and *Putrefaction* is not yet finished, and that the colours of our *Mercury*, are not as yet well mingled, and rotten with the rest. Then this *blackness*, and these colours, teach plainly, that in this beginning the matter, and compound, begins to rot and dissolve into powder, less than the *Atoms* of the *Sun*, the which afterwards are changed into *coator permanent*. And this dissolution is by the envious *Philosophers* called *Death*, *Destruction*, and *Perdition*, because that the *natures* change their *form*, and from hence are proceeded so many *Allegories* of *dead men*, *tombs*, and *sepulchres*. Others have called it *Calcination*, *Denudation*, *Separation*, *Erituration*, and *Assation*, because the Confections are changed and reduced into most small pieces and parts. Others have called it *Reduction into the first matter*, *Mollification*, *Extraction*, *Commixtion*, *Liquifaction*, *Conversion of Elements*, *Subtiliation*, *Division*, *Humation*, *Impastation*, *and Distillation*, because that the *Confections* are melted, brought back into seed, softened, and circulated within the glass. Others have called it *Xir*, or *Iris*, *Putrefaction*, *Corruption*, *Cymmerian darkness*, *a gulph*, *Hell*, *Dragons*, *Generation*, *Ingression*, *Submersion*, *Completion*, *Conjunction*, and *Impregnation*, because that the matter is black and waterish, and that the natures are perfectly mingled, and hold one of another.[1]

The animal and color symbolism of Flamel employs the same obscure language that we have encountered in the Islamic texts. Here also one can understand certain elements in terms of the masculine-feminine principles, and in analogy with other doctrines, yet many symbols still remain obscure. For the modern reader, separated by more than three centuries from the time when the alchemical tradition was still a major force in the West, one can in fact hope no more in the space of a few pages than to present a few glimpses of medieval alchemy. The period and the subject matter make a

[1] Nicolas Flamel, *His Exposition of the Hieroglyphical Figures . . . : Concerning both the theory and Practice of the Philosophers Stone* (London: 1624, chapters I and III).

complete exposition quite impossible, were one even able to understand all that the alchemists wrote. It is enough, as an introduction to alchemy, for the modern reader to realize that the alchemists were not just amateur chemists, that alchemy had a definite conception of Nature, a vast language of symbolism, an aim and a method completely different from those of modern chemistry. Instead of dealing with physical entities in themselves, it dealt with them as manifestations of the subtle domain. The alchemical work sought to establish equilibrium in the cosmos, an equilibrium symbolized by gold in the metallic state. It brought about this equilibrium by the aid of the spiritual principle—the Elixir—which, like the Divine Act, is transcendent with respect to the world of the natures and qualities. The alchemist united with the cosmos and participated in its dream, in order to awaken ultimately from all dreaming, and thereby to bring deliverance to his own soul and "salvation" to cosmic matter.

CHAPTER ELEVEN

PHILOSOPHY

PHILOSOPHY IN THE ISLAMIC WORLD began in the third/ninth century, with the translation of Greek philosophical texts into Arabic. The first Muslim philosopher, any of whose writing has survived—al-Kindī—was also celebrated in the Latin West. He was well acquainted with the main tenets of Greek philosophy, and even had a translation of a summary version of the *Enneads* made for him. It was he who initiated the process of formulating a technical philosophical vocabulary in Arabic, and of rethinking Greek philosophy in terms of Islamic doctrines. In both these respects, he was followed by al-Fārābī, through whom the basis for Peripatetic philosophy became well established in Islam. The philosophers of this school were familiar with the Alexandrian and Athenian Neoplatonists and commentators on Aristotle, and viewed the philosophy of Aristotle through Neoplatonic eyes. Moreover, there are Neopythagorean elements to be seen in al-Kindī, Shiite political doctrines in al-Fārābī, and ideas of Shiite inspiration in certain of the writings of Avicenna.

The main tendency of the Peripatetic school, however, which found its greatest Islamic exponent in Avicenna, was toward a philosophy based on the use of the discursive faculty, and relying essentially on the syllogistic method. The rationalistic aspect of this school reached its terminal point with Averroes, who became the most purely Aristotelian of the Muslim Peripatetics, and rejected, as an explicit aspect of philosophy, those Neoplatonic and Muslim elements that had entered into the world view of the Eastern Peripatetics, such as Avicenna.

From the sixth/twelfth century onward, the other major school of Islamic philosophy—or, more appropriately speaking, "theosophy" in its original sense—came into being. This school, whose founder was Suhrawardī, became known as the Illuminationist *(ishrāqī)* school, as contrasted with the Peripatetic *(mashshā'ī)* school. While the Peripatetics leaned most heavily upon the syllogistic method of Aristotle, and sought to reach truth by means of arguments based on reason, the Illuminationists, who drew their doctrines from both the Platonists and the ancient Persians as well as the Islamic revelation itself, regarded intellectual intuition and illumination as the basic method to be followed, side by side with the use of reason. The rationalist philosophers, although they left an indelible mark upon the terminology of later Muslim theology, gradually became alienated from the orthodox elements, both theological and gnostic, so that, after their "refutation" by al-Ghazzālī, they exercised little influence upon the main body of Muslim opinion. But the Illuminationist school, which combined the method of ratiocination with that of intellectual intuition and illumination, came to the fore during that very period that is generally—although quite erroneously—regarded as the end of Islamic philosophy. In fact along with gnosis it occupied the central position in the intellectual life of Islam. At the very moment when, in the West, Augustinian Platonism (which regarded knowledge as the fruit of illumination) was giving way to Thomistic Aristotelianism (which turned away from this very doctrine of illumination), the reverse process was taking place in the Islamic world.

We must, however, make a distinction between the Sunni and Shiite reactions to philosophy. The Sunni world rejected philosophy almost entirely after Averroes, except for logic and the continuing influence of philosophy on its methods of argumentation, as well as some cosmological beliefs that have remained in the formulations of theology, and certain Sufi doctrines. In the Shia world, however, the philosophy of both the Peripatetic and Illuminationist school has been taught continuously as a living tradition through the centuries in the religious schools; some of the greatest figures in Islamic philosophy, such as Mullā Ṣadrā, who was contemporary with Descartes and Leibniz, came long after the period usually regarded as "the productive phase" of Islamic philosophy.

As for the differences between the Sunni and Shiite perspectives, it should be emphasized that it was early in its history that Islam became divided along the lines of these two perspectives, both of which are orthodox and legitimate interpretations of the Islamic revelation, each suited for a particular type of mental and psychological constitution. The Shia have always been a numerical minority, and constitute today perhaps one-fifth or one-sixth of the Islamic world. Their spiritual and cultural importance during Islamic history, however, has been much greater than their number might indicate—especially during the fourth/tenth and fifth/eleventh centuries, when they ruled over large sections of the Islamic world. In Persia, Twelver Shiism has been dominant since the tenth/sixteenth century, and it is not accidental that it was in this predominantly Shiite atmosphere that philosophy found its most congenial habitat after the time of Averroes. Here, logic and the Peripatetic philosophy which is essentially based on it have become a preparation for undertaking the study of the doctrines of the Illuminationist school, and this study in turn a ladder for rising to the comprehension of the doctrines of pure gnosis.

Of the various branches of Shiite Islam, two are of particular importance for the study of Islamic philosophy, the Twelve-Imam or Jaʿfarī school, and the Ismaili, which had a great influence, both political and cultural, during the Middle Ages. The Shiite imams, who bear within themselves the prophetic light, are the interpreters *par excellence* of the inner meaning of all things, of the book of Revelation as well as of the book of Nature. They possess in principle the knowledge of all things, supernatural as well as natural, and some of them—particularly Jaʿfar al-Ṣādiq, the sixth imam—were not only masters of religious and spiritual sciences, but wrote about the natural sciences as well. As has already been mentioned, the famous alchemist, Jābir ibn Ḥayyān, claimed to be one of imam Jaʿfar's disciples. In fact, the integration of Hermeticism into Islam, and the acceptance of the legitimacy of the Greek sciences in the eyes of the Shia came as a result of the contact of several of the imams with men learned in the Greek sciences.

The Shia thereupon sought to cultivate various sciences, particularly the cosmological ones. Many of the famous Muslim scientists and philosophers—such as Avicenna, Nāṣir-i Khusrau, and Nāṣir al-Dīn al-Ṭūsī—were either Shiite, or from a Shiite background. There is, among Shiite writings, a vast literature dealing with Nature and its spiritual significance. Alchemical and numerical symbolism are used extensively in the cosmological treatises of this group, the physical domain being studied primarily as a symbol of the higher orders of reality. Nature is regarded as a book, whose inner meaning can be understood only by symbolic interpretation *(taʾwīl),* and not by "literal" observation. The Shia join the

Sufi perspective in attaching a spiritual significance to the study of Nature, and in viewing the physical world as a mirror in which spiritual realities are reflected. For them, as for the Sufis and certain philosophers, the universe consists of a hierarchy of beings, which descend from a single source and return ultimately to their unique Origin.

To illustrate the Shiite conception of Nature, we give a passage from the writings of the eighth/fourteenth century philosopher and Sufi poet, Afḍal al-Dīn al-Kāshānī, associated with Naṣīr al-Dīn al-Ṭūsī, in which the essential elements of the symbolic interpretation of Nature are clearly stated:

> Creatures are of two kinds: those who receive action, which are the created, and the original beings [the archetypes], which are eternal. The place of the created beings is called the *world of existence,* and the place of the archetypes the *world of eternity*. They also call the world of created beings, the *world of Nature,* and the world of archetypes, the *world of the Intellect;* likewise, the created world is called the *particular,* and the eternal world the *universal.* All these expressions have but one meaning, which is that there are two worlds—one, the real; the other, the symbolic. The real is the necessary, and the symbolic the contingent; the real is the universal, and the symbolic the particular. The beings of the world of particulars are symbols of the world of the universals. The creatures of this world subsist through the archetypes of the other; persons of this world have their existence through those of the other.
>
> The beings of the world of particulars each possess a measure and quantity, whereas the beings of the world of universals are without quantity or measure. The beings of the world of becoming are dead by themselves, and alive by that which is other than themselves, while the beings of the eternal world are alive by themselves. Sensible knowledge of this world, that is, the world of becoming, is a symbol of the intelligible knowledge of that world. The physical world is the symbol and image of the spiritual world.[1]

The summation and perfection of the philosophy of al-Kindī and al-Fārābī came with Avicenna, who may in a sense be regarded as the founder of what is distinctly medieval philosophy. Avicenna was perhaps the greatest philosopher-scientist, and certainly the most influential philosopher, within the Islamic world. He represents an excellent

[1] Afḍal al-Dīn al-Kāshānī, *Muṣannafāt* (Tehran: University Press, 1954), pp. 47–48. Translated by S. H. Nasr.

example of the *ḥakīm* or wise man, in whom various branches of knowledge are united. After his death, his writings soon became the source from which many different schools were to draw their ideas and inspiration.

Avicenna was not only a Peripatetic philosopher who combined the doctrines of Aristotle with certain elements from the Neoplatonists, and a scientist who observed Nature within the framework of the medieval philosophy of Nature; he was also one of the precursors of the metaphysical school of Illuminationism *(ishrāq),* whose greatest exponent was Suhrawardī. In his later works, especially the *Visionary Narratives* (or "Recitals"), and the treatise on love, the cosmos of the syllogistic philosophers is transformed into a universe of symbols through which the gnostic journeys towards his final beatitude. In *The "Logic" of the Orientals,* belonging to a larger work, most of which has been lost, Avicenna repudiated his own earlier works, which are chiefly Aristotelian, as being suitable for the common people; instead, he proposed to present, for the élite, the "Oriental philosophy." His trilogy—*Ḥayy ibn Yaqẓān (Living Son of the Awake), al-Ṭair (The Bird),* and *Salāmān and Absāl*—deals with the complete cycle of the gnostic's journey from the "world of shadows" to the Divine Presence, the Orient of Light. In these writings, the outline of the universe of the medieval philosophers and scientists remains unchanged; the cosmos becomes internalized, however, within the being of the gnostic—a "crypt," with respect to which the initiate must orient himself, and through which he must journey. The facts and phenomena of Nature become transparent, symbols which have a spiritual significance for the subject who comes into contact with them in this cosmic journey.

The totality of Avicenna's work presents a clear example of the hierarchy of knowledge within Islamic society. He was an observer and an experimenter in geology and in medicine; a philosopher of the Peripatetic school, more Neoplatonic than Aristotelian; and the author of gnostic texts which were to become the source of many commentaries by later Illuminationists. One can see in his writings the harmony of sensible, rational, and intellectual knowledge, revealed by the way of an imposing edifice based upon the hierarchy which lies in the nature of things, and which rests ultimately upon the multiple states and grades of cosmic manifestation.

The Book of Healing—the most complete exposition of Aristotelian philosophy in Islam—contains sections dealing with every branch of the natural sciences (many, such as geology, being based upon years of observation), as well as with logic, mathematics, and the first philosophy. Moreover, Avicenna describes an elaborate cosmology, in which the planets are made to correspond to various intelligences or angels, all emanating from the First Intellect. The Latin interpretations of Avicenna, as exemplified in the attacks of William of Auvergne, usually leaned toward criticism of his emphasis upon the angels. On the contrary, in the Islamic world, particularly in Persia, the cosmology of Avicenna was interpreted in the light of an angelology, so that the universe always preserved its sacred aspect, and continued to serve as the harmonious background for the realities of religion. In his narrative cycle, as well as in several poems and short treatises less well known in the Western world than his "exoteric" philosophy, Avicenna makes clear the primordiality of the intelligible or angelic world, and its superiority over the sensible and human one, as well as the necessity for the human soul to leave this world of shadows, and to return to the angelic world from which it came. Since the Intellect is the principle of the universe, the soul gains certain knowledge of the cosmos only when it is united with the Intellect—that is, only when it has regained its angelic nature. Avicenna expresses this idea in the following poem on the human soul.

It descended upon thee from out of the regions above,
That exalted, ineffable, glorious, heavenly Dove.
'Twas concealed from the eyes of all those who its nature would
ken,
Yet it wears not a veil, and is ever apparent to men.
Unwilling it sought thee and joined thee, and yet, though it
grieve,
It is like to be still more unwilling thy body to leave.
It resisted and struggled, and would not be tamèd in haste,
Yet it joined thee, and slowly grew used to this desolate waste,
Till, forgotten at length, as I ween, were haunts and its troth
In the heavenly gardens and groves, which to leave it was loath.
Until, when it entered the D of its downward Descent,
And to earth, to the C of its centre, unwillingly went,
The eye of (I) infirmity smote it, and lo, it was hurled
Midst the sign-posts and ruined abodes of this desolate world.
It weeps, when it thinks of its home and the peace it possessed,
With tears welling forth from its eyes without pausing or rest,
And with plaintive mourning it broodeth like one bereft
O'er such trace of its home as the fourfold winds have left.
Thick nets detain it, and strong is the cage whereby

It is held from seeking the lofty and spacious sky.
Until, when the the hour of its homeward flight draws near,
And 'tis time for it to return to its ampler sphere,
It carols with joy, for the veil is raised, and it spies
Such things as cannot be witnessed by waking eyes.
On a lofty height doth it warble its songs of praise
(For even the lowliest being doth knowledge raise).
And so it returneth, aware of all hidden things
In the universe, while no stain to its garment clings.

Now why from its perch on high was it cast like this
To the lowest Nadir's gloomy and drear abyss?
Was it God who cast it forth for some purpose wise,
Concealed from the keenest seeker's inquiring eyes?
Then is its descent a discipline wise but stern,
That the things that it hath not heard it thus may learn.
So 'tis she whom Fate doth plunder, while her star
Setteth at length in a place from its rising far,
Like a gleam of lightning which over the meadows shone,
And, as though it ne'er had been, in a moment is gone.[2]

This poem of great beauty in the Arabic original, has been the subject of many commentaries throughout the ages.

In the *Visionary Narratives,* Avicenna, the natural historian, scientist, and philosopher, becomes the navigator and guide through the whole cosmos, from the world of gross forms to the Divine Principle. All his wide knowledge, here illuminated by intellectual vision, serves him as the basis on which to construct with great beauty the panorama of the universe through which the initiate must journey. The sciences of Nature, previously exterior and indirect, are here transformed into an immediate and direct reality. The cosmos through which he who seeks to know effectively and not only theoretically must travel, becomes internalized within his own being; in a sense, he "becomes" the cosmos.

Avicenna begins the *Narratives* with a description of the sage, who symbolizes the light of intellectual intuition, as well as the spiritual master, who is to guide the initiate; and then, in the language of the guide, he describes the anatomy of the universe, or cosmic "crypt," through which guide and initiate, master and disciple, are to journey.

The Sage says:

[2] E. G. Browne, *A Literary History of Persia* (London: T. Fisher Unwin, 1906), II, pp. 110–111. The translation from the Arabic is by Browne. Reprinted by permission of Ernest Benn Limited, London.

"My name is *Vivens;* my lineage, *filius Vigilantis;* as to my country, it is the Celestial Jerusalem [lit., the 'Most Holy Dwelling,' *al-Bait al-Muqaddas*]. My profession is to be forever journeying, to travel about the universe so that I may know all its conditions. My face is turned toward my father, and my father is *Vigilans.* From him I have learned all science, he has given me the keys to every kind of knowledge. He has shown me the roads to follow to the extreme confines of the universe, so that since my journey embraces the whole circle of it, it is as if all the horizons of all climes were brought together before me."

He describes the Universe as follows:

"The circumscriptions of the earth are threefold: one is intermediate between the Orient and the Occident. It is the best known; much information concerning it has reached thee and has been rightly understood. Notices even of the marvelous things contained in that clime have reached thee. But there are two other strange circumscriptions: one beyond the Occident, the other beyond the Orient. For each of them, there is a barrier preventing access from this world to that other circumscription, for no one can reach there or force a passage save the Elect among the mass of men, those who have gained a strength that does not originally belong to man by right of nature.

"What aids in gaining this strength is to immerse oneself in the spring of water that flows near the permanent Spring of Life. When the pilgrim has been guided on the road to that spring, and then purifies himself in it and drinks of that sweet-tasting water, a new strength arises in his limbs, making him able to cross vast deserts. The deserts seem to roll up before him. He does not sink in the waters of the ocean; he climbs Mount Qāf without difficulty, and its guards cannot fling him down into the abysses of hell. . . .

"Thou hast heard of the Darkness that forever reigns about the pole. Each year the rising sun shines upon it at a fixed time. He who confronts that Darkness and does not hesitate to plunge into it for fear of difficulties will come to a vast space, boundless and filled with light. The first thing he sees is a living spring whose waters spread like a river over the *barzakh* [purgatory]. Whoever bathes in that spring becomes so light that he can walk on water, can climb the highest peaks without weariness, until finally he comes to one of the two circumscriptions by which this world is intersected. . . .

"At the uttermost edge of the Occident there is a vast sea, which in the Book of God is called the *Hot* (and Muddy) *Sea.*

It is in those parts that the sun sets. The streams that fall into that sea come from an uninhabited country whose vastness none can circumscribe. No inhabitant peoples it, save for strangers who arrive there unexpectedly, coming from other regions. Perpetual Darkness reigns in that country. Those who emigrate there obtain a flash of light each time that the sun sinks to its setting. Its soil is a desert of salt. Each time that people settle there and begin to cultivate it, it refuses; it expels them, and others come in their stead. Would any grow a crop there? It is scattered. Is a building raised there? It crumbles. Among those people there is perpetual quarreling or, rather, mortal battle. Any group that is strongest seizes the homes and goods of the others and forces them to emigrate. They try to settle; but in their turn they reap only loss and harm. Such is their behavior. They never cease from it.

"All kinds of animals and plants appear in that country; but when they settle there, feed on its grass, and drink its water, suddenly they are covered by outsides strange to their Form. A human being will be seen there, for example, covered by the hide of a quadruped, while thick vegetation grows on him. And so it is with other species. And that clime is a place of devastation, a desert of salt, filled with troubles, wars, quarrels, tumults; there joy and beauty are but borrowed from a distant place.

"Between that clime and yours there are others. However, beyond this clime of yours, beginning at the region in which the Pillars of the Heavens are set, there is a clime that is like yours in several ways. In the first place, it is a desert plain; it too is peopled only by strangers come from distant places. Another similarity is that that clime borrows its light from a foreign source, though it is nearer to the Window of Light than the climes we have described hitherto. In addition, that clime serves as foundation for the heavens, just as the preceding clime serves as the seat for this earth, is its permanent base. On the other hand, the inhabitants who people that other clime are sedentaries there in perpetuity. Among the strangers who have come there and settled, there is no war; they do not seize each others' homes and goods by force. Each group has its fixed domain, into which no other comes to inflict violence upon it.

"In relation to you, the nearest inhabited country of that clime is a region whose people are very small in stature and swift in their movements. Their cities are nine in number.

"After that region comes a kingdom whose inhabitants are even smaller in stature than the former, while their gait is slower. They passionately love the arts of the writer, the sciences of the stars, theurgy, magic; they have a taste for subtle occupations and deep works. Their cities number ten."

After giving a similar astronomical and astrological description for the other planets, Avicenna's Sage continues:

"Next comes an immense kingdom, with great scattered countries. Its inhabitants are numerous. They are solitaries; they do not live in cities. Their abode is a desert plain where nothing grows. It is divided into twelve regions, which contain twenty-eight stations. No group goes up to occupy the station of another except when the group preceding it has withdrawn from its dwelling; then it hastens to replace it. All the migrants expatriated in the kingdoms that we have described hitherto travel about this kingdom and perform their evolutions there.

"Marching with it is a kingdom of which no one has descried or reached the boundaries down to this day. It contains neither city nor town. No one who is visible to the eyes of the body can find refuge there. Its inhabitants are the spiritual Angels. No human being can reach it nor dwell there. From it the divine Imperative and Destiny descend upon all those who occupy the degrees below. Beyond it there is no earth that is inhabited. In short, these two climes, to which the heavens and the earth are respectively joined, are on the left side of the universe, that which is the Occident."

Describing the Orient, the Sage says:

"He who is taught a certain road leading out of this clime and who is helped to accomplish this exodus, such a one will find an egress to what is beyond the celestial spheres. Then, in a fugitive glimpse, he descries the posterity of the Primordial Creation, over whom rules as king the One, the Obeyed.

"There, the first delimitation is inhabited by intimates of that sublime King; they ever assiduously pursue the work that brings them near to their King. They are a most pure people, who respond to no solicitation of gluttony, lust, violence, jealousy, or sloth. The mission laid upon them is to attend to the preservation of the ramparts of that empire, and it is there that they abide. Hence they live in cities; they occupy lofty castles and magnificent buildings, whose material was kneaded with such care that the result is a compound that in no wise resembles the clay of your clime. Those buildings are more solid than diamond and jacinth, than all things that require the longest time to wear away. Long life has been bestowed upon the people; they are exempt from the due date of death; death cannot touch them until after a long, a very long term. Their rule of life consists in maintaining the ramparts in obedience to the order given them.

"Above them is a people that has more intimate dealings with the King and that is unceasingly bound to His service. They are not humiliated by having to fill this office; their state is preserved against all attack, nor do they change their occupation. They were chosen to be intimates, and they have received the power of contemplating the highest palace and stationing themselves all about it. It has been granted them to contemplate the face of the King in unbroken continuity. They have received as adornment the sweetness of a subtle grace in their nature, goodness and penetrating wisdom in their thoughts, the privilege of being the final term to which all knowledge refers. They have been endowed with a shining aspect, a beauty that sets the beholder trembling with admiration, a stature that has attained its perfection. For each of them, a limit has been set that belongs to him alone, a fixed rank, a divinely ordained degree, to which no other contests his right and in which he has no associate, for all the others either are above him or each respectively finds sweetness in his lower rank. Among them there is one whose rank is nearer to the King, and he is their 'father,' and they are his children and grandchildren. It is through him that the King's word and order emanate to them. And among other marvels pertaining to their condition is this: never does the course of time expose their nature to the marks and withering of age and decrepitude. Far from it, he among them who is their 'father,' though the oldest in duration, is thereby all the more abounding in vigor, and his face has all the more of the beauty of youth. They all live in the desert; they have no need of dwelling places or shelter.

"Among them all the King is the most withdrawn into that solitude. Whoever connects Him with an origin errs. Whoever claims to pay Him praise that is proportionate to Him is an idle babbler. For the King escapes the power of the clever to bestow qualifications, just as here too all comparisons fail of their end. Let none, then, be so bold as to compare Him to anything whatsoever. He has no members that divide Him: He is all a face by His beauty, all a hand by His Generosity. And His beauty obliterates the vestiges of all other beauty. His generosity debases the worth of all other generosity. When one of those who surround His immensity undertakes to meditate on Him, his eye blinks with stupor and he comes away dazzled. Indeed, his eyes are almost ravished from him, even before he has turned them upon Him. It would seem that His beauty is the veil of His beauty, that His Manifestation is the cause of His Occultation, that His Epiphany is the cause of His Hiddenness. Even so, it is by veiling itself a little that the sun can be the better contemplated; when, on the contrary, the heliophany sheds all the violence of its brightness, the sun is denied to the eyes, and that is why its light is the veil of its light. In truth, the King manifests His beauty on the horizon of those who are His; toward them He is not niggardly of His vision; those who are deprived of contemplating Him are so because of the wretched state of their faculties. He is mild and merciful. His generosity overflows. His goodness is immense. His gifts overwhelm; vast is His court, universal His favor. Whoever perceives a trace of His beauty fixes his contemplation upon it forever; never again, even for the twinkling of an eye, does he let himself be distracted from it.

"Sometimes certain solitaries among men emigrate toward Him. So much sweetness does He give them to experience that they bow under the weight of His graces. He makes them conscious of the wretchedness of the advantages of your terrestrial clime. And when they return from His palace, they return laden with mystical gifts."[3]

[3] Henry Corbin, *Avicenna and the Visionary Recital,* translated from the French by Willard R. Trask (Bollingen Series LXVI. Copyright 1960 by Bollingen Foundation, New York. Distributed by Princeton University Press), pp. 137–138; 141–143; 144–145; 148–150. London: Routledge Kegan Paul Ltd. Reprinted by permission.

CHAPTER TWELVE

THE CONTROVERSIES OF PHILOSOPHY AND THEOLOGY—THE LATER SCHOOLS OF PHILOSOPHY

THE PHILOSOPHY OF AVICENNA, especially in its symbolic and cosmological aspects, continued to be studied and cultivated in the Shiite world, while in the Sunni world the rationalistic view inherent in the Peripatetic philosophy was being refuted in the name of the tenets of Islamic Revelation. Sunni theology—like all theology, which is meant above all to protect reason from falling into error—sought to fight against certain elements of rationalist Greek philosophy by means of reason itself.

Theology began among the Muslims as the result of an attempt to defend the tenets of their faith against attacks by followers of other religions, and especially the Christians, who were armed with the tools of Greek logic. At first, it was dominated by the Mutazilites. Gradually, following an early period of intense debate over such questions as determinism and free will, the nature of the divine attributes, etc., a theological tradition became established which, after the fourth/tenth century, fell under the domination of the Asharites. The school of Scholastic theology—*Kalām* as it has become known in Islamic history—did not, like the schools of philosophy, deal with every question which presents itself to the human mind, but restricted itself, instead, chiefly to specifically religious matters. It did not attempt, however, to follow the teachings of any particular Greek school, so that the theologians were able to expound certain quite original theses. They used the logic developed by Aristotle and his school, but to different ends; their "philosophy of Nature"—their speculations regarding the nature of light and heat, the meaning of causality and the "explanation" of natural events —are quite distinct from the views of the Peripatetics.

The dominant school of Sunni theology, which arose in the fourth/tenth century in response to various currents of rationalistic thought based on Greek philosophy, was the Asharite school, named after its founder, Abuʾl-Ḥasan al-Ashʿarī, who lived during the third/ninth Islamic century. The school spread rapidly after his death, and has remained ever since the dominant theology of the Sunni world. The doctrines of al-Ashʿarī were developed and extended, especially in the domain of the philosophy of Nature, by Abū Bakr al-Bāqillanī, who was al-Ashʿarī's student.

The central idea which dominates the many aspects of Sunni theology is a "conceptual atomism," which breaks the apparent continuity of the world and of its matrices, time and space, and makes God the direct agent in all events. This "atomism" has its roots in the specific character of Islam, which asserts the absolute transcendence of the Divine Principle, and the "nothingness" of all beings, from the lowest animal to the highest Intellect, before that Principle. Secondarily, this "atomism," which stresses the discontinuity between the finite and the Infinite, is dependent upon the spiritual and psychological structure of the Arabic language, and of the Arab mind, for whom the aspect of the concrete discontinuity of things and actions predominates over any abstract continuity of cause and effect, established by examination of the relations existing between all things.

The Asharites therefore reject the Aristotelian notion of causality. For them, everything is caused directly by God; every cause is the Transcendent Cause. A fire is hot, not because it is "in its nature" to be so, but because God willed it so. The coherence of the world is due, not to the "horizontal" relation between things, or between various causes and effects, but to the "vertical" bond which connects each concrete entity or "atom" with its ontological cause. Unlike some of the philosophers, and the other schools of theology (including that of the Shia), the Asharites lay primary stress upon the discontinuity between the world and God, and the nothingness of everything in the universe before the Creator. For them, all intermediate causes and states of beings are absorbed into the Divine Principle. One may say that a particular being is "nothing" before the Infinite, but also that it is real, inasmuch as that particular being exists and therefore shares some degree of reality. The Asharites based their views on this aspect of "nothingness," while the philosophers, following the Neoplatonists, based their view on the continuity between the universe and its ontological cause. It remained for the Sufis to formulate the doctrine which contains the synthesis of these (logically speaking) "contradictory" relations, as two aspects of the same reality.

A. Al-Ghazzālī

The spread of Asharite theology curtailed the influence of rationalism in Islam and with the help of Sufism finally destroyed it as a major force. The person who was destined to accomplish the "destruction of the philosophers," and at the same time to establish a harmony between the exoteric and esoteric elements of Islam, was Abū Ḥāmid Muḥammad al-Ghazzālī (the Latin "Algazel").

Respected by the jurisprudents, theologians, and Sufis alike, and possessing a remarkable lucidity of thought and power of expression, he clarified once and for all in his writings the role which philosophy, as the attempt of human reason to explain all things in a system, was to have in Islam, and especially in Sunni Islam. After him, rationalistic philosophy continued to be taught, particularly in the Shiite world, but not as a central aspect of the intellectual life of Islam. Al-Ghazzālī died in Tus, having oriented Muslim intellectual life in the direction which it has followed ever since, and which has distinguished it from its sister civilization in Western Europe. In the Latin world, Aristotelianism was adopted by Christianity; its rationalistic structure became a half-way mark between the metaphysical perspective of the Church Father and the rationalism of the Renaissance and the seventeenth century. The growth of Aristotelianism was to lead to the Thomistic synthesis, but also to the gradual stifling of the metaphysical and gnostic element in Christianity, as represented by the Fideli d'Amore and the Rhenish Mystics.

In Islam, al-Ghazzālī, who may in a way be compared with St. Thomas, drove Aristotelianism from the inner life of Islam, thereby guaranteeing the survival of the school of Illuminationism and Sufism, which have been able to maintain themselves to this day. The radically different course of events in the West and in the Islamic world during the following centuries, despite the many similarities of the two civilizations during the Middle Ages, can perhaps be explained in part by the different attitude each civilization was to adopt with respect to Peripatetic philosophy.

The reaction of orthodox Islam, both the theologians and also certain gnostics, against the rationalistic philosophers, especially as to the sciences of Nature, is best exemplified in al-Ghazzālī's "confessions," *Deliverance from Error,* in which he enumerates the various philosophical and scientific schools and their limitations.

A. *The schools of philosophers, and how the defect of unbelief affects them all.* The many philosophical sects and systems constitute three main groups: the Materialists, the Naturalists, and the Theists.

The first group, the *Materialists,* are among the earliest philosophers. They deny the Creator and Disposer of the world, omniscient and omnipotent, and consider the world has everlastingly existed just as it is, of itself and without a creator, and that everlastingly animals have come from seed and seed from animals; thus it was and thus it will ever be. These are the Zanādiqah or irreligious people.

The second group, the *Naturalists,* are a body of philosophers who have engaged in manifold researches into the world of nature and the marvels of animals and plants, and have expended much effort in the science of dissecting the organs of animals. They see there sufficient of the wonders of God's creation and the inventions of His wisdom to compel them to acknowledge a wise Creator who is aware of the aims and purposes of things. No one can make a careful study of anatomy and the wonderful uses of the members and organs without attaining to the necessary knowledge that there is a perfection in the order which the framer gave to the animal frame, and especially to that of man.

Yet these philosophers, immersed in their researches into nature, take the view that the equal balance of the temperament has great influence in constituting the powers of animals. They hold that even the intellectual power in man is dependent on the temperament, so that, as the temperament is corrupted, intellect also is corrupted and ceases to exist. Further, when a thing ceases to exist, it is unthinkable in their opinion that the nonexistent should return to existence. Thus it is their view that the soul dies and does not return to life, and they deny the future life—heaven, hell, resurrection and judgment; there does not remain, they hold, any reward for obedience or any punishment for sin. With this curb removed, they give way to a bestial indulgence of their appetites.

These are also irreligious, for the basis of faith is faith in God and in the Last Day, and these, though believing in God and His attributes, deny the Last Day.

The third group, the *Theists,* are the more modern philosophers and include Socrates, his pupil Plato, and the latter's pupil Aristotle. It was Aristotle who systematized logic for them and organized the sciences, securing a higher degree of accuracy and bringing them to maturity.

The Theists in general attacked the two previous groups, the Materialists and the Naturalists, and exposed their defects so effectively that others were relieved of the task. "And God relieved the believers of fighting" (Koran, 33, 25) through their mutual combat. Aristotle, moreover, attacked his predecessors among the Theistic philosophers, especially Plato and Socrates, and went so far in his criticisms that he separated himself from them all. Yet he too retained a residue of their unbelief and heresy from which he did not manage to free himself. We must therefore reckon as unbelievers both these philosophers themselves and their followers among the Islamic philosophers, such as Ibn Sīna, al-Fārābī and others; in transmitting the philosophy of Aristotle, however, none of the Islamic philosophers has accomplished anything comparable to the achievements of the two men named. The translations of others are marked by disorder and confusion, which so perplex the understanding of the student that he fails to comprehend; and if a thing is not comprehended how can it be either refuted or accepted?

All that, in our view, is genuinely part of the philosophy of Aristotle, as these men have transmitted it, falls under three heads: (1) what must be counted as unbelief; (2) what must be counted as heresy; (3) what is not to be denied at all. Let us proceed, then, to the details.

B. *The Various Philosophical Sciences.* For our present purposes the philosophical sciences are six in number: mathematics, logic, natural sciences, theology, politics, ethics.

1. MATHEMATICS. This embraces arithmetic, plane geometry and solid geometry. None of its results are connected with religious matters, either to deny or to affirm them. They are matters of demonstration which it is impossible to deny once they have been understood and apprehended. Nevertheless,

there are two drawbacks which arise from mathematics. (a) The first is that every student of mathematics admires its precision and the clarity of its demonstrations. This leads him to believe in the philosophers and to think that all their sciences resemble this one in clarity and demonstrative cogency.

Further, he has already heard the accounts on everybody's lips of their unbelief, their denial of God's attributes, and their contempt for revealed truth; he becomes an unbeliever merely by accepting them as authorities, and says to himself, "If religion were true, it would not have escaped the notice of these men, since they are so precise in this science." Thus, after becoming acquainted by hearsay with their unbelief and denial of religion, he draws the conclusion that the truth is the denial and rejection of religion. How many have I seen who err from the truth because of this high opinion of the philosophers and without any other basis!

Against them one may argue: "The man who excels in one art does not necessarily excel in every art. It is not necessary that the man who excels in law and theology should excel in medicine, nor that the man who is ignorant of intellectual speculations should be ignorant of grammar. Rather, every art has people who have obtained excellence and preeminence in it, even though stupidity and ignorance may characterize them in other arts. The arguments in elementary matters of mathematics are demonstrative whereas those in theology (or metaphysics) are based on conjecture. This point is familiar only to those who have studied the matter deeply for themselves."

If such a person is fixed in this belief which he has chosen out of respect for authority, he is not moved by this argument but is carried by strength of passion, love of vanity, and the desire to be thought clever to persist in his good opinion of the philosophers with regard to all the sciences. . . .

(b) The second drawback arises from the man who is loyal to Islam but ignorant. He thinks that religion must be defended by rejecting every science connected with the philosophers, and so rejects all their sciences and accuses them of ignorance therein. He even rejects their theory of the eclipse of the sun and moon, considering that what they say is contrary to revelation. When that view is thus attacked, someone hears who has knowledge of such matters by apodeictic demonstration. He does not doubt his demonstration, but, believing that Islam is based on ignorance and the denial of apodeictic proof, grows in love for philosophy and hatred for Islam.

A grievous crime indeed against religion has been committed by the man who imagines that Islam is defended by the denial of the mathematical sciences, seeing that there is nothing in revealed truth opposed to these sciences by way of either negation or affirmation, and nothing in these sciences opposed to the truths of religion. Muhammad (peace be upon him) said, "The sun and the moon are two of the signs of God; they are not eclipsed for anyone's death nor for his life; if you are witness of such an event, take refuge in the recollection of God (most high) and in prayer." There is nothing here obliging us to deny the science of arithmetic which informs us specifically of the orbits of sun and moon, and their conjunction and opposition. (The further saying of Muhammad [peace be upon him], "When God manifests himself to a thing, it submits to Him," is an addition which does not occur at all in the collections of sound Traditions.)

This is the character of mathematics and its drawbacks.

2. LOGIC. Nothing in logic is relevant to religion by way of denial or affirmation. Logic is the study of the methods of demonstration and of forming syllogisms, of the conditions for the premises of proofs, of the manner of combining the premises, of the conditions for sound definition and the manner of ordering it. Knowledge comprises (a) the concept, which is apprehended by definition, and (b) the assertion or judgment, which is apprehended by proof. There is nothing here which requires to be denied. Matters of this kind are actually mentioned by the theologians and speculative thinkers in connection with the topic of demonstrations. The philosophers differ from these only in the expressions and technical terms they employ and in their greater elaboration of the explanations and classifications. An example of this is their proposition, "If it is true that all A is B, then it follows that some B is A," that is, "If it is true that all men are animals, then it follows that some animals are men." They express this by saying that "the universal affirmative proposition has as its converse a particular affirmative proposition." What connection has this with the essentials of religion, that it should be denied or rejected? If such a denial is made, the only effect upon the logicians is to impair their belief in the intelligence of the man who made the denial and, what is worse, in his religion, inasmuch as he considers that it rests on such denials.

Moreover, there is a type of mistake into which students of logic are liable to fall. They draw up a list of the conditions to be fulfilled by demonstration, which are known without fail to produce certainty. When, however, they come at length to treat of religious questions, not merely are they unable to satisfy these conditions, but they admit an extreme degree of relaxation (*sc.* of their standards of proof). . . .

3. NATURAL SCIENCES OR PHYSICS. This is the investigation of the sphere of the heavens together with the heavenly bodies, and of what is beneath the heavens, both simple bodies like

water, air, earth, fire, and composite bodies like animals, plants and minerals, and also of the causes of their changes, transformations and combinations. This is similar to the investigation by medicine of the human body with its principal and subordinate organs, and of the causes of the changes of temperament. Just as it is not a condition of religion to reject medical science, so likewise the rejection of natural science is not one of its conditions, except with regard to particular points which I enumerate in my book, *The Incoherence of the Philosophers.* Any other points on which a different view has to be taken from the philosophers are shown by reflection to be implied in those mentioned. The basis of all these objections is the recognition that nature is in subjection to God most high, not acting of itself but serving as an instrument in the hands of its Creator. Sun and moon, stars and elements, are in subjection to His command. There is none of them whose activity is produced by or proceeds from its own essence.[1]

B. Averroes and Philosophy in Andalusia

In Andalusia Islamic philosophy reached its peak and also termination with Averroes and began three centuries before him with Ibn Masarrah, the Sufi and philosopher who founded the school of Almería. The "pseudo-Empedoclean" writings in which the doctrine of intelligible matter and a particular cosmology based on five stages of "matter"—the universal, intellectual, psychic, natural and "second" matter—are expounded are connected with his name. His teachings were to have much influence on the Jewish philosopher Ibn Gabirol (Avicebron) as well as on the Sufi master Ibn ʿArabī.

In the fifth/eleventh century the theologian, philosopher and historian of religion Ibn Ḥazm enhanced the cause of

[1] W. Montgomery Watt, *The Faith and Practice of Al-Ghazālī* (London: George Allen and Unwin, 1953), pp. 30–36.

philosophical and theological studies in Andalusia through his voluminous writings. Besides being credited with an outstanding work on the history of religions, Ibn Ḥazm wrote several philosophic works, the most familiar being the *Ring of the Dove* which in the manner of *Phaedrus* of Plato analyzes the universal love that pervades the whole cosmos. Ibn Ḥazm in fact represents the Platonic strain in Islamic philosophy in Andalusia.

As for the Peripatetic school, it found its first outstanding representative in Avempace who was born in the north of Spain in Zaragoza and died in Fez in 533/1138. He was both a scientist and philosopher and exerted a great influence despite the loss of most of his writings. Like most other Andalusian philosophers he was more attracted to the philosophy of al-Fārābī than Avicenna while at the same time he was opposed to al-Ghazzālī who had only a few years before Avempace criticized Avicenna on certain points of his philosophy. Although himself drawn to a metaphysical interpretation of philosophy which drew it into the domain of gnosis, he represented another tendency than the perspective of al-Ghazzālī. In fact he gave what one might call an "anti-Ghazzālīan" imprint to Andalusian philosophy which culminated with Averroes who was opposed to al-Ghazzālī as well as to certain interpretations of Avicenna whom al-Ghazzālī had in turn criticized.

Avempace wrote several commentaries upon Aristotle as well as independent works on astronomy, philosophy and music and, in fact, like al-Fārābī was a competent musician. In astronomy, as we learn from Maimonides, he wrote a treatise defending the Aristotelian celestial physics against the Ptolemaic epicyclic system, thus underlining an extensive debate which was carried out by later astronomers and philosophers.

Avempace's main philosophical work is the *Regime of the Solitary* which he left unfinished. Although externally it seems to deal with "political philosophy," it is actually a metaphysical work based on the central theme of union with the Active Intellect. Avempace developed an elaborate theory of spiritual forms. He distinguished between intelligible forms abstracted from matter and intelligible forms independent of matter and believed the process of philosophical realization to be to go from the first to the second. This doctrine is of utmost importance in his physics where he applies it to the force of gravity with results that had a far-reaching historic effect.

It is in fact in the domain of the philosophical aspect of physics that Avempace is best known in the West. None of his works were translated into Latin but through quotations by Averroes and others he exercised an influence which is to be seen even in the writings of Galileo. In the early *Pisan Dialogue* there are two important elements, the impetus theory and the "Avempacean" dynamics, both of which have their basis in Islamic sources as elaborated by late medieval Latin philosophers and scientists.

As far as the impetus theory is concerned it had its origin in the criticism of John Philoponus, a sixth-century (A.D.) Christian philosopher, against Aristotle's theories of projectile motion. Discussing motion in the void—if there were to be a void—Philoponus refuted Aristotle's theory that there would be no way for a projectile to stop because of the homogeneity of the void. Rather, he asserted that the source of motion communicates a certain incorporate motive force (the Scholastic *impetus*) which when terminated causes the motion to come to an end. Avicenna—who as far as is known is the first Muslim authority to elaborate on this question—adopted the view of Philoponus against the projectile theories of Aristotle and the Muslim theologians but applied it to ordinary projectile motion encountering resistance, not just theoretical motion in the void. He asserted that the moving body borrows from the mover what he calls *mail* (the Latin *inclinatio*), literally meaning "tendency" in both Arabic and Latin, which makes violent motion possible. This *mail* is gradually used up against the resistance until it finishes and the motion terminates. In a vacuum without a resistance, therefore, the motion would continue indefinitely.

The sixth/twelfth century Jewish philosopher Abu'l-Barakāt al-Baghdādī, who is said by some to have become a convert to Islam at the end of his long life, continued this criticism of the Aristotelian theory of motion and adopted the view of Philoponus but disagreed with Avicenna on the perpetual continuity of motion in the void. He also studied the question of the accelerated motion of a falling body. As pointed out by the authority on medieval philosophy, S. Pines, in his masterly studies of Abu'l-Barakāt,[2] he is the first to have refuted the basic principle of Aristotelian dy-

2 Especially "Etudes sur Awḥad al-Zamān Abu'l-Barakāt al-Baghdādī," *Revue des Etudes Juives,* Vol. III (CIII), No. 1–2, 1938, pp. 3–64; Vol. IV (CIV), No. 1–2, 1938, pp. 1–33, upon which we have drawn in this analysis.

namics according to which a constant force produces a uniform movement whose velocity is proportional to the force causing motion. Rather, he asserted that a constant force which produces natural motion causes accelerated motion.

Later Muslim philosophers and theologians adopted the views of Avicenna and Abuʾl-Barakāt on this question and some like Mullā Ṣadrā further developed them. In Andalusia, however, the philosophers, because of their "anti-Avicennian" attitude, did not accept the impetus theory, and the Latin West, where this theory was known and defended by some like Peter Olivi, came to know of it through Avicenna's own writings as well as through certain references to it in the works of the astronomer al-Biṭrūjī.

But Avempace did develop the other criticism of Aristotelian physics which came to be known under his name. Averroes in commenting on Chapter 8 of Book IV of the *Physics* of Aristotle, which contains the heart of his discussion on mechanics and which Galileo especially attacked, turns away from the text to criticize the views of Avempace. The Stagirite held that in projectile motion the velocity is directly proportional to the motive power and inversely proportional to the resisting medium. Following E. A. Moody, whose study of this question has illuminated the debt of the early Galileo to Avempace,[3] if we set V = velocity, P = motive power and M = resisting medium, then the Aristotelian theory could be written as $V = P/M$. From the quotation of Avempace from his lost commentary on *Physics* cited by Averroes and from the original commentary in Arabic long believed to have been lost but recently recovered, it becomes clear that he believed $V = P—M$ so that in a vacuum motion would not be instantaneous. This view, known as the Avempace theory, was debated in the Middle Ages and defended by St. Thomas and Duns Scotus while Averroes and many in the West like Albertus Magnus rejected it. It was also known in the Renaissance and in fact is the exact formula which Galileo gives in his *Pisan Dialogue* against Aristotle's view of motion, without, however, mentioning the name of its discoverer.

Avempace, moreover, conceived of the force of gravity as an inner form, a spiritual form, which moves bodies from within and which he compared to the movement of the heavenly bodies by the intelligences. He thereby removed the

[3] E. A. Moody, "Galileo and Avempace," *Journal of the History of Ideas*, Vol. XII, No. 2 (1951), pp. 163–193; No. 3, pp. 375–422.

barrier between the heavens and the sublunary world. Galileo also followed him in both these questions except that he was extending the laws of terrestrial physics to the heavens, while Avempace held the opposite view. Galileo absorbed the cosmology and the theological implications of celestial physics in terrestrial physics and applied the earthly laws everywhere in the heavens whereas Avempace was seeking to absorb terrestrial mechanics in a celestial physics with all its spiritual implications by elevating the moving force of terrestrial bodies to the rank of a spiritual principle. As in so many other cases between medieval and modern science there is the correlation of ideas and in fact the influence of one set of ideas upon another while at the same time the ends for which those ideas were formulated are quite different.

Avempace's contemporary Ibn al-Sīd is also of much interest, although he was of a very different character. He was a philosopher of Neopythagorean tendencies who, perhaps under the influence of the Brethren of Purity, sought to correlate the order of existence with the series of numbers. He posited three circles, each composed of a decad symbolizing the world of the intellect, the soul and matter. He believed the number 10 to be the basis of the rhythm of life in the cosmos as it is the basis of the decimal system of numbers.

Between Avempace and Averroes there stands the figure of Ibn Ṭufail (the Latin Abubacer), physician, philosopher and statesman, who was again known to the West through the criticism of Averroes against him in the commentary upon the *De Anima (On the Soul)* of Aristotle. Besides his contributions in medicine, he is best known for his *Living Son of the Awake* which, however, must not be confused with the work of Avicenna by the same title. Ibn Ṭufail was in fact a great admirer of Avicenna, but his work has a different setting and end. It is also the quest of knowledge through union with the Active Intellect, externally resembling the *Robinson Crusoe* story which, in fact, it inspired. Not known during medieval times it was translated in the seventeenth century as *Philosophus Autodidactus* and made a deep impression upon some of the philosophers of that day as well as the mystics in England who spoke of the "inner light" and sought to discover the "light" within themselves through individual effort. The original aim of Ibn Ṭufail was not by any means the same, but he came to exert an influence on such people as the founders of the Quaker movement. More immediately, in Andalusia itself, he was to provide the link between Averroes, the most celebrated Islamic philosopher of

Andalusia, and the philosophic tradition which culminated with him.

The answer to Muslim philosophers who sought to modify Aristotle as well as the challenge of al-Ghazzālī against the philosophers was answered, but without too great an effect upon the Muslim world itself, by Averroes. The purest of Aristotelians among Muslim philosophers, he was to have, perhaps because of this fact, a greater influence in the Christian than in the Islamic world. He can, in a sense, be regarded rather as belonging even more to the philosophical tradition of the West, than to the mainstream of the intellectual life of Islam. The real Averroes, however, is quite different from his Latin image, in which he appears as the synonym for antireligious thought, practically a disciple of the Devil. Averroes actually believed, like many medieval philosophers, that both reason and revelation are sources of the truth and lead to the same ultimate end as affirmed by his book *On the Harmony between Philosophy and Religion;* unlike Avicenna and other famous Muslim philosophers, however, his thought remained much more rationalistic than intellectual. His system is the most complete and faithful exposition in the Islamic world of Aristotle and his Neoplatonic commentators. He followed Aristotle quite closely in the sciences of the sublunary region, although differing from the Stagirite on questions regarding the Intellect, the relation of God to the universe, and the connection between philosophy and religion. Yet, like the Stagirite, he believed that all knowledge could be discovered by human reason operating upon the experience of the senses, and that the existence of God could be proved by arguments drawn from physics.

The Incoherence of the Incoherence was Averroes's reply to al-Ghazzālī's attack upon the philosophers. The reply, however, was nowhere nearly as effective in the Islamic world as the attack. The ideas of Averroes have been taught in certain Islamic countries, such as Persia, ever since his death, as part of the corpus of the Peripatetic school. Yet, even in the field of Peripatetic philosophy, Averroes has occupied a secondary position by comparison with al-Fārābī and Avicenna, whose less rationalistic and more metaphysical perspectives have provided a more congenial companion for gnosis, and a more suitable background for intellectual intuition, than the more rationalistic philosophy of Averroes.

The following excerpt from *The Incoherence of the Incoherence* is from the first of four "discussions" about the natural sciences—the seventeenth through the twentieth of twenty such discussions—each of which takes up and replies to one of al-Ghazzālī's points of attack in *The Incoherence of the Philosophers.*

THE ATTACK OF AL-GHAZZĀLĪ UPON THE PHILOSOPHERS AND THE RESPONSE OF AVERROES

Ghazzālī says: According to us the connexion between what is usually believed to be a cause and what is believed to be an effect is not a necessary connexion; each of two things has its own individuality and is not the other, and neither the affirmation nor the negation, neither the existence nor the non-existence of the one is implied in the affirmation, negation, existence, and non-existence of the other—e.g., the satisfaction of thirst does not imply drinking, nor satiety eating, nor burning contact with fire, nor light sunrise, nor decapitation death, nor recovery the drinking of medicine, nor evacuation the taking of a purgative, and so on for all the empirical connexions existing in medicine, astronomy, the sciences and the crafts. For the connexions in these things is based on a prior power of God to create them in a successive order, though not because this connexion is necessary in itself and cannot be disjoined—on the contrary, it is in God's power to create satiety without eating, and death without decapitation, and to let life persist notwithstanding the decapitation, and so on with respect to all connexions. The philosophers, however, deny this possibility and claim that that is impossible. To investigate all these innumerable connexions would take too long, and so we shall choose one single example, namely the burning of cotton through contact with fire; for we regard it as possible that the contact might occur without the burning taking place, and also that the cotton might be changed into ashes without any contact with fire, although the philosophers deny this possibility. The discussion of this matter has three points.

The first is that our opponent claims that the agent of the burning is the fire exclusively; this is a natural, not a voluntary agent, and cannot abstain from what is in its nature when it is brought into contact with a receptive substratum. This we deny, saying: The agent of the burning is God, through His creating the black in the cotton and the disconnexion of its parts, and it is God who made the cotton burn and made it ashes either through the intermediation of angels or without intermediation. For fire is a dead body which has no action, and what is the proof that it is the agent? Indeed, the philosophers have no other proof than the observation of the occurrence of the burning, when there is contact with fire, but observation proves only a simultaneity, not a causation, and, in reality, there is no other cause but God. For there is unanimity of opinion about the fact that the union of the spirit with the perceptive and moving faculties in the sperm of animals does not originate in the natures contained in warmth, cold, moistness, and dryness, and that the father is neither the agent of the embryo through introducing the sperm into the uterus, nor the agent of its life, its sight and hearing, and all its other faculties. And although it is well known that the same faculties exist in the father, still nobody thinks that these faculties exist through him; no, their existence is produced by the First either directly or through the intermediation of the angels who are in charge of these events. Of this fact the philosophers who believe in a creator are quite convinced, but it is precisely with them that we are in dispute. . . .

And for what other reason do our opponents believe that in the principles of existence there are causes and influences from which the events which coincide with them proceed, than that they are constant, do not disappear, and are not moving bodies which vanish from sight? For if they disappeared or vanished we should observe the disjunction and understand then that behind our perceptions there exists a cause. And out of this there is no issue, according to the very conclusions of the philosophers themselves.

The true philosophers were therefore unanimously of the opinion that these accidents and events which occur when there is a contact of bodies, or in general a change in their positions, proceed from the bestower of forms who is an angel or a plurality of angels, so that they even said that the impression of the visible forms on the eye occurs through the bestower of forms, and that the rising of the sun, the soundness of the pupil, and the existence of the visible object are only the preparations and dispositions which enable the substratum to receive the forms; and this theory they applied to all events. And this refutes the claim of those who profess that fire is the agent of burning, bread the agent of satiety, medicine the agent of health, and so on.

I say:

To deny the existence of efficient causes which are observed in sensible things is sophistry, and he who defends this doctrine either denies with his tongue what is present in his mind or is carried away by a sophistical doubt which occurs to him concerning this question. For he who denies this can no longer acknowledge that every act must have an agent. The question whether these causes by themselves are sufficient to perform the acts which proceed from them, or need an external cause for the perfection of their act, whether separate or not, is not self-evident and requires much investigation and research.

And if the theologians had doubts about the efficient causes which are perceived to cause each other, because there are also effects whose cause is not perceived, this is illogical. Those things whose causes are not perceived are still unknown and must be investigated, precisely because their causes are not perceived; and also since everything whose causes are not perceived is still unknown by nature and must be investigated, it follows necessarily that what is not unknown has causes which are perceived. The man who reasons like the theologians does not distinguish between what is self-evident and what is unknown, and everything Ghazzālī says in this passage is sophistical.

And further, what do the theologians say about the essential causes, the understanding of which alone can make a thing understood? For it is self-evident that things have essences and attributes which determine the special functions of each thing and through which the essences and names of things are differentiated. If a thing had not its specific nature, it would not have a special name or definition, and all things would be one—indeed, not even one; for it might be asked whether this one has one special act or one special passivity or not, and if it had a special act, then there would indeed exist special acts proceeding from special natures, but if it had no single act, then the one would not be one. But if the nature of oneness is denied the nature of being is denied, and the consequence of the denial of being is nothingness.

Further, are the acts which proceed from all things absolutely necessary for those in whose nature it lies to perform them, or are they only performed in most cases or in half the cases? This is a question which must be investigated, since one single action-and-passivity between two existent things occurs only through one relation out of an infinite number, and it happens often that one relation hinders another. Therefore, it is not absolutely certain that fire acts when it is brought near a sensitive body, for surely it is not improbable that there should be something which stands in such a relation to the sensitive thing as to hinder the action of the fire, as is asserted of talc and other things. But one need not therefore deny fire its burning power so long as fire keeps its name and definition. . . .

Now intelligence is nothing but the perception of things with their causes, and in this it distinguishes itself from all the other faculties of apprehension, and he who denies causes must deny the intellect. Logic implies the existence of causes and effects, and knowledge of these effects can only be rendered perfect through knowledge of their causes. Denial of cause implies the denial of knowledge, and denial of knowledge implies that nothing in this world can really be known, and that what is supposed to be known is nothing but opinion, that neither proof nor definition exist, and that the essential attributes which compose definitions are void. The man who denies the necessity of any item of knowledge must admit that even this, his own affirmation, is not necessary knowledge.[4]

C. Al-Ṭūsī

While al-Ghazzālī's attacks against the philosophers are well known, those of Fakhr al-Dīn al-Rāzī, the influential theologian who followed him nearly a century later, have not yet been universally recognized. Yet al-Rāzī's criticism was to have a more enduring effect, from a technical philosophical point of view, than that of his predecessor. Although he was one of the most learned men of his day, and wrote what is generally considered to be the most complete commentary upon the Quran, as well as treatises on various mathematical and natural sciences, he set out to destroy the philosophical influence of the Peripatetics by writing a criticism of Avicenna's philosophical masterpiece, *The Book of Directives and Remarks*. In making his critical attacks, he took the meaning of nearly every sentence into consideration, and thereby left his mark upon all subsequent studies of this work, which has been studied and taught to the present day in the Islamic world.

It was Naṣīr al-Dīn al-Ṭūsī, whom we have already had occasion to mention as one of the leading Muslim mathematicians and astronomers, who took up the challenge of al-Ghazzālī, and especially of al-Rāzī, and sought to reestab-

4 Averroes, *Tahāfut al-tahāfut (The Incoherence of the Incoherence)*, translated by S. Van den Bergh (E. J. W. Gibb Memorial Series, New Series 19. London: Luzac and Co., 1954), I, pp. 316–319.

lish the school of Avicenna, which these men had combated so assiduously. It was this reply of al-Ṭūsī, more than *The Incoherence of the Incoherence* of Averroes, that exerted a lasting influence in the Islamic world, particularly its Eastern half, so that al-Ṭūsī is remembered in the East today more for his philosophical writings than for the mathematical ones, which have made his name famous in the Occident.

Naṣīr al-Dīn al-Ṭūsī is one of the most eminent examples of the *ḥakīm,* to whom we alluded in the introduction. He could place himself in the perspective of each school, and defend it from its own point of view; and even compose a work in that field, which later became accepted as a standard authority. He had realized fully the inner harmony of the various perspectives cultivated in Islam. He in fact displays in his writings this harmony, the result of the position that has been accorded to each science according to a hierarchical order, thus preserving the harmony of the whole and preventing the disciplines from becoming contending enemies upon an intellectual battleground. As compared with Avicenna—the sole figure with whom one could compare him—Naṣīr al-Dīn al-Ṭūsī must be regarded as a lesser philosopher and physician, but a greater mathematician and theologian. His writings in Persian are more important than those of Avicenna. In any case, he stands second only to Avicenna, the master of all Muslim philosopher-scientists, in his influence and significance for the Islamic arts and sciences and philosophy.

The universality of Naṣīr al-Dīn's genius, which some have quite erroneously taken for lack of principles, is shown by the fact that, while in the service of the Ismailis, he was able to master their doctrines and even wrote several works which contain some of the clearest expositions of Ismailism. Among these, the *Taṣawwurāt (Notions)* is particularly notable, as a simple exposition of the basic doctrines of this important branch of Islam. The second chapter concerning "the descent of the things of the world from the First Cause" bears witness to this.

TAṢAWWUR THE SECOND

On the descent of things of the world from the First Cause. (In [8] questions and answers.)

QUESTION:—Some people maintain that the source of existence

is one, some say that it is two, others three, and others again—four. What is thy idea on the matter?

ANSWER:—*My idea is that the source of existence is one, namely the volition of God the All-High, which is called "the Word." The first creation, which came into existence directly by the creative volition, without any intermediary, was the First* [*Intellect*]. *(All) other creations came into existence from the Divine volition through different intermediaries. Thus the* [*Soul*] *through the* [*Intellect*] *and the* [*Hylē*], *nature and matter came through the* [*Soul*].

QUESTION:—Some say that the creative act which emanates from the volition of the Creator the All-High—without any intermediary and not in time—must be imagined as the light spreading from the lamp. But some say that light spreads from the lamp automatically, i.e. without volition. And if this detail is also accepted along with this simile, it would neither prove the existence of the Creator, nor of the creative act. What wilt thou say about this?

ANSWER:—*What is said about the creative act from the volition of the Creator in the simile of the light of lamp is nothing but a metaphor, one of those figurative expressions which are applied either to human beings, or to God, for the purpose that the people may at once comprehend and realize from the simile the works of the Divine Volition, not in order that, in this case, they would accept this simile as exactly in reality coinciding with that to which it refers. The attributes which the people give to Him the All-High, such as absolute existence, oneness, simplicity of substance, spontaneity, knowledge, might, etc., in the same strain, are like saying that God is a Pure Light or an Absolute Bounty or generosity, liberality, a gift, a benefaction, which in the broad sense are the cause of the existence of 18,000 worlds, and in the narrow sense the cause of the perfection of their own nature. That plurality, duality or multiplicity, and the fact that all such properties as absolute existence, oneness, being, simplicity of substance, spontaneity, volition, wisdom, power, etc., are given to Him separately; this does not imply that they are not all one with Him. It follows that created (properties) refer (only) to creations, not to God. Therefore, that spontaneity or automatism which thou hast mentioned cannot be applied to the world of reality,—how then can it be binding?*

QUESTION:—We want an explanation of the coming into being of the first creation from the Divine volition.

ANSWER:—*Its explanation is this. Since God became conscious of himself as a Creator, this fact necessitated the existence of the creation. That creation was the First* [*Intellect*], *and as the*

First [Intellect] was absolute oneness, one in every respect, there arose the problem of the principle according to which "from one only one can come out" (i.e. a simple cause can produce only one effect).

. . . .

QUESTION:—Thou hast explained the origin of the First [Intellect] from the First Cause. What dost thou say of the other creations?

ANSWER:—*This question may be answered in two ways, either as a whole or in part. The full answer is that the First [Intellect] by the power of Divine assistance of the Highest Word [i.e. Divine volition], conceived the idea of all things, both spiritual and material, to the utmost limits. Thus, all that at this moment forms the world, from the outer sphere to the core of the earth, must have this particular form and appearance, constituting an organism which has to possess a soul which would keep it, regulate and control it. Such an idea of the [Intellect] became the cause of the coming into existence of the origin of all things with all that every creation required. Thus the [Intellects] with their participation in the running of the world, the [Souls'] activities, the spheres and their regulation, the elements with their influences, the kingdoms of nature with their inter-relations, with all on what depends their well-being and all that it continuously requires, all this was in the idea conceived by the [Intellect]. It was just as a suspicion arises at the first glance: no sooner had the [Intellect] conceived that idea than all instantly came into existence by the way of creation and initiation. Both these latter were one: the creation—which refers to the reason—came into being from the Divine volition without any intermediary, and the initiation refers to the spiritual and material substances which came into being through the [Intellect] and [Soul].*

The explanation of details is this:—When the First [Intellect] thought of its own cause, which had a higher affinity, its thought became the cause of the coming into existence of the second [Intellect], i.e. the [Intellect] of the outer sphere, which is also called the sphere of Aṭlas, *or the Throne. When it [the First Intellect] reflected on its own substance—which possessed intermediary affinities, i.e. understood that it is due to something else—that thought became the cause of the coming into existence of the [Universal soul], i.e. the [Soul] of the outer sphere. And when it, the First [Intellect], reflected on its own existence by possibility—which had inferior affinities, i.e. realized that it itself was merely a possibility—that thought became the cause of the existence of the outer sphere, itself.*

QUESTION:—No material body can come into existence without (the participation of) the [Hylē] and form which have precedence before it. Why, therefore, hast thou mentioned the coming into existence of the sphere without any reference to the [Hylē] and [Form]?

ANSWER:—*The* [*Hylē*] *and* [*Form*] *came into existence when the* [*Universal Soul*] *reflected on the substance of the First* [*Intellect*] *and realized the fact it was perfect. From this reflection appeared the form which comes from the field of perfection. And when the* [*Universal Soul*] *thought of its own substance, and realized its own being imperfect, from this realization the* [*Hylē*], *which comes from the field of defect, came into existence. These two regards became necessary to the* [*Soul*], *because it has a double face: one side is turned towards oneness, and the other towards plurality.*

QUESTION:—As oneness is a characteristic of the [Intellect], and plurality of the [Soul], how is it that thou hast attributed to the [Intellect] three thoughts, while to the [Soul] only two?

ANSWER:—*Because in the position of the* [*Intellect*] *all is perfection, and for it all the relative aspects are one, and that one is in the fact that it is turned towards Him, the All-High. Therefore, one idea in it means all ideas and all its ideas means one. But for the* [*Soul*], *which occupies an inferior position, and houses an imperfection in its substance, matters are different. The rest that have been mentioned, namely* [*souls*], [*intellects*], *spheres, elements, kingdoms of nature, and the Intellect of the outer sphere,* falaku'l-aflāk, *all also must have, just as in the case of the First* [*Intellect*], *three* taṣawwurs *(moments of cognition). One is needed for the bringing into being of the Second* [*Intellect*], *i.e. the* [*Intellect*] *of the sphere of fixed stars or, . . . the Throne of God. One is needed for the production of all between the* [*sphere of fixed stars*] *to the* [*Intellect*] *of the sphere* Zuhal *of (Saturn). Thence to the* [*Intellect*] *of the sphere of* Mushtarī *(Jupiter). Thence to the* [*Intellect*] *of the sphere of* Murīkh *(Mars), thence to the* [*Intellect*] *of the sphere of the Sun, thence to the* [*Intellect*] *of the sphere of* Zuhra *(Venus), thence to the* [*Intellect*] *of the sphere of* ʿAṭārid *(Mercury), thence to the* [*Intellect*] *of the sphere of the Moon. Every one of these* [*Intellects*] *needs three* [*ideas*], *which are required for bringing into being the* [*Intellect*], [*Soul*] *and the sphere which is the next in order. The* [*Hylē*] *and the form of each sphere of necessity come from those two realizations which were made by the corresponding* [*Soul*] *namely the realization of the perfection of the* [*Intellect*] *and its own imperfection. Such is the order decreed by the Great and Wise One. The creation of the world of the celestial spheres was decreed to consist of those nine rotating spheres. Each sphere was provided with a* [*Soul*] *and an* [*Intellect*] *as the controller of the latter. This was done in order that each sphere would possess an independent and direct moving agent. Such separate mover was the* [*Intellect*] *and the direct moving force was the* [*Soul*]. *This may be compared, e.g., with a magnet, which by itself does not move but brings into motion iron, attracting it to itself. And "the direct mover", is like, for example, the wind which whirls round the tree, shaking it. The last of the* [*Intellects*] *associated with the spheres, namely that of the sphere of the Moon, is called* [*Active Intellect*], *i.e. "effective," "maker," because it is this* [*Intellect*] *which brings the things of this world from the state of potentiality into the state of actuality. For the same reason it is also called "the giver of forms" because it grants them to the things of this world.*

. . . .

QUESTION:—What dost thou say: was the number of the spheres such as it was, not bigger and not smaller, by the reason of nine being the ultimate number of bodies? Or because the [Hylē] was exhausted, or for what other reason?

ANSWER:—*This world is of the kind of which it is said in the Coran (ii, 256): "They comprehend not aught of His knowledge but of what He pleases." It was so destined by the command and wisdom of God the All-High that there should be nine spheres, twelve constellations of the Zodiac, seven "fathers", i.e. planets, four "mothers", i.e. elements, and three kingdoms of nature. Only the Lords of the Truth, (i.e. Imams)—prostration be due to their mention!—know as to how and why this was done, because (only) they comprehend the creation as a whole, and are informed (about its details). The ordinary slaves of God can only discuss as much as they have learned from their* dāʿīs [*Ismāʿīlī* missionaries]. . . . *From God comes guidance, and in Him is help. With regard to the elements and kingdoms of nature the* [*Universal Soul*], *in the longing which it experiences for the perfection of the position of the First* [*Intellect*] *and imitating the latter, which it usually does, keeps the spheres continually moving. But as, with regard to perfection, the rotation of the spheres was destined to become the living force, and could only be (manifested in) individual organisms, composed of matter and its forms, who required suitable and co-related causes (for their existence). With that rotation which (every) celestial circumference was making around its centre according to its autonomous laws, the elements, i.e. fire, air, water and earth—which are the ingredients of the nature in the cavity of the sphere of the Moon—became organised into the order and system of being. Every one of these fourfold basic elements, which happened to be nearer to the sky, proved to be able to possess a substance lighter and finer (than the others), as, e.g., fire, which is above the air, is of a finer substance as compared with the latter, although more solid as compared with the substance of the sphere. Air, which stays above water, is finer as compared with the latter, while it is more solid than fire. Water, which remains above earth, is finer as compared with the latter, but more solid if compared with earth. The latter, standing the furthest from the skies, has solidity as its characteristics.*

The force of the creative act which, by the way of the creation, reached the Throne of God, through the latter reached the Kursī, *and, through the latter again, descended to the sphere of Saturn, to which it became attached. Similarly, it descended further, from one sphere to the other, until it reached the sphere of the Moon. Then the emanations and rays of the stars, by the force of that energy and through the intermediary of the sphere of the Moon, fell upon the elements, and that was certainly the cause which stimulated (the activity of) the elements. It is from this that the passive motion, which caused the association and disassociation of the elements, became necessary. The form of each of these varieties of matter was split by others, and all four, from the tendency of stressing their contrasting qualities to the extreme, turned towards the middle course, which was the balance of the mixture. Thus came into existence the product which has the ability of accepting form. And the "Giver of forms" gave the kingdoms of the nature in this world, namely minerals, plants, animals and man, each kind of them, a form which befitted them, together with their necessary special qualities, refinement of appearance, astonishing constitution and wonderful properties. All these, in proportion to their merits, received a share of the force from the energy of the [Universal Soul] and a light from the lights of the First [Intellect], e.g. compactness in minerals, growth in plants, sensibility and free movement in animals, reason and intellect in man. The categories of these kingdoms of nature consisted of individual organisms, which themselves were subdivided into different species, each differing from the others by a certain innate merit. These kingdoms of nature started with minerals, then followed plants, later animals, and then man, so that the last (i.e. highest) degree of the mineral merges in the first (i.e. lowest) degree of the plants, and so forth, while the last (highest) degree of man touches the first (lowest) degree of the angels. Such an hierarchy of creations in the periodicity of things has by the will of God the All-High reached its top and perfection in the degree of man and his ability to receive that perfection which consists of the possession of those mental means and physical possibilities which are characteristic of him. From this it is obvious that although minerals, plants and speechless animals preceded him in the order of creation, the ultimate purpose of all these (being brought into existence) was he, man, in accordance with the saying: first comes the thought, then the action.*

With regard to the differences in form of the various categories of creations, it may be explained as due to the fact that the will of God the All-High was such as to make all that was potential in individual souls come into a state of actuality by the influence of the spheres and stars. But the spheres always rotate, in a fast movement. Therefore, the difference in the conflicting action of stars could have produced different forms in the basic categories of beings.[5]

D. Suhrawardī and Mullā Ṣadrā

Although he lived nearly a century before Naṣīr al-Dīn, Shihāb al-Dīn al-Suhrawardī—as far as the influence of the school founded by him is concerned—belongs to the centuries that followed the philosopher-mathematician, upon whom he even exercised some influence. Suhrawardī lived but a few years, having been born in 548/1153, and died in 587/1191. But these thirty-eight years were enough for him to found the second major philosophical perspective in Islam, the school of Illuminationism, which became a rival of the earlier Peripatetic school, and soon even overshadowed it. Suhrawardī studied in Maragha, the future site of al-Ṭūsī's astronomical activities, and also in Isfahan, where he was a classmate of Fakhr al-Dīn al-Rāzī. He traveled extensively throughout Persia, Anatolia and Syria, finally settling in Aleppo. Here his frank exposition of esoteric doctrines, and especially his reliance upon symbolism drawn from Zoroastrian sources, as well as his harsh and outspoken criticism of the jurists, brought about

[5] Naṣīr al-Dīn al-Ṭūsī, *Taṣawwurāt,* translated by W. Ivanov (The Ismaili Society Series A, No. 4. Bombay, 1950), pp. 6–15.

a severe reaction, which resulted in his imprisonment and finally his death.

Suhrawardī, known to his compatriots as *Shaikh al-ishrāq* or "master of illuminationism," was the author of a series of philosophical and gnostic works in Arabic and Persian, of which the most important is the *Ḥikmat al-ishrāq (Theosophy of the Orient of Light)*, the basic testament of that school, which has dominated the intellectual scene in Persia ever since it was written. In this magisterial work, Suhrawardī begins with a severe criticism of Peripatetic philosophy, not only in logic (in which he cuts the ten Aristotelian categories to four), but also in natural philosophy, psychology and metaphysics. He insists upon the archetypal world, which Aristotle had laid aside in favor of the immanent form, and regards the study of Nature as the hermeneutic interpretation and penetration of cosmological symbols. Moreover, he removes the Aristotelian distinction between the sublunary and celestial regions, and places the boundary between the world of pure light or Orient, and the world in which matter or darkness is mixed with light—that is, the Occident—at the sphere of the fixed stars. The real heaven thus begins at the boundary of the visible universe, and what the Aristotelians as well as the Ptolemaic astronomers had called the heavens belongs more or less to the same domain as the world of generation and corruption.

Suhrawardī also discussed at length the question of knowledge, ultimately basing it on illumination, and proposing a theory of vision that is in a certain sense similar to that of Gestalt psychology. He combines the way of reason with that of intuition, regarding the two as necessary complements of each other. Reason, without intuition and illumination is, according to Suhrawardī, puerile and half-blind and can never reach the transcendent source of all truth and intellection; whereas intuition, without a preparation in logic and the training and development of the rational faculty, can be led astray, and furthermore cannot express itself succinctly and methodically. That is why the *Theosophy of the Orient of Light* begins with logic and terminates with a chapter on ecstasy and the contemplation of the celestial essences.

Suhrawardī also wrote a number of short symbolic narratives, mainly in Persian, which are masterpieces of Persian prose, and also depict in a highly artistic manner the universe of symbols through which the adept must journey to reach the truth, a universe reminiscent of the Avicennian cosmos, to which we have already alluded. In these treatises, many aspects of natural philosophy are discussed, especially light and light phenomena. But the aim is to pave a path through the cosmos, in order to guide the seeker of truth, and thus to free him from all entanglements and determinations connected with the natural domain. The ultimate goal of all forms of knowledge is illumination and gnosis, which Suhrawardī in unmistakable terms places at the summit of the hierachy of knowledge, thereby affirming the essential nature of the Islamic Revelation. The following passages from his *Song of the Griffin* bear testimony to this point:

PART ONE
ABOUT THE BEGINNINGS

CHAPTER ONE: On the Excellence of this Science Over all Other Sciences. Be it not unknown to the light-hearted that the preference of a science to others is due to several reasons. Firstly, the "known" should be nobler, *e.g.* goldsmithship is preferable to pack-saddle-craft; because that deals with gold and this other with wood and wool.

Secondly, because the arguments of this science are stronger than those of any other science.

Thirdly, because occupation therein should be more momentous and its advantage greater.

And in comparison to other sciences all the signs of preference are found in this science.

With regard to the "object" and the "known."—It is apparent that the object and the aim of this science is Truth. And it is impossible to compare other existant things with His grandeur.

With regard to ascertainment of argument and corroboration of proof.—It is established that observation is stronger than argumentation. The Masters of the art of Kalām consider it lawful that God the Almighty should give man the necessary knowledge about His existence, qualities and so on. Since it is lawful, the acquisition of some knowledge of this sort is undoubtedly superior to that which necessitates bearing the troubles of observation, labours of reasoning, and falling into the places of doubts and abodes of suspicion. One of the Ṣūfīs was asked, "What is the proof of the existence of the

Creator?" He replied: "For me it is the morning instead of the lamp." Also another one of them says: "The semblance of one who seeks after the Truth through arguments is like one searching after the sun with a lamp."

Since the masters of the principles have accepted and agreed that in the next world God the Almighty will create in men a perception in the sense of vision, to see God without mediation; argument, proof, and admonition are no considerations with the People of Truth. So according to these principles it befits [Him] to create in his [man's] heart perceptions of this kind in order to see Him in this world without any mediation and proof. And it is therefore that ʿOmar—may God be pleased with him—said, "My heart has seen my Lord" and ʿAlī—may God beautify his face—says, "If the veil is removed, my belief is not increased." And here secrets are concealed which are not proper [to be dealt with] in this place.

With regard to importance.—There is no doubt that for men there is nothing more important than the greatest felicity. Rather, all questions cannot be treated in this brief treatise. And the greatest of means of access is *maʿrifa* [gnosis].

So from all aspects it is proved that *maʿrifa* is nobler than all sciences. And Junayd—peace be upon him—said, "If I knew that under the sky there is a science in this world nobler than that in which the seekers of *maʿrifa* contemplate, I would have engaged myself to buy it and would have toiled in the best way to acquire it until I had got it."

CHAPTER TWO: On what appears to the Ahli-Badāyā [Beginners]. The first lightning that comes to the souls of the Seekers from the presence of Divinity is accidents and flashes; and those lights dawn upon the soul of the [mystic] traveller from the world of Divinity; and it is delightful.

Its onrush is like this: that a dazzling light suddenly comes, and soon disappears; and "He it is Who shows you the lightning."

From the second point of view it refers to the "times" of the Companions of Seclusion. The Ṣūfīs call these accidents "time" and it is therefore that one says, "Time is sharper than the sword" and they have said, "Time is a cutting sword." In the Book of God there are many references to that, as it is said: "The splendour of His lightning almost takes away the eye-sight." Wāsiṭī [a fourth/tenth century Ṣūfī] was asked, "Wherefrom is the restlessness of some people in the state of hearing music?" He answered, "There is a light which appears and is then extinguished"; and quoted this verse:

" 'From them a flash came to the heart.
The flash of the lightning appeared and dwindled away.
And therein they have food for the morning and the night.' "

These flashes do not come at all times. At times they are intercepted. And when ascetic exercise increases, lightnings come more often, until that limit is reached that whatever man looks into, he sees some of the states of the next world. Suddenly these dazzling lights become successive: and may be after this the limbs are shaken. As is well-known, the Prophet—peace be upon him—says in expectation of this state, "Verily, for your Lord there are blasts of His mercy in the days of your time, provided you expose yourselves thereunto."

At the time of break, the devotee seeks the help of gentle thought and pure commemoration, against the impurities of carnal desires, in order to regain this state. And it is possible that sometimes this state does come to one who is without ascetic discipline, but he remains unaware.

If one waits for it in the days of ʿId-festivities when men go to places of worship, and when raised voices and loud glorifications and harsh clamours take place and sounds of cymbals and trumpets prevail—if he is a man of intelligence having a sound nature and rememorizes the divine states, he will at once find this effect which is very pleasant.

And likewise it is in battles when men come face to face and the clamour of the warriors rises and there is neighing of the horses and the sounds of the drum and the military band become louder, and men engage in fight and unsheath swords: If some one has a little purity of heart, even if he is not a man of [ascetic] discipline, he will come to know of this state provided that at that time he rememorizes the divine states and brings to mind the souls of the departed and the observation of [Divine] Majesty and the rows of the high assembly.

Similarly, if somebody sits on a galloping horse and makes it run very hard and thinks that he is leaving the body aside and becoming extremely reverent and going to the presence of [Divine] Existence in the state of the soul exclusively and to be included in the rows of the saints—an effect like this state will also appear to him, although he is not a devotee of discipline. And here there are secrets which only a few men understand in these days.

When these lightnings come to man they affect the brain to some extent, and it may also appear in the brain and shoulder and back, etc.; so that the vein begins to pulsate and it is very pleasant, and he also tries to complete *samāʿ* [spiritual concert]. So far this is the first stage.

CHAPTER THREE: On Tranquillity. At length when the lights of the Secret reach the utmost extremity and do not pass away quickly and remain for a long time, that is called "Tranquillity" and its delight is more perfect than the delights of other flashes. When a man returns from Tranquillity, and comes back to [the ordinary state of] humanity, he is highly regretful at its separation; and regarding this one of the saints has said:

"O breath of the soul, how good are you,
One who is emerged in you has tasted the food of intimacy."

In the Holy Quran Tranquillity is mentioned many times, as it is said: "And God sent down His tranquillity" and in another place He says, "He it is Who sent down Tranquillity into the hearts of the faithful that they might add belief unto their belief." He who attains Tranquillity knows about the minds of men, and acquires knowledge of unknown things, and his penetration of mind becomes perfect. The Chosen—God bless and keep him and his family—informed about it, saying, "Fear a believer's penetration of mind, for he perceives with the light of God." And the Prophet—peace be upon him—says about ʿOmar—be God pleased with him—"Verily, Tranquillity speaks through the tongue of ʿOmar"; and he also said, "Verily, in my community there are mutakallimūn [theologians] and muḥaddithūn [scholars of traditions] and ʿOmar is one of them."

One who possesses Tranquillity hears very pleasant sounds from the high Paradise, and spiritual discourses reach him; and he becomes comfortable; as is mentioned in the Divine Revelation: "Verily, in the remembrance of God do hearts find rest!" And he witnesses very fresh and pleasant forms through the compact of his contiguity with the spiritual world.

Of the stages of the People of Love this is the intermediate one.

In the state between awakening and sleep he hears terrible voices and strange noises at the time of the slumber of Tranquillity and sees huge lights and he may become helpless through superabundance of delight.

These accidents are according to the Seekers [of Truth] and not in the manner of a group who close their eyes in their privacy and cherish phantasies. Had they sensed the lights of the truthful, many would have been the sorrows encountering them; "And there those who deemed it vain will lose."

PART TWO
ABOUT THE ENDS

CHAPTER ONE: On Annihilation. "And this Tranquility becomes such that if man desires to keep it off from himself he cannot do so. Then man reaches such a stage that whenever he likes, he gives up the body and goes to the world of [Divine] Majesty; and his ascents reach the high spheres. And whenever he likes or desires he can do so. So whenever he looks at himself he becomes happy, because he discerns the radiance of God's light [falling] on him. Hitherto it is a defect.

"If he exerts further, he also passes this stage. He becomes such that he does not look on himself and his knowledge of his existence is lost; this is called *'fanā-i-akbar.'* When one forgets himself and also forgets the forgetfulness it is called *'fanā dar fanā.'*

"And as long as they delight in *maʿrifa* they are at a loss. This is reckoned amongst latent polytheism. On the other hand, he reaches perfection when he loses knowledge in the 'known,' because, whoever delights in 'knowledge' likewise as in the 'known' has made that his object. He is 'alone' when in the 'known' he gives up the thought of 'knowledge.' When the knowledge of humanity also disappears it is the state of Obliteration, and is the stage of 'Everyone that is in it, will pass away and there remaineth but the face of Thy Lord, the Glorious and Beneficent.'

"One of the Seekers says that 'There is no God but God' is the unification of the common-folk, and 'There is no He but Him' is the unification of the higher class. He has erred in the classification.

"There are five grades of *Tauḥīd*. One is 'There is no God but God' and this is the unification of the common-folk who negative Deity from what is not God. These people are the commonest of the common.

"Beyond this sect there is another group, nobler in comparison to these and commoner in comparison to another sect. Their unification is 'There is no He but Him.' This [group] is higher than the first one. And their place is higher, because the first group only negative divinity from what is not God. This other group did not restrict themselves to negating Truth from what is not Truth. On the other hand, in face of the existence of God, the Almighty, they have negated all other existences. They have said: 'Heship' is for Him, none else can be called 'He' because all 'Heships' emanate from Him. So 'Heship' is exclusively meant for Him.

"Beyond these there is another group whose unification is 'There is no Thou but Thou.' This group is higher than that which addressed God as 'Him.' 'Him' is used for the absent. These negate all 'Thouships' which in occasioning 'Thouship' asserts the existence of oneself; and they refer to the presence [of God].

"There is a group above these and these are higher still. They say: When someone addresses another as 'thou' he separates him from himself, and he asserts duality; and duality is far removed from the world of unity. They lost and considered themselves lost in the appearance of God, and said: "There is no I but Me." They spoke truer than all these. I-ship, Thou-ship, and He-ship are all superfluous reflections about the essence of the unity of the Self-existant. They submerged all the three words in the sea of Obliteration and destroyed expressions and annihilated references: "And everything will perish save His face." And their place is more elevated. As long as a man has human attachments with this world he will not reach the world of Divinity above which there is no other stage since it has no end. A pious man was asked: 'What is taṣawwuf?' He answered: "Its beginning is God and as regards the end it has no end."[6]

Suhrawardī's doctrines found their congenial home in Persia, especially in the Shiite milieu, in which Islamic philosophy and theosophy developed during the latter phase of Islamic history. Suhrawardī's school approached that of the Peripatetics, especially as interpreted by Avicenna, and also the gnostic doctrines of the school of Ibn ʿArabī. In the bosom of Shiism, these diverse perspectives finally became unified in the eleventh/seventeenth century in the synthesis brought about by Mullā Ṣadrā. This Persian sage, who was both philosopher and gnostic and one of the greatest expositors of metaphysical doctrines in Islam, has been compared by Henry Corbin, the only Western scholar who has made a serious study of the doctrines of Suhrawardī and Mullā Ṣadrā, to a combination of St. Thomas Aquinas and Jakob Boehme, in the context of Islam. Mullā Ṣadrā's *Spiritual Journeys* is the most monumental work of Islamic philosophy, in which rational arguments, illuminations received from spiritual realization and the tenets of revelation are harmonized

[6] Shihābuddīn Suhrawardī Maqtūl, *Three Treatises on Mysticism,* edited and translated by O. H. Spies and S. K. Khatak (Stuttgart: W. Kohlhammer, 1935), pp. 30–38.

in a whole which marks in a sense the summit of a thousand years of intellectual activity in the Islamic world.

Basing his doctrine upon the unity of Being, and the constant "transsubstantial" change and becoming of this imperfect world of generation and corruption—without, however, in any way implying that "evolution" à la Teilhard de Chardin which has become popular today—Mullā Ṣadrā created a vast synthesis, which has dominated the intellectual life of Persia and much of Muslim India during the past few centuries. He, along with Suhrawardī, provided a vision of the universe which contains elements of the sciences of Nature developed earlier, and which has been the matrix of the intellectual and philosophical sciences, particularly in the Eastern lands of Islam. Therefore, his doctrines, like those of the master of Islamic gnosis, Ibn ʿArabī, and his followers, have provided the vision of the cosmos for the many of those in the Islamic world who have trodden the path of spiritual realization, and thus have belonged to the tradition of Sufism.

CHAPTER THIRTEEN

THE GNOSTIC TRADITION

In the Islamic world, the highest form of knowledge has never been any single science, or *scientia,* which remains at the discursive level, but the "wisdom of the saints," or *sapientia,* which ultimately means gnosis. Not only did the Muslim and in general medieval sages say, with Aristotle, that knowledge is dependent upon the mode of the knower, and therefore upon his state of being; they also asserted, conversely, and from another point of view, that one's being depends upon one's knowledge. In gnosis, knowledge and being coincide; it is there that science and faith find their harmony. A knowledge which illuminates the whole being of the knower, it differs from philosophy as understood in its usually accepted meaning today which, being theoretical, is limited to the mental plane. Philosophy had originally been that element of doctrine which, along with certain rites and the practice of spiritual virtues, makes up the totality of gnosis; later, however, it became limited to purely theoretical knowledge, divorced from spiritual realization, and the arrival at by limiting the intellect to human reason alone.

Gnosis, which has always been held to be the highest form of knowledge in Islam, as well as in other Oriental traditions, has definite conceptions of the universe, and in fact provides the only matrix within which the traditional cosmological sciences can be properly understood. It is the fountain of life from which they draw their sustenance. The gnostic sees all things as manifestations of the Supreme Divine Principle, which transcends all determinations—even Being, its first determination. All entities in manifestation, both visible and invisible, are connected with this Center by the degree to which they reflect the Intellect and also by their existence. The "intelligence" of each being is the direct bond between it and the Universal Intellect—the *Logos,* or Word, "by which all things are made." The degree of being of each creature is a reflection of Pure Being at some level of cosmic existence; it is by virtue of this reflection that a being is something, and not nothing. If the Divine Principle may be symbolized by a point, then the relation of various beings to It, as Pure Being, is like that of various concentric circles drawn about a center, while their relation to the center as Intellect is like that of the various radii from the circles to the center. The cosmos, then, is like a cobweb: each part of it lies on a circle, which is a "reflection of the center," and which relates the existence of that part to Being; at the same time each part is connected directly to the center by a radius, which symbolizes the relation between the "intelligence" of that part and the Universal Intellect or *Logos.*

The gnostic thus views the cosmos in its dual aspect of positive symbol and negative illusion. In so far as any manifestation is real, it is a symbol of a higher order of reality; in so far as it is separated from, and other than the Principle, it is merely an illusion and non-being. In Islam, this doctrine is explained in two different ways, both of which ultimately arrive at the same meaning. The school of *waḥdat al-wujūd,* or "unity of Being," founded by Muḥyī al-Dīn ibn ʿArabī, regards creation as theophany *(tajallī).* The archetypes of all things, which are aspects of God's Names and Qualities (the *aʿyān al-thābitah*), exist in a latent state in the Divine Intellect. Then God gives them being, so that they become manifested; yet what is seen in the sensible world is only the shadow of the archetypes. The school of *waḥdat al-shuhūd,* or "unity of witness" (or "vision"), established by ʿAlāʾ al-Daulah al-Simnānī, believes creation to be the reflection of the archetypes in the cosmic domain seen ultimately by the One who alone is the real Knower. In both cases creation, or the universe, is regarded as having an unreal aspect, an element of nothingness or non-being, like that to which Plato's "world of shadows" alluded. It is separated from the Divine Principle at the same time that it is *essentially* united with It.

This gnostic view of the cosmos has its positive aspect in its vision of Nature as symbol, and in the consequent cultivation of the sciences which deal with natural phenomena, not as facts, but as symbols of higher degrees of Reality. In their symbolic aspects, alchemy and astrology may in fact be regarded as cosmic supports for the gnostic's metaphysical contemplation.

Since the universe is the "body" of the *Logos,* and since the *Logos* also manifests itself microcosmically in man, the gnostic gains greater intimacy with the universe the more he becomes integrated into the luminous source of his own being. In principle, the body of man as a microcosm contains in miniature the universe, viewed as the macrocosm. Moreover, the Principle which lies at the center of man's being is that same Intellect "out of which all things are made." That is why the gnostics believe that the best way to know Nature in its essence, rather than in its details, is the purification of one's self until one's being becomes illuminated by the Intellect. Having thus reached the center, the gnostic has, in principle, the knowledge of all things. As Ibn ʿArabī says in the *Fuṣūṣ al-Ḥikām (The Bezels of Wisdom):*

> When God willed in respect of His Beautiful Names (Attributes), which are beyond enumeration, that their essences—or if you wish, you may say "His essence"—should be seen, he caused them to be seen in a microcosmic being which, inasmuch as it is endowed with existence, contains the whole object of vision, and through which the inmost consciousness of God becomes manifested to Him. This He did, because the vision that consists in a thing's seeing itself by means of itself is not like its vision of itself in something else that serves as mirror for it: therefore God appears to Himself in a form given by the place in which He is seen (*i.e.,* the mirror), and He would not appear thus (objectively) without the existence of this place and His epiphany to Himself therein. God had already brought the universe into being with an existence resembling that of a fashioned soulless body, and it was like an unpolished mirror. Now, it belongs to the Divine decree (of creation) that He did not fashion any place but such as must of necessity receive a Divine soul, which God has described as having been breathed into it; and this denotes the acquisition by that fashioned form of capacity to receive the emanation, *i.e.,* the perpetual self-manifestation which has never ceased and never shall. It remains to speak of the recipient (of the emanation). The recipient proceeds from naught but His most holy emanation, for the whole affair (of existence) begins and ends with Him: to Him it shall return, even as from Him it began.
>
> The Divine will (to display His attributes) entailed the polishing of the mirror of the universe. Adam (the human essence) was the very polishing of that mirror and the soul of that form, and the angels are some of the faculties of that

> form, *viz.*, the form of the universe which the Sufis in their technical language describe as the Great Man, for the angels in relation to it are as the spiritual and corporeal faculties in the human organism. . . . The aforesaid microcosmic being is named a man and a Vicegerent.[1]

In the Sufi perspective, the Prophet in his inner reality, the Muḥammadan Light *(al-nūr al-muḥammadī)*, is the *Logos*, the archetype of the whole of creation, containing within himself the "idea" of the cosmos just as according to the Gospel of St. John all things were made by the Word or *Logos*. He is also the perfect man, in whom all states of being, dormant and potential in most men, have become realized. These two functions—as the *Logos*, and the archetype of all creation, and as the norm of sanctity, and the perfect model for the spiritual life—are united in the "Universal Man" *(al-insān al-kāmil)*. The Prophet is the Universal Man par excellence, coming at the end of the prophetic cycle, and therefore uniting within himself all aspects of prophethood. The Sufi, Najm al-Dīn al-Rāzī, in his *Mirṣād al-ʿibād (The Path of the Worshippers)* compares the universe to a tree and the Prophet Muḥammad to a seed; he writes that, just as the seed is first planted in the earth, then the stem comes forth, then the tree, then its leaves, and finally the fruit, in which the seed is once again contained, so did the inner reality of the Prophet as the *Logos* precede all things, although he himself came into this world only at the end of the great prophetic cycle. All other prophets, however, as well as the great saints, the "poles," or *aqṭāb* in Sufi terminology, also partake of the nature of the Universal Man, and therefore also possess a cosmic function. Man himself, in fact, by virtue of his central position in the cosmos, is potentially capable of identifying himself with the Universal Man, although higher states of being remain latent for the majority of men, and become fully realized only in the person of the gnostic, or the perfect Sufi, who has reached "the end of the path."

This dual role of the Universal Man, as model of the spiritual life, and as archetype of the cosmos, gives a cosmic aspect to Islamic spirituality. The benediction upon the Prophet and his family, so common in Muslim rituals, is also a benediction upon all creatures. The contemplative presents himself before God as part of the creation to which

[1] R. A. Nicholson, *Studies in Islamic Mysticism* (Cambridge: Cambridge University Press, 1921), pp. 154–155.

he is wed, not only by the elements of his own body, but also by that Spirit which is the source of his own being, as well as of the universe. Islamic spirituality and gnosis, in their cosmic aspect, assign to Nature a positive role in the spiritual life, prefigured in the cosmic functions of the Prophet as the most perfect of all creatures, and as the archetype of the whole universe.

The various levels of Islam are united by the idea of Unity, interpreted according to different degrees of profundity. The first *Shahādah* or affirmation of faith is *La ilāha illʾ Allāh,* which may be translated as "There is no divinity other than The Divinity"; it is to be understood, on the theological level and that of the Divine Law as an affirmation of the Unity of God, and a denial of polytheism. In the Sufi perspective, however, the same formula becomes the doctrinal basis and the most perfect expression of the unity of Being, *wahdat al-wujūd:* "There is no being other than Pure Being" (because there cannot be two independent orders of reality); by extension, "there is no reality, beauty or power except absolute Reality, Beauty and Power." The first *Shahādah,* the fountainhead of all Islamic metaphysics, thus expresses, at the metaphysical level, the "nothingness" of all finite beings before the Infinite, and integrates all particulars into the Universal. At the cosmological level, it expresses the unicity of all things: the corollary to the Unity of the Divine Principle is the unicity of all manifestation and the interrelation of all beings. Just as it is the aim of all metaphysics to arrive at the knowledge of Divine Unity *(al-tawḥīd),* so it is the aim of all cosmological sciences to express the unicity of all existence. The sciences of Nature in Islam share with medieval science in the West, as well as with ancient science generally, this basic aim of expressing "the unicity of all that exists."

The Sufis express the unity of Being, and the relation of the cosmos to its Principle, in many ways—using, in each case, symbols based upon immediate experience. Some Sufis like Nasafī have employed the image of ink and the letters of the alphabet written by it, while al-Jīlī in his famous treatise on universal man compares the relation of the universe to God with that of ice to water. He writes:

> The world is comparable to ice, and the Truth to water, the origin of this ice. The name "ice" is only lent to this coagulation; it is the name of water which is restored to it, according to its essential reality.

. . . .

As a parable, creation is similar to ice,
And it is Thou who art in it the water gushing forth.
Ice is not, if we realize it, other than its water,
And it is not in this condition but for contingent laws.
But the ice will melt away, its condition will dissolve;
The liquid state will be at length established in fact.
These contrasts are unified in one beauty:
It is in it that they are annihilated; and it is from them
that it radiates.[2]

The tenth/sixteenth century Persian Sufi poet and scholar, ʿAbd al-Raḥmān Jāmī, in his *Lawāʾiḥ (Flashes of Light)*, a summary of Ibn ʿArabī's doctrines of the school of *waḥdat al-wujūd* ("unity of Being"), outlined the principles of which we have been speaking. We give a few passages below as expressions of this principle of the unity of Being whose importance in the comprehension of Sufi metaphysics and cosmology can hardly be overemphasized.

The Real Being, *quā* Being, is above all names and attributes, and exempt from all conditions and relations. The attribution to Him of these names only holds good in respect of His aspect towards the world of phenomena. In the first manifestation, wherein He revealed Himself, of Himself, to Himself, were realized the attributes of Knowledge, Light, Existence, and Presence. Knowledge involved the power of knowing and that of being known; Light implied those of manifesting and of being manifest; Existence and Presence entailed those of causing to exist and of being existent, and those of beholding and of being beheld. And thus the manifestation which is characteristic of Light is preceded by concealment; and concealment, by its very nature, has priority over, and is antecedent to, manifestation; hence the concealed and the manifested are counted as first and second.

And in like manner, in the case of the second and third manifestations, etc., as long as it pleases God to continue them, these conditions and relations always go on redoubling themselves. The more these are multiplied, the more complete is His manifestation, or rather His concealment. Glory be to Him who hides Himself by the manifestations of His light,

2 Al-Jīlī, *Al-Insān al-kāmil (Universal Man)* (Cairo: Al-Bahīyah Press, 1304 A.H.), Part I, p. 31. The translation is by S. H. Nasr based on the French translation of this and other fragments of this work from the Arabic text in a summary of it by T. Burckhardt entitled *De l'homme universel* (Lyon: P. Derain, 1953), pp. 51–52.

and manifests Himself by drawing a veil over His face. His concealment has regard to His pure and absolute Being, while His manifestation has regard to the exhibition of the world of phenomena.

"O fairest rose, with rosebud mouth," I sighed,
"Why, like coquettes, thy face for ever hide?"
He smiled, "Unlike the beauties of the earth,
Even when veiled I still may be descried."

Thy face uncovered would be all too bright,
Without a veil none could endure the sight;
What eye is strong enough to gaze upon
The dazzling splendour of the fount of light?

When the sun's banner blazes in the sky,
Its light gives pain by its intensity,
But when 'tis tempered by a veil of cloud
That light is soft and pleasant to the eye.

. . . .

It follows, therefore, that in the external world there is only One Real Being, who, by clothing Himself with different modes and attributes, appears to be endued with multiplicity and plurality to those who are confined in the narrow prison of the "stages," and whose view is limited to the visible properties and results.

Creation's book I studied from my youth,
And every page examined, but in sooth
I never found therein aught save the "truth,"
And attributes that appertain to "Truth."

What mean Dimension, Body, Species,
In Mineral, Plant, Animal degrees?
The "Truth" is single, but His modes beget
All these imaginary entities.

When one says that the multiplicity of things is comprehended in the Unity of the One Real Being, this does not mean that they are as the parts contained in an aggregate, or as objects contained in a receptacle, but that they are as the qualities inherent in the object qualified, or as consequences flowing from their cause. Take, for instance, the half, the third, the fourth, and other fractions up to infinity, which are potentially contained in the integer, one, though not actually manifested until they are exposed to view by repeating the various numbers and fractions. . . .

These modes are in the essence of the "Truth,"
Like qualities which qualify the "Truth";
But part and whole, container and contained,
Exist not where God is, who is the "Truth."[3]

The doctrine of the unity of Being was first formulated explicitly by the seventh/thirteenth century Sufi, Muḥyī al-Dīn ibn ʿArabī, who was born in Andalusia and died in Damascus. He was the most important expositor of Sufi doctrines, particularly of cosmology and the sacred sciences. In the early centuries of Islam, the Sufis had stressed the purification of the heart, as the symbolic seat of intelligence, and therefore did not occupy themselves with writing elaborate metaphysical and cosmological treatises, like the later Sufis. This apparent "weakness" and its "correction" were not due to a "development" or later "accretion" but rather arose because the need for explicit formulation grows with the increase in the lack of comprehension of doctrines, not with the increase in the ease of understanding them. Ibn ʿArabī, coming after six centuries of Sufism, was destined to formulate explicitly doctrines that had, until that time, remained more or less implicit. He expressed the Sufi conception of Nature in formulations based not only upon Quranic terminology, but also upon elements drawn from Hermetic and Pythagorean sources. It was he who explicitly expressed for the first time in Arabic the conception of Nature as the "breath of the Compassionate." As he writes in the *Futūḥāt al-makkīyah (Meccan Revelations):*

> What is called breath from the point of view of its ontological reality is not the breath except by virtue of its coming from the Compassionate or what corresponds to it among the Divine Names. . . . In reality what Allah "breathes" into creation is what is found of necessity and by inner determination, but actually by that which is His Attribute from the influence of His Will.[4]

According to Ibn ʿArabī and most other Sufis, the creation of the world is thus based upon the "compassion" *(al-raḥmān)* of the Infinite. It is by His Compassion that God gives being to the Names and Qualities which are the arche-

[3] Jāmī, *Lawāʾiḥ, A Treatise on Sufism,* translated by E. H. Whinfield and Mīrzā Muḥammad Ḳazvīnī (Oriental Translation Fund, New Series, Vol. XVI. London: Royal Asiatic Society, 1914), pp. 14–15, 20–21.

[4] Ibn ʿArabī, *Futūḥāt al-makkīyah* (Cairo: Al-ʿĀmirah Press, 1329), II, p. 566. Translated by S. H. Nasr.

types of creation. As the sacred saying of the Prophet Muḥammad puts it: "I [God] was a hidden treasure; I wanted to be known. Therefore, I created the world." This desire to be known arises from the Compassion of the Divine Being for Himself. The word "compassion" *(al-raḥmān)* is therefore the principle of manifestation, the "expansive" aspect of the Infinite; the substance of which the universe is made is thus called the "Breath of the Compassionate." Each particle of existence is immersed in this breath, which endows it with a "sympathy" with other beings, and above all with the source of the breath, the Divine Compassion. That is why the Sufis say that each atom of the universe is a "theophany" *(tajallī)* of the Divine Being. Maḥmūd Shabistarī, in the *Gulshan-i Rāz (The Mystic Rose Garden)* expresses the presence of the Divine Being in all things when he writes:

Non-being is a mirror, the world the image [of the Universal
Man], and man
Is the eye of the image, in which the person is hidden.
Thou art the eye of the image, and He the light of the eye.
Who has ever seen the eye through which all things are seen?
The world has become a man, and man a world.
There is no clearer explanation than this.
When you look well into the root of the matter,
He is at once seen, seeing eye, and thing seen.
The holy tradition has declared this,
And "without eye or ear" demonstrated it.
Know the world is a mirror from head to foot,
In every atom are a hundred blazing suns.
If you cleave the heart of one drop of water,
A hundred pure oceans emerge from it.
If you examine closely each grain of sand,
A thousand Adams may be seen in it.
In its members a gnat is like an elephant;
In its qualities a drop of rain is like the Nile.
The heart of a barley-corn equals a hundred harvests,
A world dwells in the heart of a millet seed.
In the wing of a gnat is the ocean of life,
In the pupil of the eye a heaven;
What though the grain of the heart be small,
It is a station for the Lord of both worlds to dwell therein.[5]

Nature, according to Sufi cosmology of the school of Ibn

[5] Maḥmūd Shabistarī, *Gulshān-i Rāz (The Mystic Rose Garden)*, translated by E. H. Whinfield (London: Trübner & Co., 1880), pp. 15–16. Some modifications of the translation of this passage have been made by S. H. Nasr.

ʿArabī, is the third member of the cosmic hierarchy, following the Intellect and the Universal Soul. Ibn ʿArabī writes in the *Meccan Revelations:*

> Know that Nature is for us in the third state of existence, with respect to the First Intellect. Its existence is intelligible, but its essence does not exist [it is in a latent and non-differentiated state]. The meaning of our saying "it is created" is that it is determined, because creation is determination, and to determine something is to bring it into being.[6]

Universal Nature is a limitation, when considered with respect to the Divine Principle Itself; yet it is also the productive and feminine aspect of the Divine Act, or Universal Essence. The Divine Act creates all the worlds of existence out of the womb of Universal Nature, which Ibn ʿArabī calls "the Mother of the Universe." Since the Divine Act, is however, permanent and pure actuality, it is Universal Nature that is responsible for bringing things from potentiality to actuality. Nature is the "dynamic" aspect of the passive pole of Being; it is therefore the active cause of change in this world, in spite of its being passive with respect to the Divine Act. Matter, which Nature moves, is the "static" aspect of this same feminine and passive pole, the plastic substance of which the formal world is shaped. Nature, seen in this light, is a divine power, molding this substance and directing the changes in the universe. The regularities and logical coherence of Nature are inverted reflections of the absolute freedom of the Divine Act, which "acts without acting" upon Nature.

Just as the first *Shahādah* (affirmation of faith) of Islam, which means ultimately the unity of Being, opens the faith of the Muslim, so the second *Shahādah* of Islam, *Muḥammadun rasūl Allāh,* "Muḥammad is the messenger of God," completes his declaration of faith. The Divine Law interpretation considers the formula to signify simply that Muḥammad was the Prophet of God and received the revelation from Him. The Sufis add to this interpretation the esoteric significance of the formula, which involves the inner reality of the Prophet as the *Logos,* the archetype of Creation. From this latter point of view, the second *Shahādah* means that the universe is a manifestation of God.

ʿAbd al-Karīm al-Jīlī in his *Universal Man* writes:

6 Ibn ʿArabī, *Futūḥāt,* II, pp. 565–566.

> The Universal Man [the *Logos*] is the pole around which all the spheres of existence from the first to the last evolve. He is unique as long as existence lasts. However, he appears in different forms and reveals himself by diverse cults, so that he receives multiple names. . . .
>
> Know that the Universal Man bears within himself correspondences with all the realities of existence. He corresponds to the superior realities by his subtle nature, and to the inferior realities by his gross nature. . . . The Divine Throne corresponds to his heart; moreover, as the Prophet has said, the heart of the believer is the throne of God; the Divine Pedestal corresponds to his "I-ness"; the Lotus Tree of the Extreme Limit [referring to the Quranic description], to his spiritual state; the Supreme Pen to his Intellect; the Guarded Tablet [the tablet upon which God has written all events of the cosmos before the creation of the world] to his soul; the elements to his body and the *hylē*—to his receptivity.[7]

Considered metaphysically, the first *Shahādah* "annihilates" all things as separate realities before the Divine Unity; the second relates all multiplicity, in so far as it possesses a positive aspect, to Unity through the Universal Man, the archetype of all existing things. For the Sufi, the world is not God, but neither is it other than God; it is not God who is in the world but, to quote a contemporary Sufi, the world which "is mysteriously plunged in God."

The Universal Man, the "Light of Muḥammad," who is essentially the *Logos* or Supreme Spirit, is the theater of the theophany of all the Divine Names and Attributes, and the archetype of the cosmos. Creation thrives upon him and derives its sustenance from his being. He is also the archetype of the children of Adam, all of whom are potentially the Universal Man, although it is only among the prophets and the greatest saints that this potentiality becomes actualized. In them, the inner reality of the microcosm becomes illuminated, so that the Divine realities are reflected in it. As the Universal Man, the archetype of the cosmos, contains in himself all the Platonic "ideas," so does the gnostic, who has realized his inner oneness with his archetype, become the mirror in which God contemplates His own Names and Qualities. As al-Jīlī writes:

> Know that it is the Universal Man to whom in principle the

[7] Al-Jīlī, *op. cit.*, Part II, pp. 48–49. Translated by S. H. Nasr. A somewhat different and full translation of this section is given by Nicholson in his *Studies in Islamic Mysticism*, p. 105.

Names of the Essence and Divine Qualities belong, as does the kingdom [universal existence] by virtue of his essence. . . . Therefore he is to God what a mirror is to a person who does not see his face except in it. . . . The Universal Man is the mirror of God because God has imposed upon Himself the condition of not contemplating His own Names and Qualities except in the Universal Man. And this is the meaning of the Divine saying, "Lo! We offered the trust unto the heavens and the earth and the hills, but they shrank from hearing it and were afraid of it. And man assumed it. Lo! he hath proved a tyrant and a fool." [Quran 33: 72.] That is to say, he did wrong to his own soul and fell from such a high rank ignorant of his own capacity since he is the locus of Divine Trust of which he is not aware.[8]

In still another passage, al-Jīlī describes the creation of the universe from the Idea of Ideas (which, from the cosmic point of view, may be identified with the Universal Man), in these symbolic terms:

Before the creation God was in Himself, and the objects of existence were absorbed in Him so that He was not manifested in anything. This is the state of "being a hidden treasure" or, as the Prophet expressed it, "the dark mist above which is a void and below which is a void," because the Idea of Ideas is beyond all relations. The Idea of Ideas is called in another Tradition "the White Chrysolite, in which God was before He created the creatures." When God willed to bring the world into existence, He looked on the Idea of Ideas (or the White Chrysolite) with the look of Perfection, whereupon it dissolved and became a water; for nothing in existence, not even the Idea of Ideas, which is the source of all existence, can bear the perfect manifestation of God. Then God looked on it with the look of Grandeur, and it surged in waves, like a sea tossed by the winds, and its grosser elements were spread out in layers like foam, and from that mass God created the seven earths with their inhabitants. The subtle elements of the water ascended, like vapour from the sea, and from them God created the seven heavens with the angels of each heaven. Then God made of the water seven seas which encompassed the world. This is how the whole of existence originated.[9]

The doctrine of the Universal Man is the alpha and omega of all esoteric sciences of the universe, because the Universal

[8] *Ibid.*, Part II, p. 50.
[9] R. A. Nicholson, *Studies in Islamic Mysticism* (Cambridge: Cambridge University Press, 1921), pp. 121–122.

Man contains the archetypes of creation, in terms of which the gnostic seeks knowledge of all things. Moreover, the Universal Man is the archetype of the gnostic himself; to the degree that the latter gains knowledge in terms of the archetypes, he is realizing an aspect of his own being. His knowledge and his being thus become identified. He gains "sympathy" with the cosmos to the degree that he approaches his own inner reality. The universe itself is in fact manifested because of the Divine Compassion, which has created a sympathy between all things. The sympathy between the gnostic and God includes all the other cosmic sympathies: it is the same compassion which causes the universe to be manifested that also draws the gnostic, and through him all other creatures, back to their Divine Source.

The seventh/thirteenth century Sufi Nasafī, writes:

> To travel the path is not an exclusively human thing. All the species of the existent world are journeying, to reach their goal and end. And the aim of each thing is perfection, and the end of all things is the human species, which is the perfection of the whole. To their goal they journey in obedience and natural movement . . . but to their end they can also go against their will, in violent movement. All things in the world of existence are on a journey to attain to their goal, and man too is on a journey. But the goal of man is maturity, his end freedom. The motive for the traveling of all these things is love. O dear friend, the seed of all plants and the sperm of all animals is filled with love, indeed all the parts of the world of existence are drunk with love; for if there were no love, the sphere would not turn, the plants would not grow, the animals would not be born. All are full of love for themselves, strive to behold themselves, desire to see themselves as they really are, and to disclose the beloved to the eyes of the lover.[10]

We have undertaken to state briefly the doctrines of the unity of Being and of the Universal Man, which are for the most part alien to modern readers, in order to indicate the theoretical aspect of Islamic metaphysics, without a knowledge of which the comprehension of the gnostic perspective would be impossible. But the reader should never identify the theoretical formulation with gnosis itself, for the Sufis

[10] *Spirit and Nature: Papers from the Eranos Yearbooks,* translated by Ralph Manheim; "The Problem of Nature in the Esoteric Monism of Islam (1946)" by Fritz Meier, who translates on page 197 Nasafi, *Tanzil al-arwah* (*The Descent of Spirits*). Bollingen Series XXX, 1., copyright 1954 by Bollingen Foundation, New York. Distributed by Pantheon Books), I, 197. London: Routledge & Kegan Paul Ltd. Reprinted by permission.

always emphasize that something must happen to the soul of the seeker, even more than to his mind: he must stop being what he now is, and become a new being. Theories and books are thus merely an aid, not the "thing" itself. Regarding the inadequacy of books, Nasafī writes,

> . . . in this book, I have not set down my own opinion and my own point of view. And this is because a man does not know everything; because it is not fitting for him to say everything he knows; and because it is not fitting for him to write everything he says. Of a hundred thousand men, there may be one who knows; of a hundred thousand things this man knows, there may be one that he should utter, and of a hundred thousand things he utters, there may be one that he should write. . . . And thus, since Muḥammed, or indeed since Adam, everyone who has had knowledge of the essence of things obtained it through personal association with one who knew. . . .[11]

Even the book of Nature is only an aid toward the ultimate goal of the gnostic. Again, to quote Nasafī:

> Each day destiny and the passage of time set this book before you, sura for sura, verse for verse, letter for letter, and read it to you. . . . like one who sets a real book before you and reads it to you line for line, letter for letter, that you may learn the content of these lines and letters. This is the meaning of the words: "We will show them our signs in different countries and among themselves until it become plain to them that it is the truth" (Sura 41:53). But what does it avail if you have no seeing eye and no hearing ear, i.e., no eye that sees things as they are, and no ear that hears things as they are? This is the meaning of the words: "They are like the brutes: yea, they go more astray: these are the heedless" (Sura 7:178). But if you yourself cannot read, then you must at least listen when someone reads to you, and accept what he reads. But you do not accept it because you have not the ear for it. "Who heareth the signs of God recited to him, and then, as though he heard them not, persisteth in proud disdain" (Sura 45:7), "as though his ears were heavy with deafness; announce to him therefore things of an afflictive punishment" (Sura 31:6). . . . But he who finds for himself the eye of the eye and the ear of the ear, who transcends the world of creatures and attains to the world of the commandment [the spiritual world], he obtains knowledge of the whole book in one moment, and he who has complete knowledge of the whole book, who frees his heart

11 Nasafī's *Kashf al-ḥaqā'iq (The Revelation of Spiritual Realities)* in *Spirit and Nature, op. cit.*, p. 171.

> from this book, closes the book and sets it aside, he is like one who receives a book and reads it over and over until he fully knows its content; such a man will close the book and set it aside.[12]

The spiritual journey of man in quest of the ultimate science of things, of certainty of knowledge, thus means a transformation of the soul and involves a "phenomenology" of its own. Nasafī writes that

> spirit and body are in the beginning as butter in milk and at the end as rider and mount. That is to say, in the beginning they are in one another, at the end they are with one another, in the beginning there is mixture, at the end contiguity.[13]

Once the butter and milk are separated, i.e., once the chaos of the soul of ordinary man is transformed into the order or "cosmos" illuminated by the Intellect, then man becomes a gnostic, a mirror in which all things are reflected, because he becomes himself, what he always "was" without being conscious of it. As Nasafī expressed it:

> Although each individual being in the existent world is a goblet, the knowing man is the goblet that reveals the whole cosmos. Thus the knowing man is the union of all stages (of being), the "great electuary," the goblet that reveals the world . . .
>
> In quest of the goblet of *Djām* [the cup of Solomon which contained the world], I journeyed through the world.
>
> Not one day did I sit down, and not one night did I give myself to slumber,
>
> When from the master I heard a description of the goblet of *Djām*,
>
> I knew that I myself was that goblet of *Djām*, revealing the universe.[14]

The final stage of science is the "subjective" realization of "objective" knowledge which itself lies beyond such a subject-object distinction. A change must take place within the soul of the knower; he must cast aside the ordinary consciousness, by which man lives during his everyday life, in order to become illuminated by a new form of consciousness which, until the moment of effective realization, lies hidden

12 *Ibid.*, p. 203.
13 Nasafī, *Tanzīl, op. cit.*, p. 196.
14 *Ibid.*, p. 189.

and latent within the soul. His theoretical and discursive knowledge must become immediate and intuitive. As Jalāl al-Dīn Rūmī, the incomparable seventh/thirteenth century Persian poet of Sufism, writes in his *Mathnawī,* which is an ocean of gnosis:

> Come, recognize that your sensation and imagination and understanding are like the reed-cane on which children ride.
> The spiritual man's knowledge bears him aloft; the sensual man's knowledge is a burden. . . .
> Do you know any name without a reality? Or have you ever plucked a rose from R.O.S.E.?
> You have pronounced the name: go, seek the thing named. The moon is in the sky, not in the water.
> Would you rise beyond the name and letter, make yourself entirely pure,
> And behold in your own heart all the knowledge of the prophets, without book, without learning, without preceptor.[15]

All the arts and sciences that the human mind can master cannot replace or even lead to gnosis, if these disciplines are regarded as independent modes of knowledge. Again, to quote Rūmī, this time his prose masterpiece, *Fīhi mā fīhi* (*Discourses,* in its English translation):

> One person comes to the sea and sees nothing but salt water, whales and fish. He asks, "Where is the jewel [the pearl which symbolizes gnosis]"? Perhaps there is none. But when can the pearl be found by just looking at the sea? If that person takes out a hundred thousand pails of water from the sea, he will not find the pearl. One needs a deep sea diver to discover the pearl, and then not just any diver at all, but one who is clever and fortunate. These arts and sciences are like taking out the water of the sea in pails; the way of finding the pearl is something else. There are many who possess all the arts, as well as wealth and beauty, but not that meaning [gnosis]; there are many whose appearance is in ruins, who do not have a handsome face or elegance of speech, yet the meaning which is immortal is in them. It is by virtue of that meaning [gnosis] that man is ennobled and honored, and has superiority over other creatures.[16]

The "prayer of the gnostic" is to "see" that the knowledge of each particular being and each domain leads to the knowl-

[15] R. A. Nicholson, *Rumi, Poet and Mystic* (London: George Allen & Unwin, 1950), p. 98.
[16] Rūmī, *Fīhi mā fīhi* (Tehran: Majlis Press, 1330), p. 186. Translated by S. H. Nasr.

edge of its ontological cause, to see in the arts and sciences the vehicle and support for the realization of gnosis. The famous prayer of the Prophet as orchestrated and expanded by Jāmī, sums up the end toward which the gnostic strives with all his mind, soul and body:

> O God, deliver us from preoccupations with worldly vanities, and show us the nature of things "as they really are." Remove from our eyes the veil of ignorance, and show us things as they really are. Show us not non-existence as existent, nor cast the veil of non-existence over the beauty of existence. Make this phenomenal world the mirror to reflect the manifestation of Thy beauty, not a veil to separate and repel us from Thee. Cause these unreal phenomena of the Universe to be for us the sources of knowledge and insight, not the causes of ignorance and blindness. Our alienation and severance from Thy beauty all proceed from ourselves. Deliver us from ourselves, and accord to us intimate knowledge of Thee.[17]

17 Jāmī, *Lawāʾiḥ*, p. 2.

SELECTED BIBLIOGRAPHY

General Background

Arnold, Thomas W., and Alfred Guillaume (ed.). *The Legacy of Islam.* Oxford: Clarendon Press, 1931.

Browne, Edward G. *A Literary History of Persia.* 4 vols. London: T. Fisher Unwin, and Cambridge, The University Press, 1902–24.

Carra de Vaux, Bernard. *Les penseurs de l'Islam.* 5 vols. Paris: P. Geuthner, 1921–26.

Corbin, Henry, with S. H. Nasr and O. Yahya. *Histoire de la philosophie islamique,* Vol. I. Paris: Gallimard, 1964.

Dermenghem, Emile. *Muhammad and the Islamic Tradition.* Trans. by J. H. Watt. New York: Harper and Brothers, 1958.

Duhem, Pierre. *Le système du monde, histoire des doctrines cosmologiques de Platon à Copernic.* 10 vols. Paris: A. Hermann et fils, 1913–59.

The Encyclopaedia of Islam, New Edition. Leiden: E. J. Brill, vols. 1–2, 1960–65. To be completed in 5 vols.

Gibb, Hamilton A. R. *Mohammadanism.* London: Oxford University Press, 1949.

———. *Studies on the Civilization of Islam.* Ed. by S. J. Shaw and W. R. Polk. Boston: Beacon Press, 1962.

Ibn Khaldūn, *The Muqaddimah.* Trans. by F. Rosenthal. 3 vols. New York: Pantheon Books, 1958.

Levy, Reuben. *The Social Structure of Islam.* Cambridge, The University Press, 1957.

Mieli, Aldo, *La science arabe et son rôle dans l'évolution scientifique mondiale.* Leiden: E. J. Brill, 1938.

Nasr, Seyyed Hossein. *Ideals and Realities of Islam*. London: Allen & Unwin, 1966.

———. *An Introduction to Islamic Cosmological Doctrines*. Cambridge: Harvard University Press, 1964.

———. *Three Muslim Sages*. Cambridge: Harvard University Press, 1964.

O'Leary, DeLacy. *How Greek Science Passed to the Arabs*. London: Routledge and Kegan Paul, 1949.

Rosenthal, Franz. *A History of Muslim Historiography*. Leiden: E. J. Brill, 1952.

Sarton, George. *Introduction to the History of Science*. 3 vols. Baltimore: The Williams and Wilkins Co., 1927–48.

Schroeder, Eric. *Muhammad's People*. Portland, Me.: The Bond Wheelwright Co., 1955.

Schuon, Frithjof. *The Transcendent Unity of Religions*. Trans. by P. Townsend. London: Faber and Faber, 1953.

———. *Understanding Islam*. Trans. D. M. Matheson. London: George Allen & Unwin, 1963–66.

Sharif, Miyan Muhammad (ed.). *A History of Muslim Philosophy*. 2 vols. Wiesbaden: O. Harrassowitz, 1963.

Shustery, A. Mahomed Abbas. *Outlines of Islamic Culture*. 2 vols. Bangalore City: Bangalore Press, 1938.

von Grünebaum, Gustave E. *Islam—Essays in the Nature and Growth of a Cultural Tradition*. London: Routledge and Kegan Paul, 1955.

Zaki, Ali, and Prince Aga Khan. *Glimpses of Islam*. Geneva: The Authors, 1944.

NATURAL AND MATHEMATICAL SCIENCES

Avicenna. *Le livre de science*. Trans. by M. Achena and H. Massé. 2 vols. Paris: Société d'édition "Les Belles Lettres," 1955–58.

Avicenna Commemoration Volume. Calcutta: Iran Society, 1956.

Al-Bīrūnī, *Alberuni's India*. Trans. by E. C. Sachau. 2 vols. London: Kegan Paul, Trench, Trübner & Co., Ltd., 1910.

———. *The Chronology of Ancient Nations*. Trans. by E. C. Sachau. London: W. H. Allen and Co., 1879.

———. *The Book of Instruction in the Elements of the Art of Astrology*. Trans. by R. R. Wright. London: Luzac and Co., 1934.

Al-Biruni Commemoration Volume. Calcutta: Iran Society, 1951.

Deyer, John L. E. *A History of Astronomy from Thales to Kepler.* 2nd ed. New York: Dover Publications, Inc., 1953.

Hartner, Willy, in Arthur U. Pope (ed.). *A Survey of Persian Art.* 6 vols. London and New York: Oxford University Press, 1938–39, Vol. 3, pp. 2530–2554.

Ikhwān al-Ṣafāʾ. *Dispute between Man and the Animals.* Trans. by J. Platts. London: W. H. Allen and Co., 1869.

Karpinski, Louis C. *Robert of Chester's Latin Translation of the Algebra of al-Khowarizmi.* New York: The Macmillan Co., 1915.

Al-Masʿūdī. *El Masʿudi's Historical Encyclopaedia Entitled "Meadows of Gold and Mines of Gems."* London: Oriental Translation Fund, 1841.

Mingana, Alphonse (ed. and trans.). *Book of Treasures, by Job of Edessa.* London: W. Heffer and Sons, Ltd., 1935.

Niẓāmī-i ʿArūḍī. *Chahār Maqāla.* Trans. by E. G. Browne. (E. J. W. Gibb Memorial Series, Vol. XI, 2.) London: Luzac and Co., 1921.

Al-Qazwīnī. *The Zoological Section of the Nuzhatu-l-Qulub of Hamdullah al-Mustaufi al-Qazwini.* Trans. by J. Stephenson. (Oriental Translation Fund, New Series, Vol. XXX.) London: Royal Asiatic Society, 1926.

Rhazes. *The Spiritual Physick of Rhazes.* Trans. by A. J. Arberry. London: John Murray, 1950.

Sayīlī, Aydīn M. *The Observatory in Islam.* Ankara: Türk Tarīh Kurumu Basimevi, 1960.

Suter, Heinrich. *Die Mathematiker und Astronomen der Araber und ihre Werke.* Leipzig: B. G. Teubner, 1900.

Winter, Henri J. J. *Eastern Science.* (Wisdom of the East Series.) London: John Murray, 1952.

MEDICINE

Avicenna. *A Treatise on the Canon of Medicine of Avicenna Incorporating a Translation of the First Book.* Trans. by O. C. Gruner. London: Luzac and Co., 1930.

Browne, Edward G. *Arabian Medicine.* Cambridge, The University Press, 1921.

Campbell, Donald E. H. *Arabian Medicine and Its Influence on the Middle Ages.* London: Kegan Paul, Trench, Trübner and Co., Ltd., 1926.

Elgood, Cyril E. *A Medical History of Persia and the Eastern Caliphate from the Earliest Times until the Year A.D. 1932*. Cambridge: The University Press, 1951.

Leclerc, Lucien. *Histoire de la médicine arabe; exposé complet des traductions du grec; les sciences en Orient, leur transmission à l'Occident par les traductions latines*. 2 vols. Paris: Librairie des Sociétés Asiatiques, 1876.

ALCHEMY

Aniane, M. "Notes sur l'alchemie, 'yoga' cosmologique de la chrétienté médiévale" in *Yoga, science de l'homme intégral*. Paris: Cahiers du Sud, 1953.

Burckhardt, Titus. *Alchemie, Sinn und Weltbild*. Olten: Walter-Verlag, 1960.

Eliade, Mircea. *The Forge and the Crucible*. Trans. by S. Corrin. New York: Harper & Bros., 1962.

Evola, Giulio. *La Tradizione ermetica*. Bari: G. Laterza e Figli, 1948.

Flamel, Nicolas. *His Exposition of the Hieroglyphical Figures*. London: Eagle and Child in Britans Bursse, 1624.

Grillot de Givry, Emile A. *Witchcraft, Magic and Alchemy*. Trans. by J. C. Locke. London: Harrap, 1931.

Holmyard, Eric J. *Alchemy*. London: Penguin Books, 1957.

Al-ʿIrāqī. *Kitāb al-ʿilm al-muktasab fī zirāʿat adh-dhahab*. Trans. and ed. by E. J. Holmyard. Paris: P. Geuthner, 1923.

Jung, Carl G. *The Collected Works of C. G. Jung*. Vol. XII: *Psychology and Alchemy*. Trans. by R. F. C. Hull. (Bollingen Series XX.) New York: Pantheon Books, 1953.

Kraus, Paul. *Jābir ibn Ḥayyān*. 2 vols. Cairo: Imprimerie de l'Institut français d'archéologie orientale, 1943.

Nasr, Seyyed Hossein. *Islamic Studies*. Beirut: Librairie du Liban, 1967.

Read, John. *Prelude to Chemistry: An Outline of Alchemy, Its Literature and Relationships*. New York: The Macmillan Co., 1937.

Ruska, Julius F. *Tabula Smaragdina, ein Beitrag zur Geschichte der Hermetischen Literatur*. Heidelberg: Carl Winter, 1926.

Scott, Walter (ed.). *Hermetica*. 4 vols. London: Oxford University Press, 1924–36.

Stapleton, H. E., R. F. Azo, and M. Hidāyat Husain.

"Chemistry in Iraq and Persia in the Tenth Century A.D.," *Memoires of the Royal Asiatic Society of Bengal,* Vol. VIII, No. 6 (1927).

Stapleton, H. E., and M. Hidāyat Husain. "Three Arabic Treatises on Alchemy by Muhammad ibn Umail al-Tamīmī," *Memoires of the Royal Asiatic Society of Bengal,* Vol. XII, No. 1 (1933).

Waite, Arthur E. *The Secret Tradition of Alchemy, Its Development and Records.* New York: Knopf, 1926.

———. *Turba Philosophorum.* London: George Redway, 1896.

Philosophy and Theology

Averroes. *Tahāfut al-tahāfut.* Trans. by S. van den Bergh. (E. J. Gibb Memorial Series, New Series 19.) London: Luzac and Co., 1954.

de Boer, Tjitze J. *The History of Philosophy in Islam.* Trans. by E. R. Jones. London: Luzac and Co., 1961.

Corbin, Henry. *Avicenna and the Visionary Recital.* Trans. by W. Trask. (Bollingen Series LXVI.) New York: Pantheon Books, 1960.

Fakhry, Majid. *Islamic Occasionalism and Its Critique by Averroës and Aquinas.* London: Allen and Unwin, 1958.

Gardet, Louis, and M. M. Anawati. *Introduction à la théologie musulmane, essai de théologie comparée.* Paris: J. Vrin, 1948.

Gibb, Hamilton, A. R. "The Structure of Religious Thought in Islam," *The Muslim World,* Vol. XXXVIII (1948), pp. 17–28; 113–123; 185–197; 280–291.

Iqbal, Sir Muhammad. *The Development of Metaphysics in Persia; a Contribution to the History of Muslim Philosophy.* London: Luzac and Co., 1908.

Macdonald, Duncan B. *Development of Muslim Theology, Jurisprudence and Constitutional Theory.* New York: C. Scribner's Sons, 1903.

Munk, Salomon. *Mélanges de philosophie juive et arabe.* Paris: J. Vrin, 1927.

Pines, Salomon. *Beiträge zur islamischen Atomenlehre.* Berlin: A. Heine, 1936.

Quadri, Goffred. *La philosophie arabe dans l'Europe médiévale des origines à Averroès.* Trans. by R. Huret. Paris: Payot, 1947.

Suhrawardī. *Opera Metaphysica et Mystica, I.* Ed. by H. Corbin. (Biblioteca Islamica, Band 16A.) Istanbul: Maarif Matbassi, 1945. *II.* Ed. by H. Corbin. Tehran-Paris: Institut Franco-Iranien—Adrien-Maisonneuve, 1952.

Walzer, Richard. *Greek Into Arabic; Essays on Islamic Philosophy*. Cambridge: Harvard University Press, 1962.

Watt, William M. *The Faith and Practice of al-Ghazālī*. London: George Allen and Unwin, 1953.

Wolfson, Harry A. *Crescas' Critique of Aristotle: Problems of Aristotle's Physics in Jewish and Arabic Philosophy*. Cambridge: Harvard University Press, 1929.

THE GNOSTIC TRADITION

Anawati, Georges C., and Louis Gardet. *Mystique musulmane; aspects et tendances, expériences et techniques.* (Etudes musulmanes, VIII.) Paris: J. Vrin, 1961.

Arberry, A. J. *Discourses of Rumi.* London: John Murray, 1961.

Asin Palacios, Miguel. *Islam and the Divine Comedy*. Trans. and abridged by H. Sunderland. London: John Murray, 1926.

Burckhardt, Titus. *An Introduction to Sufi Doctrine*. Trans. by D. M. Matheson. Lahore: Muhammad Ashraf, 1959.

Corbin, Henry. *L'Imagination créatrice dans le soufisme d'Ibn Arabī*. Paris: A. Flammarion, 1958.

Guénon, René. *Symbolism of the Cross*. Trans. by A. Macnab. London: Luzac and Co., 1958.

Hujwīrī. *The Kashf al-Maḥjūb*. Trans. by R. A. Nicholson. (E. J. W. Gibb Memorial Series, Vol. XVIII.) Leiden: E. J. Brill, 1911.

Ibn ʿArabī. *La Sagesse des prophètes*. Trans. by T. Burckhardt. Paris: Editions A. Michel, 1955.

Jāmī. *Lawāʾih, A Treatise on Sufism*. Trans. by E. H. Whinfield and M. M. Ḳazvīnī. (Oriental Translation Fund, New Series, Vol. XVI.) London: Royal Asiatic Society, 1914.

Al-Jīlī. *De l'homme universel*. Trans. by T. Burckhardt. Lyon: P. Derain, 1953.

Lings, Martin. *A Moslem Saint of the Twentieth Century: Shaikh Ahmad al-Alawi, His Spiritual Heritage and Legacy.* New York: The Macmillan Co., 1961.

Massignon, Louis. *La Passion d'al-Ḥallaj.* 2 vols. Paris: P. Geuthner, 1922.

Nicholson, Reynold A. *Studies in Islamic Mysticism*. Cambridge, The University Press, 1921.

Rūmī. *Mathnawī*. 8 vols. Trans. by R. A. Nicholson. (E. J. W. Gibb Memorial Series, New Series, Vol. 4.) London: Luzac and Co., 1925–40.

Schaya, Léo. *La doctrine soufique de l'unité*. Paris: A. Maisonneuve, 1962.

Schuon, Frithjof. *Gnosis, Divine Wisdom*. Trans. by G. E. H. Palmer. London: John Murray, 1959.

Sirāj al-Dīn, Abū Bakr. *The Book of Certainty*. London: Rider and Co., 1952.

Supplementary Bibliography

A number of books pertaining directly to the subject of this work and published during the past twenty years are noted below. This list is not at all exhaustive but includes only the most pertinent titles. A fairly complete list of works on Islamic science and related fields in both book and article form can be found in the *Index Islamicus*.

Burckhardt, T. *Moorish Culture in Spain*. Trans. A. Jaffa, London: Allen & Unwin, 1972.

Craig, William L. *The Kalam Cosmological Argument*. London: The Macmillan Press, 1979.

Cruz Hernández, Miguel, *Historia del pensamiento en el mundo islámico*. 2 vols., Madrid: Alianza Editorial, 1981.

Diwald, Suzanne. *Arabische Philosophie und Wissenschaft in der Enzyklopädie Kitāb Ihkwān aṣ-Ṣafā' III. Die Lehre von Seele und Intellekt*. Wiesbaden: Otta Harrassowitz, 1975.

Fakhry, Majid. *A History of Islamic Philosophy*. New York: Columbia University Press, 1983.

Hamarneh, Sami K. *Health Sciences in Early Islam*. Ed. M.A. Anees, 2 vols., Blanco (Texas): Zahra Publications, 1983.

Hartner, Willy. *Oriens–Occidens*. Hildesheim: Georg Olms Verlags Buchhandlung, 1968.

Kennedy, Edward S. *Studies in the Islamic Exact Sciences*. Beirut: American University of Beirut, 1983.

King, David. *Islamic Mathematical Astronomy*. London: Variorum, 1986.

Matvievskaya, Galina P. and Rozenfel'd, Boris A. *Matematiki i astronomy musul'manskogo srednevekov'ya i ikh trudy (VIII–X–VII v.v.),* 3 vols., Moscow: Nauka, 1983.

Nasr, Seyyed Hossein. *Islamic Science–An Illustrated Study*. London: World of Islam Festival Publishing Company, 1976.

______. *An Annotated Bibliography of Islamic Science*. 3 vols, Tehran: Imperial Iranian Academy of Philosophy, 1975, 1978, and 1991.

Pines, Shlomo. *Studies in Arabic Versions of Greek Texts and in Medieval Science*. Leiden: E.J. Brill, 1986.

Sezgin, Fu'ād. *Geschichte des arabischen Schrifttums*, Vol. 3–5. Leiden: E.J. Brill, 1970-74.

Ullmann, Manfred. *Islamic Medicine*. Edinburgh: Edinburgh University Press, 1978.

______. *Die Natur- und Geheimwissenschaften im Islam*. Leiden: E.J. Brill, 1972.

Wiedemann, Eilhard. *Aufsätze zur arabischen Wissenschaft-geschichte*. 2 vols., ed. W. Fischer, New York: George Olm Verlag, 1970.

INDEX

as part of program of al-Azhar University, 72;
al-Ghazzālī on, 311 (*quoted*)
"Logic" of the Orientals, The, of Avicenna, 297
Logos, or Word, 338, 339, 340, 346, 347
Lully, Raymond, 244

Macrocosmic view of cosmology, 94
Madāris (colleges): chain of, 71;
teaching personnel of, 72;
relation between teacher and student in, 73–74
Madrasah, see Madāris
Maghrib, the, Islamic medicine in, 214–16
Al-Maghribī, 81, 174
Maghribī method of child instruction, 67, 68
Magi, 31
Al-Māhānī, 149
Mahdi, M., as translator, 79*n.*
Maḥmūd, of Ghazna, 50, 234
Maḥmūd Shabistarī, *see* Shabistarī
Maier, Michael, 244
Maimonides, 175, 184, 215, 313
Maître Conches, 285
Majlis, see Circle or "gathering"
Al-Majrīṭī, 51, 171
Al-Majūsī (Holy Abbas), 204–5 (*quoted*), 208–9
Maktab, see Elementary school
Malakūt, see Psychic manifestation
Malay Archipelago, 103
Malikshāh, 53, 80
Al-Ma'mūn, 42, 45, 69, 70, 79, 169
Ma'mūnic astronomical tables, 169
Man, science of, 78, 230–41
Manichaeism, 268
Al-Manṣūr, 88;
caliph, 168, 193
Manṣūrī hospital, in Cairo, 89
Mapmakers, 100
Maps, geographical and celestial, 45
Al-Maqdisī, 100–1
Maragha observatory and scientific institution, 55, 80-81, 150, 172, 174
Al-Māridīnī, 151
Al-Marwazī, 112
Māsarjoyah, 194
Māsawaih al-Mārindī, 194
Māsawaih (Māsūyah) family, 193–94
Māshā'allāh, 168
Mashshā'ī, see Peripatetic school
Al-Mas'ūdī, 47–48, 97, 101, 106, 108, 118, 230
Māsūyah, *see* Māsawaih
Materia medica: guide on, 111;
Greek authorities on, 191;
of Dioscorides, 214
Materialists, al-Ghazzālī on, 308 (*quoted*)
Mathematics, 25, 28, 146–67;
two types of, practiced by Muslims, 26;
Sabaeans' knowledge of, 31;
influence of Indian and Persian sciences on, 31;
of Illuminationist school, 36;
of Islam, influence of, on West, 39;
of al-Khwārazmī, 45, 157–59;
of Bahā' al-Dīn, 57–58;
in curriculum of institutions of higher learning, 73;
history of, in Islam, 148–52;
Islamic, summary of achievements of, 152;
and Brethren of Purity, 152–57 (*quoted*);
of 'Umar Khayyām, 160–67;
al-Ghazzālī on, 309–11 (*quoted*)
Mathematikoi of Pythagorean school, 34
Mathnawī, of Rūmī, 352 (*quoted*)
Mazdaean angelology, 97
Al-Māzinī, 101
Meadows of Gold and Mines of Precious Stones, of al-Mas'ūdī, 48, 101, 106–8 (*quoted*)
Meaning of the Glorious Koran, The, an explanatory translation by Pickthall, 24*n.*
Measles, 204
Mecca, annual pilgrimage to, 90
Meccan Revelations, of Ibn 'Arabī, *see Futūḥāt al-makkīyah*
Mechanica, of Archimedes, 139
Mechanics: science of, 75, 315;
studies of, 138, 139
Medical encyclopedias, 212, 215, 217, 218
Medical History of Persia and the Eastern Caliphate, of C. E. Elgood, 190*n.*, 205*n.*, 214*n.*
Medicine of Dārā Shukūh, The, of 'Ain al-Mulk, 218
Medicine, Islamic, 184–229;
of Illuminationist school, 36;
Rhazes' contribution to, 46, 196–207;
Avicenna's contribution to, 49, 51, 56, 196, 209–12;